REGNUM EDINBURGH 2010 SERIES

Interfaith Relations after One Hundred Years

REGNUM EDINBURGH 2010 SERIES

The Centenary of the World Missionary Conference of 1910, held in Edinburgh, was a suggestive moment for many people seeking direction for Christian mission in the twenty-first century. Several different constituencies within world Christianity held significant events around 2010. From 2005, an international group worked collaboratively to develop an intercontinental and multi-denominational project, known as Edinburgh 2010, and based at New College, University of Edinburgh. This initiative brought together representatives of twenty different global Christian bodies, representing all major Christian denominations and confessions, and many different strands of mission and church life, to mark the Centenary.

Essential to the work of the Edinburgh 1910 Conference, and of abiding value, were the findings of the eight think-tanks or 'commissions'. These inspired the idea of a new round of collaborative reflection on Christian mission – but now focused on nine themes identified as being key to mission in the twenty-first century. The study process was polycentric, open-ended, and as inclusive as possible of the different genders, regions of the world, and theological and confessional perspectives in today's church. It was overseen by the Study Process Monitoring Group: Miss Maria Aranzazu Aguado (Spain, The Vatican), Dr Daryl Balia (South Africa, Edinburgh 2010), Mrs Rosemary Dowsett (UK, World Evangelical Alliance), Dr Knud Jørgensen (Norway, Areopagos), Rev. John Kafwanka (Zambia, Anglican Communion), Rev. Dr Jooseop Keum (Korea, World Council of Churches), Dr Wonsuk Ma (Korea, Oxford Centre for Mission Studies), Rev. Dr Kenneth R. Ross (UK, Church of Scotland), Dr Petros Vassiliadis (Greece, Aristotle University of Thessalonikki), and coordinated by Dr Kirsteen Kim (UK, Edinburgh 2010).

These publications reflect the ethos of Edinburgh 2010 and will make a significant contribution to ongoing studies in mission. It should be clear that material published in this series will inevitably reflect a diverse range of views and positions. These will not necessarily represent those of the series' editors or of the Edinburgh 2010 General Council, but in publishing them the leadership of Edinburgh 2010 hopes to encourage conversation between Christians and collaboration in mission. All the series' volumes are commended for study and reflection in both church and academy.

Series Editors

REGNUM EDINBURGH 2010 SERIES

Interfaith Relations after One Hundred Years:

Christian Mission among Other Faiths

Edited by Marina Ngursangzeli Behera

First published 2011 by Regnum Books International

Regnum is an imprint of the Oxford Centre for Mission Studies
St. Philip and St. James Church
Woodstock Road
Oxford OX2 6HR, UK
www.ocms.ac.uk/regnum

09 08 07 06 05 04 03 7 6 5 4 3 2 1

British Library Cataloguing in Publication Data
A catalogue record for this book is available from the British Library

ISBN: 978-1-506476-02-5

Typeset by Words by Design

Distributed by 1517 Media in the US and Canada

Contents

TOWARDS EDINBURGH 2010
PRE-EDINBURGH CENTENARY CELEBRATION CONSULTATION
UNITED THEOLOGICAL COLLEGE, BANGALORE
JULY 17-19, 2009

ACKNOWLEDGEMENTS

I acknowledge my sincere gratitude to those organizations and bodies who had collaborated with The United Theological College, Bangalore and financially helped support the Pre- Edinburgh Consultation on Study Theme II: Christian Mission Among Other Faiths held at the The United Theological College from 17th to 19th July 2009; viz., the Edinburgh 2010 Celebration Committee; the National Council of Churches in India; the Methodist Church of India (South India Regional Conference); Henry Martyn Institute (Hyderabad).

My thanks are also due to: Dr Joseph George, the Acting Principal of the United Theological College, Bangalore; members of the Faculty coordination committee – Dr I.J. Mohan Razu, Dr Abraham Stephen, Dr P.T. George, Dr Evangeline Anderson Rajkumar, and Dr Siga Arles and my other Faculty colleagues; my sincere thanks are also to Dr Kirsteen Kim, Research Coordinator, Edinburgh 2010 who encouraged me and took the responsibility of getting this book published. And most importantly Dr Daryl Balia, representing the Edinburgh 2010 Celebration Committee without whose support and encouragement the Consultation would not have taken place.

I would also like to thank all the contributors without whom the consultation and the publication of these papers would not have been possible.

Dr Marina Ngursangzeli Behera
Editor & Coordinator
Pre-Edinburgh Consultation on Study Theme II
The United Theological College, Bangalore

Foreword

Andrew Wingate

The question of Mission and Other Faiths played a major role at Edinburgh 1910. It was the 4th of the commissions, and the evidences gathered from serving missionaries were amongst the richest put together before the conference. These replies came particularly from India and China, and they reveal major advances in mission theology and practice, with much more inclusive understandings of the place of other faiths, particularly Hinduism. It is surprising how little comparatively was said of Islam. In general, there is a move towards Fulfilment Theology, though clearly this was not universal. Long experience in 'the mission field' had brought this about, and studies by Kenneth Cracknell (*Justice, Courtesy and Love*, Epworth 1995), and Wesley Ariarajah (*Hindus and Christians, a century of Protestant Ecumenical Thought*, Eerdmans, 1991) emphasise how Edinburgh in some ways was ahead of its time in this area of mission.

Much has happened in the century since, not least with Vatican 2, and the crucial importance of *Nostra Aetate* for all churches. In spite of growing conservatism in the Roman Catholic Church, there has been no back sliding from this aspect of Vatican 2. It had brought a dramatic reversal of the doctrine, going back to Cyprian, that *extra ecclesiam, nulla salus (*Outside the church there is no salvation) and began the official endorsement of Catholic inclusivism as regards people of other faiths. The journey has been more complex within the protestant churches. The WCC has played a key role in the pursuit of dialogue and theological change. But conservative churches have grown stronger throughout the world, with their generally exclusive view of other faiths.

This conference in Bangalore was the place where preparations were made for Edinburgh 2010, in terms of the area of Inter Faith Dialogue and of Mission with People of Other Faiths. Logistics were not easy beforehand, which led to a dominance of Indian delegates, and only limited participation from foreigners, though overall women were in balance with men, and a large proportion had earned doctorates! If the task was to prepare by considering issues globally, across six continents, the conference did not really work. But it proved to be an in depth engagement with the context of India, and in a way therefore repeated positively the experience of Edinburgh 1910, where also the primary focus proved to be on India.

As in 1910, also, primary inputs related to Hindu issues. There was a balanced programme, but the issue in particular of Dalits came up again and again. This is quite understandable, but was not ideal as a preparation for Edinburgh. I felt for Father Aleaz, from Bishop's College, who gave a paper on classical Indian Christian Theology, which was not taken as seriously as it should be. Such theology has been extremely rich, and it is not good enough merely to dismiss it as 'Brahminic'. Of course, the sufferings of 200 million Dalits need to be taken ever seriously, but it is also important to engage with the 80% of Hindus who are not Dalits or tribals. Within the non-Catholic or Orthodox churches, the majority of Bishops are now from Dalit background, and all the difficulties in the church cannot any longer be projected upon caste questions.

Striking also was the highlighting of how inter faith issues bear particularly hard on women, as shown in the contributions of the women participants. Gabrielle expressed the danger of the hard line tactics used by the President in Sri Lanka to suppress the Tamil Tigers, being seen as a very successful precedent by those in India who wished to suppress dissident groups by force.

I was surprised especially with the lack of focus upon Islam, and mission amongst Muslims. I gave a major paper on Mission and Muslims in Europe. Other papers were expected but not forthcoming, and I felt quite isolated in this respect. At one point, someone said from the floor that matters to do with Islam were a western agenda. I reacted strongly, pointing to the Mumbai bombings, Kashmir, Pakistan, the Hindutva agenda of combining the second largest Muslim population in the world (Indian) with Christians as followers of foreign religions, and therefore not to be trusted as Indians. More locally, I pointed out the enormous new mosque that has come over the last two or three years just across the road from UTC. This was visited by a few of us, but could well have been visited by more, and a dialogue held there with leading Muslims. This could have enabled more balance in the programme.

An area much discussed was the appropriateness of the word 'Mission' to describe Christian involvement with people of other faiths. In several parts of the world, including India, this could be misunderstood. Discussion focused on whether it can be 'mission with...', and not only 'mission to...' But overall, the word 'mission' cannot and should not be removed, with its strong biblical base, as well as being in the title of the Edinburgh conferences of 2010, as well as 1910.

Positively, I would like to commend the participation of Daryl Balia, the link with Edinburgh and of Shanta, from the Dialogue commission of the WCC. Both distinguished themselves by being listeners, and in no way wishing to impose their agendas. Shanta preached effectively in the chapel, in a service for which the UTC students had prepared with great care. Daryl, in his capacity of being the focal person for Edinburgh 2010, provided helpful insights on the topics being discussed, explained well the links between Edinburgh 1910 and Edinburgh 2010, revealing a strong sense of historical reflection. He was fully loyal to 2010, though open about certain wishes he may have had, for example, that the conference should be held in Asia or Africa.

Daryl also responded positively to the suggestion I made, endorsed by the whole conference, that a small number of appropriate observers from other faiths could be at Edinburgh, be observers in the group where inter faith issues were discussed, and make their comments on the outcomes of the conference. This was not acceptable to the main conference planning group/committee. Hence, I was invited to bring some Muslims to Edinburgh, and we made a presentation on Mission to or with Muslims, where they fully participated – a challenge inspired by the debate in Bangalore above. Unfortunately, though this was on the conference alternative programme, and received support, it was in the evening, before mainly the converted. It would have been wonderful to have made our presentation to the groups concerned with dialogue and mission, within the main schedule.

I would like to commend the care taken by UTC, at a difficult time in its life. Here I mention particularly the Acting Principal Dr Joseph George, and faculty member Dr Marina Ngursangzeli Behera, the coordinator of the consultation, who did a sterling job in holding the conference together, and working on the papers afterwards. In terms of educational method, it would have been good to have more time for groups to discuss the rich diet of papers. But this happened only one occasion, which was a pity. It would have enabled all to participate more, and not just those who can speak up in a group of 40 to 50.

I was disappointed by the outcome statements from the main Edinburgh Conference on this theme. This was perhaps inevitable, granted the desire to enable the ecumenical agenda, of holding the vast spectrum of world Christianity together. This meant that this Bangalore Conference was all the more important, and I commend this book to its readers, with its varied diet of papers.

Andrew Wingate

INTRODUCTION

Marina Ngursangzeli Behera

Indian Christians have made important and significant contributions to the ecumenical movement in terms of promoting interfaith relations or interfaith dialogue. It can be argued that the emphasis of the ecumenical movement has shifted as a result of the input made by Indian Christians. India being a country where pluralism is a way of life, Indian Christians were therefore more appreciative of other cultures and faith communities. Prominent ecumenical Indian thinkers, writers and workers such as P.D. Devanandan, M.M. Thomas, Stanley Samartha, Russell Chandran to name a few, have voiced this perspective of Indian Christians in the global arena. In this manner, the life experience of Indian Christians has opened the eyes of Christians globally and has helped redefine the range and scope of the ecumenism they are striving for.

These life experiences of being a minority in a vast sea of plurality in all spheres of life has ingrained in them the necessity for building relationships with their neighbours of other faiths in all aspects of life and work. This has made them appreciate the plurocentric approach to religio-cultural relationships and is reflected in their attitude towards each other as well as towards adherents of other living faiths. So it was befitting that the Edinburgh 1910 Centenary Celebration Coordination Committee asked the United Theological College, Bangalore, India, to organise a preparatory consultation on Study theme II: Christian Mission among Other Faiths under the theme "Interfaith Relations with People of Other Faiths" This was done in the hope of taking stock of the past and to plan for a future with greater knowledge and confidence.

This book consists of essays by prominent theologians in India and elsewhere, who struggle with the realities of inter-faith relations in the contexts they live in and therefore this book is not only academic but offers a glimpse of the academics grounded and influenced by day-to-day events in the lives of the contributors. These papers were presented and studied at the Pre-Edinburgh 2010 consultation that was held from 17th to 19th July 2009 at the United Theological College, Bangalore. The book has been divided into seven sections based on the theme of each study group of the Consultation.

The first section **"Interfaith Relations from Muslim Perspectives"** consists of papers written/presented by Andrew Wingate, David Emmanuel Singh, Martha Frederiks and, Steve Cochrane.

Andrew Wingate briefly examines the historical factors in Europe that have affected Christian-Muslim interactions before 9/11 as well as subsequent changes in the Christian and Muslim communities themselves and Christian responses to Islam. He devotes considerable space to contemporary mission approaches to Islam and suggests practical and theological approaches in ten areas viz., (1) Mission, Evangelism and Theology of religions; (2) Mission and Inter faith dialogue; (3) Mission and the scriptures; (4) Mission and sharing of basic Christian convictions; (5)Mission and Apologetics; (6) Mission, Ethics and Social engagement; (7) Mission and spirituality; (8) Leadership structures; (9) Mission as Pastoral care; (10) Mission and the Education of children and young people. Emphasizing the urgent need to stand together against a new militant atheism which is increasingly strident in Europe, he states that Muslims and Christians need each other, which would mean trusting each other.

David Emmanuel Singh focuses on the evolution in thinking among Christians from traditional missions to interfaith relations since Edinburgh 1910. He suggests that in today's context where Islam is largely associated with violent *Jihad*, traditional missionary Christianity might be quite irrelevant and even dangerous. He offers a possible solution by putting forward the idea of 'zones of contact' or 'exchange' in circles that overlap each other to encourage an exchange of ideas instead of circles that are separate and so result in conflict. According to him, one can imagine that each circle could contain diversity within and representing the different intra-religious/cultural theologies. Whilst one can expect a continuing exchange and dialogue within each circle, the extent to which different religions will intersect with each other can be a source of potentially valuable interfaith theologies.

Martha Frederiks gives a brief overview of Christian-Muslim relations in sub-Sahara Africa which are both diverse and complex. She identifies three current trends in Christian-Muslim relations: an increase in polarization and polemics, the debate on the implementation of the *Shari'a*, and joint social action programmes. She explains how in recent years, because of the growing influence of Pentecostal Christianity on one hand and Muslim fundamentalism on the other, there has been a steady deterioration in relationships between people of the two faiths. But on the other hand it has stimulated the more moderate minded Christians and Muslims to work together to diffuse the tensions and strive towards peaceful coexistence and mutual respect accepting the religious diversity of the continent as a part of the African reality.

Steve Cochrane is specifically concerned with the presence of Christian monks and monasteries in Islamic countries and how these illustrate aspects of interfaith relationships particularly between Christianity and Islam. He points out that by the 9th century C.E. the interaction of Muslim Sufis and Christian monks was developing and providing contacts and exchanges in ways often overlooked in the historical overview of Christian-Muslim relations and consequently suggests that one of the paradigms for strengthening dialogue and relationships could be to regard the monastery as a signpost pointing to the mutuality of faith encounters. He poses the question whether it would be possible to build new bridges through a re-birth and renewal of Christian monasticism, even in Islamic countries.

Arising out of these papers and the discussions that followed were several concerns such as:

1. Muslims want to be partners with Christians; are we willing to enter into such partnership?
2. Muslims are often looked at with suspicion in the context of global events; the stereotypical image of the Muslim is on the increase.
3. Though in India both Muslims and Christians are considered foreigners, in Europe Christians are 'at home' while Muslims are not.
4. The purpose of dialogue is to continue to be engaged in the liberative mission of God for all creation.
5. This engagement takes place in the day-to-day lives of people in society as people face different challenges of life.
6. The problem of poverty and the situation of Muslim women in India could be two possible areas for inter-religious relations.
7. Conversion from one religious community to another is not the focus of dialogue.[1]

In the second section **"Interfaith Relations from Hindu Perspectives"** we have a paper written by K.P. Aleaz which gives an overview of major trends in ecumenical responses to other faiths, from the 18th and 19th centuries with Christian missionary attitudes to other faiths to the WCC Assembly at Vancouver in 1983. In examining some 19th and 20th century Indian Christian dialogues with Hinduism, he points out how Indian Christians sought to engage positively with Hinduism, rather than adopt the standpoint of discontinuity between Christianity and other faiths that the various early Missionary Conferences advocated. He also looks at a few Indian Christian exclusivists who viewed Hinduism negatively, before concluding that overall, Christian dialogue with Hinduism has been positive, encouraging and rewarding.

During the discussion that took followed, a note of caution was made about the generalization of the term "Hindu" and "Christian". For interfaith dialogue to take place meaningfully at the ground level, the particular

---

[1] See Report of the Bangalore Consultation. http://www.edinburgh2010.org/en/study-themes/main-study-themes/2-christian-mission-among-other-faiths/bangalore-conference.html

identities of Hindus and Christians need to be taken into account. It is also possible that a particular Hindu, Christian, Muslim or Buddhist may transcend his or her given religious identity and embrace meaningful and empowering elements from the neighbouring traditions.[2]

In the third section **"Interfaith Relations from Sikh Perspectives"** we have papers written by James Massey and John Parry.

James Massey deals with four areas namely, a personal reflection on Sikh-Christian relations, a re-look at the Edinburgh 1910 Document, the development of Sikh-Christian dialogue and looking beyond Edinburgh 1910. He explains how during the last quarter of the 19th century the *Singh Sobha* was founded as a response to the work of the missionaries in Punjab. Its main purpose was to create awareness of the Sikh religion and social life among the Sikhs. This development forced the Christians to rethink their approach to other religions as well as to their mission work.

The first Sikh-Christian Dialogue organised by the Christian Institute for the Study of Religion and Study (C.I.S.R.S.) in December 1962 through a seminar on 'Sikhism and Christianity in Panjab', laid the foundations for Sikh-Christian Dialogue in the country. Massey explains that in recent years the followers of the Sikh religion have also been concerned with inter-religious dialogue. In this regard a few major universities in Punjab and research institutes in and outside the state have played important roles in fostering interfaith relations through meetings and seminars. He also urges us to ponder the fact that the younger religious movements including the 'Sikh faith' have not been a priority for the Christian world.

John Parry begins by explaining how Sikhs migrated to places such as the U.K., East Africa, Canada, the U.S., Malaysia, Singapore, Hong Kong and other parts of Europe in search of work and better prospects. Tracing the Sikhs' encounters with Christians from the time of the Mughal Emperor Akbar into the 1980s, Parry then focuses on the Diaspora Sikhs in the UK where there was renewed interest in Sikhism in contrast with the rejection the community faced in India because of the assassination of Indira Gandhi. Parry points out how a series of meetings sponsored by the Reformed Church led to the understanding that if dialogue was to be worthwhile, there had to be a careful, specific, non polemical articulation of the Christian faith alongside a growing realisation among Christians that there were issues which required further exploration in the articulation of a Christian apologetics to the Sikhs.

A significant point that arises out of the two papers was that Sikhs have started taking initiatives for interfaith-dialogue, especially through the programmes of the universities in Patiala and Amritsar, with the objective of discerning the impact of religion on the lives of the people in society. It is also to be noted that the Guru Granth Sahib is an expression of spirituality drawn from various traditions. Another important observation

---

[2] Ibid.

was that in relating to people of other faiths, one has to insightfully discern "How 'other' is the other?" One may well realize that much of the 'otherness' is part of one's 'I-ness'. Such discernment would help in strengthening interfaith relations. A concern was raised whether the Church in general and the presbyters were willing to engage in serious dialogue. Such a commitment would require a deep study of Sikhism and Hinduism rather than depending on the traditional missionary understanding and stereotypes of Hindus and Sikhs.[3]

In the fourth section, **"Interfaith Relations from Subaltern Perspectives"** papers were presented by Fr A. Alangaram, Jhakmak Neeraj Ekka, B. Bolinkar Sohkhlet, Wati Longchar, and T. Swami Raju.

Fr A. Alangaram restricts the term 'Subaltern Movements' to the understanding of conversion movements of the oppressed 'castes' and 'classes' of the people of Tamil Nadu, India from Hinduism to Roman Catholicism. He also attempts to explain the reasons, the cultural impacts of conversion including the opposition to conversion and points out some movements towards revolutionary change.

Jhakmak Neeraj Ekka delineates the relationship between Christianity and the tribal religion and community in Jharkhand in terms of proclamation, self-definition and transformation. He opines that Christianity's encounter with the tribal community led to the creation of a new reality i.e. the indigenous tribal Christianity and argues that Christianity must continue to seek transformation by self-imposing questions about whether the Christian faith has truly become an indigenous tribal Christian faith in Jharkhand. In his opinion, there is still a long way to go in this regard.

B. Bolinkar Sohkhlet discusses Christian mission with regard to Primal faith in the Khasi-Jaintia context of the Northeast Indian state of Meghalaya. In his examination, Sohkhlet highlights the essential features of the primal religion before tracing the advent of Christianity, its interaction with the primal religion of the people, the Church's laxity of its perception of the theological significances and values of the indigenous religion leading to various social and religious problems. The paper concludes with proposals for the Church to enable a more meaningful and successful mission today.

Wati Longchar points out that a Jubilee year like Edinburgh 2010 must be an occasion for revision and participation in God's mission. This is particularly important when we remember that in Edinburgh 1910 the mission motif that was reiterated was an expansionist one and understood in terms of planting and organising the Church among non-Christians. With the spread of Christianity coinciding with colonial expansion, it is little wonder that Christianity even today is identified as part of Western imperialism. He points out that without negating the role and dedication of

---

[3] Ibid.

missionaries, it must also be accepted that the Church has been an ally of empires in the marginalization, oppression, exploitation and even the obliteration of indigenous communities. In today's context of corruption, the misuse and abuse of political power and where peace and justice remain distant for many, he suggests that the way forward in mission is by considering four things – affirming life, transforming life, building solidarity and affirming the integrity of creation.

T. Swami Raju points out the practical difficulty of joining insights from the perspective of subaltern movements for interfaith dialogue as many subaltern movements originated and further evolved as the movements of 'liberation' rather than 'dialogical' or 'inter-faith' concerns. Nevertheless he looks at the topic from three angles – a conceptual clarification of key terms, important subaltern movements and cults and investigating insights for interfaith dialogue. He makes the stand that the Church in the 21st century needs to continue its dialogical journey until it fulfils the bold ecumenical vision of "oneness of humanity" irrespective of differences – oneness not in terms of uniformity but of "unity in diversity" in its truest sense.

During the discussion that followed, it was affirmed that interfaith dialogue is a given reality at the grass-roots level and is a dialogue of life, though at times it becomes confrontational. Tribals, adivasis and dalits are subject to much discrimination, oppression and suffering. While Christian mission has brought the gospel of love, equality and inclusion in society to the subalterns, it has also done harm to them. For instance their religions and cultures have been neglected. The Church and even the ecumenical movements have engaged only in acts of tokenism in addressing the issue of the subalterns. While scholarships, opportunities, positions and desks are created, power still remains in the hands of the 'upper castes' and 'classes'.[4]

The Church needs to identify with the subalterns. We need incarnational ministries. The subalterns should not be treated as objects of mission who are granted charity. Rather they should be the subjects of mission. There is much spiritual value in terms of realizing the presence of God in the communitarian solidarity, hospitality, ecological integration, etc. from subaltern traditions. A note of caution was however sounded that in the engagement for justice and the reclamation of subaltern traditions, there could be a danger of false constructs being fabricated.[5]

In section five, **"Interfaith Relations from Feminist Perspectives"** we have papers written by T. Vanlaltlani and R.L. Hnuni.

T. Vanlaltlani, says that though the Church in Mizoram does not positively view the few non-Christians in Mizoram, it is the Mizo women who have reached out to these people through inter-religious marriages thus

---

[4] Ibid.
[5] Ibid.

opening up new opportunities for inter-faith relations and mission. She points out that the Church in Mizoram, being patriarchal in nature has neglected its women congregation and advocates more use of the talents and abilities women have to offer for the mission fields, especially when there can be no gender barriers from holding any position of responsibility.

R.L. Hnuni firstly points out the hill people of the Northeastern part of India lived largely in isolation from the rest of India and so there was little or no interfaith dialogue with others. The indigenous people who are converted by the missionaries were mainly animists. She points out that women played an important role as liberators, educators, evangelists and small entrepreneurs and continue this role by breaking barriers in terms of cultural, religious and communal differences. She suggests that if women were given greater responsibility in the Church today, there would be better relationships between denominations and with people of other faiths.

A point was made during the discussion that in spite of obstacles, women are positively engaged in the day-to-day struggles of life in society. Women are more interested in "diapraxis" rather than in "dialogue". A redefinition of ecumenism can be seen in women's movements where all boundaries are transcended. It was suggested that there be a strengthening of networking among women of different religious traditions.[6]

In section six, **"Christian Relationship with Marxist/Humanist/ Secular Ideologies"** we have papers written by Gabriele Dietrich and Pieter Verster.

Gabriele Dietrich explores Christian-Marxist Dialogue in her paper "On the Need to end Capitalism and built a just Society of Sharing". In dividing her paper into six segments she traces the history and significance of Christian-Marxist relations and dialogue from India's anti-colonial struggle, through the 60s and 70s of India's social and political history, class polarizations in Indian society, 9/11 and the war on terror. She concludes by pointing out that alliances need to be built with dalits, adivasis, women, small peasants and workers in the unorganised sectors if Christians are to show solidarity with the poor.

During the discussion that followed, the conflict between God and *Mammon* (the 'god' of globalization, etc.) was seriously noted. Just as Jesus was engaged in a movement against *Mammon*, people following different religious traditions and ideologies are also engaged in similar struggles. It was pointed out that here is an opportunity for working together with them.[7]

Pieter Verster points out that in South Africa's history of conflict and oppression, mission in South Africa meant a struggle to make people aware of human rights. Missionaries were often rejected because they pleaded for human rights for the indigenous people of South Africa. He further points

[6] Ibid.

[7] Ibid.

out that mission in South Africa must be a proclamation of the ministry of reconciliation. The task of the Church in South Africa is to reach out to people so that they can be established as a people living with one another and so proclaim the word of God.

In the discussion that followed, a point was made that while we in India are quick to condemn colour racism in Africa, Australia and elsewhere, we are silent about the evils of caste racism in our country. We have been advocating a pacifist theology for so long; the question that was consequently raised was should violence not be used as a deterrent or as a prophetic protest whenever it is required?[8]

In section seven, **"Perspectives and Issues in Mission and Interfaith Dialogue"** we have papers written by Shanta Premawardhana, Roger Gaikwad, Jonas Adelin Jorgensen, D.K. Sahu, and P.S. Jacob.

Shanta Premawardhana explores the idea that in today's world inter-religious dialogue is not simply a sober conversation about ideology and about power and meaning in our sacred texts but a complex dynamics of culture, language, ethnicity, social location and political affiliations are brought to the dialogue table. In wondering how the ecumenical movement can navigate these tensions, Premawardhana identifies three areas in which Christians have expressed concerns – firstly, wider ecumenism would eventually replace Christian ecumenism, secondly, that there is the fear that wider ecumenism is an implicit universalism and leads to a tacit admission that "all religions are the same" and thirdly, that Christian mission has divided the world into those who are "saved" and those who are "in need of salvation" with the implication that other religious traditions are inadequate paths of salvation.

Roger Gaikwad places the thoughts and contributions of Samartha with regard to interfaith dialogue in a world that is increasingly pluralistic and beset with communal problems. In his paper he examines Samartha's contributions to religious traditions and their response to the mystery of the Ultimate, his contributions and thoughts on inter-religious dialogue, his advocacy of a theocentric Christology which does justice to the Christian experience of Jesus Christ as well as to the empirical reality of religious plurality and what Samartha's opinions on Christian mission were. He suggests that one of the watchwords of Edinburgh 2010, in line with Samartha's thoughts could well be "Dialogical Evangelization of the Pluralistic World of Our Times".

Looking at the issue of Mission and Interfaith Dialogue, Jonas Adelin Jorgensen discusses three main missiological challenges – the political, the ecumenical and the challenge from other religions. He focuses on the third challenge and argues that the main challenge for missiology from the existence of other religions is an answer to the question, "What is the goal

[8] Ibid.

for Christian mission in relation to believers from other religious traditions?"

D.K. Sahu points out how the impact of the national struggle for freedom developed a new sense of selfhood in Indian churches and as a result they began to see the Church transcending the western cultures and western Christian denominations. Despite the diversities and disparities in India, Christian contribution to nation building in terms of education, the press and journalism, in medical and social fields has been widely acknowledged and appreciated. However challenges remain in terms of Indian Christians making their mark in the political life of the nation, in industry and commerce and in the fields of art, architecture, literature and the media.

P.S. Jacob points out that higher education in India brings people of divergent faiths together in a campus context. Such a situation could be used for comprehending and appreciating the increasing impact of an interfaith environment and the nurturing of an interfaith dialogue. Tracing the three stages of the arrival of Christianity in India he further traces the manner in which the western system of education introduced by western missionaries has contributed immensely to nation building. He points out that the major areas of Christianity's service to India has been in enhancing the modern character of restoration, educational opportunities for the disadvantaged, special attention to women's education and innovative educational efforts to name a few.

During the discussion that took place on this theme a serious concern was raised about the nature and source of Christian Mission as practised by the churches. The Church in India has not progressed much from the earlier missional commitments to nation building, education and health. There is urgent need for relevant indigenous mission theologies. Questions were raised about the relationship between mission and dialogue as well as the appropriateness of the term mission because of its colonial and communal overtones.

It was mentioned that while being committed to God's reign, as we engage in dialogue with people of other faiths, we continue to draw identity, inspiration and strength from the Bible, the life and work of Jesus and our Christian tradition; however we are also open to 'conversion.' There could be something from the life and faith of our neighbours that could edify us. So we need to have porous identities. We should be 'at the border' where new things can happen and where God's reign could find expression. [9]

At the final open plenary session the following issues were raised during the session:

- Whereas in the global environment Christian-Muslim relations have been given priority, the Indian subcontinent has its

[9] Ibid.

agenda. Both these concerns must be taken into consideration.

- Witness to Christ must be at the grassroots level and should not be confined to the academic and intellectual community.
- Both the terms 'mission' and 'witness' have been questioned due to their limitations and misuse. Likewise the term 'conversion' and the language of conversion need further reflection and clarification.
- There are however, expectations that can be made for mission during the 21st century. These include elimination of oppression and poverty and the establishment of justice and righteousness.
- Any understanding of mission and witness must be rooted firmly in the Bible.
- There is a duty of listening, paying close attention to local realities. This would mean that theologians and other thinkers may then facilitate the creation of contextual theologies and liturgies.
- Is 'mission' to be confined to the Church or may it be conducted with people of other faiths in terms of solidarity with the poor and the transformation of the marginalized?
- The Church in India is not alone but is in partnership with churches all over the world. Thus, international collaboration is to be encouraged so that we may learn from the experiences of others.
- Together with the people of other faiths we share areas of common concerns, for example, HIV and AIDS, sexual abuse, human trafficking, environmental issues etc. Thus can common projects be established as we struggle against these concerns together?
- Dalit, tribal and subaltern agendas must receive careful attention and be pursued in order to enable the establishment of justice and the renewal of human beings.
- Our experience of dialogue is that our own faith can be enhanced through the questions of people of other faiths. However, there are many Christians who maintain an exclusivist attitude.
- Thus there is an undoubted need for education for life and witness in a pluralistic society to be an inherent part of theological education and preparation for church leadership and ministry both lay and ordained.
- It may be that the challenges we face may be summed up in terms of the sharing of food, water, shelter and good news for the life of the world.[10]

---

[10] Ibid.

SECTION I

INTERFAITH RELATIONS FROM MUSLIM PERSPECTIVES

Issues in Christian Dialogue with Muslims in European Context

Andrew Wingate

Abstract

The paper looks historically at factors in Europe that affected Christian interaction with Muslims before 9/11. It then considers what has happened since, with the greatly increased profile of Islam caused by several factors outlined. It considers changes within Christian and Muslim Communities, and at Christian responses to Islam. An extensive section considers contemporary approaches to mission with Muslims theologically and practically, in ten areas. The conclusion provides evidence for why Europe in general, and Britain in particular, are pivotal for the development of a constructive approach to Muslim Christian relations, and a sensitive approach to mission.

Mission and Muslims in the Contemporary British and European Contexts

The context has changed drastically since the Edinburgh Conference of 1910. At that point, engagement with Islam was something happening elsewhere, within the old 'mission field.' This meant, in the main, the Middle East, parts of Africa and the Asian sub continent. Feelings about Islam or about Muslims were not to the fore as the previous millennium developed. There were few Muslims living in Western Europe, and issues within Europe were focused upon the Ottoman Empire, as it came to an end in the aftermath of the Second World War. The secularisation of Turkey under Ataturk was aggressive in its impact, with Islamic practice officially removed from public life. In other parts of South East Europe, Orthodox Christians lived alongside Muslims in peace, provided each left the other alone.

This is largely how things remained through the ideological conflicts of the Fascist period and World War Two, and then through the confrontation between East and West during the cold war. Questions related to Islam hardly met the public eye, either in media or political circles. Exceptions included the turmoil caused by the partition of India in 1947, and the break up of Pakistan in 1973. Amongst other significant events were the creations of the state of Israel in 1948, and consequent expulsion of the Palestinian majority into neighbouring Muslim countries, and the seemingly endless wars and violent incidents over the next 60 years which have disturbed all attempts to broker any sort of permanent or even temporary peace in the so called Holy Land. Also, led by the Middle East, there came the oil crisis of the early 1970's, with the formation of OPEC, and the realisation of the economic power that part of the world could hold over the West. But this was not yet seen as a Muslim-Christian confrontation. Equally dramatic was the Islamic revolution in Shiite Iran in 1979, an event that casts its shadow over Europe and the USA until today.

It was likewise with other post colonial conflicts in Malaysia, Indonesia, and several parts of Africa, where the rhetoric of Islam has been used within the power struggles of these areas. So also the radicalisation of Muslims in Afghanistan and surrounding areas, in the phase of Soviet invasion, and the creation of a Taliban ideology, and an emphasis on Jihad to expel the Soviet invader, using weapons supplied by the USA. Islam was brought directly onto the agenda by Pakistan, where its success in becoming a nuclear weapon state was heralded as their acquiring an Islamic bomb, in a way that was not paralleled by India's bomb normally being named as a Hindu bomb.

Mention should also be made of the break up of Yugoslavia. This brought to the fore, for the first time in Europe in recent times, deadly examples of ethnic cleansing based upon religious labels, as Serbian Orthodox and Muslim confronted each other across new frontiers. The consequence was that large numbers of Muslims moved to Western Europe as refugees, and governments were forced to take into account religious divides as a basis for state making in modern Europe.

Another major event was the publication of the Satanic Verses in 1988, and the subsequent *Fatwa* issued from Iran pronouncing the death penalty upon Salmaan Rushdie. This had a dramatic effect in Britain where he is a citizen and is in residence, and more widely in Europe. One significant effect was the mobilisation of Muslims as communities, focused around the burning of books in Bradford streets. There was a polarisation amongst liberal opinion, between those who championed freedom of expression, and those who wanted to defend the vulnerabilities of a minority community. The most prominent Muslim leader of the time, the Egyptian Zaki Bedawi, said he might hat the book, but would invite Salmaan Rushdie to stay in his own house for protection. The long term effects were considerable – was there an inevitable clash of values between Islam and those of liberal democracy? Crucially, the conscientisation of British Muslims as a force to be reckoned with had begun. And had an external power any right to pronounce against a British citizen?

These are some of the external events that had a profound effect upon Europe during the century preceding what became known as 9.11.

Equally important were migration factors. Millions of Muslims moved from Turkey to Germany, from North Africa to France, from Indonesia to Holland, and from the Asian sub continent to Britain. More recently large numbers of Muslim refugees have come to more open societies such as Scandinavia, from Syria, Iraq, Palestine and elsewhere. Estimates of population figures give up to 30 million Muslims within Western Europe. The expansion of the EU has brought in more Muslims from Eastern Europe. The question of Turkey's application to the EU is not seen just as a political or economic question, but as a religious challenge, affecting the demography of Europe radically, as 70 million Muslims would potentially have access to the EU in terms of movement of population. Another significant migration is that of Somalis, who have come in vast numbers because of the push factor of civil war, to Holland and Scandinavia. Many of these have then made a second migration, as EU citizens, to Britain, to cities such as London, Birmingham and Leicester. For example, around 12,000 have come to Leicester, a city of 300,000, in the last few years, seeking an easier place to practice their faith, and to learn English.

Since 1990, however, and more and more, since 2001, there has come the challenge about living together permanently. Jonathan Sacks, the Chief Rabbi of the United Kingdom, has written a number of key prophetic books. The first was *The Dignity of Difference*. Faced with the challenge of living together as different faiths, he suggests that religions can either be part of the problem, or part of the solution of the problem. They can only become the second if they recognise the dignity of difference – difference is not something to be feared, but to be welcomed – see my own book, *Celebrating Difference, Staying Faithful – how to live in a multi faith world* (DLT, 2005).

Sacks more recent book is entiled *The Home we build together* (Continuum, 2007), and he outlines three models of living. In his first model, Britain or Europe is like a country house. There is a host and owner. Guests come for a weekend or so, and are treated well, but are then expected to go. The second model is that of a 5 star hotel. Each culture or faith has a room. They are independent of each other, and are not expected to communicate with those in the next room. They may not speak each other's language, and there is no incentive to learn the language of the other. This is *multiculturalism* in its least attractive guise.

The third model is that of the Home. All who are part of a home contribute to the whole, each is valued for their own sake, and each needs the other. No-one possesses the home, all possess it together. There is a common narrative which all own, and they suffer or rejoice together. But each person in the home is valued for their own sake. In terms of society, this model is of *integration without assimilation.*

Applying this to the multi religious context, Jews have spent centuries in Europe being accepted as a community who are integrated, but are not required to assimilate. There were deep traumas on the way. But, for example, in Britain, they became valued for what they contribute to the whole, and much of this comes from the nature of their community of faith.

Muslims in Europe are on the same journey, and one of the mission challenges for the churches is how far they can provide them a helping hand on this journey. The journey is a different one in each country, and full of possibilities but also of pitfalls. How can the churches become advocates for such a model of integration without assimilation, rather than one of the major obstacles to this?

To take the example of Britain, the Muslim communities (note, communities, not community, since they are very varied) are about 2.5 million people, (estimate of 2010, census figure of 2001 is 1.6 million) out of a population of 55 million. More than half were now born in Britain – if you ask them to go 'home', they would remain where they are since home is Britain. But incidents like 9/11, and 7/7, the London bombing, and riots in northern cities in 2001, involving poor Muslims and poor whites, have led to negative stereotyping, in the media and amongst the general public. The challenge for the churches is how far they follow such negatives, or how far they can become advocates for a new way of thinking and behaving.

In my educational work with Christians, I have found that the kind of words used by many congregations mirror those of society – say the word Muslim, or Islam, and the description of how they are seen contains these kinds of words – confrontation, fear, suspicion, rivalry, exclusivity, terrorist and fundamentalist – or different worlds (different rooms?). Understandable. But how far can the church play a role in not mirroring the attitudes of society, but going out ahead and breaking these down. How far too can they enable the large proportion of the Muslim population who want to integrate, to contribute to British and European life as fellow citizens in a common home, not to set themselves against the democratic model of society? How far can the church provide facts, and not add to false rumours? An example is that in 2009, Europol reported that there were 294 terrorist incidents in Europe, of which only one was suspected to be Islamic in origin.

Here, mission as dialogue becomes relevant. Dialogue can only happen through meeting. Meeting and encounter with Muslim can lead to friendship and friendship to honesty and trust. 'Speaking the truth in love' means also 'hearing the truth in love.' And through such encounter, we can reach the point of mutual witness to the distinctiveness of our faiths. And from that difference, acknowledged with mutual respect, we can get to the point of contributing together to the common good.

I outline here some pan European realities, within which we need to consider mission with Muslims. Here I am drawing on a document of which I was chief Editor – *Embracing a New Reality – Muslims in Europe and training of clergy and lay people* (prepared for the Committee for

Relations with Muslims in Europe, of the Conference of European Churches and Catholic Bishop's Conferences).

The Profile of Islam has Increased Greatly

Islamic issues: These have become politicised in many European countries – questions of the Hijab, style of marriage, call to prayer, faith schools, minarets, Halal meat, have had to be tackled in each country. The European Union has had to reflect, not least through the constitution debate, on the place of religion within the European Union and the Council of Europe. The place of modified *sharia* personal law, within one legal system, has also begun to be discussed and this is highly controversial, for example, in Britain with the misunderstood reflections of the Archbishop of Canterbury about personal law and *sharia.* The building of mosques has taken place in varying speeds in different countries – for example, there are many in Britain and France, fewer in Germany or Sweden.

International incidents: These have significantly increased the profile of Islam. 9/11, Madrid, the London bombings, Mumbai and Gaza are dramatic examples of this. So also the response to what is seen as Islamic terrorism, in Afghanistan and Iraq, in Lebanon and potentially Iran; the continuing impasse in Israel/Palestine; radicalisation in Pakistan, and also a range of issues involving Muslims in Africa. Some have claimed that the cold war has been replaced by a clash of civilisations, between the Christian world and Islam (the Huntington thesis). But it is clear that most of these conflicts are about political power and economic resources, whatever the religious rhetoric.

The media: Some sections of the media have become somewhat obsessed with Islam, with endless programmes, books, films, press articles, about Muslims. These can be well produced and informative, and positive. But often they have a negative spin. These media outlets are often also negative to churches and to Christians. The cartoon controversy, begun in Denmark, was a sign of how sensitive feelings are, with polarisation between those for and those against publication. Clearly this becomes a confrontation between the right of freedom of expression, and artistic license, and the need to consider religious feelings and to act responsibly. The media ensure that what happens in one country is immediately internationalised. The BBC has recently appointed a Muslim as its Director of Religious Affairs for TV. What this will mean remains to be seen.

The Internet: Positively, the Internet enables dialogue, and education: for example, the use of Face Book enables cross religious chat rooms. There are also international programmes through BBC, Doha Talks, Al Jazeera English channel. There are challenging films of a social or documentary kind, though they are not marketed widely. At the same time there is a danger that Muslims in Europe (and, indeed, Christian immigrants from Africa and elsewhere) watch only or mainly satellite TV programmes from their countries of origin. Doing this may be harmless but it discourages integration, and may create a linguistic and generational gap. Some programmes also may not be fair about political developments in Europe. Worse, they can fire up radical movements, particularly amongst the young.

Schools and education: Schools now give teaching about Muslims and Islam, as a routine, along with Christianity and other faiths, in some countries. In other countries the school system divides religious teaching, or includes it in history or art or literature (France). In some countries there are government financed Muslim schools (England, Sweden, Holland). In a range of countries in Europe there are private Muslim schools, some residential.

Islamophobia: There has been documented growth in Islamophobia in some countries across Europe, as Muslims are demonised as a threat to European, Christian, or national ways of life. The entry of right wing explicitly anti Muslim parties into parliament, and in some cases providing support to governments, has been seen in Holland, Denmark, Norway and Sweden, all of them traditionally tolerant countries. Some countries also report a phenomenon they name as 'Christianophobia', where Christians are mocked and denigrated.

Mobility: Cheap international flights have led to many more people travelling to Muslim countries on business, or, notably, on holidays. This may increase appreciation or prejudice.

Changes within Muslim Communities

(1) Some have a growing self awareness, and wish to identify with being European, French, British, Norwegian etc, and to take part in local and national politics. They have been working at what it means to live as a minority Muslim community within a plural society In general, and at differing speeds in different countries, Muslims have become more organised. This is partly their own wish, partly responding to government needs for partners to work with. At the same time they remain diversified in culture, ethnic background, language, educational proficiency, Islamic tradition, degree of identity with modern society. At times these can lead to significant divisions. A minority wish to have nothing to do with European life and values, though benefiting economically from living in Europe.

(2) Probably the largest group of Muslims have adjusted to life in Europe, and are making their way as workers, shopkeepers, restaurant owners, service industries etc. Their children are rising in the educational field, and the local language is now their first language. In some countries – Germany, France, Britain, for example, there are a growing number of Muslim entrepreneurs, professionals, advocates. Also financial capital from Muslim entrepreneurs does much to undergird the investment markets. They are beginning to be elected as members of local, regional or national

parliaments in Germany, France, Holland, Britain and Denmark, and have taken up ministerial responsibilities in some cases.

(3) Others feel marginalised and economically passed over, and disaffected, as seen in the riots in France and in the North of England. Factors include failure in education, unemployment, and poor housing. For some this leads to drugs, violence or crime, for others to increasing radicalisation, particularly of young people.

(4) There are a slowly growing number of converts from the indigenous populations, and these are sometimes high profile in their various countries. Many are through mixed marriages. Others, of course, convert to be Christians, or become indifferent to Islam.

(5) There are often links with countries of origin. Ease of travel and IT keeps such engagement going. This is particularly the case in Germany, where the Turkish state has strong influence on the large Turkish population, especially through the DIYANET network of mosques, and Turkish culture. is deliberately maintained. Influence of other economic, social and political links with Middle Eastern countries, including Saudi Arabia, and with groups in Pakistan, is found in several European countries, and is seen as a source of radicalisation of young people.

(6) There are major debates about the position of Muslim women. These have increased as women have become more educated, and in many cases now, more educated than men. Are they oppressed by social and cultural traditions, or free to choose their own path and identity?

Some Changes within Christian Communities

(1) Increasing secularisation in Western Europe has lead to some marginalisation of churches in public dialogue, and reduction in Sunday attendance. At the same time, the vast attendance at the German Kirchentag, and the immense appeal of ecumenical centres such as Taize, and pilgrimage journeys to places as Santiago di Compestella, shows continuing interest in spirituality in Europe.

(2) There has been a growth in the relative importance of Eastern Orthodox churches. This is not only because of the revival in Eastern Europe, and conversions in the West, but also through migration to western European countries of Orthodox Church members such as to Spain, Italy and Sweden. Some of these, for ex ample in Sweden, are often anti-Islamic.

(3) Migration of Poles and others within the EU, and immigration from Africa, South America and parts of Asia such as the Philippines, have increased the size of the Roman Catholic church in many countries. So also there has been a large increase of protestant migrants from Africa, providing significant increases in church attendance within mainline churches, and the formation of many independent African churches.

(4) Theological polarisation between so called liberals, and conservative evangelicals has increased in some churches, such as the Anglican

Communion, and attitudes to other faiths is often one of the places of divide. The ecumenical movement has receded in some places, with the weakening of churches leading to a withdrawal within themselves, and mission and ecumenism taking a secondary place.

Developments in Christian Response, and Muslim-Christian Engagement

(1) *Response to secularism:* Secularism has become a central reality in national life in most countries, and in some, such as France, it is enshrined in legislation. It is amongst several reasons which affect attendance at all religious places of worship, especially amongst the young. More aggressive attacks on religion and religious values have led to a coming together of some Muslims and Christians, in defence of the appropriate place of religion in public life. Various approaches to religious experience have found a following across a range of people, not all of them young, and some of these are linked with Sufism or spirit movements in Christianity.

(2) *Response to violent extremism:* Fear of Islamic extremism has penetrated many Christian individuals and groups, and also affected moderate Muslims' confidence in dealing with the issue.

(3) *Solidarity with the persecuted:* There is a higher profile of those working to highlight persecution of Christians in Muslim lands, and their appropriate challenge to Christian and Muslim leaderships in Europe. . These stories influence Christian congregations, whether through the media coverage, or through refugees. This can lead to polarisation, but also to joint statements by Muslims and Christians condemning such extremist actions.

(4) *Statements:* Positively, there have been a wide range of statements by Christian churches, in response to a number of issues and conflicts that have arisen. There has been lively intra Christian debate within the churches in most countries, with the presence of Islam being an energising factor in such discussion. More Christians are willing to engage with Muslims at all kinds of levels. These include the academic level, and inter faith dialogue. They include common actions – events, demonstrations for peace etc. They also include working together in the issues of life, 'the dialogue of life'. Muslim-Christian women's interaction has increased.

(5) *Exchange programmes:* These have become more frequent. An example is that between EKD, Germany, and Iran, and between the Church of England and Iran. There are a range of joint programmes related to Israel/Palestine. The Anglican Church has a joint programme with Al-Azhar in Egypt. Many groups have been to Turkey to visit holy sites, for example a Muslim-Christian group from Leicester. Indonesia has also been involved in such programmes, and there have been student exchanges with Algeria. There are also university faculty contacts between countries.

(6) *Local and national forums:* In some countries, Christian-Muslim forums have been established at a national, or city level – for example in Britain with the Christmas-Muslim Forum, of which the Archbishop is President, in France with GAIC (Groupe d'Amitie Islamo-Chretien), and in Norway and Denmark. In Germany, the Christian-Muslim Working Group (ICA) was established on a national level as early as 1976. In Germany also notable is the Christian/Jewish/Muslim initiative 'Invite your Neighbour' (1999-2003) followed by 'Do you know where I am?' (since 2004). This has encouraged supported some hundreds of local initiatives. There are also many city level or local district initiatives such as those in Paris, Gothenburg, Leicester, Drammen, Arhus and in a number of German cities. Individual church leaders have been appointed with responsibility for Muslim-Christian relations in several countries.

(7) *Training opportunities:* Initiatives in training have increased, for lay people perhaps more than yet for clergy. From the Christian clergy side, these include the training of future pastors, or in service training, in Islam and in Muslim-Christian relations.

(8) *Academic study:* There has been a growth in academic interest in Islam and in Muslims in Europe – not primarily in textual work, but over a wide range of areas. Growth of 'scriptural reasoning' dialogue groups. Initiatives like *A Common Word* (2007) bring a wide response. This was the remarkable letter of 138 Muslim scholars and religious leaders, addressed to the Pope and other Christian leaders. Since the number has risen to around 400, with numerous Christian leader responses, and its web site can be read with great profit as an example of a major Muslim initiative in dialogue.

Mission and Muslim Communities

It should be remembered that Christianity, as Islam, was born into a multi faith context. We need therefore to go back to our roots in reflecting theologically on how to relate to the Islamic presence in Europe. Change is not uniform, and there is enormous diversity across Europe. Attitudes need to be encouraged that are prepared to embrace change positively, and to trust in God to guide us to a way forward. For God embraces all humanity in the creation stories, and we need not be afraid of working together with Muslim brothers and sisters.

(1) *Mission, Evangelism and Theology of religions:* There are clearly a variety of understandings of the status of people of other faiths, as found in Christian traditions, and these can loosely be summarised in three ways. For some, the imperative is to preach the gospel since it is the only door to salvation ('exclusivism') For others, all religions are expressions of various relationships to God, and that human beings cannot judge between such expressions ('pluralism'). For a third group, Christ is at the centre of any understanding of God's salvific will, but above all, Christ reveals the

openness of God's love for all ('inclusivism'). He remains the unique Saviour, but we cannot determine how this eventually is achieved and where are its boundaries. That depends upon God's mysterious will, and the breadth of the operation of God's Spirit (cf *Nostra Aetate*, Vatican II). Christian mission is about expressing that love in word (evangelism) and action.

These understandings all have their implications in relating to Muslims, and Christians need to face the challenge of reflecting on these possibilities. How to respond when a Muslim desires baptism? Is this what we seek? Christians must also be prepared to be 'evangelised' by Muslims (*da'wa)*. The right to share one's faith, and the right to convert are part of the human rights as they are enshrined in the UN Charter and guaranteed in Europe by the Convention on Human Rights of the Council of Europe. This right is not fully accepted by all Muslims living in Europe. But we can see acceptance agreed in the final declaration of EU sponsored Christian Muslim Conference in Mechelen, Belgium, October 2008, atteneded by 25 Muslims and 20 Christians from across the wider Europe, organised by the Churches Committee for Relations with Muslims in Europe (CRME) – 'As Christians and Muslims (of Europe) we acknowledge the right of freedom of conscience, of changing one's religion or deciding to live without a religion, the right to demonstrate publicly and to voice one's religious convictions without being ridiculed or intimidated into silence by prejudice or stereotyping intentionally or through lack of knowledge.'

(2)*Mission and Inter faith dialogue:* There are various ways of analysing dialogue between faiths. Two examples follow here. The Roman Catholic church has distinguished between four levels of dialogue (*Dialogue and Proclamation – 1991). Dialogue of life, dialogue of engagement, dialogue of theology, dialogue of the spirit/heart.* These are simple and self explanatory, and provide a basis for a holistic approach to Muslim-Christian interaction. It is made clear that dialogue is not opposed to proclamation. A parallel model, based upon the WCC guidelines, also has four principles – dialogue begins when people meet people; dialogue depends upon understanding and trust, dialogue leads to common action; dialogue is the means of authentic witness. It should be noted that witness is likely to be two way, listening to the other, as well as proclaiming Christ. We must be ready to be transformed by the encounter. Dialogue with the unexpected and radically different other, leads to 'surprise and joy', as we talk about what matters most – holiness, being at peace, and what truly is (Rowan Williams). God alone is truth. We are all on the way, and are to be open to learning from the other.

The Orthodox theology of dialogue centres upon their wide understanding of the place of the Holy Spirit in creation and redemption. The Muslim will fully understand the centrality of the search for holiness, peace and truth, in the dialogical encounter. Christians in Europe have usually made the first steps, which is not surprising, as they hold the historically powerful position, and remain the main faith in Europe. Also, dialogue for a Christian, is following in the steps of Jesus in his ministry, reaching out to others. The Trinity emphasises dialogue within the heart of God (*intra*), and this flows outwards (*ad extra) (missio Dei)*. A significant minority of Muslims are now responding to the challenge of dialogue.

(3) *Mission and the scriptures:* There are differences in the approach to scripture found within the Christian world. We should recognise that there is a growth in conservatism within some European churches. This has been increased through the immigration of Africans to many European countries. Many of them have had difficulties with Muslims in their own country. There has also been a growth in Pentecostalism, which had had similar effects. Most of these groups are very wary of those who make relationships with Muslims a priority. At the same time, others are finding a new excitement about reading the Bible in a multi faith world. For some this is found in a fresh discovery of the Old Testament (Hebrew Bible), and its commonalities with parts of the Quran. Reflection on a commonality between the values of the Kingdom of God, and the ethics found in the Quran has proved fruitful. Comparison can be found between the stories of the Gospels and some of the traditions related to Mohammed in the Hadith. Christians have also been challenged to justify and indeed to rejoice in the diversity of our gospels and the writings of Paul, in terms of their witness to Jesus Christ. Muslims will of course also vary in how they use the Qur'an in today's European world.

(4) *Mission and sharing of basic Christian convictions:* Christians are challenged to explain how they can believe in Christ as more than a prophet, by questioning from Muslims. They are led to understand why Muslims reject the sonship of Christ through dialogue with Muslims. This forces Christians to explain in understandable terms what we mean by 'Son of God.' The same applies to the explanation of the cross and resurrection as being at the centre of the Christian story, and the place of the suffering God (as per Bonhoeffer). God coming in the flesh is a deeply disturbing concept for Muslims, but is the heart of Christian faith. The 'second coming of Christ' is also a rather different concept in Islam, and Christians are led to think about their own understanding of this difficult, but credal concept.

The paradox of the Trinity stems from the early church as a picture or symbol of how Christians experience God. Muslims need to be reassured that affirmation of the Trinity does not mean we are dividing God, or believe in three gods. Christians are absolutely committed to the oneness of God, but this does not limit the language of how that oneness is experienced. Within the Trinity, the place of the Spirit needs to be emphasised, and the breadth of God's presence through history and in the wider world beyond the church. The contribution of East European and Syrian Orthodox churches, and of theologians such as Jurgen Moltmann, from Germany, and JV Taylor, from England, can be noted here. Here the concept of *logos spermatikos* ('without Him was not anything made that was made', can be introduced as a potentially inclusive concept.

(5) *Mission and Apologetics:* Christians can learn from Muslims about the importance of defending their faith. Many Muslims know only about Christian beliefs, as taught by fellow Muslims, and the information they pass on is what Christians would see as misinformation or misperception. Understanding the 'other' is a vital challenge. But at times dialogue can no longer proceed with any benefit, where there appears to be a dialogue of the deaf. Christians should be prepared to explain the faith within them, or as St Paul puts it to 'confess the faith of Christ crucified', which was 'foolishness to the Greeks and a scandal to Jews.' They should be prepared for what they say as being radically unacceptable to Muslims. But they should also at the same time be prepared to listen to the Muslim, and hear how they define themselves. Defending the faith does not mean defending everything that has happened in Church History, or in the actions of the contemporary church, even less of so-called 'Christian nations.' This will help Muslims to feel they do not have to defend everything done in the name of Islam – 'not in our name'! Sometimes it is necessary sometimes 'to tell the truth in love.' We must hold to relationships while standing firm against distortions of what we see as the truth about Christian faith. An example is the use of the Gospel of Barnabas, composed, serious scholars of this document agree, in the early 17th century. If Muslims quote this as if it is the gospel, Christians should be prepared to express clearly our dissension from its use in dialogue.

(6) *Mission, Ethics and social engagement:* Both religions are concerned about how to live a good life under God. There is more than a human referent for ethical standards. There are important commonalities between Muslims and Christians. So also the general command to 'love our neighbour as ourself', as highlighted in *A Common Word.* Both also have universal ethical norms, though with contextual working out of those norms in a given situation. In decision making, both involve reflection on scripture, tradition and reason. Christianity, however, should not revert to 'proof texts', and simply referring to 'God's law.' Nor should Christians adopt an attitude that is confrontational to the secular, or be over ready to dismiss the 'the enlightenment'. The UN Declaration on Human Rights is vital for today's approach to ethics, for a Christian, even though it does not spell out any God reference.

Sensitive areas in ethical discussion are likely to include the relationship between the individual and society, the place of democracy and freedom of the individual, the ethics of conversion, and gender issues. Perhaps most sensitive will be the approach to questions of human sexuality, including marriage and divorce, homosexuality, cohabitation, polygamy, sex education etc. Included also will be questions of gender understanding, the upbringing of children, the care of the elderly. All these are seen by

Muslims, as by Christians, as being religious questions, even if the two faiths sometimes come to different conclusions.

Common approaches can be developed towards ecology and the environment, reverence for life, and how to prevent the breakdown of law and order, and the increase in crime. So also there can be common approaches to the evil of racism, and the rise of the far right in several European countries. Responsibility for the use of money, and God's gifts on the earth can centre around the common concept of stewardship given to human beings. Consideration of waste and litter, and conservation, can be approached together to 'save the earth'. There needs to reflection upon the place of personal responsibility, and the place of conscience in ethical decision making.

(7) *Mission and spirituality:* Spirituality is at the heart of both Muslim and Christian faiths. Both centre upon public times of worship – *salat* for a Muslim, the daily offices and the Eucharist (mass, divine liturgy, holy communion). These can be observed by the other, but are not normally participated in by the other faith, which can lead to confusion. But the intention behind both is the praise of God, the acknowledgement of our dependence upon Almighty God, our prayers for others, the expression of solidarity with our fellow believers, and the sense of being protected by others. Alongside these times, through dialogue there can arise times of mutual spirituality. These may be controversial, and not acceptable to all, for theological reasons. No-one should be forced to join anything they are not comfortable with. Examples of prayer alongside each other include famous public occasions such as prayers for peace at Assisi (1986), attended by Pope John Paul 2nd, and the regular prayers Sant Egidio held ever since; the Commonwealth service held every year in Westminster Abbey, attended by the Queen of England; prayers held in many places after disasters such as the tsunami in 2005, or prayers before the Iraq war. In Holland there have been Assisi style prayers for the opening of parliament since 1986, and annual prayers in Leeuwareden. Some such prayer events are civic, some are within churches. But all include many faiths, and prayer is alongside, and not mixed together.

Prayer can also arise in long standing dialogue groups, or between individuals who need each others' prayers. Here, it is important to be sensitive to the group, and to feel when prayer becomes appropriate. It is also important that words are carefully chosen and are as inclusive as possible. Another type of engagement is with Sufi movements, or with *dhikr* chanting, or Shia chanting during the month of *muharram*. The phenomenon can be compared with the use of the Jesus prayer in Orthodox tradition. The use of the rosary can also be seen as a common practice, where the names of God or Hail Mary (Ave Maria) are chanted. Prayer at the tombs of saints in popular catholic and Islamic traditions is another apparent commonality of practice.

(8) *Leadership structures:* Muslims have often gone through a major challenge on coming to Europe. In some contexts, they are used to tribal or family leadership, in others, to the dominance of the state authorities, as in Turkey or Iran. Leadership in religion and within the state are not separate in various places. Muslims in Europe are faced with the challenge of being a Muslim in a state without an all embracing Islamic framework. The Imam is traditionally a teacher and leader of prayer. In Europe, there is a pressure for him to become like a Christian priest or pastor. Christian clergy can assist imams in their development to a wider role, but should not impose their own models. The movement towards chaplaincy has also led to some Imams, as well as lay people including women, becoming facilitators of pastoral care within a range of institutions and communities. This role requires different forms of training, from the old purely scholarly schools of training, and Christians can assist in this.

(9) *Mission as Pastoral care.* Muslims often come with structures of family, and community care. They have not had experience of pastoral care in a different kind of society, where life tends to be individualistic, with the young going their own way. Where the family holds together, the problems may be lessened, though those who opt out of this can be very lonely. Another area of challenge is the nature of marriage, for societies which are used to arrange marriage, often to cousins. Bringing brides from the home countries leads to significant problems if they are not educated and do not know the European languages. Divorce is growing fast.

How are Christian and Muslim care structures responding? One way is clearly through the role of chaplains in institutions, whether clergy or lay. The Christian chaplains/pastors find themselves responding to a range of these problems – for example in prisons, hospitals and universities. For example, in the Netherlands there are official army, hospital and prison Imams, paid for by the government, as also in Britain. Christian care of immigrants is a major calling in many countries. How to advise in cases of inter faith marriage, particularly when children come, is a delicate ministry. The convert coming from Islam, needs special care, not just from the priest but from the congregation, to provide a new 'family' often. The convert away from Christianity needs to be known that they are still loved, his/her family need to be reassured that they are not 'responsible' for what they see as apostasy. The challenge also of how to pray with the bereaved or sick from another faith, can arise for a Christian pastor. How to offer new hope to those without hope through alcohol or drug addiction, or through long years of imprisonment. How to show love in a way that 'sets people free'. This may include affirming them as Muslims, and introducing them to appropriate pastoral or community care, it may on occasions to respond to their request to know more about the Christian faith. This situation must never be exploited in the quest for converts.

(10) *Mission and the Education of children and young people:* The situation varies from country to country. Secularism has led to ignorance in

understanding the religious facts and cultures throughout Western Europe, and in several East European countries. Some countries such as France include the teaching of religious facts in various disciplines, such as history, literature, art etc. The purpose is to understand the cultural heritage of Europe, as well as of France, of the world as well as the local. In France confessional teaching is given in private schools or in chaplaincy within public schools. In Norway, the emphasis is upon Christianity – 50% – and other faiths and philosophies and ethics – 50%. Few schools are faith schools. In Britain, the government is encouraging the opening of many more faith schools, whether Christian or Muslim or Hindu or Jewish or Sikh. However, there is a clear distinction between Anglican schools which cater for the whole community, and Muslim, Catholic or Jewish schools which are largely or completely confessional. Religious education is broad, as in Norway, and is required in all schools. Confessional teaching has been compulsory in Romania since 1990. There are significant developments in Germany, where the partnership between religious organisations and state religious education has a firm place in the public educational system. Efforts are being made to include Islam within this system, and there are now established professional training programmes for future Muslim religious teachers at several German universities. The syllabus in Madrassas is under scrutiny in several places, with an encouragement or requirement to include citizenship education, as well as traditional subjects.

Conclusion

Europe has become a key area for Muslim-Christian relations, and within Europe, Britain is in the forefront of most issues, with its variety of communities, and British commonwealth connections focused upon the vast number of Muslims living in the Indian subcontinent. For Holland the connections with Indonesia is central, for Germany Turkey, for France the Magrib. Recent asylum movements have brought the whole world to Europe, with Scandinavia to the fore in receiving Muslim refugees. Freedom of movement within the EU has led to migration across the EU, wherever the orginal point of entry. Europe is also the continent where Muslim scholars, as mentioned above, are struggling towards new European interpretations of Islam which work at making it compatible with liberal democracy and with living as a minority within a multi faith society where Christianity is main partner or protagonist. The challenge for Christians is which of these they are to be. This is why an Indian Christian I met on a train in South India a couple of years ago, shook hands with me after a long conversation, and wished me well on my return to Britain – 'You are going back to the most important country in the most important continent for the future of the world. If religions and cultures cannot live together there, they cannot do this anywhere.'

It is not surprising therefore that the majority of responses to the Common Word (see above) have come from Europe, from a range of sources (see the web site of Common Word). There have been other common documents of significance. The Mechelen statement above contains this challenge:

> Identity has many strands, of which religion is one. Strength in a rope comes from many strands being intertwined, including our identity as Europeans, as citizens of particular countries, and our ethnic background. We are challenged to build bridges across cultures and faiths. Europe is called to be a laboratory of learning for both Muslims and Christians.
>
> As Christians and Muslims we believe in the principle of integration. This does not and must never carry with it the demand to forsake our religious identities. For example this may happen through prohibiting the wearing or display of religious symbols in public places or neutralising religious festivities with the pretext that their being allowed would harm the sensitivities of other believers or that they would go against the principles of the secular state.

There is also an urgent need to stand together against a new militant atheism which is increasingly strident in Europe, even though the number of its followers may not be large. Richard Dawkins is the most prominent. A summary is found in an article in the Guardian (1.6.2002):

> Since it is no longer permissible to disparage any single faith or creed, let us start disparaging all of them. To be clear: an ideology is a belief system with an inadequate basis in reality; a religious is a belief system with no basis in reality whatever. Religious belief is without reason and without dignity, and its record is near universally dreadful.

Here Muslims and Christians need each other. And this means trusting each other. It is good that important that in Norway and Britain, Muslims and Christians have agreed together statements about mission. The British statement affirms the right of both faiths to share their faith. It lists 10 different guidelines on how this can be done which recognises the need for compassion and transparency, and ends 'Whilst we may feel hurt when someone we know and love chooses to leave our faith, we will respect their decision and will not force them to stay or harass them afterwards.'

A young Muslim leader, Dilwar Hussein,and a colleague from Leicester, writes for this European context in the modern Muslim journal EMEL (July/Aug 2004) as follows:

> Muslims are now part of the West, so the discussion is not between 'them' and 'us', but between 'us' and 'us', among ourselves, with our common humanity. Talk of 'clash of civilisations' in this context is not only dangerous and irresponsible (for the false line it perpetuates), it is also foolish…Muslims living in the West may not agree with certain material motivations in the West or the way the family is being neglected, and on these issues they may stand together with many of their fellow citizens of Christian and other faiths and non-faith backgrounds. Muslims living in the West may take issue with the current state of social and international justice,

and they would again stand with the majority of their fellow citizens. On concerns abut the environment, again Muslims would stand with the people.

A last word from Rowan Williams, the Archbishop of Canterbury, about dialogue:

> The Christian is struck and challenged by the fact that outside the visible fellowship of faith, lives are lived which look as though they are in harmony with the Christian Universe.... We have to see how very other our universes are; and only then do we find dialogue a surprise and joy as we also discover where and how we can still talk about what matters most – holiness, being at peace, and what truly is.

A joint commitment to holiness, peace and truth – where better to end this study of mission amongst Muslims in the contemporary British and European context. And how central this is in the light of the economic and political uncertainties we live under in Europe.

Hundred Years of Christian-Muslim Relations: Mission to Interfaith Relations

David Emmanuel Singh

In this paper, the phrase 'Christian-Muslim' is understood as being part of the broader academic and activist notion of 'interfaith'. The terms, 'interfaith' and 'intercultural', will be used interchangeably but the focus here will not be on the reflections of local religion/culture on Christianity or the history of or efforts at the development of a culturally sensitive Christianity nor on the academic and pluralist theology but on the development of the idea of relations or exchanges (which to many can be/are a source of intercultural/interfaith theologies of religion).

The phrases, 'Interfaith' and 'Christian-Muslim' are used often as terms denoting an actual example or potential state of 'relations' and are seen by many to be a positive strand of development in Christian thinking from 'confrontation' to 'understanding, reconciliation-peace and collaborative action' for common human good. In Christian theology these may represent movements from stark 'dualism' (people are saved apart from their religion through Christ and his Church) to 'qualified pluralism' (religions play a significant and positive part in human salvation in Jesus Christ) to 'absolute pluralism' (religions have a central role in God's single plan of salvation). Clearly, whilst the first two theological positions do fall within what might be described as Christian Mission Theology, the last position transcends any notion of particularity (see Dupuis 2001). The traditional ways of thinking and approaching Islam (and other faiths) as was also supremely endorsed by Edinburgh 1910 however continue not least in many churches and among many Christians.

The idea of interfaith/Christian-Muslim relations is not new. Cragg, in his lecture in Oxford (2009) argued that academic centres, even in the 30s subscribed to a theologically neutral approach to religions. This to him contrasted with the religious and theological approaches which tended to be absolutist. In 'the post-colonial' and the 'post-western Christian' context, this relational approach has gradually been growing out of academia. This has not replaced the traditional mission but reflects the priorities of peace and collaborative action for common human good. Edinburgh 1910's section on 'Carrying the Gospel to all the Non-Christian World' serves as a fair summary of the traditional approach.

Our focus here is not on traditional mission or theologies of religions on their own but on the evolution of thinking among Christians from traditional mission to interfaith relations since Edinburgh 1910.

Mission to the 'Non-Christian World': Edinburgh 1910

W.H.T. Gairdner's account of Edinburgh 1910 was published for the 'World Missionary Conference' in 1910 (Gairdner 1910). Its interpretation of the conference is based primarily on an over 300 pages report which was a result of a two year long process leading up to the conference. Gairdner's work is accessible and is generally reliable not only because it was published in the year of the conference but also because it was published for the conference. The interpretation given it therefore most closely dovetails with the official position. Chapter VII of this work deals with faiths other than Christianity (Gairdner 1910:68-92). Christian missions are founded on biblical-theological and historical foundations. Edinburgh 1910 represented a renewal of a long-held goal the foundations of which were seen to be biblical and yet it was seen as something 'largely unfulfilled'. Every age believes it is standing on the cusp of history, uniquely positioned to make a mark on history itself in fulfilling aspirations of the ages. Unsurprisingly, the conference saw itself as being in a unique point of history to 'make Christ known' to the world. The world was carefully segmented in to different regional, geographical, racial, religious etc. type. The most fundamental division was that of the Christian and Non-Christian world. The centre of the Christian world was still acknowledged to be Europe and the 'Non-Christian world' was out there, largely the two-thirds world or the global South. The main purpose of the conference was seen to be to 'scientifically' investigating the faiths in their present contexts and the 'problems' they posed. The study was not to understand or learn from them or to relate with them but to make 'the Gospel known' and thereby fulfill the command of Jesus Christ in St. Matthew's Gospel.

To be fair, Gairdner's synopses of the report does capture the emerging realization of the fact that: Firstly, although, the centre of Christianity was still the historic European and North American regions, the so-called 'Christian world' was facing internal challenges in the form of luxury and materialism. The belief was that the future of the mission to the 'Non-Christian' world was dependent on the health and earnestness of the 'Churches of Christendom' (Gairdner 1910:87-88). The centre of gravity of Christianity and the true measure of 'the pure faith of Christianity' was still believed to be in the West. The 'conquest' of the 'Non-Christian world' was seen to be necessary and the Western Church was seen to be the prime mover of this process. There was nothing of the sort of vigorous support for the idea that the 'centre of gravity of Christianity' was already tilting toward 'the South' as it has been in recent times in the writings of Buhlmann (1978) and Walls (2002: 118). There is however some interest in the increasingly significant role being played by the churches of 'the mission-field': 'Evangelization of the world….is not chiefly a European and American enterprise, but an Asiatic or African enterprise. Therefore our hearts have been filled with hopefulness and confidence as we have studied the reports from all over the world showing the growing evangelistic and missionary spirit in the Church in the Mission-field.' (Gairdner 1910:84)

The acknowledgement of the continuing centre role of the European and American churches and the significance for evangelization of the 'Non-Christian World' in 'the South' by the 'Church in the Mission-field' (in the South) led to the led to the call for churches to be engaged in 'united planning and concerted efforts' (Gairdner 1910: 83).

A good part of Gairdner's review of the report to the conference however actually deals with clearly re-mapping the 'Mission-field' in 'the South'. What is interesting is that this re-mapping is done along geographical, racial and religious lines. This is where Islam gets defined as a priority area for Christian mission. In terms of geography, certain 'neglected' mission fields also called the 'unoccupied fields' were specifically named such as Mongolia and strangely, India! Specific countries were named as the priority areas; as for example, in Africa, particular emphasis was paid to the 'problem of Islam' in Africa. Islam was seen as a problem both because of its resistance to the Gospel but also because it was inhibiting Christian work in the borderlands. Islam was seen both as an object of an impossibly difficult mission and a competitor. In the case of the borderland 'heathens' Islam was seen as winning the battle in being ahead of Christianity in 'Islamizing' the 'heathens' (Gaidner 1910: 73). Colonial policy of favouring Muslims/Islam in terms of political power, especially in Nigerian and Congo regions was seen to be another serious problem for mission work. Contrary to popular belief about missions being facilitated by colonialism, the Edinburgh report suggested that it was in fact working against Christian mission interest. This was because, it was believed that the presence of the colonial authority was removing the 'natural barriers of resistance' and since Islam was being favoured in colonial political patronage here it had, from the report's perspective, an 'absolutely free Play'. The challenge to Christianity was, according to the report, that there was no competing force to neutralize the influence of Islam in this region. This 'problem of Islam' was being exacerbated by the internal Islamic political and religious movements such as the Sanussi which started in the 18th century and was influenced by the 18th century Wahhabi movement. The pro-Islamic colonial policy coupled with the resurgent Islam in Africa was seen as the bane of the Church, an 'impossibility which only mountain-moving faith could remove' (Gairdner 1910:74). The mood was sensational: 'unless the present drift is reversed, we shall probably before long *see Islam assuming the attitude of the heaven-sent uniter and vindicator of the African race,* reaping most of the harvest sown by the Ethiopianism of to-day (italics in the original) (Gairdner 1910:74). Some of the recommendations for this to happen can seem rather simplistic, even laughable. As for example the idea proposed by a participant that in Nigeria the dominant Hausa clan be won for Christ with the establishment of a force consisting of forty workers and focusing primarily on education to 'stem the tide of Islam'! (Gairdner 1910: 73) A call was raised therefore for all Christians to 'unite in 'facing the common problem of Islam!' all over colonial Africa (Gairdner 1910: 73).

Outside Africa, it is not clear from the report if Edinburgh 1910 was entirely aware of the far greater presence of and significance of Islam in the Indian subcontinent or the Far East. When speaking of India or the Far East, the conference seems to have had either, the Indian and the great 'yellow' races or, Hinduism, Buddhism, Confucianism and Shintoism in mind. They were certainly aware of the presence of Islam in this region but just did not think this was as significant as the African and more importantly the Middle Eastern Islam. The report therefore speaks of the great 'Problem of Islam' especially in terms of the Middle East. The West seems to have had a special interest in the Middle East and is not simply limited to faiths. Subconsciously, the West has never lost its sense of loss of a thriving Christian presence before the advent of Islam. Crusades were, among other things, an attempt to regain this lost world. The Middle East is an abiding reminder of this loss and a latent force that can potentially overrun the world again with disastrous consequences for Christianity's missionary potential and its very survival. The lands, peoples and religions in the east and west of the Middle East are no challenge. The real problem is 'that great, central, unsympathetic, alien and hostile wedge [Islam]' (Middle Eastern Islam). If the world were to be thought of as a 'seamless robe', the Middle East was like a tear in the middle isolating the 'Catholic Church' on the two halves of it (Gairdner 1910:75).

For this reason, the conference made a special appeal to focus on this region. The strategy seems at best quite general and at worst almost humorous. Thus, for example, it suggested that the existing centres of Christian presence and activity needed strengthening and new ones established. The plan was in line with the old Western commercial tactic of founding mission centres like 'trading posts' along the coast of Arabia. This had worked spectacularly in India. The Mughals never thought much of these posts but these very posts became a start of a power that would replace them in the subcontinent. So far so good; but then it was suggested, by no mean a person than Zwemer, that the purpose of the advance of Christianity thus was to 'try the effect of a mission to Mecca and Medina'! (Gairdner 1910:75)

In the conference itself no specific references were made to Indian Muslims. When a reference to India was made it was still a 'jewel in the crown'. Most people, even rulers have limited memory of history. The 'sepoy mutiny' (war of independence) was in part religious in nature. The exile of the last Mughal to Burma was symbolic of the full British victory over Islamic India and the formal start of the Raj. By the time of the Edinburgh conference, Muslims in India were more numerous than in the Middle East (and they still are), but they were subjects of 'the great civilizing force' of the Raj. They were not a problem like the 'other'

Muslims. Simplistic though their solutions for mission were, they demonstrate to us a greater sense of confidence and reach under the Raj. Thus, when they speak of one missionary for every 25000 (a supposedly 'scientific' and 'prayerful' calculation), they were not thinking of placing them on the margins of India – i.e. on the coasts but in the very heartland. The strategies here (Gairdner 1910:76) were in line with the tested 19th century missionary methods of John Wilson[1] and Alexander Duff's[2] education!. In speaking of the so-called 'storm-centres' of interest, India as an undifferentiated whole was seen to be *a* focus of 'the ecumenical crusade'; the others being 'the Yellow Farther East' and 'Islam' (Middle East and Africa) (Gairdner 1910:72).

Mission Paradigm in Change

It is not surprising that Edinburgh 1910 identified the 'storm-centres' for mission to be in the global South. It did acknowledged challenges of 'luxury' and 'materialism' in the West but continued to be optimistic about the central role to be played by Europe and North America in world mission. 'Mission world' was supposed to be vast and out there. This world was still simplistically divided into the Christian and 'Non-Christian' worlds. The notion of the 'Christian Church' however, transcended this generalized division. Although, the Church was mainly located in 'the Christian World', it was also present in many parts of the 'Non-Christian' world (although, many areas remained 'unoccupied' and needed to be part of the new strategic mission).

This acknowledgement of the presence of the Church in the 'Non-Christian world' assumed the Church to be a distinct entity untouched by cultures. There was therefore a lack of serious interest in things to do with interfaith or intercultural. Not many seemed to question the idea of Mission simply as fulfilling the Great Commission or a lack of recognition of possible continuities or interfaces between religions. Three forms of Fulfillment ideas however were proposed, though largely within academic theology: the first assumed an essence of religion (such as Otto's *numinous*) seeing underlying linkages between religions. Critical theorists and historians would understandably not take this seriously as they would assume ideas are historically formed and conditioned. The second form supposed that Christianity fulfilled aspirations in other religious traditions. Perhaps this was the form that came closest to the Protestant Fulfillment

[1] Early John Wilson is also known for his polemical approach to religions which involved refuting religious beliefs in public debates (and then often printed). See O'Hanlon 2002: 65. A PhD work on Wilson being completed through OCMS/Wales by R. Gabriel argues that Wilson gradually changed his methods from overt polemics to more sophisticated method of education as a means for change.

[2] See Venn 1970: 85-125 on Duff

theology. The third form was idealistic like the first. It supposed all religions to be part of a subtle process of dialectical development towards 'the Cosmic Christ.' (See Whaling 548-49).

Protestant Fulfillment theology which would just be making its appearance in informal discussions at this point seemed confined to academic discourse (see Farquhar 1913; Hedges 2001; Sharpe 1965). The great followers of Jesus Christ like Sunder Singh and N.V. Tilak 'experimented' with Christian life and thinking that seemed quite at home with their mother religion and culture. They seemed to assume their traditional faith was both linked spiritually and was fulfilled in Christ. They were critical of the missionary enterprise, the foreignness of the institutional Church and generally their antithetical and polemical mission methods that had not much regard for other religious traditions and cultures.

Early Christianity was missionary but it was lived and practiced on the margins. It was often persecuted and was characterized by powerlessness. Growth in numbers despite suffering was affirming and would have been an important source of hope and a proof of its truth. Christendom changed Christianity beyond recognition. As power became part of the equation, ideals of self-sacrifice and suffering became dogmatized as ideal to celebrate but not necessarily to participate in. Power and the new sense of self encouraged martial attitude and practices. Actual, verbal or written Crusades and polemics against Islam (indeed all religions) became commonplace.

The institutional Church, Christian states and missionaries aside, even the great Orientalists have been accused of seeking to undermine other religions and civilizations and serving Christendom. We know that the Orientalist discourse was varied and was not always engaged in the service of Christendom. Western missionary movements have been accused of legitimizing colonial ideology and 'piggy-backing it to spread Christianity without seriously engaging with faiths. To be fair, missionaries were a product of their time and there are many significant examples of the missionary critique of colonialism (Bartolome de las Casas in South America) and colonial antipathy to missionaries and missions (the Serampore Trio in India). Political power and religious patronage do however collaborate more often than not. Colonial enterprise did contribute to a sense of separateness, superiority and temporal-spiritual power over others. Its effects on Mission thinking therefore cannot be denied. It was all part of a general sense of God being on the side of Christianity and, thus, traditional mission was not seen as arrogant, grandiose or self-absorbed. It was natural and normal.

Why is this changing? The world wars showed the underlying hatred human beings were capable of. In the subcontinent, the Partition showed another face of the human capacity for violence. As millions migrated across the new nations states, thousands were butchered on both sides of the border. The violence between Hindus and Muslims (others too) has continued sporadically since Independence. The contemporary image of Islam has suffered much from its association with violent Jihad and 'belligerence'. This image is in stark contrast to the Meccan and prophetic phase of Muhammad (see Cragg 2009). In such a context, fundamentalist and confrontational versions of faith including traditional missionary Christianity might seem to be quite irrelevant, even dangerous.

The experience of political freedom and the re-discovery of ancient texts and their translations not only brought the great religious traditions and their wisdom back to the surface (for others to see and appreciate) but it also accorded greater degree of confidence, identity and self-respect to the adherents. The increasing reduction in the dependence of non-western Christianity on the West, its contact, awareness and appreciation of the richness of these traditions encourages the rise of contextual theologies. This also encourages greater efforts at exchange and relations.

In the majority world, freedom from colonialism furthered the resurgence (some of it extremist) of indigenous and historical religions and cultures. Christianity too is firmly rooted in many of these contexts and is widely understood to be more populous here than in Europe. This encounter of Christianity with other living forms of the same faith and other living faiths can create isolationistic tendencies in some but it can also create a form of Christianity that is knowingly or unknowingly taking the shape of the local culture. Thus, both in terms of culture and theology, one can speak of this sort of Christianity as authentically African, Indian, Chinese, and Korean as it reflects greater sensitivity to and continuity with the local cultures. In post-colonial India although, 'religious studies' have not become widespread in secular academies, it has now become possible to study Christianity and Islam not simply as part of other 'hard scientific' disciplines such as social science, history and politics but on its own terms as Christianity and Islam (Hinduism, Jainism and Buddhism continue to be taught as part of philosophy). Although, mission theology/missiology continues to be popular in seminary contexts, changes are taking place even here towards more intercultural and interfaith relations direction.

In Europe, secularization led to modernity which in turn has contributed to the increasing reduction of religion (Davie 2002). One expected that the same would happen elsewhere in the world such as in Africa and Asia where the post-colonial state, in varying degrees, were aspiring to change their economic and political destinies. Modernity does seem to have become quite commonplace in these regions, even secularism in places like Turkey, India and Kenya. This has not however led to the marginalization of religion as it did in Europe. America too followed a different trajectory from Europe and hence, this led to Davie's idea that Europe was an exceptional case, in that secular and modern ideas do not necessarily lead to the reduction of the influence of religion. Even in contexts such as the United Kingdom where the Anglican Church has been closely identified with the state, and where displays of any single religion in state schools (for example) are not considered appropriate. It is true that here the state's association with the Church has more to do with 'traditional forms' yet, religion here has not been abandoned. Most white people see themselves as Christian and people of other faiths such as Islam, Sikhism, and Hinduism etc. are as alive as ever. As a multi-religious society, Britain too has seen its own share of violent religious conflicts as also France, Netherlands and Spain on the continent.

Works by the scholars such as Smart contributes to the realization that Christianity is after all a historical religion like any other with characteristic dimensions common to all. Such approaches enable people of faiths or no faiths to speak of religions without necessarily having to take sides or offer judgments (Smart 1998). Cragg has argued this point too but instead of relying on 'descriptive phenomenology', he recommends the use of 'philosophy' in place of 'religious or theological' discourse. His reason for this is that religious and theological discourse tends to be 'absolute'; the adherents feel the need to defend its tenets as timeless and exclusive truths and when taken to extremes, can lead to conflicts, physical Jihad or Holy Wars. Philosophy helps to maintain neutrality (Cragg 2009).

Globalization is also a force to reckon with. The world is becoming smaller and people of faiths are increasingly moving across the world and changing demographics. Never before has the world needed a more concerted effort at building a common future of humanity on this tiny globe. Peace, environmental concerns, and common human good are not simply seen as the tasks of 'Nation States' but of the 'United Nations' transcending regional, religious and ideological boundaries. Increasingly, the people of faiths are being asked for their contributions to these goals. Human survival and the survival of the planet depend on everyone making their contribution. Faith based initiatives in areas of development and environment for instance are being increasingly recognized world over, not least efforts where multi-faith and interfaith work is making a difference in situations of poverty, natural disasters and political or religious crises.

Interfaith/Christian-Muslim Relations

Broader Debate

Hardt and Negri (2001) published a book titled *Empire* which has generated considerable discussion. This new Empire is not inspired or legitimized by religion (e.g. Byzantine, Mughals, and Ottomans etc.) or ideology (Communist) and yet is more widespread in its reach and effects than any others in the past. It seems quite able to function relatively freely across the nation states and seems relatively free of political constraints as a sovereign power in its own right. This is significant in a world also seeing a resurgence of religion and culture in many parts. The idea of 'interculture' is consequently a new watchword for banking and world business (as is evident from the HSBC advertisements). The ability of the new empire to operate across nations may be a cue for religious people and theologians to take into account religious and cultural plurality in their vision for humanity. This may involve appreciating that Christians in the south have theologies too and other religions too have their theologies. In this world of diversity, social praxis can perhaps provide a way of inter-connecting people and their theologies expressly for the sake of a more critical goal: Peace.

Skepticism about traditional missions with its dualistic suppositions comes from academies traditionally considered strongholds of Christian theology (Wijsen and Nissen, eds. 2002). The main argument has been to replace missions with liberation theology, intercultural/religious theology and faith inspired development. This probably explains why some academic faculties have ceased to have chairs in Missiology. Missiology as a discipline continues however in some faculties but largely in seminaries. In seminaries of free colonies however, there is a renewed re-conception about whether mission should become 'dialogue' (see Monte & Lang 1998) or 'interfaith/cultural relations' and mission theology/missiology should become intercultural theology. Dupuis' argument in his 'Christian theology of religious pluralism' about mission being dialogue is an example of this transition in post-colonial/post (western) Christian Christianity (see Dupuis 1996).

In Western academies Christian theology is often twinned with 'Religious Studies'. This means that religions are studied on their own terms and not anymore through the glasses of Christian Theology. Theology is thus gradually losing its traditional position of privilege. This is roughly the same in Germany where some chairs combine Mission (Christian Theology) with the Study of Religions (as in Heidelberg) whereas in others Mission and Theology have given way completely to 'Intercultural Theology' and the 'Study of Religion' (e.g. in Salzburg).

Hollenweger is credited with having renamed 'mission' as 'intercultural theology'. This renaming is intended to reflect the actual international (rather than western Christian) character of Christianity today. It acknowledges the need for Christian theology to actually allow the inputs from diverse Christian backgrounds and cultures where Christianity today flourishes. It also means that Christian theology needs to seriously engage with the real questions and issues from these contexts as sources for theological reflections. Hollenweger's concerns stemmed from his engagements with students from the majority world who were required to rehash Western theology (he called it 'mono-cultural imperialism'). Much of this theology was said to be simply irrelevant or ill suited for non-Western contexts (Hollenweger 1989 & 1984).

But, Intercultural theology is more complex than this as Kuster and Grayson have argued. It involves three aspects of a single process of development: 'Missiology' looks at how Christianity takes form in different cultures and although this may be the case, it is not necessarily concerned with providing missionaries with a substance for mission. It is concerned with the 'first contact'. 'Ecumenics' is concerned with intra-Christian and inter-faith relations at the early stages following the contact. These may be characterized by 'conflict'. 'Comparative religions' is concerned with genuine 'exchange' between religions (see more Kuster 2003 and Grayson 2007 & 2009). This process involving Contact, Conflict and Exchange not just describes how Christianity encounters another religion-culture and is 'emplanted' but also how this can serve as the model and source of intercultural theology (Geertz 1973).

Clearly, therefore, intercultural theology is understood to be an umbrella term denoting 'inter-confessional, intercultural and inter-religious' engagements (see also Wiksen 2001). It is today understood to be an important task for Christians belonging to the Ecumenical Association for Third World Theologians. These are men and women of faith rooted in their cultures but also exposed to Western academies. They recognize the narrowness of a mono-cultural theology, which is often blind to or inimical to local cultures and subcultures (see Fahlbusch 2008).

Christian-Muslim Relations

This is the broader context for Christian-Muslim relations. The shared history of Christians and Muslims shows that it does not matter who is politically or culturally dominant, Muslims or Christians, perhaps with some exceptions in the 9th century, conflict and confrontation has been a norm (Goddard 2000). The principle of 'exchange' has rarely been explored.

In the early Arab Middle East, which experienced the Muslim conquest and was integrated within the expanding Muslim rule, only Muslims had full rights. This may have partly contributed to the decline of Eastern Christianity. Their migrations, even today (e.g. in Turkey and Iraq) are perhaps a sign of the continuing conflicts (most of it avoidable, as in Iraq). Both religions have been guilty of taking their notion of truth and reality to extremes and in hating the other enough wage wars.

Perhaps there is something for modern Christians and Muslims to learn from the 9th century dialogues. Beaumont's work on Christology shows how Christian presented 'Christ for Muslims' in what he called 'the most creative period of Christian-Muslim dialogue' (9th century) (Beaumont 2005). What is interesting is that he compares it with the 20 century dialogue which follows similar trajectory and this is where his significant contribution lies. Christians believed there were continuities between the two faiths. Islam already had the Christ and their task was to build on this pre-understanding. In such an open and honest context even the seemingly intractable problems of Jesus' divinity and crucifixion could be explained and people were civil enough to hear them speak. They may eventually reject it but not before they had properly heard them.

The comparative framework for Beaumont's study was intended to serve as a model for dialogue. According to him, what characterized Christians from these periods was their ability to listen to Muslims and their objections and take their 'concerns seriously'. There was genuine commitment to engaging with them and although, they might eventually reject Christian claims, Christian commitment to continue fostering this relationship and creative exchange held promise. This sort of friendly persistence was precisely what Jesus intended in 'the Parable of the Sower' in Mark 4. Jesus spoke creatively in parables not to confuse people and prevent them from understanding but to secure understanding. The question of acceptance was for the listener to choose. Some thinkers go a step further in seeking to understand and secure understanding of their respective faiths in the spirit of friendship and service. Apostolov (2004), for example, in his 'Christian-Muslim frontiers' searches for an interface between Christianity and Islam from the new perspective of intercultural theology. The key notions in this approach are 'interface' or the 'zone of contact' where theologies intersect.

The idea of 'interface' or the 'zone of contact' or 'exchange' (rather than conflict) is interesting. It conceives of religions as representing, as it where, different circles. Much of these circles are unique to the religions they represent; i.e. the greater space in these stands on its own may owe to the unique trajectories they have traversed in their political, social, cultural and economic history. There appear however, between these circles, 'zones of contact' or 'interfaces' which too may owe to historical contacts between them, natural osmosis of ideas and possibly also the common operations of a just and loving God, the creator of all beings and the spirit of Christ. In terms of the idea of exchange through such zones of contact, we have the example of W.C. Smith who purposefully worked hard to emphasize 'interfaith' and particularly Christianity's relations with Islam. To him it did not mean sacrificing religious distinctive – that was the greater part of religious identities anyway (Ipgrave 2002). The traditional approach, according to Smith assumed Islam and Christianity to be two distinct religions and civilizations (thus representing them as separate circles). It is not surprising therefore that confrontation and conflict have characterized their history. Their relationship as a result is still largely understood and constructed in terms of clash rather than cooperation and acceptance (see Huntington 1998). Smith's call therefore, was for 'a new mental map'. Here the 'operative metaphor' was 'relations' the object of which was not simply 'understanding' the other and securing their understanding of another's faith but to lead to genuine relations expressed in and through a common theology ('world theology')(Smith 1981). This theology would be dynamic and developmental. It would be based on the premise that truth was a 'humane' and 'not an objective' concept. It was not contained in 'beliefs or doctrines' but was 'a function of the inner person.' If the nature of truth was concrete and not abstract then it was something that grew in human engagement with it (see Netland 2001).

Whether we agree with this extent of the idea of relations and a kind of pluralistic theology it engenders needs discussion. One might suggest however that there are historical and methodological problem in thinking of Islam and Christianity as being two distinct circles. We know there is a continuing effort on the part of the Christian minorities to create a place for themselves as equals in Arab-Islamic states. Common culture and history are powerful means in this process (see Pacini 1998). In the pre-19th century period Christian minorities in the Ottoman Empire lived under Islamic law. There was no sense of necessary conflict between them. In the 19th century, conflicts between Muslims and Christians in the empire became commonplace and to a large extent continue until today in modern Turkey (Masters 2001). One would not be far wrong in asserting that much of the current Muslim use of biblical material and vice versa remains explicitly negative and polemical. In one of my recent studies I highlight two passages from Isaiah and Deuteronomy that are used by Muslims for their assumed connection with the earliest call narratives in Surat 96 and 74 (see Singh 2008). My argument was that the parallel narrative exposition of the Qur'anic passages in canonical traditions and the earliest *Sirat* suggests a relational narrative/theology, not a polemical one; this narrative/theology involves the issue of Muhammad's identity as a prophet like Moses. Thus, addressing the issue of Muhammad's prophetic identity, early on, was inextricably linked to the Jewish and Christian traditions of Moses. A change from a relational to a polemical approach owed partially to the early post-Meccan developments in Islam and may be explained, at least partly, as a later "rereading" of an earlier tradition. There was therefore an element of deliberation and pre-meditation in seeking a distinct identity or an identity forged in opposition to things that otherwise might have actual relations. Conflicts and reasons for these thus evolved and were encouraged.

Perhaps Coptic Christianity in Egypt and Ethiopia serves as a good example of intentional disjunction and separation (see Hasan 2003). Indeed Coptic Christianity is a brave survivor in a context dominated by Islam. Its marginalization in Egypt does not make for a pleasant spectacle. However, one of the contemporary responses to this has been a reaffirmation of a distinct identity that is rooted in an ancient culture that does not have another living parallel. This identity serves to assert their unique discourse on Egyptian-ness and Coptic Christian identity that is not shared by Egyptian Islam. Separateness is emphasized in order to inspire revival of a distinct identity and communal pride. This sort of recollection or coming together does have its advantages in a context of overt discrimination and outright hostility but only for a time. It almost seems like Coptic Christianity is reliving a period of first 'contact' and 'conflict'. What it needs to further its relevance in Egypt will require an immense sense of faith to transcend to the level of 'cooperation' and 'exchange' with Islam.

The way of seeing Christianity and Islam in absolute circles may have been fine in an age of political conflicts of the Western Christianity with the East, but we like to think we live in a different world today. We have the benefits of hindsight. We know the crusades and the World wars (and in our own age), the Iraq war were not necessary conflicts, they were made to happen. They owe to certain ideological positions sometimes religiously legitimized. They could all have been avoided. Today, a majority of the Christians live in the East where Christianity is also growing. Christianity can no longer be equated with the West. The great ideologically conflicting axes of the West and Islam cannot be simplistically equated with Christianity versus Islam. This way of thinking has serious consequences for the ancient Christian minorities living in 'Islamic' lands and generally for Christians and Muslims in Africa and Asia alike. In these regions, Christians live with Muslims and are often part of the same cultural and civilizational 'circles'. There is often a greater degree of overlap between them and Muslim neighbours than between them and Western Christians. Our emphasis therefore, needs to shift to relations something that Bennett (2008) persuasively argues as he searches for bases for peace and justice and reconciliation.

Christian-Muslim Relations: Cases

Henry Martyn Institute (HMI)

Following Edinburgh 1910, in 1926, the National Christian Council (NCC) (later to become NCCI) formed a committee to explore the possibility of establishing a centre dedicated for 'work among Moslems'. Subhan (1972), a former director, in his story of HMI tells us that HMI was the product of this process. Since NCC was involved, it was clear that it would share the prevailing traditional Edinburgh 1910 position in respect to Christian mission among Muslims. From 1930-38, it was located in Lahore but later moved to Mussoorie (1938-40) (present state of UP), Aligarh (1940-62) (present state of UP), Jabalpur (1962-66) (MP), Lucknow (1966-71) (UP) and then Hyderabad (1971-present) (AP).

In the first three decades of HMI's existence it continued this early position both in terms of its essential ideology and practice (D'Souza 1998:8). HMI was conceived as a 'school' (later changed to 'Institute') of 'Islamic Studies'. This reflected the 'scientific' angle of Edinburgh 1910 towards: India, 'Yellow race' and Islam (see Gairdner 1910:76). Research and study was therefore one of three main tasks of the 'school'; the other task being preparing Christians for work among Muslims and the writing of gospel literature for use among Muslims (Isaiah 1980: 651-53). In line with Edinburgh 1910 and underlying the 'scientific' exterior, there was the fundamental belief in the 'Crescent faith' (Islam) being a 'problem', which could not be entirely overcome but could be 'neutralized' (see Gairdner 1910:73). Interestingly, 'the Tambaram debate' that took place in 1938 did not change or affect HMI in this phase. Kraemer's work outlining his position on religions (and Hinduism) was one of the main contexts for debate at this conference. Kraemer's brief was to write a preparatory material for discussion on the question of 'Christian approach to non-Christian religions'. Ariarajah speaks of the responses from Chenchiah and Chakkarai which were then published as *Rethinking Christianity in India* where they questioned Kraemer. Karemer's response was published in *The Authority of the Faith* (Ariarajah 1991:69). The fundamental problem (from the Indian perspective) with Kraemer's position was that he saw no 'continuity' or compatibility between Christianity and religions (Hinduism in particular).[3] Despite appreciating the historical nature of Christianity as a religion he distinguished it from others as the 'bearer of revelation'. He rejected the notion of Fulfillment and emphasized 'discontinuity'. In this context the task of mission was not to look for continuities but to focus on how to make the Gospel as a radically 'new/true news' relevant (Ariarajah 1991:70). Kraemer, a firm believer in 'realism', unabashedly saw Christian mission as 'the third redeeming factor' after 'western oriental science' and 'colonialism' (Kraemer 2002; repri.). It is clear from this work that he was responding to the growing interest in and talk of the 'meeting of Christianity and the great non-Christian religions'. He believed this idea of 'meeting' and 'dialogue' was too fuzzy and unhelpful. He was interested in establishing the clear line between Christianity and other faiths. As the 'universally valid' and bearer of revelation, Christianity was the 'normative standard of truth'. This to him removes the fuzziness in the fashionable use of the ideas of dialogue, encounter and meeting (Kraemer 2002; repri.).

The 1960s began, D'Souza argues, with a new focus in the work of HMI – 'dialogue' (14). This phase saw a promising start of real contact between Christians and Muslims as is evidenced from the first joint seminar of Christians and Muslims organized by HMI in 1965 at the NCC offices in Nagpur. It was a four-day consultation between nine Christians and nine Muslims focusing on both aspects of 'faith' and 'works'. We do not know what this consultation really led up to in terms of clear outcomes on the question of faith and works. What is significant is not that any agreement towards a joint statement was reached but that such a meeting took place. One of the concrete outcomes however was the organization of a series of seminars on the 'relational' theme of 'Islam and Christianity'. Both Muslims and Christians saw this as a sign of a changing relationship and respectful attitude (see D'Souza 1998:16). D'Souza, quoting from Subhan,

[3] See Kraemer's details of Kraemer's position on religions including Islam in Kraemer 2002.

notes that dialogues like these were seen as evidence of a positive movement from 'polemics', 'debates' and 'controversy' to 'inter-faith fraternization and a better religious understanding' (see Subhan 1972:12 and D'Souza 1998:17). The goals of conversion and discipleship were seen to be consistent with this positive, respectful and honest approach.

The 1980's began a new phase in HMI's evolution. Largely in the light of the dangerously incendiary communal context particularly involving Muslims and Hindus in India, the idea of peace and reconciliation were considered and later adopted as the goal of mission (see D'Souza 1998:24-31). On the ground, this led to not just interfaith academic studies but also interfaith living (journeys), joint work during and in the aftermaths of Hindu-Muslim communal violence (*aman-shanti* forum). Today, this focus continues and besides these HMI is also involved in joint development work in the violence prone areas of Hyderabad. HMI has a permanent presence in these locations where it works closely with both Hindus and Muslims. The ideological/theological under-shoring for this sort of work was provided by what was called the 'Constructural Theology of Reconciliation' (D'Souza 1998:29) an approach interfaith theology which closely reflected the reality of interfaith work and staffing. This was called 'Construal' as is being figured out through actual action process and remains incomplete.

The Burnley Project

Another actual working of Christian-Muslim relations comes from the South Asian (Muslim) dominated region of Lancaster, UK. It shows how a respectful exchange between Christians and Muslims can work to promote 'religious cohesion' in a region of the UK that is hopelessly divided in socio-religious terms and has also witnessed actual communal conflicts in 2001 (see Holden 2009).

After the communal conflicts of 2001, Building Bridges Burnley (BBB) was constituted by the Burnley Lane Fellowship of churches. These were a not part of mainstream Anglican but rather fellowships of 'Trinitarian Christians'. BBB invited the Muslims leaders who were on their own part seeking to bring things under control after the violence. This initiative received much enthusiastic participation in due course from mainstream denominations such as the Catholics, Methodists, Anglicans and Free Churches. Along with the Muslim groups, BBB evolved over a two-year period and was formally registered as a charity. The impact of BBB was broadened through their networking with likeminded charities and organization across the religious divide. It began with addressing the tension following the conflict but this initial task gradually broadened with the institutionalization of BBB and the transfer of its offices to a local mosque. This was not only the first interfaith organization but the first one to be housed in a mosque where people of all faiths were freely welcome. Funds poured in both from Islamic as well church based groups. Among its activities was an initiative called the *Bridge Project.* It task was to work with children as young as 8-13 who were understood to be vulnerable to extremist influences. Another group within BBB looked after the affairs of the interfaith work, which included a series of Christian-Muslim seminars, church and mosque visits, interfaith parties etc. The *New Schools Working Group* jointly oversaw faith-based activities in six schools in town. Special emphasis was laid on certain groups of the youth most vulnerable to social alienation. Young people were involved in community activities such as sports, drama, and outdoor activities. Over time not only primary schools but also secondary became involved in the BBB. Holden notes: 'What had begun as a largely reactive partnership in the months following the disturbances had become a proactive one within a 4-year period. The organization had gained recognition for its work at local, regional and national levels and had received visits from [other] interfaith groups....' (Holden 2009:184/Apendix 1)

The question of cohesion was significant in such a charged and mutually exclusive multi-faith/culture context. Communities used to isolation and absolute difference, have been the 'breeding ground' of terrorist sympathizers and homegrown South Asian terrorists as the London bombings amply demonstrate. In such contexts, obviously, the idea that faith can somehow be allowed to remain a private matter, simply will not work. Politicians and have shown how serious it is to engage the people of other faiths at the level of ideas (Muslims in this case) and in joint work out of 'political necessity' (Holden 2009:viii). This is the pragmatic goal of the state and its public representatives. The project shows, Christian and Muslims may have different goals when it comes to essentials of faith and ideas but this difference is not going to prevent them from engaging with each other at any level. Holden's work is a serious piece of social-action research. It shows, based on actual empirical evidence by working together and engaging with each other, that they are responsible for what happens to faith communities. They can choose to remain separatist and suffer its consequences or choose to engage and thereby promote reconciliation and wellbeing even in a context to segregation and conflict. This was called the *The Burnley Project.*

Holden, as a sociologist, partially borrows from theology of religion discourse four typologies of 'religious attitude': religious inclusivists, religious exclusivists, secular integrationists and secular aversionists. Secular and religious people strangely demonstrate not too dissimilar preferences. There are people in both camps who support or oppose engagement. Religious people open to interfaith relations/action are wary of proselytization (especially if it is a hidden as the real motive for engagement) not of open and honest conversations on faith (including differences). Many of them are wary too of infringing on 'worship' aspects of faith which obviously are deemed to be an inside matter. Otherwise most on both sides of the divide are most happy to engage. The attitudes may be wide-ranging and complex but it is the lack of willingness and initiatives to actually make engagement that is responsible for segregation and conflict.

Conclusion

The purpose of this paper was not to argue for the validity of one approach over the other but rather to present a survey of the idea of 'interfaith relations' with reference to traditional mission since Edinburgh 1910.

'Traditional mission' and 'relations' approaches seem to follow different paradigms. They are however not necessarily different and there need not be any competition between them.

Believers across Christianity and Islam rightly hold to truth being independent of the observer. Traditionally, however, many Christians and most Muslims have held a rather naive position on how this truth is revealed and received. They have assumed truth to remain unaffected by this process of descent and reception. They have also assumed that somehow our historical and contextual location does not shape truth as we perceive it. This results in a religious or theological discourse which tends to be absolute and exclusivist. In interfaith contexts this position translates into rigid and polarized positions respecting the truth and its ownership. Relations between people of faiths (also between people from within the same faith) in such encounters are often characterized by conflict or disjunction.

A qualified variant of this position would adopt a more realistic and critical approach to the process of revelation and its apprehension. It would query human capacity to receive truth without affecting its apprehension by means of their location in history and culture. This is not a terrible thing to acknowledge. It is instead humbling. This attitude has the potential for believers to be in a better position to acknowledge continuities between faiths than those sure of possessing truth as it is. Furthermore, the descriptions of what is received through theologies too are shaped by the history and context of the theologian. This does not mean that the truth itself is relative. This means however, that theologies need to be understood as provisional statements on truth and in need of ongoing review in different periods and contexts.

The metaphor of religions being circles was also reviewed. One can imagine each circle to contain diversity within and representing the different intra-religious/cultural theologies. Whilst one can expect a continuing exchange and dialogue within each circle, the extent to which different religions will intersect with each other, these intersections can be a source of potentially valuable interfaith theologies. This process will not affect the uniqueness of religions since the greater parts of each religion would seem to be free of interfaces. Scholarly studies of contact between Christianity with other cultures/religions shows (as we pointed out) there to be three levels: first contact, conflict and exchange. A review of the

Christian-Muslim contacts over the ages and particularly in the last 100 years show conflict to be a primary effect. Conflict is not necessarily negative. It is part of the story though, not the complete story, as the examples of the Burnley Project and HMI showed. Sustained and deliberate efforts at contact for common good and peace need not result in conflict. Conflict in the tripartite story of interfaith contact is therefore, neither necessary nor inevitable.

The outcomes of conflict and exchange depend on the goals one nurtures and the belief about truth one subscribes to.

Bibliography

Apostolov M 2004
The Christian-Muslim Frontier: A Zone of Contact, Conflict, or Cooperation. NY: Routledge Curzon

Ariarajah, W. 1991
Hindus and Christians: A century of Protestant Ecumenical Thought (Rodopi Bv Editions)

Beaumont, M. 2005
Christology in Dialogue with Muslims: A Critical Analysis of Christian presentation of Christ for Muslims from the Ninth century and twentieth centuries (Oxford: Regnum)

Bennet, C 2008
Understanding Christian-Muslim Relations (Continuum)

Buhlmann, W. 1978
Wo der Glaube lebt (Where the faith flourishes), Freiberg

Chandler, P-G 2007
*Pilgrims of Christ on the Muslim Road: Exploring a new path between two faiths (*NY: Cowley)

Cragg, K. 2009
'70 Years' Study of Islam'; a lecture at Song School, St Stephen's Hall, Oxford; 6 May, 2-4 Pm

Davie, G. 2002
Europe: The Exceptional Case (Darton Longman and Todd)

D'Souza, D 1998
Evanegelism, Dialogue, Reconciliation: The Transformative Journey of the Henry Martyn Institute (Hyderabad: HMI)

Dupuis, J. 2001
Christianity and the Religions: From Confrontation to Dialogue (Maryknoll: Orbis)

Gairdner, W.H.T. 1910
Edinburgh 1910: An Account and Interpretation fo the World Missionary Conference (Edin. Lond.: Oliphant, Anderson and Ferrier)

Grayson, J. 2007

'The Kwallye Samga of Korea: A Failed attempt at Christian Accomodation to Confucian Culture' in *Asian Folklore Studies,* 66, 125-140

Grayson, J. 2009

A lecture given on 12.3.2009 at OCMS, oxford on 'A Failed attempt at Christian Accommodation to Confucian Culture'

Farquhar, J.N. 1913

The crown of Hinduism (London: 1913)

Goddard H 1995

Christians and Muslims: From Double Standards to Mutual Understanding Surrey: Curzon Press

Goddard, H. 2000

History of Christian-Muslim relations Edinburgh University Press

Let Us Understand Our Differences: Current Trends in Christian-Muslim Relations in Sub-Sahara Africa

Martha Th. Frederiks

Abstract

This article gives a brief overview of Christian-Muslim Relations in sub-Saharan Africa. It points out that in recent years, due to the pentecostalisation of Christianity and the increased influence of more fundamentalist Islamic groups, relations in sub-Sahara Africa seem to deteriorate, despite initiatives to work on harmonious interfaith relations. The article then identifies three current trends in Christian-Muslim relations: an increase in polarisation and polemics, the debate on the implementation of *shari'a* and joint social action programmes.

Introduction

Anecdotal history relates of an encounter in the mid 1960s between Dr. Nnamdi Azikiwe, Nigeria's first president and Alhaji Ahmadu Bello, one time premier and Sarduna of Sokoto. The story, related by Johnson Mbillah, general coordinator of the Programme for Christian Muslim Relations in Africa, is transmitted as follows:

The two leaders had met to discuss the growing tensions between coalition partners in central government (the Northern People's Congress and the National Council of Nigerian citizens). The tension brought into the open divergences between the majority Muslim north and the majority Christian south which was degenerating into ethno-religious antagonism. In the cause of dialogue to restore some understanding, Dr. Azikiwe is quoted to have said to Ahmadu Bello, "Let us forget our differences." Ahmadu Bello replied, "No, let us understand our differences… By understanding our differences we can build unity in Nigeria."

And Mbillah continues: 'This short conversation between the two leaders provides the real grounds in which interfaith relations in Africa can be carried out – accepting our differences and living with such differences in harmony.'[1]

When assessing current trends in Christian-Muslim relations in Africa the shift from 'let us forget our differences' to 'let us understand our differences and live with those differences in harmony' can be used as a characteristic for recent developments in African interfaith relationships. The agenda of Christian-Muslim relations in sub-Sahara Africa seems to have changed from an emphasis on information and intellectual dialogues, to reducing communal tensions and stressing the need for joint social action despite differences.

This contribution gives a brief historical overview of Christian-Muslim relations in sub-Saharan Africa in order to position current developments and then proceeds to identify and discuss three main trends on the contemporary interfaith agenda: concern over the increase in polarisation and polemics, reflections and debates about the implications and introduction of *Shari'a* and joint social action programmes such as peace-building projects and programmes to combat the HIV epidemic and its consequences.

Before embarking on this scheme however, a few introductory remarks are in order. Whilst the topic 'current trends in Christian-Muslim relations in Africa' might seem self-evident, the question needs to be asked: which Christians, which Muslims and which Africa are we talking about.[2] The aspirations in Christian Muslim-relations of the Church of Pentecost in Ghana or of Mensa Otabil's International Central Gospel Church will differ substantially from the stance of the Presbyterian Church of Ghana or of the Roman Catholic Church in Ghana on interfaith relationships. Likewise a Nigerian Muslim of the Qadariyya or Tijaniyya fraternity will have a different outlook on interfaith relations than a member of one of the newer Islamic fundamentalist movements such as Izala or Maitatsine.

Not only are denominational allegiances important for understanding Christian-Muslim relations in Africa, historical and regional differences also play a crucial role. Whereas both Islam and Christianity have a long history in the North, North-East and West of Africa, Christianity and/or Islam are of much more recent date in South-East, Central and Southern regions. As such, the South African Muslim community consisting of mainly Indian and Malay Muslims who joined other South Africans in the strife for abolition of Apartheid[3] has a distinctly different history from the

---

[1] J. Mbillah, 'African Churches and Interfaith Relations. Food for Thought', in J. Mbillah and J. Chesworth (eds), *From the Cross to the Crescent*, Nairobi, Procmura 2004, 7-8 (1-14)

[2] J. Voll, 'African Muslims and Christians in World History' in B.F. Soares (ed.), *Muslim-Christian Encounters in Africa*, Leiden, Brill 2006, 18-19 (17-38).

[3] M. Haron, 'Christian-Muslim Relations in South Africa (ca. 1986-2004). Charting out a pluralist path', *Islam and Christian Muslim Relations*, 18/2 (2007), 257-273. The South African Muslim community consists of two groups: those who were

Muslim community in Tanzania with its direct link between Islam, Arab merchants and Swahili culture[4] and both are again different from the Senegambian 'black' Islam[5]. These differences in development and history are also manifest in interfaith relations.

As Africa is a huge continent and both Islam and Christianity have a wide diversity, it is virtually impossible in one single contribution to discuss Christian-Muslim relations in Africa in their broadest sense. Therefore, this contribution will mainly focus on Christian-Muslim relations as perceived from a Christian perspective with particular attention for Christian mainline traditions. Though not exclusively a Protestant perspective, this chapter will first of all focus on the relations and reflections of Protestant mainline churches with some excursions into Roman Catholicism and Pentecostalism, thus honouring the Edinburgh 1910 legacy in its widest interpretation. Regionally, the emphasis will be on the developments in the Western and Eastern regions of Africa, where both Islam and Christianity have a long history and where at times the tension between the two communities have risen high.

Christian Muslim Relations: A Brief History

In order to assess current trends in Christian-Muslim relations in Africa, a short historical positioning seems appropriate. Christian-Muslim relations in Africa go back to the days of prophet Muhammad (pbuh). With Christianity well established in North Africa, the valley of the Blue Nile (Nubia) and present day Ethiopia (Axum), newly professed Muslims in 615 sought political asylum with the *Negus* of Axum. Though traditions vary somewhat, Sura al-Maryam (S. 19) is said to have played an important role; the result of the audience was that hospitality was granted to the group of Islamic refugees. One of the traditions recounts:

> On further questioning by the king on what they believed about Jesus Christ, Ja'fer proceeded to quote some passages from the Qur'an about Jesus Christ: 'Verily Christ Jesus, son of May, is the apostle of God and his word which he conveyed into Mary and a spirit proceeding from him.' And when the Emperor asked him about Mary, he recited the Qur'an XIX, 16-34 (…) When the Emperor heard that, he wept so that his beard was wet with his tears… Then said the Negush to them, 'Verily this and that which Moses brought

---

brought to South Africa as slaves (Malay Muslims) and those who came as merchants (Indian Muslims). Both groups suffered under the Apartheid regime and joined other Africans in the strife for liberation.

[4] L. Rasmussen, *Christian-Muslim Relations in Africa. The cases of Northern Nigeria and Tanzania compared*, London, British Academic Press 1993, 9-12, 21-26 and 55-61.

[5] M.T. Frederiks, *We have toiled all night. Christianity in The Gambia 1456-2000*, Zoetermeer, Boekencentrum 2003, 113-157.

> emanate from one Lamp, go, for by Allah I will not suffer them to get at you, or even contemplate this.[6]

Hence, the first Christian-Muslim encounter on African soil was peaceful in nature and this hospitality and interreligious acceptance is still frequently referred to as the African matrix for interfaith encounters. Whether described as 'that tolerance that was once traditional in Africa'[7] or as 'the innate African spirituality that focuses on existential matters and has thus become the bedrock of African religiosity, which is live and let live with our religious diversities in harmony'[8], the basic message conveyed is that relationships in Africa are in principle harmonious and that conflict is the exception, instigated by influences from elsewhere. Benjamin Soares contests the usefulness of this point of departure, stating:

> …many studies, in particular those in theology and missiology, employ a decidedly outmoded social model that assumes that the "normal" state of affairs is one of peaceful coexistence and mutual tolerance between Muslims and Christians. While such attempts to understand and possibly promote religious "tolerance" are perfectly understandable in a world where conflict between members of different religious communities seem increasingly prevalent, interactions between Muslims and Christians, in Africa and elsewhere, cannot be understood as simply coexisting at a point on a one-dimensional continuum that runs from coexistence to conflict.[9]

Soares no doubt has a point when he argues that relations were much more complex than can be expressed by a simple coexistence-conflict model. Neither the Muslim community nor the Christian community are monolithic and though possibly most African Muslims and most African Christians have gotten along harmoniously most of the time, this is certainly not the case for all African Christians and African Muslims all of the time. Relations were unquestionably more multifaceted than the smooth 615 encounter. The seventh century Arab conquest of North Africa for example had distinct violent traits, though at the same time many of the Christian communities welcomed the Arab-Muslim rulers for the stability they brought.

The inclusion of North Africa in the Umayyad empire eventually led to the virtual disappearance of the North African churches, with the noted

---

[6] Quoted as in A. Mehari, 'Christian-Muslim Relations in Ethiopia', *Christian-Muslim Relations in East Africa. Report of a seminar/workshop sponsored by the Lutheran World Federation and the Project for Christian-Muslim Relations in Africa*, Geneva, Lutheran World Federation 1987, 79 (77-81).

[7] O.A. Onwubiko, *Echoes from the African Synod. The future of the African church from present and past experiences*, Enugu (Nigeria), Snaap Press 1994, 117.

[8] J. Mbillah, 'African Churches and Interfaith Relations. Food for thought' in J. Mbillah and J. Chesworth, *From the Cross to the Crescent*, Nairobi, Procmura 2004, 5 (1-14).

[9] B. Soares, 'Introduction', in B. Soares (ed.), *Muslim-Christian Encounters in Africa*, 3 (1-16).

exception of the Coptic Church in Egypt; lack of inculturation, internal divisions and conversions for practical reasons e.g. acquittal from *jiziya* all contributed to the gradual Islamization of Northern Africa.[10] Expeditions from North Africa and the conversion of the Berbers who controlled the trans-Saharan trade routes led to a slow but sure dispersion of Islam (or, as some prefer: of Muslims) to sub-Saharan Africa from the 10th century onwards,[11] resulting in the conversions of the kings of Gao (985 AD) of Tekrur (1040 AD) and of ancient Ghana and Mali to Islam.[12] By late 14th or early 15th century there were small settlements of Muslim Africans in all of West Africa up to the edge of the tropical rainforest,[13] including Kanem-Bornu where Muslim traders (called *wangara* or *dyula*) had brought Islam and Islam had become the religion of the ruling class.[14]

Thus, by the time the Portuguese started exploring the west coast of Africa, Islam had settled as the religion of the elite in many of the Sahel and Savannah kingdoms and chieftaincies. The account of Diogo Gomes, a Portuguese who visited the Senegambia in 1456 and 1458, relates of his discussion with the Muslim advisor of Niumi *mansa,* a chief ruling over the Gambia estuary; it is probably one of the earliest sub-Saharan reports of a Christian-Muslim encounter that has been preserved, apart from the 615 Axum encounter. Gomes writes:

> A certain bishop of their church was there, a native of Mali, who asked me about the God of the Christians, and I answered him according to the intelligence God had given me. I finally questioned him respecting Muhammad, in whom they believe. What I said pleased his lordship the king so much that he ordered the bishop within three days to leave his kingdom.[15]

The account does not tell the response of the Muslim advisor, but not much imagination is needed to guess that he can hardly have been pleased with the outcome.

The encounter in a way is typical for much of the Christian-Muslim 'relations' in sub-Saharan Africa up till the mid 20th century, where

---

[10] L. Sanneh, *West African Christianity*, London, C. Hurst and Company 1983, 15-17.

[11] P.B. Clarke, *West Africa and Islam. A study of religious development from the 8th to the 20th century*, London, Edward Arnold 1983, 10.

[12] J.S. Trimingham, *A History of Islam in West Africa*, Oxford, Oxford University Press 1992 (1962), 28.

[13] J. Kenny, *West Africa and Islam*, Takoradi (Ghana), AECAWA 2000, 88-102. The tropical rainforest hosted the tse-tse fly whose bite was deadly for the camels and horses of the traders; thus the spread of Islam through the dispersion of traders (e.g. cola nuts) stopped at the edge of the rainforest.

[14] P.J. Ryan, 'In My End is My Beginning. Muslim and Christian traditions at cross-purposes in contemporary Nigeria', in B. Soares (ed.), *Muslim Christian Encounters in Africa*, 189 (187-220).

[15] D.P. Gamble, P.E.H. Hair, *The Discovery of the River Gambra (1623) by Richard Jobson*, London, Hakluyt Society 1999, 263.

essentially Islam and Christianity considered each other to be competitors 'for the soul of Africa'. Despite missionary endeavours on both sides, with Christians trying to convert Muslims and both Muslims and Christians trying to convert the adherents of the African traditional religions, Christianity as well as Islam remained minority religions in West Africa throughout most of the period from the 15th to the mid 18th centuries; guests hosted by African traditional religions. This period of accommodation in which both religions learned to adjust to conditions set by the traditional rulers or the majority of the populations is sometimes considered to be one of the reasons for the often harmonious and accommodative interfaith relationships in the sub-region;[16] a relationship which Mbillah, quoted above, characterized as 'live and let live with our religious diversities in harmony'.

Only from the late 18th century onwards and throughout the 19th and early 20th centuries, by means of a series of *jihads*, was Islam popularised. Propagated by a method of resistance against Western (read: Christian) colonialism, it became the majority religion in large parts of West Africa, in particular the earlier mentioned Sahel and Savannah areas.[17] The popularisation of Islam in West Africa coincided with the 19th and 20th century Western colonial expansions as well with the modern missionary movement. Encounters during this period were therefore more often than not polemic by nature, with Christian missionaries being identified with the colonial powers and Christians and Muslims seeing each other as rivals in the field. Many of the present-day tensions find their origin in this period of Western imperialism.[18]

In order to minimize expenditure and curtail chances of conflict the colonial governments (especially Britain) closed off many of the predominantly Muslim areas of West Africa to Christian mission work (e.g. Northern Ghana, Northern Nigeria etc.), leading to incongruity in levels of development in the countries at independence.[19] This inequality, often reinforced by religious and ethnic disparity, has at times proven to be the seed of contemporary conflicts. In areas that were not predominantly Muslim, *jihads* and other internal wars unsettled the region and precluded extensive missionary work. Hence, by the beginning of the 20th century, when the 'pacification' of the hinterlands in West Africa enabled the expansion of Christian mission to the non-coastal areas, the die had already been cast for large parts of West Africa; they had become predominantly Muslim.

The South African Muslim scholar Farid Esack considers much of contemporary mission and *da'wah* to be a continuation of this so-called 'colonial scramble for Africa'. In sharp words he condemns both Christian

---

[16] M.T. Frederiks, *We have toiled all night*, 123-124.
[17] M.T. Frederiks, *We have toiled all night*, 130-136, 150-153.
[18] J. Voll, 'African Muslims and Christians in World History', 28-29.
[19] L. Rasmussen, *Christian-Muslim Relations in Africa*, 16-21.

and Muslim missionary endeavours for their hypocrisy, accusing them of focussing on the propagation of a religious group rather than on the welfare of Africa(ns):

> Muslims and Christians encounter each other on this continent over the remains of a carcass. (...) It is the rawness of Africa that motivates us, that age-old perception of African as 'fertile territory'. (...) We, the ones who drive it, we never own Africa in the Sobukwean sense of the word, the way Robert Sobukwe uses it. We try to own it in the colonial sense of the word. (...)our main concern in the midst of this is not for the potholes, not for the lives of people dying around us. In mission and *da'wah* often our main concern is a competition for converts. We live on a continent where millions are dying because of AIDS or other poverty-engendered diseases, and yet our main concern is: How will my cap look like when I arrive at the scene of the accident so that I may possibly attract some of the people to my religion?[20]

In East Africa a somewhat different development took place. Christianity had established itself in the Nubian kingdoms of Nobatai, Makurrah and Alwa from the third century onwards and was only to disappear gradually in the 15th century due to intermarriage, whilst the Christian Axum legacy is continued up to the present day by the Ethiopian Orthodox Church.[21] It was this Christianity that Arab traders met when they began their settlements on the East Coast. Lilli Rasmussen dates the earliest Muslim community back to the 9th century[22], whilst Sigvard von Sicard gives the 8th century as date for Muslim settlements on the East coast. He attributes the Muslim reticence to conquer East Africa to a treaty made with the Negus in Axum:

> Because of the kind treatment they received at the hands of the Negus, there is a tradition in which Muhammad is reported to have said "Leave the Habashi in peace as long as they do not take to the offensive" (Abu Daud 2:133). As a result there was no Muslim expansion in the area until the time of the Caliphs Sulaiman and Yazid 'Abd al-Malik in the first quarter of the eight century. By this time Muslims had also established themselves in various trading settlements along the East African coast. Recent archaeological work near Pate and Lamu in Kenya indicates the existence of purpose built mosques in the middle of the eight century.[23]

Gradually however, Arab and Indian Muslims extended their areas of influence, first on the islands before the East African coast such as Zanzibar, but later also on the mainland itself, creating towns such as

---

[20] F. Esack, 'Islamic *Da'wah* and Christian Mission. A Muslim perspective' in K.T. August & C. Sauer (eds), *Christian-Muslim Encounter in Africa*, Johannesburg, AcadSA Publishing 2007, 27 (21-30).

[21] K. Ward, 'Africa' in A. Hastings (ed.), *A World History of Christianity*, Grand Rapids, Eerdmans 1999, 196 (192-237).

[22] L. Rasmussen, *Christian-Muslim Relations in Africa*, 10.

[23] S. von Sicard, 'Islam in Eastern Africa', *Christian-Muslim Relations in East Africa*, 43 (42-49).

Mombassa and Malindi.[24] From there, they explored the inland trade routes, in search for ivory, slaves, timber and foodstuff.[25] But where in West Africa the Muslim merchants not only traded with the local population but also intermarried with Africans and settled among them, Arab traders in East Africa observed strict segregation. Only in the late 19th century did Islam begin to spread amongst Africans in East Africa[26], about the same time that Christian missions (re)started work in East Africa, as Portuguese missionary endeavours did not make a lasting impact in East Africa.[27] Thus, East Africa in the 19th and 20th centuries was the stage for Christian-Muslim competitions for the African soul; it was an era characterized by polemic exchanges and the fostering of mutual suspicion[28], resulting in plural religious East African societies with substantial Muslim and Christian population groups as well as communities of adherents of the African traditional religions, societies where at times tensions flair up fiercely.

John Voll summarizes the situation for both East and West Africa fairly adequately when stating that 'in most cases of Muslim-Christian encounters in Africa during the period from the sixteenth century until the late nineteenth century, these encounters were basically a part of the encounters between Europeans (Christians) and Africans who were Muslim.'[29] Only from the Upper Guinea Coast, where both Christianity and Islam were long-standing traditions, there are reports from actual encounters between African Christians and African Muslims in this period, but these were nearly always polemic in nature.[30]

Relationships between Christians and Muslims in Africa gained a new momentum when from the mid 20th century onwards Christian mainline churches began to reflect on and revise their attitude towards Islam (and to a lesser extent also to the African Traditional Religions). For Protestant Church this process can be traced to the International Missionary Council meeting in 1957 in Accra, Ghana, where concern was expressed about the lack of reflection on the relationship between Christianity and Islam.[31] The theme was reiterated less than a year later at the 1958 All African Conference of Churches meeting in Ibadan. This led in 1959 to the establishment of the Islam in Africa project (in 1987 renamed as Project for Christian Muslim Relations in Africa and in 2003 as Programme for Christian Muslim Relations in Africa), a project related to but not part of

---

[24] I.A. Lapidus, *A History of Islamic Societies*, Cambridge, Cambridge University Press 2002 (second revised edition), 433.

[25] S. von Sicard, 'Islam in Eastern Africa', 43-44.

[26] L. Rasmussen, *Christian-Muslim Relations in Africa*, 10.

[27] K. Ward, 'Africa', 213-216.

[28] L. Rasmussen, *Christian-Muslim Relations in Africa*, 36-37.

[29] J. Voll, 'African Muslims and Christians in World History', 26.

[30] E.g. M.T. Frederiks, *We have toiled all night*, 207-213

[31] For details see www.procmura-prica.org (Accessed: June 30 2009).

the AACC. Procmura started work in Nigeria in that same year 1959, soon followed by programmes in Kenya, Cameroon and Ghana. The project focussed on the training of specialists in Islam and Christian-Muslim relations, the study of Islam in the various contexts and aided the churches in their reflections on Christian witness to Muslims.[32] Presently, Procmura, with slightly updated goals, is working in 24 countries in sub-Saharan Africa, Anglophone as well as Francophone.[33]

In the Roman Catholic Church the second Vatican Council brought about a major change in the relationships with Muslims, stating in *Nostra Aetate*

> Although in the course of the centuries many quarrels and hostilities have arisen between Christians and Muslims, this most sacred Synod urges all to forget the past and to strive sincerely for mutual understanding. On behalf of all mankind, let them make common cause of safeguarding and fostering social justice, moral values, peace, and freedom.[34]

The Vatican II statements gave an impulse to Christian-Muslim relations worldwide. For Africa it has meant that the various Episcopal conferences have invested in Christian-Muslim relations by publications, the training of personal and active participation in dialogue programmes and encounters with Muslims; at times these goals are realised in close collaboration with organisations like Procmura.[35] Also at the 1994 African Synod Christian-Muslim relations became one of the leading themes of the gathering.[36]

Much more recent but nevertheless significant are endeavours of a number of Muslim leaders advocating dialogue and participating in interfaith initiatives. Religious leaders from Nigeria were among the initial signatories of the 2007 declaration *A Common Word*, together with Muslim leaders from North Africa. Meanwhile also Muslim leaders from Chad, Gambia, Sudan and other African countries have signed the declaration,

---

[32] J. Haafkens, 'Project for Christian Muslim Relations in Africa (formerly the Islam in Africa project)', *Christian-Muslim Relations in East Africa,* 5 (5-7).

[33] www.procmura-prica.org. (Accessed: June 25 2009). The Ghanaian Muslim Rabiatu Ammah has critiqued Procmura as 'totally unrelated to the traditions of the countries and therefore do not appear to be based on a very solid foundation.' R. Ammah, 'Christian-Muslim Relations in Contemporary Sub-Saharan Africa', *Islam and Christian-Muslim Relations*, 18/2 (2007), 150 (139-153).

[34] Cited as in M. Borrmans, *Interreligious Documents I. Guidelines for dialogue between Christians and Muslims*, New York, Paulist Press 1990, 2.

[35] See e.g. the AECAWA publication J. Kenny, *West Africa and Islam*, Takoradi, AECAWA 2000 or AECAWA, *Islam and Christianity in Dialogue*, Jos (Nigeria), Imico Books 1987.

[36] H. Teissier, 'Christians and Moslems in Africa. Challenges and chances for a genuine relationship', in Africa Faith & Justice Network (ed.), *African Synod. Documents, Reflections, Perspectives*, Maryknoll, Orbis Books 1996, 152-153 (152-159).

thus indicated their commitment to harmonious relationships between Muslims and Christians.[37]

Despite the dialogue efforts of the mainline churches and initiatives like *A Common Word*, many see a deterioration of relationships since the mid 1970s. Agwu Kalu points to an Islamic resurgence in Africa from the mid 1970s onwards, due to increased influences from abroad and facilitated by the large quantities of oil money that are poured into Africa.[38] Others such as Matthews Ojo point to the impact of the Pentecostalisation of African Christianity on interfaith relationships. He observes that the antagonistic stance of Charismatics and Pentecostals towards people of other religious traditions, including Islam, has made relationships more precarious.[39] It is against this multi-facetted background of historical and regional diversities, of new initiatives in Christian-Muslims relations was well as of groups within Islam and Christianity seeking to redress their identities that current trends in Christian-Muslim relations take place.

Concern Over the Increase in Polarisation and Polemics

The history of Christian-Muslim relations can hardly be called a past of smooth relationships. Though at the grassroots level individual Muslims and Christians have often lived and worked together quite harmoniously, the official discourses between the two religious communities were mostly characterised by exclusivist, polemic and offensive language. Jean-Marie Gaudeul's *Encounters and Clashes*[40] gives a chronological overview of the key participants and texts on both the Christian and Muslim side while Norman Daniel's *Islam and the West. The making of an image*[41] provides insightful background information to understand many of the European colonial and missionary (mis)perceptions of Islam, that still linger on in many of Africa's churches.

During the colonial period, when Christianity was often associated with the colonial powers, polemics was the main form of interaction. Independence however brought emancipation and more equitable societal participation for Muslims in many countries; thus in most places, the atmosphere was optimistic and relations improved. The process of decolonisation and its aftermath of disillusions coincides, as mentioned above, with two other developments. The first was a shift in outlook of the

[37] www.acommonword.com (Accessed: July 1 2009).

[38] A. Kalu, 'Nigeria', in H.S. Wilson (ed.), *Islam in Africa. Perspectives for Christian-Muslim Relations*, Geneva, WARC 1995, 79 (79-84).

[39] M.A. Ojo, 'Pentecostal Movements, Islam and the Contest for Public Space in Northern Nigeria', *Islam and Christian-Muslim Relations* 18/2 (2007), 175-188.

[40] J.M. Gaudeul, *Encounters and Clashes. Islam and Christianity in history*, Rome, PISAI 1990.

[41] N. Daniel, Islam and the West. The making of an image, Edinburgh, Edinburgh University Press 1980.

mainlines churches from the midst of the 20th century onwards to tone down the polemical approach to Islam and adopt a more respectful and dialogical attitude[42]. Though this change was welcomed by Muslims, it was also regarded with scepticism and the suspicion, that dialogue was just another form of mission and still had conversion as its aim.[43] The second was the emergences of groups in Christianity and Islam that, disillusioned that Independence did not bring the hoped-for change, turned to fundamentalist religiosity as an alternative for society, religiosity which was characterised by an exclusivist and often antagonistic stance towards both more liberal representations of their own traditions[44] and towards people of other religious persuasions. This surfacing of animosity amongst certain groups of Christians and Muslims in Africa fits into the wider, global developments where with the decline and the fall of communism, Islam seems to have been branded as the new 'enemy' threatening world peace. The bombings of the U.S.A. embassies in Dar-es-Salam and Nairobi, of the Khobar Towers in Saudi Arabia, the attacks on the World Trade Centre in New York, on the hotels in Bali and the undergrounds in Madrid and London as well as the invasions in Afghanistan and Iraq can all be seen as symptoms of these increasingly strained relationships between what is perceived to be 'Christians' and 'Muslims'. The effects of these worldwide developments can also be detected in Africa.

From the late 1970s onwards, a growing concern can be identified in Christian circles over what is called 'an Islamic resurgence' or 'Islamic integrism', which is considered to enhance and invigorate polarisation. Cuthbert Omari and Lilli Rasmussen signal fundamentalist tendencies in e.g. Tanzania as early as the 1980s.[45] Throughout the 1980s and 1990s more and more voices express alarm over the 'Islamic resurgence'. The African synod for example calls the attention to what Henri Teissier describes as 'Islamic integrism'.[46] The church fathers attribute this development mainly to 'foreign influences', thus affirming the idea that traditionally interfaith relations in Africa are harmonious. The Senegalese Cardinal Hyacinth Thiandoum stresses that 'most of the time the difficulties with Islam have their source in influences beyond Africa and

---

[42] See e.g. Secretarius pro non-Christianis, Guidelines for a Dialogue between Muslims and Christians, Rome, Ancora 1971 or J. Haafkens, 'Christian-Muslim Relations in Africa,' in H.S. Wilson (ed.), *Islam in Africa. Perspectives for Christian-Muslim Relations*, Geneva, WARC 1995, 19 (7-33).

[43] M.T. Frederiks, *We have toiled all night*, 402.

[44] For Christianity see e.g. S. Grodz, '"Eleventh Hour Christianity". Issues raised by the growth of neo-Pentecostalism in Ghana', *Verbum SVD*, 48/1 (2007), 35-49.

[45] C.K. Omari, 'Christian-Muslim Relations in Tanzania' *Christian-Muslim Relations in East Africa*, Geneva, Lutheran World Federation 1987, 64-66 (61-68); L. Rasmussen, *Christian-Muslim Relations in Africa*, 100-102.

[46] H. Teissier, 'Christians and Moslems in Africa. Challenges and chances for a genuine relationship', 154.

from outside Islam as a religion'[47], thus expressing concern over the developments whilst at the same time cautiously not estranging those Muslim groups with whom good relationships exist and whom he considers 'important but difficult dialogue partner[s]'.[48]

The 'Islamic resurgence' has also had a direct effect on Christian-Muslim relations. Both Johnson Mbillah and Laurenti Magesa draw attention to the so-called *mihadhara* in East Africa, a phenomenon which Magesa kindly defines as 'public lectures by Muslim scholars, addressing issues to do with Christianity' in East Africa[49] but for which 'vicious polemics' might seem a more adequate description. Polemics are also conducted in other forms: tapes and movies of the famous debates of the Muslim polemicist Ahmad Deedad with Christian evangelists from the 1980s and 1990s are again reproduced and redistributed lavishly Africa-wide; events during which the movies are shown 'often end in chaos and sometimes stone-throwing – the beginning of hatred between the two communities.'[50] Polemical pamphlets written by Ahmad Deedat and others are reprinted, sponsored by oil money from e.g. Saudi Arabia, and distributed across the continent in large quantities.[51]

However, fuelling polarisation between Christians and Muslims through polemics is not just the monopoly of certain Muslim groups. These trends have their equivalent in Christianity. As early as 1987 Paul Rajashekar, then working at the LWF Desk for interfaith relations, observed during a workshop in Nairobi that 'while many Christians may feel that such missions are a threat to the future of Christianity in Africa, it should not be forgotten that Christian churches are also actively engaged in mission to convert Muslims in Africa and they too are recipients of financial assistance from the West.'[52] As already mentioned above, Matthews Ojo has pointed out that also the Pentecostalisation of Christianity in sub-Saharan Africa has had its impact on interfaith relations, as generally

---

[47] O.A. Onwubiko, *Echoes from the African Synod*, 112.

[48] O.A. Onwubiko, *Echoes from the African Synod*, 110.

[49] J. Mbillah, 'Interfaith Relations and the Quest for Peace in Africa', in C. Hock (ed.), *The Interface between Research and Dialogue: Christian-Muslim relations in Africa*, Münster, Litt Verlag 2004, 69 (66-79); L. Magesa, 'Contemporary Catholic Perspectives on Christian-Muslim Relations in Sub-Saharan Africa. The case of Tanzania, *Islam and Christian-Muslim Relations*, 18/2, 171 (165-173).

[50] J. Mbillah, 'Interfaith Relations and the Quest for Peace in Africa', 69. For growing tension in Kenya see also A. Kubai, 'Christian-Muslim Relations in Kenya since Independence' in C. Hock (ed.), *The Interface between Research and Dialogue: Christian-Muslim relations in Africa*, 43-44 (32-66).

[51] D. Westerlund, 'An Outline for Research on Christian-Muslim Relations', in C. Hock (ed.), *The Interface between Research and Dialogue: Christian-Muslim relations in Africa*, 130-133 (125-144). Note: the South African polemicist Ahmad Deedat died in 2003 but his work is still reprinted intensively.

[52] J.P. Rajashekar, ' Introduction', *Christian-Muslim Relations in East Africa*, Geneva, Lutheran World Federation 1987, 3 (1-4).

speaking Pentecostals have a 'strong negative attitude towards other religions'. According to Oyo in Nigeria this has resulted into 'an overt demonization of Islamic groups'.[53] In response to the perceived threat to Christianity by the developments in the 1980s and 1990s in Northern Nigeria, Pentecostals in recent years have increasingly ventured in the public arenas of politics and media to combat what they see as an 'Islamization agenda', leading in turn to protests and retaliation by Muslim groups.[54]

Also individuals have contributed to the increase in tension: David Westerlund considers the evangelist Reinhardt Bonnke the evangelical counterpart of Ahmad Deedat, whose 'crusades' have strained interfaith relationships and on occasions led to serious violence. The clashes in Kano in 1991 over the intended crusade of Bonnke might serve as an example.[55] Less pronounced but nevertheless unhelpful is ignorance of Islam by Christian religious leaders and their use of inflammatory and offensive language in official speeches, signalled for example by Laurenti Magesa in Tanzania and Anne Kubai in Kenya.[56] Instead of propagating peaceful relations, church leaders call upon the faithful to stop the spread of Islam in Africa or claim that Muhammad was a Christian before he founded Islam, thus fuelling the tensions.

Mbillah has observed yet another trend on the continent, that of what he calls 'religious tribalism', 'a wind blowing across the African continent that tends to categorise African heads of state according to their religious affiliations, especially Christian and Muslim'.[57] Where in the past African leaders were identified and identified themselves as leaders, the trend of polarisation now seems to extend to include 'religio-partisan politics'. This increase rather than decrease in polarisation and polemical language and actions on all levels and the invigorating role of the media in these tensions, has led both Muslim and Christians to underscore the urgency of interreligious as well as intra-religious dialogues.[58] Further education and sensitization of people, with special attention for opinion makers such religious and political leaders and the media and attempt to moderate the opinions of more radical groups within Islam and Christianity as well as stressing the importance of tolerance, respect, interreligious cooperation

---

[53] M.S. Ojo, 'Pentecostal Movements, Islam and the Contest for Public Space in Northern Nigeria', 175, 176.

[54] M.S. Ojo, 'Pentecostal Movements, Islam and the Contest for Public Space in Northern Nigeria', 176.

[55] D. Westerlund, 'An Outline for Research on Christian-Muslim Relations', 129.

[56] L. Magesa, 'Contemporary Catholic Perspectives on Christian-Muslim Relations in Sub-Saharan Africa. The case of Tanzania', 169; A. Kubai, 'Christian-Muslim Relations in Kenya since Independence', 54.

[57] J. Mbillah, 'African Churches and Interfaith Relations', 12.

[58] R. Ammah, 'Christian-Muslim Relations in Contemporary Sub-Saharan Africa', 152; J. Mbillah, 'African Churches and Interfaith Relations', 6.

and harmonious co-existence are deemed imperative. For religious diversity has come to stay; in the words of Johnson Mbillah:

> Whatever the case, religious diversity has become the lot of the human race. God-given freedom allows free human beings to choose the religious path they wish to tread; the churches in Africa and like elsewhere therefore, cannot be impatient with the religious diversity around them since arguably, religious variety will remain the lot of the human race until the end of time. A credible question for the churches to ask therefore, is not how to eradicate religious diversity (for that will mean attempting to eradicate the God-given freedom of human beings) but how to constructively relate with religious diversity.[59]

Issues of Religious Freedom: Shari'a

The themes of religious diversity and religious freedom link up with another current trend in Christian-Muslim relations: the debate on the implementation of *shari'a*. In a variety of countries there is the call for the introduction of *shari'a* either on the regional or national level, a quest which the Ghanaian Rabiatu Ammah interprets as a 'search for a voice, a search for justice and a search for identity' over and against the colonial legacy; in the same paragraph however she queries whether the mode and manner in which and the extent to which *shari'a* has been applied to African societies so far, does not 'undermine or contradict the very principle of justice which the *shari'a* espouses.'[60]

The most well-known cases where *shari'a* has been introduced and where there has been an ongoing debate about *shari'a* for quite some time now are Sudan and Nigeria. As both case-studies have been elaborately described and discussed elsewhere, there seems no need to repeat the historical developments leading up to the present situation in these countries.[61] However, a number of the more general issues raised in the

---

[59] J. Mbillah, 'African Churches and Interfaith Relations', 3-4.

[60] R. Ammah, 'Christian-Muslim Relations in Contemporary Sub-Saharan Africa', 145-146.

[61] For a study of both countries, see e.g. J.O. Hunwick (ed.), *Religion and National Integration in Africa. Islam, Christianity and politics in the Sudan and Nigeria*, Evanston, Northwestern University Press 1992. For Nigeria specifically see e.g. J. Kenny, 'Shari'a in Nigeria. A historical survey', *Bulletin for Islam and Christian Muslim Relations in Africa*, 4/1 (1986), 1-17; M. Oduyoye, 'The Shariy'ah Debate in Nigeria', in C. Hock, *The Interface Between Research and Dialogue*, 98-113; J. Idowu-Fearon, *The Shari'a Debate in the Northern Sates of Nigeria and Its Implications for West Africa Sub-Region*, in J. Mbillah & J. Chesworth, *From the Cross to the Crescent*, 15-24; P.J. Ryan, 'In My End is My Beginning. Muslims and Christian Traditions at Cross-Purposes in Contemporary Nigeria' in B. Soares, *Muslim-Christian Encounters in Africa*, 187-220; P. Ostien, 'An Opportunity Missed by Nigeria's Christians. The 1976-1978 Sharia debate revisited', in B. Soares, *Muslim-Christian Encounters in Africa*, 221-255; F. Kogelmann, 'The

discussion on *shari'a* by Muslims and Christians have relevance for the wider context of Africa, if only because the discussions on the implementation of *shari'a* are not limited to Sudan or Nigeria, but also features intermittently in other countries, such as Senegal, Tanzania and Kenya.

Muslims have often advocated that the *shari'a* in no way limits the religious freedom of Christians as it is meant to apply to Muslims only.[62] Often, like in the case of Nigeria, the calls for *shari'a* have been accompanied by statements the state has a distinct Christian orientation. Josiah Idowu-Fearon, bishop of Sokoto states that 'the Nigerian Muslim feels that the State and the Christian faith are not separate but that one is an extension of the other'[63]; the organisation of the week, with Saturday and Sunday as the weekend-days off, the long recesses for Christmas and Easter and short breaks for Id al-Fitr and Id al-Adha, the school calendar and uniforms are all considered to be Christian oriented. These complaints are often retorted by Christians who protest that the governmental foreign currency is used to sponsor the *hajj*, that grand *qadis* are paid by public funds and that Nigeria has become an OIC membership.[64] It is not without reason that Johnson Mbillah has observed that 'in interfaith relations for peaceful co-existence, the most difficult area in Africa is that of religious freedoms and rights as ones exclusive rights could easily turn out to be a violation of another's religious rights.'[65]

Critical areas, that raise concern amongst Christians vis-à-vis the introduction and implementation of *shari'a* are the lack of freedom of (re)building religious buildings, the restrictions in travel of Christians and particularly of clergy, the confiscation of church property, the Arabisation and Islamisation of school curricula, the limitation of the right of religious freedom, including the right to convert, the status of non-Muslims under *shari'a,* the applicability of *shari'a* for multi-religious and modern states and the possible introduction of blasphemy laws.[66]

"Sharia Factor" in Nigeria's 2003 Elections', in B. Soares, *Muslim-Christian Encounters in Africa*, 256-274. For Sudan see e.g. S.N. Ador, 'Shari'a. Historical and Contemporary Perspectives in the Sudan', in J. Mbillah & J. Chesworth, *From the Cross to the Crescent*, 25-47; M. Mahmoud, 'When Shari'a Governs. The impasse of religious relationships in Sudan', *Islam and Christian Muslim Relations*, 18/2 (2007), 275-286.

62 See e.g. M. Mahmoud, 'When Shari'a Governs. The impasse of religious relationships in Sudan', *Islam and Christian Muslim Relations*, 18/2 (2007), 275-286.

63 J. Idowu-Fearon, 'The *Shari'a* Debate in the Northern States of Nigeria', 19-20.

64 A. Kalu, 'Nigeria', 81-84.

65 J. Mbillah, 'Interfaith Relations in Africa', 10.

66 J. Idowu-Fearon, 'The *Shari'a* Debate in the Northern States of Nigeria', 20-23; O.A. Onwubiku, *Echoes from the African Synod*, 114-116; S.N. Ador, 'Shari'a. Historical and Contemporary Perspectives in the Sudan', 58-59.

So far most steps seem to have been taken to address these issues rather than to proffer ways to resolve them. The bishops at the African synod have pleaded for a 'modernisation of Islam' rather than an 'islamisation of modernity'.[67] Others have met in conferences and workshops to study the teaching of *shari'a* with regard to non-Muslims[68] Also amongst Muslims the theme of the applicability of *shari'a* to multi-religious societies is queried. Rabiatu Ammah states that *shari'a* can only offer an acceptable alternative to the present legal system in Africa if it is modernised and contextualised. She states that,

> in this pluralist situation, it is imperative for *fiqh* and its teachings on *dhimmis* to be seen in their proper context. (…) The questions relating to the *jizya*, the concept of citizenship, and the penalty for the apostate are typical examples that must be explained contextually to be meaningful in the contemporary world. In this way the fears and apprehensions of Christians would be minimized.[69]

Only thus, by guaranteeing religious freedom and justice for all, according to Ammah, Christians can be convinced that they have very little to loose and much to gain by the implementation of *shari'a*. The African reality of the implementation of *shari'a* at the moment however seems to be a far cry from the optimistic and rather rosy picture painted by Ammah and therefore the topic still poses a profound challenge to Christians and moderate Muslims alike.

Joint Societal Action

The last trend that can be identified is the ever more powerful call by Muslims and Christians to join hands in societal action.[70] Considering the context of Africa, where poverty, diseases and war seem to multiply day after day and considering the fact that the message of both Islam and Christianity speaks about peace and justice, this is not surprising. Nor is this trend entirely new. In the past South African Muslims joined South African Christians in their fight against Apartheid.[71] In the early 1990s Muslim and Christian leaders in Liberia took the initiative to set up the Interreligious Council of Liberia to work towards peace in Liberia, an example that was emulated in second half of the 1990s by the establishment

[67] O.A. Onwubiku, *Echoes from the African Synod*, 113

[68] E. Oyelade, 'The *Shari'a* and National Unity in Nigeria', in J. Mbillah & J. Chesworth, *From the Cross to the Crescent*, 40, (25-47).

[69] R. Ammah, 'Christian-Muslim Relations in Contemporary Sub-Saharan Africa', 148.

[70] See e.g. R. Ammah, 'Christian-Muslim Relations in Contemporary Sub-Saharan Africa', 149.

[71] M. Haron, 'Christian-Muslim Relations in South Africa (ca. 1986-2004)', 265.

of a similar platform in war-torn Sierra Leone.[72] Both in Liberia and Sierra Leone, the Councils contributed significantly to the signing of a cease-fire and later the peace-treaties, as well as disarmament programmes after the war. Meanwhile related councils have been set-up in Ivory Coast, Ghana and Guinea.[73]

Peace initiatives and proactive interventions to prevent an escalation of violence play a prominent role in the interreligious cooperation. In 1994 for example, Procmura sent a delegation of four Christians and four Muslims to Sudan on a peace mission, an event that became known as the Sudan Peace Initiative.[74] Though the initiative did not succeed in bringing about peace or reconciliation, it was indicative for a new direction in Procmura, as similar interreligious ventures were undertaken in Nigeria, Ghana and Tanzania in later years.[75] In 2008 Procmura, in cooperation with Trust Africa, called a high profile interreligious conference for East Africa on *Religion and Conflict Prevention*, thus underlining its commitment to contribute towards interreligious peace initiatives in the continent.[76] Mbillah in his opening address stated that Procmura for nearly two decades has participated in interreligious peace-initiatives, some of which were successful, whilst others were not. Key to the success of these peace-missions, according to Mbillah however, is the awareness that 'unless and until Christians and Muslims are at peace with one another as religious communities, they have no rights to engage in peace building and conflict transformation with other actors.'[77] Hence Procmura's continued dedication to building interreligious relationships at all levels of society.

Also other organisations have brought together groups of Muslims and Christians to work towards peace. In Northern Nigeria from the mid 1990s onwards, interreligious groups, some consisting of religious leaders, others of young people or women, were set up in an attempt to work towards peace. Hajiya Yusuf describes and evaluates a number of these initiatives in her article *Managing Muslim-Christian Conflicts in Northern Nigeria*, with a particular focus on the successful Kaduna Peace Initiative.[78]

Joint interreligious societal action has not only taken the form of peace initiatives though these have often been most visible. Several people have

---

72 For Sierra Leone see e.g. M.T. Frederiks, 'Op de Bres voor de Vrede. Interreligious Council of Sierra Leone', *Begrip Moslims Christenen*, 29/1, 29-34.

73 www.rfpusa.org/interviews (Accessed: July 1 2009).

74 J. Mbillah, 'Interfaith Relations and Peace in Africa', 73.

75 J. Mbillah, 'Interfaith Relations and Peace in Africa', 74-78.

76 For the report see J. Mbillah, *A Journey for Peace. Report of Conference on Religion and Conflict Prevention: Peace Building and Reconciliation in Eastern Africa, Dar-es-Salaam, Tanzania 2008,* Nairobi, Procmura 2008.

77 J. Mbillah, *A Journey for Peace*, 61.

78 H.B. Yusuf, 'Managing Muslim-Christian Conflicts in Northern Nigeria. A case-study of Kaduna State', *Islam and Christian-Muslim Relations*, 18/2 (2007), 252-255 (237-256).

also pushed the interreligious agenda for programmes on poverty alleviation, gender violence and more recently the HIV epidemic. Earlier on Farid Esack was quoted regarding his appeal to religious communities to work together for the betterment of society. Esack, a Muslim liberation theologian, has recently done groundbreaking work in the field of Islam & HIV, AIDS and has taken on a pioneering role in setting up the association Positive Muslims, in producing literature and in his advocacy for interreligious cooperation in the context of HIV and Aids.[79] Similarly in Senegal Christian and Muslims religious leaders in 1999 joined hands in fight against HIV and established the *Alliance des Religieux et Expert Medicaux Contre le SIDA.*[80] More recently, also Procmura has put the HIV and AIDS epidemic on the agenda and has organised a series of national interfaith seminars for young people on HIV in e.g. Liberia, Sudan and an interfaith consultation for women in West-Africa.[81]

The peace initiatives and interreligious cooperation in the field of HIV and AIDS are just two examples of the much wider trend of interreligious action on topics like human rights, gender violence and domestic violence. The trend for joint social action seems to be *the* trend in Christian Muslim relations in sub-Saharan Africa.

Final Remarks

Christian-Muslim relations in sub-Saharan Africa are both diverse and complex. In some areas harmonious relationships reign, whereas in other countries the tension are high. Even within countries and amongst groups the perception of the necessity of interreligious relationships varies considerably, as in both Christianity and Islam those groups that take an exclusivist and intolerant position seem to expand. The increased polarisation through the influence of fundamentalist and other radical groups in sub-Sahara Africa form part of a wider, global polarisation of relations between what are perceived as 'Christians' and 'Muslims'. At the same time, the increased polarisation has also stimulated more moderately minded Christians and Muslims to work together to diffuse the tensions and strive towards peaceful coexistence and mutual respect. They have accepted the religious diversity on the continent as part of the African

[79] F. Esack, *HIV, AIDS and Islam. A workshop manual based on compassion, responsibility and justice*, Cape Town (South Africa), Positive Muslims 2007; F. Esack & S. Chiddy (eds), *Islam and Aids. Between scorn, pity and justice*, Oxford, Oneworld Publications 2009; www.positivemuslims.org.za (Accessed: June 20 2009)

[80] S.S. Gilbert, 'The Influence of Islam on HIV prevention among Senegalese University Students', *Aids Education and Prevention*, 20/5 (Oct. 2008), 399-407.

[81] A. Dogbe (ed.), *An Interfaith Approach for Women in the Fight against HIV/Aids.* Anglophone West African Women Regional Consultation, Fajara, The Gambia, May 4-9 2008.

reality and endeavour through interreligious collaboration to work towards the betterment of societies as a whole. The trends in Christian-Muslim relations that were identified – increase in polarisation and polemics and the *shari'a* debate on the one hand and joint social action on the other – reflect the ambiguity that is part of the 21st century reality of interfaith relationships in sub-Saharan Africa.

Historical Overview of Interfaith Relations in the Islamic Countries: The Presence of Christian Monks and Monastries as Signposts of Faith

Steve Cochrane

Abstract

This paper examines a little known aspect of the history of inter-faith relations in Muslim countries; the presence and role of Christian monks and monasteries. Particular attention is given to Muslim attitudes and writings on monasticism, including in the Qur'an and Hadith., the 9th century in Iraq as an important period of Muslim-Christian interactions, and present and future implications of Christian monasteries in inter-faith relations. By describing these institutions and their place in Islamic society, it is hoped that an alternate story can be told to the usually dominant paradigm of Crusade/Jihad based discourse.

Introduction

The almost millennium and a half story of inter-faith relations in Muslim lands can be told in many ways and from many perspectives. One multi-voiced telling would be that of the Islamic rulers, from the 7th century in the Arabian Desert spreading to the far corners of North Africa and Spain, and to Indonesia, India and China. Another diverse perspective would be from the standpoint of the "dhimmi"[1] communities in these lands, whether Jewish or Christian.

This paper will survey historical developments of the interaction of Early Islam with Christian monasticism including the ambivalence of the Qur'an and Hadith to it. The interest of Muslim writers in the monasteries and even a sub-genre of historical writing on them will be noted as well. A section will then highlight the 9th century context in Northern

[1] Dhimmi has the idea of "protected" communities, particularly the "People of the Book" referring to Jews and Christians. More problematic is the status of non-Monotheistic religions in Islamic countries like Hindus and Buddhists. Bat Ye'or (1985) writes extensively on dhimmi communities in history and present times, but has a strong polemic edge to her writing.

Mesopotamia, where monasteries abounded and provided places for some inter-faith relationships. The final part of the paper will bring us up to the 21st century, where monasteries still provide those signposts of faith to non-violent opportunities for relationships and reconciliation. Due to the scope of this article, many places and stories will not be mentioned, in what is a very rich yet often overlooked history of Christian monasteries in Islamic lands.

Early Islam and Christian Monasticism

From the 5th century Christian monasticism exerted "a powerful influence on the Arabs" (Shahid 1990:404), and "they took kindly to monasticism and its representatives who penetrated their deserts." The Christian historian Sozomen (Schaff 1952) writing in the mid-5th century comments on how instrumental these monks were "in leading most of the Saracens among others into the straight path of Christianity." (Ecclesiastical History, pg. 7) According to Bell (1925), in the area east of the Jordan "the monk in his cell was one of the things that attracted the attention of the Arabs." By the time that Prophet Muhammad began to preach in the early 7th century, monastic centres existed in places like Hira[2] and it is an important question how much or how little contact he actually had with monks. Shahid (2002:215) feels that there is "no doubt that Muhammad as a caravan leader had visited many of these monasteries." But unfortunately we are left with little to no evidence of that assertion, as fascinating as it may be to consider the ramifications. The Prophet's meeting with the Christian monk Bahira, though probably a legend, does illustrate the possibility of an encounter of this nature. (See Griffith 1995)

In the Qur'an itself, there is a basic understanding of monasticism, as in Surahs 5:82-86, 9:29-35, and 57:27, with particularly Surah 5 offering the "most striking praise." (McAuliffe 1991:204) In this seminal work, McAuliffe analyzes several Muslim commentators on the Qur'an and Hadith for specific themes, including how they view Christian monasteries and monks. From her study, she concludes that "the focal discussion on monasticism that emerges from the commentaries on this verse (Surah 57:27) is "exceptional ambivalence", but that monasticism remains a "source of fascination for these commentators." (1991:282) The phrase "exceptional ambivalence" could perhaps be used overall to describe the Prophet's feeling about Christian monks, and even the general attitude of Muslims throughout the history of inter-faith relations. Christian monks and monasteries have seemed to provoke from Muslims the ambivalence of respect on one side for their devotion, and yet questions on the other about

---

[2] Hira, the capital of the Christian Arab Lakhimid kingdom, had several churches and monasteries, some of which have been excavated in recent years.

their practice[3] and identity within the dhimmi community. Though much fewer than at their apex in the 13th century, Eastern Christian monasteries in Islamic countries continue to exist, and their very existence testifies to the resilience of the ambivalence after so many centuries.

An interesting and understudied genre of Muslim writing up to and including the medieval era is on the Christian monasteries. Tragically the only fully extant source from these writings is the "Kitab al-Diyarat" (Book of Monasteries) by the 10th century author al-Shabushti. (See Awaad 2007) Two other writers, Hisham (d. 990) and Isbahani (d. 972), also wrote extensively on Christian monasteries but their works are lost to us except in quotes and references of later authors. Isbahani seems to have written about the monasteries in a tone more sensual with an intention to entertain and amuse his readers. Shahid (2002:160) calls this work a "turning point in the development of this genre in Arabic literature, where the main interest of the authors was no longer the monastery itself as a place where Muslim visitors, including Caliphs, princes and governors relaxed."[4] Isbahani was perhaps responding unfavourably to Hisham, as he was rumoured to dislike him, as the latter had written a more serious work on the monasteries. It is extremely unfortunate that we do not have Hisham's work today, as it may have given us a more solid and substantive view of the monasteries from the Muslim perspective. Shabushti in "Kitab al-Diyarat" carries on in the entertainment mode of writing, but as Kilpatrick (2003:19) writes, these 10th century works "show a remarkable openness of Muslims toward Christian customs and institutions." But Shabushti's book also "conveys a sense of the (Christian) monasteries' place in pre-Islamic and Islamic Arab history and in Arab culture." (:36)

Through these Muslim writings, the Christian monasteries up to medieval times were seen as places where Muslims could go to relax, be amused and receive hospitality, including at times even wine! Mutual conversations and prayer could also result in an environment that seemed to be non-threatening to either faith. The monasteries appeared to be places where Muslims would be welcomed not as strangers but as neighbours, in a mutuality of the common journey of faith.

---

3 McAuliffe (1991:263) brings out that virtually all the Hadith commentators she studied felt that the Christians did not "observe it correctly", speaking of monasticism, but it does not seem clear what practicing it correctly would actually entail.

4 And even drank wine, as Isbhani, and later Shabushti , seemed to emphasize. Lovejoy (1957:56) says that these "moral lapses" were not considered at the time by Muslims a sign of dissoluteness on the part of the Christians (or the Muslims taking part), but "on the contrary looked upon as having a certain charm and eloquence."

Ninth Century Interactions in Northern Mesopotamia

One of the most extensive regions having Christian monasteries was in Northern Mesopotamia (modern Iraq), both of the East Syrian and West Syrian branches of the Eastern Church tradition. Shabushti in the 10th century writes of 40 different monasteries, and Iraqi Christian Bahija Lovejoy finds accounts of at least 163 more. Many of these monasteries became centres for intellectual excellence, where Iraqi Christian scholars "built outstanding schools all attached to well-stocked libraries. These centres of learning were used for transplanting the seeds of Greek culture to the land of Mesopotamia," (Lovejoy 1957:17), through a stellar translation movement from Syriac to Arabic, and then to the West from Arabic to Latin. This period in the history of inter-faith relations is often forgotten or ignored, though it was in some ways a "golden age" of creativity and intellectual sharing between Muslims, Christians and Jews. One Eastern Christian writer puts it this way: "From their very beginning monasteries have been high places for inter-religious and inter-cultural understanding and exchange. Many bridges have been built in the monasteries not only among monks who came from far and wide, but also among the many visitors and sympathizers to whom this irresistible Charismatic power of loving exchange is intended." (Boniface 1993:58)

This inter-faith exchange is illustrated in an anonymous document composed in Syriac in probably the first part of the 8th century, set in a monastery named Bet Hale near Hira in western Iraq. It recounts the dialogue between a monk of Bet Hale and a Muslim Emir. One of the most arresting comments from this dialogue that is of relevance to this study is when the Arab Emir says to the monk, "Even Muhammad our Prophet said about the inhabitants of the monasteries and the mountain dwellers that they will enjoy the kingdom." (Griffith 2000:34) Griffith finds this remark "intriguing because it does echo the positive things said about Christians, and particularly the monks, in both the Qur'an and the Hadith." (:34) While this disputation text is written with a polemical aim in mind from the Christian perspective, it again seems to show the kind of encounters going on between monks and even Muslim leaders. Patriarch Timothy (d. 823) of the Church of the East, trained in part at the famous monastery of Beit Abhe near Mosul, had a two-day debate with Caliph al-Mahdi (d. 785), probably one of the most famous of such encounters in history. (See Mingana 1928)[5]

A century later during the reign of Abbasid Caliph al-Ma'mun (d. 833), it was on a regular basis in Baghdad that inter-faith dialogues were held, called "majlis", which were "salon-like sessions in a Caliph or Emir's

---

[5] Patriarch Timothy (d. 823) of the Church of the East, trained in part at the famous monastery of Beit Abhe near Mosul, had a two day debate with Caliph al-Mahdi (d. 785), probably one of the most famous of such encounters in history. (See Mingana 1928 for the debate in Syriac and English translation)

court, in which scholars were often summoned for debate." (Lazarus-Yafeh 1999:13) Monk-scholars were involved in these gatherings from the Christian side, and at times perhaps even hosted a similar meeting at the monasteries. These kinds of developments going on between the 9th-11th centuries did lead some prominent Christian intellectuals in Baghdad, according to Griffith (2007:67), "to think for a season that on the basis of reason and the philosophical life, a measure of peaceful convivencia between Christians, Muslims and Jews would be attained in the world of Islam they all shared." In recent years it has become popular to describe a possible "golden age" in Muslim-Christian relations in the Spain of the pre-15th centuries. (See e.g. Menocal 2002) but, those same writers usually completely ignore the context of the 9th century in the east.

This possible "golden age" unraveled over the coming centuries with the impact of the Christian crusaders to the West in the 12th century, and the Mongol rampages from the East in the 13th.

Christian Monasteries in Islamic Countries in the 21st Century

The institution and practice of Christian monasticism has endured in Islamic lands through almost 15 centuries, albeit in a highly reduced form. In inter-faith relations today it is imperative to find new/old paradigms for strengthening dialogue and relationship. One of these possible paradigms could be the monastery as a signpost pointing to a mutuality of faith encounters. Boniface likens the monastery to the inn of Luke 10:33, and portrays the monk as the host or inn-keeper. He writes (1993:59) "It is a place where everyone is gathered and welcomed…it is an inn for all pilgrims travelling lightly towards the Lord's return." The monastery as inn could be a possible "zone of contact" (See Singh 2009) and perhaps the Sufi khanqah as well.

One of the monasteries that continues to exist in Muslim lands today is Rabban Hormizd, located in Northern Iraq near Mosul. Though it has only 4 monks at present in residence, it has had an illustrious history. Hope remains that as the Iraqi Church passes through this dark season in its history, the future could mean the strengthening and expansion of the monastic call in places like Rabban Hormizd and other monasteries.

In places like Kottayam in South India where a living St. Thomas Christian community traces their existence back to the Apostle, a renewed vision of monasticism fills the hearts of some of the priests there belonging to the Syro-Malabar Church. Church of the East monasticism in India may have existed at least back to the 6th century, when links with a strong monastic missionary minded Persian church meant an exchange of monk missionaries into India. Whether there was an indigenous expression of monasticism is difficult to prove, due to no ruins of monasteries available or written histories, as is the case with the widespread presence of Buddhist missionary monasticism throughout India. (See Heitzman 1980) It will be interesting to see how this renewed monasticism may result in enhanced exchanges with the Hindus and Muslims of Kerala state and beyond.

We have seen in various contexts throughout history that Muslims have visited monasteries for diverse reasons, whether aesthetic, religious, or for pleasure. Even today, as detailed by one Western Benedictine monk who spent time in the Coptic monasteries of Egypt, "many Muslims come to the monasteries" and some of those came "in the evening" to receive exorcism from demonic possession. This monk explains these Muslims' rationale as they explained it to him: "They say that their own sheikhs do not deal with this kind of power, but only with the One God, so they appeal to the Christian monks instead. By this kind of explanation, they get the help they need, yet preserve a sense of their own religious integrity." (Gruber 2002:80)[6]

A fascinating novel written by an Egyptian in 1996 is set around a Coptic monastery just after the Israeli-Arab war of 1967. Titled "Aunt Safiyya and the Monastery," author Bahaa' Taher weaves a touching story of familial love, revenge and betrayal in the midst of the revolutionary changes in the broader Middle East. The monastery becomes a symbol and actuality of refuge and protection for a local Muslim who has unjustly been beaten. He then kills the leading official responsible, and now the official's wife, Safiyya, seeks her revenge. At one point, when some are seeking the murderer at the monastery, another Muslim leader says, "Do you want me, Hinein, to turn on these monks, whose protection, according to the Qur'an, is enjoined by our Lord?" (Taher 1996:101) and later "The monks are mentioned in the Holy Qur'an" (:102) As we have described earlier in this paper, this again reveals the "exceptional ambivalence" in the understanding of a contemporary Egyptian novelist towards the hospitality, protection, and refuge represented by the Christian monastery.

In the still unfolding story of the history of inter-faith relations, the "exceptional ambivalence" towards institutions like the Christian monastery will continue. But it can also provide in that ambivalence those signposts towards hospitality of faith. Gruber (2002) has described very interesting modern encounters of Muslims with monasteries in the Coptic context. Dalrymple (1997) too has some fascinating tales of his travels to existing monasteries in the East. Boniface, an Eastern Christian prelate, goes so far as to write, "Monasticism could function more and more as a bridge between those religions and Christianity... as it stands by definition in the heart of all religion." (1993:205) As Panikkar (1982: 1X) has written, "Dialogue between Christian and non-Christian monks has to remain an

[6] The idea of Muslims coming for peaceable reasons to the monasteries must also be balanced with the struggle at times in history of attacks occurring, whether due to religious persecution or because of power dynamics related to identity. For example in recent years there have been renewed problems for the Coptic monasteries in facing persecution from more fundamentalist Muslim movements.

integral part of a larger inter-religious dialogue, which in its turn must be set within the context of a more global intercultural dialogue."

Conclusion

Perhaps the most dominant story told of inter-faith relations in Muslim lands concerns the Christian crusades of the 11th-13th centuries, and though the ramifications continue to this day, it was not the only kind of encounter happening between Muslims and Christians.

This paper was specifically concerned with the presence in Islamic countries of Christian monks and monasteries, and how these monasteries illustrate aspects of the interfaith relationship particularly between Islam and Christianity. Some of these monastic establishments predated the beginning of Islam by over two centuries, and others have even continued up to the present day in places like Egypt and Iraq. By the 9th century C.E. (3rd century A. H.) the interaction of Muslim Sufis and Christian monks was developing and providing contacts and exchanges in ways often overlooked in the historical overview of Christian-Muslim relations. These interactions often centered on the monasteries, and provided signposts to a mutuality and hospitality of faith that is often overshadowed by stories of more violent encounters through the centuries. Though many of these monasteries are in ruins today or gone completely, still others exist and provide places where Muslims still come for relaxation, prayer, and even to have demons exorcised, as in the Wadi Natrun desert of Egypt and the Tur Abdin of Eastern Turkey and Northern Iraq.

Could it be possible that through a re-birth and renewal of Christian monasticism, even in Islamic countries, that new bridges could be built? What we can see through this brief study of a neglected part of inter-faith history is an alternate story that could perhaps provide a signpost to a needed alternate future, one that emphasizes "zones of contact and exchange" rather than mutual exclusion and conflict.

Select Bibliography

Awaad, George 2007
Al-diyarat by al-Shabushti, reprint. Piscataway: Gorgias Press

Bell, Richard 1925
The Origin of Islam in its Christian Environment, London: MacMillan and co.

Boniface, Archimandrite 1993
Eastern Monasticism and the Future of the Church, Vadavathoor: Oriental Institute

Dalrymple, William 1998
From the Holy Mountain, London: Flamingo

Griffith, Sidney H. 1995

'Muhammad and the Monk Bahira,' in *Oriens Christianus*, 79, 146-174

Griffith, Sidney H. 2000
'Disputing with Islam in Syriac: The Case of the Monk of Bet Hale and A Muslim Emir,' *Hugoye Journal of Syriac Studies*, 3.1, January; at http://syrcom.cua.edu/Hugoye/VolInd.html accessed on 20.05.09

Griffith, Sidney H. 2008
The Church in the Shadow in the Mosque: Christians and Muslims in the World of Islam, Princeton: Princeton University Press

Gruber, Mark 2002
Journey Back to Eden, Maryknoll: Orbis books

Heitzman, James 1980
The Origin and Spread of Buddhist Monastic Institutions in South Asia 500 B.C.-300 A.D., Philadelphia: University of Pennsylvania

Kilpatrick, Hilary 2003
'Monasteries through Muslim eyes: The Diyarat Books,' an article in Thomas, David, ed. *Christians at the Heart of Islamic Rule*, 19-37, Leiden: Brill

Lazarus-Yafeh, Hava 1999
The Majlis: Inter-religious Encounters in Medieval Islam, Weisbaden: Harrassowitz Vering

Lovejoy, Bahija Fattuhi 1957
'Christian Monasteries in Mesopotamia,' Unpublished PhD dissertation Radcliffe College, Harvard

McAuliffe, Jane Damen 1991
Quranic Christians: An analysis of Classical and Modern Exegesis, Cambridge: Cambridge University Press

Menocal, Maria Rosa 2002
Ornament of the World, Boston: Little, Brown and company

Mingana, Alphonse 1928
Timothy's Apology for Christianity, Woodbrooke Studies No. 2, Cambridge: W. Heffer and Sons

Panikkar, Raimundo 1982
Blessed Simplicity: The Monk as Universal Archetype, New York: Seabury Press

Shahid, Irfan 1990
Byzantium and the Arabs in the 5th century, DC: Dumbarton Oaks

Shahid, Irfan 2002
Byzantium and the Arabs in the 6th century, DC: Dumbarton Oaks

Singh, D.E. 2008
'Hundred years of Christian-Muslim Relations: Mission to Interfaith Relations;' a paper presented to 'Towards Edinburgh 2010,' commission two on Interfaith at the United Theological College, Bangalore, Friday 17 to Sunday 19 of July 2009

Sozomen, Salanius 1952
The Ecclesiastical History, ed. Schaff, Philip Grand Rapids: Eerdmans
Taher, Bahaa' 1996
Aunt Safiyya and the Monasteriy, Berkeley: U of Cal press
Ye'or, Bat 1985
The Dhimmis: Jews and Christians under Islam, London: Associated University Press

SECTION II

INTERFAITH RELATIONS FROM HINDU PERSPECTIVES

Christian Dialogues with Hinduism

K.P. Aleaz

In this paper some highlights on the Indian Christian dialogues with Hinduism are presented. To begin with some trends in ecumenical responses to other faiths are analyzed. The second section is on a few 19th c. Christian dialogues with Hinduism. The third section deals with the thought of some 20th c. Christian theologians, on how they had dialogues with Hinduism and the fourth and final section provides our concluding observations.

Major Trends in Ecumenical Responses to Other Faiths

It would be worthwhile here to outline some of the major trends of the past ecumenical discussions on the Christian response to the plurality of world religious faiths. During 18th and 19th centuries the Christian missionary attitude to other religions and cultures was marked by a spirit of certainty about the superiority of the Gospel of Jesus Christ and the doctrines held by Christians. At the World Missionary Conference of 1910 at Edinburgh the missionaries who had come from lands of living faiths could not avoid the question of the Christian response to other faiths. They stated that on all lands the merely 'iconoclastic attitude' is condemned as radically unwise and unjust. The conference recognized the spirit of God working in the higher forms of other religions and affirmed that all religions disclose the elemental needs of the human soul, which Christianity alone could satisfy.[1]

The fact that missionary as well as scholarly interest continued on the subject after the conference is evident from the writings of missionary theologians like J.N. Farquhar[2] and A.G. Hogg.[3] According to Farquhar Christ provides the fulfillment of each of the highest aspirations and aims of Hinduism. Hogg disagreed with this 'fulfillment' theory through his

---

[1] J.R. Chandran, "Christianity and World Religions – The Ecumenical Discussion", *The Indian Journal of Theology*, Vol.30, Nos. 3 and 4, July-Dec. 1981, 186-7.

[2] Cf. J.N. Farquhar, *The Crown of Hinduism*, London: Oxford University Press, 1913; *Gita and the Gospel*, Third Edition, Madras: CLS, 1917.

[3] Cf. A.G. Hogg, Karma and Redemption. As essay toward the interpretation of Hinduism and the re-statement of Christianity, London: CLS, 1909; The Christian Message to the Hindu. Being the Duff Missionary Lectures for 1945 on the Challenge of the Gospel in India, London: SCM Press, 1947.

theory of 'contrast', which tried to present the gospel of Jesus through high lightening the differences between Hinduism and Christianity.

The second meeting of the Missionary Conference, at Jerusalem in 1928 thought that the enemy of the Christian mission was communism and secularism. The conference regarded other religions as allies of the Christian faith. Worship and reverence in Islam, sympathy over the world's sorrow in Buddhism, the moral order of Confucianism and the desire for contact with Ultimate Reality in Hinduism etc. were considered as 'rays of the same light'. The European Continental missionaries and theologians were later critical of this view of the conference, but the American and the British supported this view.[4]

A significant contribution came from the American Laymen's Report of 1932, *Rethinking Missions, a Laymen's Enquiry after a Hundred Years,* chiefly through W.E. Hocking[5] according to whom the task of the missionary should be to see the best in other religions. The missionary should aim at the emergence of the various religions out of their isolation into a world fellowship in which each will find its appropriate place. The aim should not be conversion. Hocking rejected the methods of 'radical displacement' and 'synthesis', and instead favoured the method of 'reconception'. The Continental missionary theologians reacted against such a standpoint and the clearest type of their reaction we see in H. Kraemer[6] who wrote *The Christian Message in a Non-Christian World* as the preparatory volume for the Third World Missionary Conference held at Tambaram in 1938. According to Kraemer Biblical revelation, God's self-disclosure in Jesus Christ, is *sue generis.* His Biblical Realism was influenced by Karl Barth and it stressed the absoluteness, finality and otherness of the Gospel. He emphasized the discontinuity between the Gospel and religions including Christianity.

The Tambaram Conference more or less adopted the line of Kraemer's theology. In Christ alone is the full salvation which humans need. Though in other religions may be found values of deep religious experiences and great moral achievements, though in them may be found glimpses of God's light as God did not leave Himself/Herself without witness in the world at any time, yet all religious insight and experience including those of Christians have to be fully tested before God in Christ. Humans have been seeking God all through the ages, but often this seeking and longing have been misdirected. The Conference 'boldly' called people 'out' from world religions to the feet of Christ.[7]

---

[4] J.R. Chandran, *Op. Cit.*, 191.

[5] For Hocking's thought Cf. William Ernest Hocking, *Living Religions and a World Faith*, New York: Macmillan Co., 1940.

[6] Cf. H. Kraemer, *The Christian Message in a Non-Christian World*, London: The Edinburgh House Press, 1938; *Religion and the Christian Faith*, London: Lutterworth Press, 1961.

[7] J.R. Chandran, *Op. Cit.*, 191.

The 'Rethinking Group' of Indian theologians P. Chenchiah, V. Chakkarai etc. were highly critical of Kraemer and the Tambaram message, specially the standpoint of 'discontinuity' between the Gospel and religions. According to them God and human person have met and fused together in the incarnation of God in Jesus and we should not have any 'Barthian nervousness' about it. The convert of today regards Hinduism as his/her spiritual mother. He/She discovers the supreme value of Christ, not in spite of Hinduism but because of Hinduism. Loyalty to Christ does not involve the surrender of a reverential attitude towards the Hindu heritage.[8]

Internationally also the debate continued in the 1940s and 50s and the overall outcome was an open-minded approach to other religions and cultures. Though the relevance of the call for conversion to the Christian faith was affirmed, many theologians openly departed from the traditional exclusive and authoritarian approach to other religions and this paved the way for a willingness for dialogue with other religions. Wide ecumenical recognition has been given through both the World Council of Churches and the Second Vatican Council, for this dialogue-approach. According to the Fourth Assembly of the World Council of Churches, which met at Uppsala in 1968, the meeting with people of other faiths must lead to dialogue. In dialogue we share our common humanity. Dialogue for a Christian, neither implies a denial of the uniqueness of Christ, nor any loss of his/her own commitment to Christ. Following the Uppsala Assembly, the WCC established a Department for Dialogue with People of Living Faiths and Ideologies.[9]

Since the meeting of the Central Committee at Addis Ababa in 1971, dialogue with people of living faiths has been part of the work of the World Council of Churches, it being understood as the common adventure of the churches. The consultation held in Chiang Mai, Thailand, in 1977 on the theme 'Dialogue in Community' proved ton be a significant stage in the very conception of dialogue. Dialogue in community has meant entering into dialogue with our neighbours of other faiths in the communities we as Christians share with them, exploring such issues as peace, justice, and humanity's relation to nature. *The Guidelines on Dialogue* adopted at the Central Committee meeting at Kingston, Jamaica, in 1979 since then has served as a guiding document for all churches. It has pointed out the relationship between Christian witness and dialogue. To quote:

> In giving their witness they (Christians) recognize that in most circumstances today the spirit of dialogue is necessary. For this reason we do not see dialogue and the giving of witness as standing in any contradiction to one another. Indeed, as Christians enter dialogue with their commitment to Jesus Christ, time and again the relationship of dialogue gives opportunity for authentic witness. Thus, to the member churches of the WCC we feel able

---

[8] Cf. G.V. Job et al, *Rethinking Christianity in India*, Madras: A.N. Sundarisanam, 1938.

[9] J.R. Chandran, *Op. Cit.*, 191-5.

> with integrity to commend the way of dialogue as one in which Jesus Christ can be confessed in the world today; at the same time we feel able with integrity to assure our partners in dialogue that we come not as manipulators but as genuine fellow pilgrims, to speak with them of what we believe God to have done in Jesus Christ who has gone before us, but whom we seek to meet anew in dialogue.[10]

Dialogue has been defined in the document as "witnessing to our deepest convictions and listening to those of our neighbours."[11]

Dialogue with people of other living faiths leads us to ask questions on Christian Theology of Religions. How do Christians theologically account for the diversity of the world's religious quest and commitment? What is the relation of the diversity of religious traditions to the mystery of the one Triune God? At both the Nairobi (1975) and Vancouver (1983) assemblies of the WCC, dialogue became a controversial point primarily because of the implicit assumptions made in dialogue about the theological significance of other faiths. At Vancouver, for example, a major stream within the Assembly rejected the possibility of God's presence and activity in the religious life of people of other faiths. Consequently the Dialogue sub-unit of the WCC undertook a four-year study programme on 'My Neighbour's Faith and Mine – Theological Discoveries through Interfaith Dialogue'.[12] As the apex of this study a document has been brought out by WCC through a significant ecumenical consultation in Barr, Switzerland in 1990. The Baar Statement says:

> We need to respect their religious convictions (i.e., of people of other living faiths), different as these may be from our own, and to admire the things which God has accomplished and continues to accomplish in them through the Spirit. Inter-religious dialogue is therefore a 'two-way street'. Christians must enter into it in a spirit of openness prepared to receive from others, while on their part, they give witness of their own faith. Authentic dialogue opens both partners to a deeper conversion to the God who speaks to each through the other. Through the witness of others, we Christians can truly discover facets of the divine mystery which we have not yet seen or responded to. The practice of dialogue will thus result in the deepening of our own life of faith. We believe that walking together with people of other living faiths will bring us to a fuller understanding and experience of truth.[13]

---

[10] *Guidelines on Dialogue with People of Living Faiths and Ideologies*, Geneva: World Council of Churches, 1979, 11.

[11] *Ibid.*, 16.

[12] Cf. *My Neighbour's Faith – And Mine. Theological Discoveries Through Inter-Faith Dialogue. A Study Guide*, Delhi: ISPCK, 1988.

[13] "Baar Statement", *Current Dialogue*, 18, June 1990, 7.

Some 19th Century Christian Dialogues with Hinduism

Krishna Mohun Banerjea (1813-1885) was the first Protestant Christian to interpret Jesus Christ and Christianity in terms of the Vedic thought.[14] In 1860s his thought on the relation between Hinduism and Christianity underwent considerable changes; he started taking a positive attitude to Hinduism. The purpose of his book *The Arian Witness*[15] written in 1875 was to show the striking parallels between the Old Testament and the Vedas and then to conclude that Christianity was the logical conclusion of Vedic Hinduism. The fundamental principles of the Gospel were recognized and acknowledged both in theory and practice by the Brahminical Arians of India. The original home of the Arians and Abraham was the same namely Media. There are striking parallels between Hebrew and Sanskrit. There are parallels to the Biblical creation stories in the Vedas. The legend of the Deluge is there in the Old Testament and *Satapatha Brahmana.*

The original sacrifice of the Vedas refers to the self-sacrifice of Prajapati, which foreshadowed the Cross of Jesus Christ. In the two Supplementary Essays[16] and in the booklet *The Relation between Christianity and Hinduism*[17] published in 1881, he further expounded the similarity between Hindu and Christian thought with respect to the understanding of sacrifice. The two theses of Banerjea were as follows:

> 1stly.That the fundamental principles of Christian doctrine in relation to the salvation of the world find a remarkable counterpart in the Vedic principles of primitive Hinduism in relation to the destruction of sin, and the redemption of the sinner by the efficacy of Sacrifice, itself a figure of Prajapati, *the Lord and Saviour of the Creation, who had given himself up*as an offering for that purpose.
>
> 2ndly. That the meaning of *Prajapati*, an appellative, variously described as a Purusha begotten in the beginning, as *Viswakarma*, the creator of all,singularly coincides with the meaning of the names and offices of the historical reality *Jesus Christ*, and that no other person than Jesus of Nazareth has ever appeared in the world claiming the character and position of the self-sacrificing *Prajapati*, at the same time both mortal and immortal....[18]

---

[14] For K.M. Banerjea's life and thought Cf. K.P. Aleaz (Comp. & Intro.), *From Exclusivism to Inclusivism. The Theological Writings of Krishna Mohun Banerjea (1813-1885)*, Delhi: ISPCK, 1999; T.V. Philip, *Krishna Mohan Banerjea. Christian Apologist*, Madras/Bangalore: CLS/CISRS, 1982.

[15] Cf. K.M. Banerjea, *The Arian Witness*, London: Thacker Spink & Co., 1875.

[16] Cf. K.M. Banerjea, *The Arian Witness. Supplementary Essays*, London: Thacker Spink & Co., 1880.

[17] Cf. K.M. Banerjea, *The Relation between Christianity and Hinduism*, Calcutta: Oxford Mission Press, 1881.

[18] K.M. Banrjea, "Selected Writing" in Kaj Baago, *Pioneers of Indigenous Christianity*, Madras/Bangalore: CLS/CISRS, 1969, 98.

Banerjea's exposition of Christ as the *True Prajapati* was an attempt to establish the fact that Christianity is not a foreign religion but rather the fulfillment of the Vedas. In fact thirty eight years before J.N. Farquhar it was Krishna Mohun Banerjea who first proposed 'Fulfillment Theory' or Inclusivism in Indian Christian Theology of Religions, that again without any negative criticisms of Hinduism as are found in Farquhar's book.[19] Also, some eighty-four years before Raimon Panikkar,[20] K.M. Banerjea was the first person to hint at Prajapati as unknown Christ of Hinduism, that again without any negative criticisms of Vedanta as are found in Panikkar's thesis. Again, sixty-three years before H. Kraemer proposed his theory of discontinuity between Revelation and religions[21]here is an Indian theologian in the person of Banerjea expounding a point of contact and continuity between Christianity and Hinduism.

The thought of the Indian Christian poet H.A. Krishna Pillai who had a conversion experience during the period 1857-59 shows that in understanding the work of Christ he was unable to find meaning in the idea of expiation and juridical justification; rather he expressed the function of Jesus as releasing precious life for humanity and making people his devotees.[22] Krishna Pillai was originally from the Vaishnava tradition and Ramanuja's thought had influenced him. Hence he could understand salvation only as a recentring of one's relationship to God in such a way that the individual self becomes a focal point for the expression of the glory and love of the divine Self, which is human fulfillment.[23] When such a vision is applied in interpreting Christ the end result would be the emergence of something totally new. Christopher Duraisingh explains:

> Within such a theology, the role of Christ is not of one that mediates the propitiatory requirement to satisfy a righteous God. Rather, the mediatory potency of Christ is that of a potency of the most decisive paradigm case, classic instance, and unique manifestation in the plane of history of such a radical recentring and self-knowledge. Jesus' acknowledgement of the divine Self as his true Self was so complete and his recentring so maximal that in and through his life, death and continuing presence in the faith of the

---

[19] Cf. J.N. Farquhar, *The Crown of Hinduism, Op. Cit.*

[20] Cf. Raimundo Panikkar, *The Unknown Christ of Hinduism*, London: Darton, Longman & Todd, 1964 (Revised and Enlarged Edition by the same Publisher in 1981). For a summary of his thesis Cf. "Isvara and Christ as a Philosophical Problem*", Religion and Society*, Vol. VI, No. 3, October1959, 8-16.

[21] Cf. H. Kraemer, *The Christian Message in a Non-Christian World, Op. Cit.*

[22] D.D. Hudson, "Hindu and Christian theological Parallels in the Conversion of H.A. Krishna Pillai. 1857-1859", Journal of the American Academy of Religion, Vol. 40, June 1972, 196-205.

[23] Christopher Duraisingh, "Reflection on Theological Hermeneutics in the Indian Context", *The Indian Journal of Theology*, Vol. 31, Nos. 3 & 4, July-Dec. 1982, 271-75.

believing community a potency for the self-realization of the believer as centres in God,his only true self is released.[24]

A.S. Appasamy Pillai born in orthodox Hindu family in Tinnevelly in 1848, baptized in 1871, entered into a process of rediscovering Hinduism which gave him new insights into the Christian faith. In Rig Veda he found an anticipation of Christianity and hence it was for him like the Old Testament. The Rig Veda points to God the one behind the many, all-powerful, all-loving and all-merciful.[25] Rig Veda, also, through the teaching on Hiranyagarbha prefigures Christ. Hiranyagarbha the Golden Egg is for him the golden Child who created everything and asked the question 'to whom shall I sacrifice'. Thus according to him the germ of the doctrines of logos and atonement is found in the Rig Veda.[26]

A.S. Appasamy Pillai made use of Indian yoga technique in Christian meditation and prayer.[27] Through Saiva Siddantic Yoga, he had the experience of receiving Holy Spirit and gaining a clearer vision of Christ.[28] Later he practiced Advaita Vedantic Yoga and recommended it for use by Christians though without accepting the Vedantic philosophy as a whole.[29] On the basis of the revelation of Christ through yoga he tried to reinterpret the doctrines of the Trinity and the Logos. He experienced God as light, Spirit as Sakti and Christ as a spiritual body or a Suksma Sarira which reflects God.[30] He had the conviction that the Holy Spirit is working through yoga not only among Christians but also among the Hindus.[31]

The contributions of Brahmabandav Upadhyaya (1861-1907) to Indian theology lie in his interpretation of Trinity as Sat-chit-anandam and Creation as Maya. It is the Upanishads and Sankara's writings which Upadhyaya takes as the basis for his explanation of the Vedantic concept Sat-chit-anandam. To speak of Brahman as Sat-chit-anandam means that Brahman knows Himself/Herself and from that self-knowledge proceeds His/Her eternal beatitude. Brahman is related of necessity only to the Infinite Image of His/Her own being, mirrored in the ocean of His/Her knowledge. This relation of Being (Sat) to Himself/Herself in self-

---

[24] *Ibid.*, 273.

[25] A.S. Appasamy Pillai, *Fifty Years' Pilgrimage of a Convert*, London, 1924, 89-92.

[26] *Ibid.*, 92-94. Cf. Rig Veda 10. 121.

[27] Kaj Baago, *Pioneers of Indigenous Christianity,Op. Cit.*, 19ff.

[28] A.S. Appasamy Pillai, *The Use of Yoga in Prayer*, Madras: CLS, 1926, 10-13.

[29] *Ibid.*, 17.

[30] Appasamy Pillai published two pamphlets. The Eternal Divine Son and The Divine Birth of the Eternal Son. Cf. A.J. Appasamy, *An Indian Interpretation of Christianity*, Madras: CLS, 1924. 4-8.

[31] *Fifty Years'Pilgrimage of a Convert, Op. Cit.*, 97ff.

knowledge (Chit) is one of perfect harmony, bliss (Anandam).[32] Upadhyaya then proclaimed that the Christian doctrine of God as Trinity is exactly the same as the Vedantic conception of Brahman as Sat-chit-anandam because in the Trinity the Father's knowledge is fully satisfied by the cognition of the Logos, the Infinite Image of His Being, begotten by thought and mirrored in the ocean of His substance and His love finds the fullest satisfaction in the boundless complacency with which He reposes on His Image and breathes forth the spirit of bliss. The knowing Self is the Father, the known Self or the self-begotten by His knowledge is the Son; and the Holy Ghost is the Spirit of reciprocal love proceeding from the Father and the Son.[33]

Upadhyaya would point out that Revelation of god in Jesus Christ is the further clarification of God conceived as Sat-Chit-Anandam. Reason can only know that self-existent Being is necessarily intelligent. But only Revelation can tell us how Self-Existent Being's intelligence is satisfied within the term of its being. Revelation teaches us that the differentiating note in Divine knowledge is the response of intelligence. Jesus Christ acknowledges responsively his eternal thought generation from the Father.[34] The relation between the father and Jesus Christ is the revelation of the true relation between Sat and Chit as well as the revelation of anandam, the result of that relation. And this revelation of the inner life of God is for humans to attain the goal of life, which is beatific vision, beholding God as He/She is in Himself/Herself.

Regarding the doctrines of Human Person, Sin, Fall, Grace, Atonement and Salvation Upadhyaya maintained the traditional Christian position and hence he tried to explain the traditional understanding of the person of Jesus Christ in terms of the Vedantic understanding of human nature also. According to the Vedanta, human nature is composed of five sheaths or divisions *(kosa)* namely physical *(annamaya)*, vital (*pranmaya*), mental (*manomaya)*, intellectual *(vijnanamaya)* and spiritual (*anandamaya*). In a human being these five sheaths are presided over by a created personality (*aham)*. Jesus Christ is also composed of five sheaths, but in him the five sheaths are acted upon directly by the Logos-God instead of a created

---

[32] B. Upadhyaya, "A Vedantic Parable", *Sophia*, Vol. V, No. 8, Aug. 1898, 119; "Being", *Sophia*, Vol. 1, No. 7, July 28, 1900, 7; "Notes", *Sophia*, Vol. 1, No. 2, June 23, 1900.

[33] B. Upadhyaya, "An exposition of Catholic Belief as compared with the Vedanta", *Sophia*, Vol. V, No. 1, Jan. 1898, 11; "Our New Canticle", *Sophia*, Vol. V, No. 10, Oct. 1898, 146; "Hinduism and Christianity as Compared by Mrs. Bezant", *Sophia*, Vol. IV, No.2, Feeb.1897, 8; "Question and Answers", *Sophia*, Vol. 1, No. 11, Aug. 25, 1900, 7.

[34] Summary of the lecture by Upadhyaya: "Hinduism, Theosophy and Christianity", *Sophia*, Vol.1V, No. 12, Dec.1897, 2, 4-5; "The Incarnate Logos", *The Twentieth Century*, Vol.1, No. 1, Jan. 1901, 6-7; "Christ's claim to attention", *The Twentieth Century*, Vol. 1, No. 5, May 1901, 115-6.

personality. The Incarnation was thus accomplished by uniting humanity with Divinity in the person of the Logos and this incarnate God in human person we call Jesus Christ.[35]

Upadhyaya also interpreted the Christian doctrine of creation in terms of the Vedantic concept *Maya.* He pointed out that according to Advaita Vedanta, the world originates by *vivarta*, a kind of communication which does not modify the communicator. *Vivarta* implies creation by will-causation *(sankalpa*). This is also the meaning of Maya. Maya signifies the will-power (*sankalp*a) of God. It means that creation is by the power (*sakti*) of the will (*sankalpa)* of God.[36] For Upadhyaya the term Maya involves three truths: (a) God is not necessarily a creator; (b) Creatures are non-beings, transformed as it were into being; (c) the transformation is caused by the mysterious power of the will of God. He then declared that this Vedantic doctrine of Maya which explains creation and the Christian doctrine of creation are identical because, according to the Christian doctrine of creation also, God does not create out of necessity but through the overflow of his perfections; creation has no being in itself; what it has is derived being and creation is the effect of the divine thought.[37] Upadhyaya even said that the term Maya could express the meaning of the doctrine of creation in a far better way than the Lain root *creare.*

Highlights on the 20th Century Christian Dialogues with Hinduism

S.K. George (1900-1960) and Manilal C. Parekh (1885-1967) held pluralism in theology of religions since 1920s and 1930s respectively and S.J. Samartha joined them in the 1990s.[38] For S.K. George redemptive suffering love manifested in the Cross of Christ is the central principle of Christianity and the manifestation of it in practice and not the preaching of any dogma, is what is needed. Mahatma Gandhi's satyagraha movement was for him Cross in action and he joined it wholeheartedly in 1932 resigning a secure teaching job at Bishop's College, Calcutta.[39] Even prior to this as a Bachelor of Divinity student of Bishop's College (1924-27), he had his doubts about the exclusive divinity of Christ. As early as 1937 S.K. George helped in organizing the All Kerala Inter-religious Students

---

[35] B. Upadhyaya, "The Incarnate Logos", *The Twentieth Century*, Vol.1, no. 1, Jan. 1901, 6-8; "Notes", *Sophia*, Vol. 1, No. 4. July 7, 1900, 6-7.

[36] Cf. B. Upadhyaya, "Maya", *Sophia*, Vol. 1, No. 18, Oct. 27, 1900, 6-7.

[37] Cf. B. Upadhyaya, "The True doctrine of Maya", *Sophia*, Vol. V1, No.2, Feb. 1899, 226-28; Vedantism and Christianity", *Sophia*, Vol. 1, Nos. 15 and 16, Sept. 29, 1900, 6.

[38] Cf. S.J. Samartha, *One Christ Many Religions*, Bangalore: Sathri, 1992.

[39] Cf. K.P. Aleaz, "S.K. George: A Pioneer Pluralist and Dalit Theologian", *Bangalore theological Forum*, Vol. XXX11, No. 1, June 2000, 91-111; S.K. George, *Gandhi's Challenge to Christianity*, 2nd Edition, Ahmedabad: Navajivan Publishing House, 1947.

Fellowship, which tried to bring together students of various religions for mutual understanding and co-operation. The first conference of the Fellowship was held at Alwaye in May 1937 and adopted its Aim and Basis which says:

> Amidst the conflicting claims made on behalf of different religions… we believe there is an urgent need for a full and free exchange of our differing religious experiences, in a spirit of mutual respect, appreciation and sympathy. We consider that for such mutual respect and sympathy to be real it is absolutely necessary that no member of the Fellowship should claim for his religion any exclusive and final possession of truth. We believe that such an interchange of experience will lead to: enrichment of one another's religious life; Mutual respect, understanding and tolerance; and Cooperation in purifying and strengthening the religious attitude of mind …from which our …problems have to be tackled.[40]

The Fellowship will explore fully the value of all the different religious traditions and disciplines and present them for the benefit of all. But at the same time nobody in the Fellowship is persuaded to join another's religious belief and practice. To weaken the hold of the truth of any religion upon humankind was considered as to weaken religion itself and hence the Fellowship is to strive for the opposite. The Fellowship was to help one another to understand and to live up to the best in all religions.[41]

S.K. George had the conviction that the hope of world unity and human fellowship lies through inter-religious cooperation. Inter-religious movement can eliminate religious conflicts and intolerances. The spirit of co-operation, which he found among Christians, he wanted to be extended to include the different religions as well.[42] In his view inter-religious movement faces many misunderstandings. One Charge is that it is syncretistic and will but result in adding one or more new fancy religions to the crowded world of religions. The clarification given by George in this context is:

> The inter-religious movement does not aim at evolving a single universal religion for all mankind. That … is the dream of the militant missionary faiths, which would blot out all other religions. What inter-religionism stands for is the acceptance of the need and the fact of variety in religious experience, of diversity in man's approach towards and realization of the One Eternal Reality, which is the common object of religious quest throughout the ages. It admits the limitation of all human understanding of the Divine – even unique revelations are mediated through human channels – and is, therefore, humble and willing to accept light from various sources. It accepts the revelation through the spiritual geniuses of all mankind and while it does not aim at, or believe in, evolving a uniformity of creed and conduct, it looks forward to a time when the spiritually minded of all religions will unite in the

---

[40] *Ibid.*, 80.

[41] *Ibid.*, 80-91.

[42] *Ibid.*, 52.

appreciation of all known truths and is welcoming fresh revelations from the unspent deep resources of God.[43]

The Fellowship of the Friends of Truth started in 1951 and whose secretary for the first seven years was S.K. George, was functioning in such a spirit as an inter-religious movement.

According to George the place of Jesus Christ in the Hindu religious heritage of India is as one of the *Ishta Devatas* or chosen deities or favorite deities. Hinduism readily grants such a place to Jesus Christ. From the side of a disciple of Jesus what is needed is, he/she must not deny other mediators between God and humans, other experiences of God's presence in the human heart, the validity of other *Ishta Devatas.* Such denials lie outside the positive experience of the Christians and therefore have no validity.[44]

Manilal C. Parekh was born in a Jain home in Rajkot, Gujarat. He was introduced to Hindu Vaishnava Bhakti by his father. A serious illness helped him to experience Theism. He came under the influence of the writings of Keshub Chunder Sen and served for some years as a *pracaraka* of the Church of the New Dispensation in Sindh and Bombay. The next stage in his pilgrimage was his growing interest in Christ, towards whom Keshub had so firmly pointed. The serious illness tuberculosis gave him opportunity for study and reflection. He studied the Bible and the *Vacanamrit* of Swami Narayana, the famous Gujarati Vaishnava religious and social reformer of the early 19thc. The study of Vaishnava Bhakti led him beyond the rationalism of the Brahmo Samaj to the conviction that God becomes incarnate and this belief in turn pointed him on to Christ of whom he read in the New Testament.[45]

Parekh was baptized in the Anglican Church in Bombay in 1918. He considered baptism as only a spiritual matter. He became disillusioned with the Westerization of the Indian Christian community. He wanted a 'Hindu Church of Christ' free from Western influence. He now strongly felt that the new disciple of Christ should remain within his/her own community, witnessing from there. He drew a clear distinction between 'evangelism' i.e., proclamation of the Gospel to individuals and 'proselytism' by which he meant mass-conversion by dubious means. He like Brahmabandhav Upadhyaya (1861-1907) of Bengal made a distinction between *samaja dharma* (social aspect of religion) and *moksha dharma* (spiritual aspect). Christianity should be *moksha dharma* only[46]

---

[43] *Ibid.*, 53-54.

[44] *Ibid.*, 48; S.K. George, "Christianity in Independent India" in *S.K. George Souvenir, The FFT Quarterly*, Vol. 7, Nos. 1&2, Oct. 1959 and Jan. 1960, 37.

[45] Cf. R.H.S. Boyd (ed.), *Manilal C. Parekh 1885-1967 Dhanjibhai Fakirbhai 1895-1967. A Selection*, Madras: CLS, 1974.

[46] K.P. Aleaz, *Religions in Christian Theology*, Kolkata: Punthi Pustak, 2001, 95-96.

By the end of 1930s, Parekh came to the final stage of his spiritual pilgrimage, namely *Bhagavata Dharma*. He conceived *Bhagavata Dharma* as a universal personal religion of devotion in which Christian devotion is one element among others, perhaps the central and organizing element. He used this term to describe a religion of personal *Bhakti*, which is seen at its clearest in Christianity and Vaishnavism, but is also seen in all other theistic faiths. He included in it Christianity, Judaism, Islam, Zoroastrianism and all the religions, which believe in God. His bitter experiences in both Brahmo Samaj and Christian Church had eventually brought him to the conclusion that change of religion is undesirable, since it tends to lead to exclusiveness and communalism. For the New Harmony which he was evolving, he wanted a name, which avoids the implication that one particular tradition had a monopoly of the truth, and this he found in Bhagavata Dharma.[47] Bhagavata Dharma truly represents a spirituality of pluralism.

The convert of today, according to P. Chenchiah (1886-1959) of the Madras Rethinking Group that flourished in the first half of 20[th]c. regards Hinduism as his/her spiritual mother who has nurtured him/her in a sense of spiritual values in the past. He/She discovers the supreme value of Christ, not in spite of Hinduism but because Hinduism has taught him/her to discern spiritual greatness. Emancipation from double bondage, namely to the traditions of Hinduism on the one hand and to the traditions of Christianity on the other, gives him/her the freedom to study the question of the meaning and significance of Jesus untrammeled by doctrines and dogma and seek in the living forces of Hinduism a positive key to the still inaccessible riches in Jesus.[48] The Christian is a new man/woman. He/She is a new creation. The Holy Spirit is the new cosmic energy; the Kingdom of God the new order; the children of God, the new type that Christ has inaugurated. The Gospel is that God in Jesus has made a new creation.[49] In Chenchiah's view human history has turned a new revolutionary chapter in Jesus. Christianity is not primarily a doctrine of salvation but the announcement of the advent of a new creative order in Jesus. The good news of Christianity is the birth of Jesus and the problem of the Christian is how to reproduce him. If we want to establish the kingdom of God, we must reproduce Jesus. Christianity is not a juridical or legal problem but a problem in genetics.[50] The Christian has to develop the Yoga of the Holy Sprit with a new *sadhana* of eternal life.[51]Today we have to realize Jesus as

---

[47] *Ibid.*, 97. Cf. Manilal C. Parekh, *A Hindu Portrait of Jesus Christ*, Rajkot: Sri Bhagavata Dhrama Mission, 1953; *Christian Proselytism in India – A Great and Growing Menace*, Rajkot, 1947.

[48] P. Chenchiah, "Jesus and Non-Christian Faiths" in *Rethinking Christianity in India*, ed. by G.V. Job et al, Madras: A.N. Sundarisanam, 1938, 49.

[49] *Ibid.*, 54-55.

[50] *Ibid.*, 58-59.

[51] *Ibid.*, 60.

the head of a new world order; or as the creative expression of God's higher purposes with regard to humans.[52]

According to Chenchiah two categories of interpretation of Jesus namely the juridical and the genetic or the creative are possible. He rejects the former and accepts only the latter. In the juridical conception of Christianity the cross is understood as a sacrifice for the atonement for the sins of humankind. But as we accompany Jesus we never get 'the Kalighat' feeling of sacrifice.[53] "Neither in my studies of the Gospel, not even in my private devotion, can I capture the feeling that in Jesus I am in a temple where he is sacrificed for me to satisfy a terror inspiring deity. No Indian gets this feeling".[54] We can never get to the heart of Christianity by the way of juridical theology. It is the genetic or creative aspect of Jesus, it is the Holy Spirit as a creative energy, that takes the Indian into the new 'given' in Jesus.[55]

The attempt to interpret Jesus exclusively in terms of justification by faith or reconciliation has resulted in the view that the ultimate effect of the ministry of our Lord was to *restore* humanity to its original condition i.e., to its primal stage before fall. But for Chenchiah Christian faith is much more than this. The fact of Christ is the birth of a new order in creation. It is the emergence of life partaking the immortal nature of God beyond sin and death. It is the birth of a new race in the creation of children of God.[56] In the company of Jesus we do not feel the gulf that separates God and humans. His own consciousness reveals the total lack of this sense of separation and his teachings do not emphasize the awful gulf between God and humans. God and human person have met in Jesus; not merely met, but fused and mingled into one and let there be no Barthian nervousness about it. To be Christian is to gain this consciousness and this sense of harmonious blend with the divine.[57] Jesus stands in relation to human person as a new creation stands towards the old. He is the New Man. He is the 'new given' that has entered the world. He is the first fruit of the new creation. Christianity brings into evolution the new Sakti of the Holy Spirit.[58] Jesus is never the absolute, unapproachable, incomprehensible. He does not stand as the absolute to human person. On this point the Church has wronged our Lord from the beginning: "We have been always anxious to turn him into a God, place him over against us, and worship him. While

[52] P. Chenchiah, "The Christian Message in a Non-Christian world. A Review of Dr. Kraemer's Book" in *Ibid.*, Appendix, 19.
[53] *Ibid.*, 21-22.
[54] *Ibid.*, 22.
[55] *Ibid.*, 22-23.
[56] *Ibid.*, 23-24.
[57] *Ibid.*, 26-27; 35-36.
[58] *Ibid.*, 42-43.

he wanted to step out of God to be with us in fellowship, ours is a worship which militates against his fellowship".[59]

In the view of A.J. Appasamy (1891-1975), Ramanuja realized with certainty that God is a personal being who loves us and to his grace we should surrender ourselves. Also, out of love God becomes incarnate in order to satisfy the longing of the humans for God. Further, Ramanuja emphasizes the immanence of God. God is the inner ruler of the universe and souls. Just as the soul is within the body, controlling it and directing it, God is within the world of nature and of humans, ruling over these from the inner depth. God immanent in the individual soul (*Tvam*) is identical with Brahman who is the author of all creation (*Tat)*. Ramanuja was the first to give a constructive and elaborate philosophical formulation of the doctrine of Bhakti. Ramanuja's convictions were entirely opposed to those of Sankara. Ramanuja believed in a God endowed with the attributes of power, knowledge, love and bliss. For him Bhakti or love is the most effective to reach the Divine and even in the highest stage of the spiritual life individual souls continue to exist and derive their bliss from their intimate relation to the Ultimate Reality. Brahman's Being, Knowledge and Bliss are in relation to others and Brahman is not limited to the attributes. Bhakti involves continuous recollection of God, which is also specified by the words vision (*darsana)* and meditation (dhyana).[60]

As these doctrines of Ramanuja make an unfailing appeal to the heart of India, in the light of them Appasamy has suggested a line along which Christology could be built up in India. The farewell discourses of John13 to 17 have to be made the focus for Christology and 'abide in me and I in You' is the Christian *mahavakya* expressing the intimate relationship between Christ and the believer. Christian faith is communion with Jesus who lived on this earth long ago and now, as the eternal Christ, dwells in the depth of the human heart. The experience of the living Christ takes place in the depths of the individual soul. The living Christ continues to do in one human heart after another what the Jesus of history did in Palestine.[61]Appasamy also thought that fundamentally the Hindu doctrine of *Avatara* is akin to the Christian doctrine of Incarnation. But he also reminds us that when speaking of Jesus as *Avatara,* we should also bear in mind the distinctiveness that he is the Incarnation of the whole Being of God for all times and he came to redeem the sinners. For Appasamy the identity between Jesus and the Father was one of will and not of essential nature. Further we may note that he has inter-related Ramanuja's doctrine

---

[59] *Ibid.*, 16-17.

[60] Cf. A.J. Appasamy, *The Theology of Hindu Bhakti*, Madras: CLS, 1970.

[61] A.J. Appasamy, "Christological Reconstruction and Ramanuja's Philosophy", *The International Review of Missions*, Vol. XLI, No. 162, April 1952, 170-76.

of the Indwelling God (*Antaryamin*) or the Inner Ruler with the Christian understanding of the Holy Spirit.[62]

Swami Abhishiktananda (1910-1973) has interpreted Jesus Christ as *Cit* in the context of his interpretation of Trinity as Saccidananda. While Brahmabandhav Upadhyaya holds that with regard to the concept of Supreme Being the advaitic and Christian doctrines are identical, Abhishiktananda would point out that a reinterpretation of the Hindu concept Saccidananda is necessary to make it Christian. The Hindu experience of Saccidananda should be remolded to attain the Christian experience of Saccidananda and once that is actualized the renewed experience of Saccidananda would be the Trinitarian culmination of advaitic experience.[63]

In the view of Abhishiktananda when the advaitic Saccidananda is considered in the light of Christian experience of the trinity, it gives the impression of being essentially monistic and of terminating in unbroken silence.[64] Advaita conceives Being as monad. Because of the advaitic understanding of Being as monad, advaita faces the antinomy and paradox of created being. Only in the light of the Trinitarian revelation of Being as communion we are able to resolve the mystery of Creation. Revelation of God in Jesus Christ as trinity is the solution to the paradox of created being. Jesus Christ provides us the revelation that 'Being is communion'.[65] Hence Creation can be understood as the 'expansion' of God's inner self-manifestation. In the very mystery of God, the Father, Son and Holy Spirit, human person discovers himself/herself as a unique and irreplaceable manifestaton of God's Being and love.[66]

Abhishiktananda explains the Hindu Advaitic experience of Saccidananda as follows:[67] a person realizes Being, *Sat*, as himself/herself as well as infinitely beyond himself/herself. A person *is*, and he/she knows that he/she *is*. This is the mystery of pure awareness, *Cit*, of Self. When pure self-awareness is sufficiently realized, the whole being is flooded with an inexpressible sense of completion, peace, joy and fullness and this is what the Hindu tradition calls *Ananda.* Thus if one descends into the successive depths of one's true self namely being, awareness of being and joy in being, then finally nothing will be left but he/she himself/herself, the only one, infinitely alone, Being, Awareness and Bliss, Saccidananda.

---

[62] A.J. Appasamy, *The Gospel and India's heritage*, London & Madras: SPCK, 1942, 256-58, 75-93.

[63] Cf. Swami Abhishiktananda, *Saccidananda. A Christian Approach to Advaitic Experience*, Delhi: ISPCK, 1974; *Hindu-Christian Meeting Point. Within the Cave of the Heart*, Bombay/Bangalore: The Institute of Indian Culture/CISRS, 1969.

[64] Swami Abhishiktananda, *Saccidananda, Op. Cit.*, 43, 174.

[65] *Ibid.*, 98, 103, 109, 117, 135.

[66] *Ibid.*, 103-104, 124, 130; Swami Abhishiktananda, *Hindu-Christian meeting Point, Op. Cit.*, 84; *Prayer*, Delhi: ISPCK, 1967, 3.

[67] Swami Abhishiktananda, *Saccidananda, Op. Cit.*, 167-70.

The claim of Abhishiktananda was that in Jesus Christ we get a different picture.[68] In the relationship between Jesus Christ and God the Father there is the expression of oneness as well as the expression of the distinct face-to-face relation. In awaking to himself at the centre of his being, Jesus awoke to the Father. And because He is pre-eminently the representative 'Son of Man', humanity shares in everything that he does and all that he achieves. Jesus Christ achieved for all his brothers and sisters the right to utter their 'I' and 'you' in perfect truth, within the 'I' and 'you' which are eternally exchanged between the Father and the Son. And moreover, Holy Spirit is the expression of the mystery of the non-duality of the Father and the Son as well as the expression of the mystery of non-duality of the whole humanity and the Father actualized in and through the Son. Thus in Christian Saccidananda i.e., in Trinity, Being, *Sat* opens itself at its very source to give birth eternally to the Son and in Him to countless creatures, each of which in its own way will for ever manifest and celebrate the infinite love and mercy of God. According to Christian Saccidananda self-awareness, *Cit* comes to be only when there is mutual giving and receiving between the Father and the Son and between the Father and the whole humanity in Jesus Christ, for the *I* only awakes to itself in a *thou*. And according to Christian Saccidananda, joy, *Ananda* is there because of the mutual giving and receiving, because of the reciprocal love between the Father and the Son, God and human person, and a person and another.

The spiritual dairy of Swami Abhisiktananda now available in English more or less shows that the transformation Advaitic experience brought in him as early as 1952 was to stay throughout his life. Though through his books *Saccidananda* and *Hndu-Christian Meeting Point*, he projected externally an Inclusivist position, there was a second internal Abhishiktananda, a Vedantin-Christian Abhishiktananda, according to whom it is the Christian Trinitarian experience which has to be remolded in terms of Advaitic experience.[69] Also to be noted that towards the end of his life Abhishiktananda could experience the saving Christ only as pure self-awareness – *I AM*, going beyond religious distinctions.[70]

According to Raimon Panikkar the role of Isvara in Vedanta corresponds functionally to the role of Christ in Christian thought. It is precisely this correspondence that provides Indian philosophy with a locus for Christ and

---

[68] *Ibid.*, 79-80, 82, 88, 91, 95, 97, 98, 176-79, 184-85; Swami Abhishiktananda, *Hindu-Christian Meeting Point, Op. Cit.*, xvi, 80, 96-97.

[69] Raimon Panikkar (ed.), Abhishiktananda. Ascent to the Depth of the 'Heart': The Spiritual Diary (1948-1973) of Swami Abhishiktananda (Dom H. Le Saux) A Selection (English translation by David Fleming and James Stuart), Delhi: ISPCK, 1998, 63, 73, 109, 124, 268, 388.

[70] James Stuart, *Swami Abhishiktananda. His Life told through his letters*, Delhi: ISPCK, 1989, 293, 294, 305, 306, 317, 318, 321, 329, 342, 346, 348, 350, 353.

Christian theology for Isvara.[71] If we start with the historicity of Christ, essential though it may be, we are liable to be gravely misunderstood. The Christ of Hinduism is one who is 'hidden and unknown' as the Isvara of the Vedanta. Isvara is the unknown Christ of Hinduism.[72] In Vedanta the concept Isvara is one which is put forward to explain the problem of the relation between Brahman and World. But the concept Isvara cannot solve the problem satisfactorily. Sankara's Isvara cannot be a true mediator as he is only real from one end and not real from the other. In Sankara's Advaita, the diversity between Brahman and Isvata is overstressed in order to save the absolute purity of the former.[73] In Ramanuja's Visistadvaita, it is the identity between Brahman and Isvara which is overstressed to save the reality of the world. And hence again Isvara is not a satisfactory 'link'.[74] According toPanikkar only Christ can be the true link between the World and God. The Isvara of Panikkar's interpretation, he claims, is really 'human' without ceasing to be divine and it points towards a reality which not only connects the two poles of God and world, but which 'is' the two poles without permitting them to coalesce and in the Christian language this Isvara of his interpretation points towards the Mystery of Christ.[75] In other words, Panikkar is reinterpreting the concept Isvara of Vedanta so that it becomes the already formulated traditional Christian understanding of Christ.

Of course it is also true that by the name 'Christ' Panikkar now means more than Jesus of Nazareth, even though Jesus is the manifestation of Christ for the Christian. Christ is the supername. Christic principle for him is the center of reality as seen by the Christian tradition in a theanthropocosmic vision. Though Chistic principle is still central for him, Panikkar is today more positive and open to other faiths, more or less moving away from Inclusivism to Pluralism.[76]

---

[71] Raimundo Panikkar, *The Unknown Christ of Hinduism. Towards an Ecumenical Christophany*, Revised and Enlarged Edition, London: Darton, Longman & Todd, 1981, 164.

[72] Raimundo Panikkar, *The Unknown Christ of Hinduism*, First Edition, London: Darton, Longman & Todd, 1968, 137.

[73] *Ibid.*, 125,128, 129.

[74] *Ibid.*, 129.

[75] Raimundo Panikkar, *The Unknown Christ of Hinduism, Revised and Enlarged Edition, Op. Cit.*, 159-60.

[76] Raimundo Panikkar, "The Jordan, the Tiber, and the Ganges. Three Kairological Moments of Christic Self-consciousness" in *The Myth of Christian Uniqueness. Toward a Pluralistic Theology of Religions*, ed. by John Hick and Paul F. Knitter, Maryknoll: Orbis, 1987, 92,113-14; "The Meaning of Christ's Name in Universal Economy of Salvation" in *Service and Salvation. Nagpur Theological Conference on Evangelization*, ed. by Joseph Pathrapankal, Bangalore: TPI, 1973, 258-59, 262-63; "Indian Christian Theology of Religious Pluralism from the Perspective of Interculturation" in *Religious Pluralism. An Indian Christian Perspective*, ed. by Kuncheria Pathil, Delhi: ISPCK, 1991, 292.

There have been some Indian Christian thinkers who were negative in their approach to Hinduism and P.D. Devanandan and Surjith Singh may be taken as their representatives. P.D. Devanandan (1901-1962) had the view that the classical Hindu Vedantic theology is incapable of giving an ideological basis for the new anthropology emerging in independent India[77] and where it is failing to find a solution, the revelation of God in Jesus Christ has got an answer to give. The different aspects of the answer are: When God became human person, that effects a revolutionary significance for the world. A person gets an understanding of life as one in which God Himself/Herself is purposely involved. Christ gives meaningful ideological basis for service *(diakonia)* as one in which God's redemptive power is at work in our day-to-day life liberating the individual and renewing human society. If human being is God's creature and God is human being's creator, God is the God who involves in world life and history. Christian thought stands for the idea of personality as applied both to finite and infinite being. Individuals can enter into creative relationship in community due to their being bound together as persons in relation to the Person.[78] Lack of emphasis of the sinful nature of human person and the purposive will of a personal God as well as over-emphasis on the gulf between the transcendental Being and Karma-samsara-life are the characteristic limitations of Hinduism[79] which can be overcome by the following facts related to the revelation of God in Jesus Christ: Human Person is fallen and sinful, God is actively involved in world history and God's redemptive plan is cosmic in its scope.[80]

In Surjit Singh's view, the values at stake in Advaita Vedanta are of personality, of history and of time. It is confusing to call God personal in Advaita system. Also, according to Advaita, ultimately individuality of a person is lost in the Absolute.[81] Hence Surjit Singh wishes to safeguard the reality of personality, human and divine, of history, of time and of the world by recapturing the New Testament significance of the person and work of Jesus Christ. Christian thought has maintained that God-human Person is an eternal fact, thus preserving the importance of human nature as

---

[77] P.D. Devanandan, The Concept of Maya. An Essay in Historical Survey of the Hindu theory of the World, with special reference to the Vedanta, London: Lutherworth Press, 1950, 227.

[78] P.D. Devanandan, *The Gospel and the Hindu intellectual. A Christian Approach*, Bangalore: CISRS, 1958, 23-27; *The Gospel and Renascent Hinduism*, London: SCM Press, 1959. IMC Research Pamphlets No.8, 57-59; Preparation for Dialogue. A Collection of Essays on Hinduism and Christianity in New India, ed. by Nalini Devanandan and M.M. Thomas, Bangalore: CISRS, 1964. Devanandan Memorial Volume No. 2, 39-40, 164-68.

[79] P.D. Devanandan, *Preparation for Dialogue, Op. Cit.*, 38.

[80] *Ibid.*, 170; P.D. Devanandan, *Christian Concern in Hinduism*, Bangalore: CISRS, 1961, xi.

[81] Surjit Singh, *Christology and Personality*, Philadelphia: The Westminster Press, n. d., 19, 139, 140, 141, 143-51, 151-58.

well as historical existence. Ultimate reality is not only divine but also divine-human. If some determinate aspects of the Real are involved and grounded in the actual, then the features of the actual are preserved in the Real beyond the cosmic process. It means that individuality in so far as it aligns itself with the pattern of Ultimate Reality, will be affirmed and preserved.[82]

The Divine-Human relation in Jesus Christ has the characteristics of involvement, interaction, interpenetration and a new paradigm.[83] Divine-human relation in Jesus shows the capacity of relatability in the inner structure of God; God is Saguna, personal. It shows the working of God in both an individual human person and also in socio-historical groups. Moreover, Jesus shows that God and a concrete human·person move towards each other through the valley of the cross to the mountaintop of the resurrection. Christ is the foundation which enables human movement from estrangement with God, self, and the world to reconciliation with God, self and the world.[84]

The present author's Christian thought in relation to Indian philosophy, specially Sankara's Advaita Vedanta which spreads over the 1990s to the present, is a practical demonstration of an Indian dialogical theology in terms of the perspective of Pluralistic Inclusivism for the relational convergence of religions an well as for the emergence of the new in Christian thought, conceiving all the religious experiences of the world as the common property of humanity.[85] Our hermeneutical context, a major

---

[82] *Ibid.*, 155, 158, 159, 162-63.

[83] Surjit Singh, *A Philosophy of Integral relation (Samyagdarsna)*, Madras/Bangalore: CLS/CISRS, 1981. Indian Christian Thought Series, No. 15, 32-34.

[84] *Ibid.*, 34-35, 39.

[85] Pluralistic Inclusivism is a perspective in theology of religions that inspires each religious faith to be pluralistically inclusive i.e., on the one hand each living faith is to become truly pluralistic by other faiths contributing to its conceptual content and on the other hand Inclusivist is to transform its meaning to witness the fulfillment of the theological and spiritual contents of one's own faith in and through the contributions of other living faiths. In the opinion of the Exclusivist school, one's own religious faith is the sole criterion by which other faiths are understood and evaluated. Other religious paths are defective and one's own faith is the only valid path to liberation. An either or model of truth is adopted here and the room for mutual enrichment between religions is ruled out. The Inclusivist approach affirms the salvific presence of God in other religions while still maintaining that one's own religious faith is the definitive and authoritative revelation of God. Inclusivism accepts the divine presence in other faiths, but rejects them as not being sufficient for liberation apart from one's own faith. All the truth in other religions belongs ultimately to one's own faith, which is its fulfillment. Pluralism holds that other religions are equally salvific paths to the one God. The Ultimate Reality upon which the faith of all believers is focused in every religion is the same, though interpretations of its essential nature may vary. Truth-claims, for this school, are of a complementary nature and not of a conflicting nature. Cf. K.P. Aleaz, "Religious

factor of which is Advaita Vedanta decides the content of our theology. The present author has tried to make the very content of the revelation of God in Jesus truly pluralistic by elaborating the contributions of Sankara's Advaita Vedanta to it.[86] He demonstrates that there is a possibility of understanding the person of Jesus as the extrinsic denominator (*upadhi*) of Brahman, the name and form (*namarupa*) of Brahman, the effect (*karya*) of Brahman, as well as the reflection (*abhasa*) and delimitation (*ghatakasah*) of Brahman.[87] There is also a possibility of interpreting the function of Jesus as to re-present the all-pervasive (*sarvagatatvam*), illuminative (*jyothi*) and unifying (*ekikrtya*) power of the Supreme Atman; as to re-present that the Supreme Brahman as Pure Consciousness (*prajnana-ghanam)* is the Witness (*saksi)* and Self of all (*sarvatma)* and as to re-present the eternally present (*nityasiddhasvabhavam*) human liberation.[88]

We have also indicated an Indian Christian epistemology in terms of the six *pramanas* (sources of valid knowledge) of Indian philosophy namely perception, inference, scripture, comparison, postulation and non-cognition. If scripture (*sabda*) can be classified under revelation, the other five *pramanas* come under reason and there is an integral relationship between reason and revelation in Indian epistemology and consequently in Indian Christian thought. Perception (*pratyaksa)* proclaims the integral relation between humans, nature and the Innermost Reality, Atman and makes theology rooted in day-to-day experience. Inference (*anumana)* challenges us to identify the invariable concomitances (*vyaptis*) in Christian theological issues in terms of the present day Indian context. A word (*sabda)* signifies the universal class character (*jati* or *akrti*) over against the particular (*vyakti)* and so we are enabled to crossover from the particular Bible to the universal Bible, from the particular Jesus to the universal Jesus, avoiding dogmatism. On perceiving Jesus to be like the person pointed out by the Old Testament and the Upanisads, we come to know that the Old Testament and the Upanisads definitely point to Jesus through comparison (*upamana*) .By means of postulation (*arthapatti*) we can arrive at theological statements that explain seemingly inexplicable phenomena in

---

Pluralism and Christian Witness: A Biblical-Theolgical Analysis", *Bangalore Theological Forum*, Vol. XXI, No. 4 and Vol. XXII, No. 1, Dec.-March 1990, 48-67; *Harmony of Religion. The Relevance of Swami Vivekananda*, Calcutta: Punthi Pustak, 1993, 154-65; *Theology of Religions. Birmingham Papers and Other Essays*, Calcutta: Moumita, 1998, 168-99.

[86] For a detailed study on Sankara's thought Cf. K.P. Aleaz, *The relevance of Relation in Sankara's Advaita Vedanta*, Delhi: Kant Publications, 1996.

[87] K.P. Aleaz, *An Indian Jesus from Sankara's Thought*, Calcutta: Punthi Pustak, 1997, 33-102.

[88] *Ibid*., 105-162.

Christian theology and non-cognition (*anupalabdhi*) recommends an apophatic Indian Christian theology.[89]

We have also suggested how Advaita Vedanta can dynamically enrich Eastern Christian theology in its further developments. The insight that Brahman/Atman pervades, illumines and unifies all he levels and layers of human personality as well as the whole of creation enables Eastern Christian theology to arrive at new insights regarding the energies of God through which God is knowable and through which deification is actualized. The divine willing, the ideas of created things, the *logoi*, the words, are in the energies of God and not in His/Her essence. The Advaita Vedantic view that before creation this universe pre-existed in Brahman as potential seed (*bijasaktih*) and undifferentiated name and form (*avyakrtanamarupa*) clarifies this understanding of creation in the energies of God. The *neti neti* theology of Advaita, the experience of Brahman/Atman as the subject and knower of all and every thing who cannot be known, enables Eastern Christian theology to develop its apophatic theology. The Orthodox conception of deification is enriched through Advaitic insights. Deification is in terms of the implantation (*mayah*) of the Atman in the five human sheaths, is in terms of the pervasion of the Atman in the total human personality. The luminous Atman (*atmajyotih*) imparts His/Her luster to the intellect and all other organs and thus deification is effected. Brahman/Atman unifies every thing and every one in His/Her homogeneity (*ekarasata)* and the result is again deification. Brahman/Atman as Pure Consciousness and Witness pervades, illumines and unifies the whole human person by means of His/Her reflection in it. The awareness that Brahman/Atman Himself/Herself is reflected at all the levels of our personality gives new vigour to the interpretation of the human person as created in the image of God, taught by Eastern Christian theology.[90]

Conclusion

The Missionary Conferences were struggling to respond to the issue of the relation between Christian faith and other faiths and the Tambaram Conference of 1938 upheld the standpoint of discontinuity between the Revelation and religions. The Madras Rethinking Group opposed such a perspective and asserted that because of Hinduism the convert from that religion is able to arrive at new meanings regarding the person and function of Jesus. P. Chenchiah explained that a new creation has begun in the birth of Jesus and we are incorporated in it through the power of the Holy Spirit;

---

[89]Cf. K.P. Aleaz, *The Role of Pramanas in Hindu-Christian Epistemology*, Calcutta: Punthi Pustak, 1991.

[90] Cf. K.P. Aleaz, *A Convergence of Advaita Vedanta and Eastern Christian Thought*, Delhi: ISPCK, 2000.

God and humans have united in Christ and we should affirm this without any Barthian nervousness going beyond the Atonement Theories. Before Chenchiah, H.A. Krishna Pillai who hailed from Hindu Bhakti background, going beyond expiation and juridical justification expressed the function of Jesus as releasing precious life for humanity and making people his devotees in terms of a radical recentring of their life in God. Going beyond Atonement Theories, the present author also has interpreted the function of Jesus in terms of Advaitic experience, as to re-present to humans and the whole creation the all-pervasive, illuminative and unifying power of the Supreme Atman. In the thought of Brahmabandav Upadhyaya again we can identify new creative theological insights emerging in terms of the Vedantic interpretation of Trinity as Saccidananda and Creation as Maya. All these thinkers were upholding the creative perspective of Pluralistic Inclusivism in theology of religions.

In their response to Hinduism we have two prominent Indian thinkers S.K. George and Manilal C. Parekh upholding Pluralism in theology of religions as early as the 1920s-30s. Decades before the WCC or the Roman Catholic Church arrived at the idea of dialogue with people of other faiths, S.K. George was organizing All Kerala Inter-religious Fellowship. He was of the view that we should not deny other mediators between God and humans, other experiences of God's presence in the human heart, the validity of other *Ishta Devatas*. Manilal C. Parekh conceived *Bhagavata Dharma* as a universal personal religion of devotion in which Christian devotion is one element among others, perhaps the central and organizing element. *Bhagavata Dharma* truly represents a spirituality of pluralism.

Krishna Mohan Banerjea was a pioneer Inclusivist interpreting Jesus Christ as the True Prajapati as early as 1875. A.S. Appasamy Pillai conceived the techniques of Saiva Siddantic as well as Advaita Vedantic Yoga as helpful in Christian experience. A.J. Appasamy presented an understanding of Christ in the light of the Bhakti philosophy of Ramanuja. Abhishiktananda held the view that the Hindu experience of Saccidananda should be remolded to attain the Christian experience of Saccidananda and once that is actualized the renewed experience of Saccidananda would be the Trinitarian culmination of Advaitic experience. Raimon Panikkar is of the view that the role of Isvara in Vedanta corresponds functionally to the role of Christ in Christian thought. It is not Isvara but Christ who can be a proper link between the world and God, Christ who transcends Christianity and is the center of reality in a theanthropocosmic vision. All these thinkers, to some extend represent the school of Inclusivism in theology of religions.

Also, we find a few Exclusivists who reject Hinduism in a negative way. For example P.D. Devanandan thought that the Hindu Vedantic theology cannot give an ideological basis for the new Indian anthropology; only the revelation of God in Jesus can. In the view of Surjit Singh the values at stake in Advaita Vedanta are of personality, of history and of time, which can be restored by recapturing the New Testament significance of the person and work of Christ.

But we must admit that over all the Christian dialogues with Hinduism have been positive, encouraging and rewarding. Learning from the past, it is hoped that we may take in future a perspective of Reception of Hinduism going beyond the perspectives of Reinterpretation or Rejection of it.

Questions for further reflection:

1. Is it possible to imbibe at least a little of the faith experience of your Hindu neighbour with empathy? In the light of it how would you creatively reconceive your own faith experience?
2. How do you think God is working among the Hindus? Is it possible for a Christian to participate in the work of God among the Hindus, upholding the liberative resources of Hinduism to counter the forces of evil and oppression?

Suggested Further Reading

K.P. Aleaz, *Christian Responses to Indian Philosophy*, Kolkata: Punthi Pustak, 2005.

" , *For a Christian Philosophy from India. Cambridge Teape Lectures – 2005,* Tiruvalla: CSS Books & BTTBPSA, 2006.

Section III

Interfaith Relations from Sikh Perspectives

A Review of 1910 Edinburgh Document from the Perspective of Sikh-Christian Dialogue

James Massey

Introductory Remarks

At the outset I want to offer my sincere thanks to the United Theological College, the Principal, the Faculty and the whole UTC family particularly Dr. Marina, the coordinator for this consultation, for inviting me to be the Convener of Group III dealing with 'Interfaith relations from Sikh Perspective', which is a part of the programme of the Edinburgh Centenary Celebrations. I am also grateful for the invitation extended to me to present this paper on the occasion.

The discussion of this paper on the theme 'A Review of the 1910 Document from the Perspective of Sikh-Christian Dialogue' will be carried out under the following four sub-themes:

- A Personal Reflection on Sikh-Christian Relations
- A Look at the Edinburgh 1910 Document
- The development of Sikh-Christian Dialogue
- Looking beyond Edinburgh 1910

A Personal Reflection on Sikh-Christian Relations

2008-09 was a year of celebration for the Sikh community for the Tercentenary of the Gurta *Gaddi* (Guruship) of Sri Guru Granth Sahib for which I had a number of invitations to deliver lectures and keynote addresses in various national seminars organized by the Sikh academia both in Delhi and in other parts of the country. On these occasions (and even earlier), a number of my Sikh friends, as well as Christians, asked me why I have become interested in such a serious study of the Sikh religion, particularly as a Christian. I have tried to answer this question in the Preface of my new book entitled *'A Contemporary Look at the Sikh Religion'* (at present in the press). I am reproducing part of this answer here as the starting point to the discussion of this paper:

> It is true that I am not only a Christian, but a fully committed Christian. My answer to the question always includes my being a Panjabi Christian, who is very proud to be a Panjabi. But I am an Indian as well, for which also I am equally proud. Now the answer to the above question is actually hidden

among these identities which I am carrying in my being, because as it stands today, I have become fully aware of my identities which have actually contributed to my 'thinking' or what can be called my 'ideology' or 'theology' of life. Among these identities, one that is very special to me is my being a 'Panjabi'. As a Panjabi, the Panjabi culture, including the Panjabi language is a part of my life and these factors constitute the core of my Panjabi identity. One factor which also influenced the formation of such an identity is the religious traditions that form a part of my 'cultural heritage'. Now there exists a very thin line between a religion and culture; any culture may draw substantially from religion or religions, but it cannot be 'identical' with 'religion' as such. However, it is actually the cultural elements which keep us together: but at the same time, unconsciously we continue to imbibe those religious elements as well which come to us as a part of the package called culture. And it is these religious elements which inevitably influence all those who share the 'common cultural identity'.

In the case of 'Panjabi' or 'Panjabiat' as an identity, it certainly carries in it the 'values' of the Sikh religion, because it has been a religion of the majority or of the dominants in the Panjab for more than 500 years. It is these culturally inherited Panjabi Sikh values, which I carry in my being. I became conscious gradually of these elements of 'Panjabi identity' from the mid 70s, and these influenced my being as a Christian as well. The symptoms of this can be seen in my book which I wrote in 1976. The book was 'Christianity: An Introduction' written in Panjabi. It had 'Panjabi thought forms' that were clearly rooted in the 'Sikh Religious traditions' and can be seen as the contribution of 'Sikh religion' to the 'Panjabi culture' or 'Panjabi Christianity'.

My becoming more and more conscious of my 'Panjabi identity' was responsible for my getting steadily and surely drawn to the 'Sikh religion'. This factor made me abundantly richer as a Panjabi Christian on the one hand, and also helped me identify myself as a part of 'Panjabi Dalit Community", as well as to see if both the Sikh faith and the Christian faith offer any message of hope for such a community (the Dalits). It was among the people of this community with whom Guru Nanak Devji placed himself when he called himself "the lowest among the low-caste" *(neech)* (SGGS, p.15).[1]

So much for the 'personal reflections'; now I shall move to the topic of this paper.

A Look at the Edinburgh 1910 Document

General Review

For my reflection of this section, I have chosen a primary document entitled *Edinburgh 1910 – An Account and Interpretation of the World Mission*

[1] Massey, James: *A Contemporary Look at Sikh Religion*, Manohar Publication, New Delhi, 2009 (in press).

Conference by W.H.T. Gairdner (19 10).[2] Rev Gairdner, who was a missionary from the Church Mission Society in Cairo, Egypt, was invited officially by the Committee of the World Missionary Conference to write 'this interpretative account' (Prefatory note p.vi).

Behind ***Edinburgh 1910*** was, "A vision of Earth – as one world, waiting, surely, for who shall carry to it and plac in its empty hands one Faith – the only thing that can ever truly and fundamentally unite it or deeply and truly satisfy it, bringing its one human race into one Catholic Church, through the message of the

> One Body and One Spirit,
> One Lord, one Faith, One Baptism,
> One God and Father of all, who is over all, and
> through all, *and in* all.

Such was the vision which called together the World Missionary Conference of 1910." (pp.6, 7). It is against this vision that the review in this paper is being undertaken.

The Organizing Committee was very clear about the nature and purpose of Edinburgh 1910. To them it was "mainly a consultative gathering". Its primary purpose was the study of the great missionary problems of the day by leaders in the missionary enterprise, at home and abroad, in order that they might see more clearly what was immediately required for fulfilling the charge to 'disciple all nations" (Prefatory note p. v). By looking closely at the words of the vision of the Conference as well as its nature and purpose, and even while going through 281 pages of the account written by Rev Gairdner, it becomes very clear that Edinburgh 1910, neither was expressly an ecumenical gathering nor could it have been brought directly within the purview of 'Inter-Faith *Concern'.* But careful study of the Document will reveal that the seeds of a number of later movements, including the inter-faith movement, were sown during this Conference. In this paper since we are concerned with inter-faith relations or dialogue, therefore we will look mainly at that section of the *Account of Edinburgh 1910* which deals with our concern at hand. But before that we will list a few other general concerns expressed in this Document, which had a future bearing upon the whole issue of inter-faith dialogue, including Sikh-Christian relations.

While relating to the two realities of the time of this Conference, viz. the 'World History' and the 'World Mission', the author of the *Account of Edinburgh 1910* raised an issue, which was 'open ended' and could lead the Conference in any direction against its set vision, nature and purpose. It said: "The issue to which the consideration of the world task of Christianity drives us back is *whether the Church really possesses Christ's thought*

[2] Gairdner, W.H.T.: *"Edinburgh 1910" – An Account and Interpretation of the World Mission Conference, Edinburgh, 1910*, vi, v; 6, 7; 18, 19; 33; 57, 58; 76; 82, 83; 109; 111; 135; 148; 139; 137, 138; 228.

about God, and, if not, whether it can get it back. The only limits to the new visions which the approaching Conference may unfold, and the new faith and devotion which it may inspire, are those set by our own unworthy and impoverished conception of God." (p. 16).

The International Committee, which prepared the core programme had 18 members (5 from North America, 10 from Great Britain and 3 from Europe). It is this Committee that met for four days in Oxford during July, 1908 and identified the following eight areas or subjects:

1. Carrying the Gospel to all the non-Christian worlds.
2. The Church in the Mission-field.
3. Education in relation to the Christianization of national life.
4. The Missionary Message in relation to non-Christian religions.
5. The Preparation of Missionaries.
6. The Home Base of Missions.
7. Relation of Missions to Governments.
8. Co-operation and the Promotion of Unity.

To prepare the study materials in advance, eight 'Commissions' were appointed with 20 members each, consisting of a total of 160. All these members were taken from North America, Great Britain and Europe (pp.18, 19). The reports of these Commissions were to be presented during the Conference.

The Conference began on 14th June 1910 and continued for 10 days, (p.33). The official delegates were 1200 in number, who represented many communions and were from about 160 Missionary Boards or Societies. It is interesting to note that representing the country like India were the names of the prominent missionary delegates from the West (p.56), but when it came to introducing the delegates representing such a country, their names were omitted; instead, the colour, caste and ethnic backgrounds of the indigenous members of the delegation were very clearly highlighted. For example about the Indian delegates, Rev Gairdner's account says: "From India came some whose light brown colour and clear-cut features proclaim the Aryan, and some whose Dravidian blood is shown by their darker skin. Belonging to the former is yonder venerable one might say high-priestly figure, a pure Brahman by descent, with long, silky-white beard, tall, upright figure, aristocratic, gentle features, and mild Indian voice; a Bengali convert of the great Dr Duff..." (pp.57, 58).

The report of the Commission on 'The Gospel to the non-Christian World recognized that as far as India is concerned "the national and spiritual movements in India today present a strong challenge to Christian mission to enlarge and deepen their work" (p.76) The report also recognized that the missionary work was carried out not uniformly but with variations, specially with less emphasis on North India as compared to South India (pp.82, 83).

The serious issue of relationships between the western missionary and the Indian Christian workers can very clearly be seen in the way, the Indian delegates such as J.R. Chitamber argued against the domination of the western missionaries (p.109 top). On this the most powerful address came one evening from V.S Azariah, who pleaded "for a deep readjustment of the personal relation that sometime existed (he alleged) in India for a more real co-operation of spirit between Western and Eastern, – in one word, for 'friendship" (p.109 middle), Rev. Gairdner quoted in his account V.S. Azariah's own words as follows:

> This will be possible only from spiritual friendship between the two races.... Through all the ages to come the Indian Church will rise up on gratitude to attest the heroism and self-denying labours of the missionary body. You have given your goods to feed the poor. You have given your bodies to the burned. We also ask for love. Give us FRIENDS! (p.111)

The response to V.S. Azariah's address was not very good. In this regard Rev Gairdner says: "Possibly some of the men – Indian missionaries they were – whose dissent and even more than dissent, boiled every now and then to surface, did not quite understand what speaker was intending." (p.109 bottom).

The Missionary Message in Relation to the Non-Christian Religions

The report of the Commission dealing with the subject of 'Missionary message in relation to the non-Christian religions' divided it into prevailing religious traditions: e.g. Chinese Religions, Japanese Religions, Islamism, and Hinduism (p.135). In the case of India, the Edinburgh 1910 was concerned only with Hinduism and did not take cognizance of other Indian religious traditions, particularly Buddhism, Jainism and Sikhism. Even the understanding of Hinduism in the Edinburgh 1910 circle was limited to the doctrinal level only (p.148). Here was the typical European form of ideology, which limits the Indian religious ethos to classical Hinduism alone. Such an understanding of Indian religious traditions had continued till the first half of 20th century, which also influenced the inter-faith dialogue process in India limiting it to the Hindu classical traditions for a long span of time.

The report of the fourth Commission was very positive while dealing with the Tribal or Adivasis religion or what it labeled as 'animism' (p.139). The report says that "the Christian faith itself may learn from even animism.... The animist sees his environment riddled and shot through and through by spirits – does the Christian see *his* environment steeped through and through by the Spirit? – a world controlled throughout by the Spirit of a Personal God, with whom the human spirit should be in complete touch by faith?" (p.141) The positive 'openness' shown here became one of the basic principles for inter-faith dialogue.

The other general principle which this Commission's report prescribed was that 'the non-Christian religions" must be approached with very real sympathy and respect; they must be *studied,* if only to bring the evangelist into touch with the minds of his hearers". The report continued to expand this principle further, saying that the other religions were also endowed with the glimmers of 'Light', although these are but 'shot, through and through as broken lights of a hidden sun'. It further adds: "Christianity the religion of the Light of the World can ignore no lights, however 'broken' – it must take them all into account, absorb them all into its central glow. Nay, since the Church of Christ itself is partially involved in the midst of the unbelievers, their failing aspirations and imperfect realizations, this quest of hers among the non-Christian religions, this discovery of their 'broken lights' may lead her to…the discovery of a facet of her own truth, forgotten or half-forgotten, perhaps even never perceived at all save by the most prophetic of her own. Thus 'by going into all the worlds', Christ's Church may recover all the Light that is in Christ, and become, like the Head, as it is His will she should become." (pp.137, 138). Here very clearly the contribution of other faiths in making Christ's Church faith-richer and complete is stressed.

After giving such positive views for 'the preparation of Missionaries' the Edinburgh 1910 further laid stress on 'the Study of Comparative Religion' which should be undertaken with "the conviction that this study of Christianity in its reciprocal relation to other religions is fraught with the most profound significance and importance, not only for the missionary but even for the church itself"(p.228). This statement in fact is the basis of our study today of inter-faith dialogue including one from the perspective of a Sikh-Christian dialogue.

On this note, we can move to the next section of our reflection.

Development of Sikh-Christian Dialogue

Historical Background of Christian Initiatives

The history of the role of the Christians in promoting inter-religious dialogue in India, as it is understood today, has been influenced variously, both by sources inside and outside our country. As far as the Roman Catholic Church is concerned, the major influence came from the positive approach in the 1965 Vatican Council shown toward other non-Christian religions including Hinduism, Buddhism and Islam. In its Declaration the Vatican Council had .said, "The Catholic Church rejects nothing of what is true and holy in these religions…The Church, therefore, urges her sons to enter with prudence and charity into discussion and collaboration with members of other religions. Let Christians, while witnessing to their own faith and way of life acknowledge, preserve and encourage the spiritual and moral truths found among non-Christians, also their social life and culture."[3] Based upon this Declaration, the General Meeting of the Catholic Bishops' Conference in India (C.B.C.I.) in 1974 at Calcutta, gave a call to the Church in India to be the pioneer in inter-religious dialogue, because "it is in the response of the Christian faith to **show?** God's saving presence in other religious traditions and the expression of the firm hope of their fulfillment in Christ." [4]

In some ways the Christians belonging to various Protestant traditions also have a similar history. The world body representing major Protestants and Orthodox traditions, the World Council of Churches (W.C.C.), has been influencing inter-religious dialogue in India. However, in some areas of dialogue the major contributions were made independently by the Indian Christians as part of their tradition of ecumenical and inter-religious dialogue history. The National Council of Churches in India (N.C.C. I), has played a very positive role in encouraging both its member churches as well as research institutes in the area of inter-religious dialogue. For example, it was N.C.C.I that started the present Henry Martyn Institute (H.M.I.) of Islamic Studies in 1930 with one of the specific objectives to work and research Islam with special reference to its Indian context.[5] Again it was the N.C.C.I. which facilitated the formation of the Christian Institute for the Study of Religion and Society (C.I.S.R.S.) between 1953-1957, which later on became one of the main sources for the development of inter-faith dialogue in India.[6]

Behind these initiatives of the N.C.C.I. and various other institutes like C.I.S.R.S. and Henry Martyn Institute, there is quite a long history of efforts for inter-religious dialogue in the Christian community of our country which runs parallel with the ecumenical history of the Church. One of the major historical factors behind the development of dialogue had been the Religious Revivalism in our country which began in the early decades of the 19th century, particularly among the followers of Hinduism, Buddhism and Islam. P.D. Devanandan had pointed out in his work 'Preparation for Dialogue' and 'Christian Concern in Hinduism' that the reason behind this revivalism was the work of missionaries and the various conversion movements. According to Devanandan, at that time each of these religions began claiming independently that each had the answer to the world's problems where the Christian religion had failed. It was then

[3] Flannery, Austin (Editor): Vatican Council II – *The Conciliar and Post Conciliar Documents*, Bombay, 1992, 654.

[4] *Guidelines for Inter-Religious Dialogue*, CBCI Centre, New Delhi, October, 1989 (Second Revised Edition), 7.

[5] Lindell, David T: "The Henry Martyn Institute of Islamic Studies", in the *Bulletin of Henry Martyn Institute of Islamic Studies* (H.M.I.I.S.) vol. III, Nos. 104, January-December 1980, 134-135.

[6] Taylor, Richard W. (Editor): *Religion and Society, The First Twenty-Five Years 1953-1978*, Bangalore, 1982, 1-2.

that the plea was also put forward that the followers of all religions should work for peaceful co-existence. The revivalism also resulted in the followers of every religion becoming socially conscious.[7] This was equally true with the Sikh religion. One of the main Sikh organizations, the *Singh Sabha* came into existence during the last quarter of the 19th century as a response to the work that Christian missionaries were doing in the Punjab at that time. The main purpose of the *Singh Sabha* was to create both awareness in the areas of the Sikh religion as well as of the social life among the Sikhs through their education.[8]

The above developments forced the Christian missionaries and churches to rethink their approach to other religions and to their mission work. A number of national and international conferences and consultations were held. The most well known are: (a) The World Missionary Conference at Edinburgh 1910 in which semi-liberal views were expressed *(as already referred to in detail above).* In the report of the Conference, though it was mentioned that Christianity is the absolute and Jesus Christ fulfils and supersedes all other religions, it was also suggested that Christianity should be enriched by the treasure available in other religions; (b) The International Missionary Council of Jerusalem 1928 was another important event, in which missionary imperialism was condemned and emphasis was laid on respecting the sentiments of the people of other religions; and (c) The International. Missionary Council held during 1938 at Tambaram, India was the third important event in the development of inter-religious dialogue. For this Council, the famous Dutch theologian of the time, Hendrik Kraemer, who belonged to the neo-Orthodox School produced a sizeable volume entitled *'The Christian Message in a Non-Christian World'.* In short the thesis which this work put forward was that the revelation of God in Jesus Christ was absolute and final.[9] Such views were questioned by Indian thinkers such as G.V. Job, P. Chenchiah, V. Chakkarai, D.M. Devasahayam, S. Jesudason, Eddy Asirvatham and A.N. Sudarisanam, who in reply to Hendrik Kraemer also brought out a sizable work entitled *'Rethinking Christianity in India'* in 1938.

In his article in this volume 'Jesus and Non-Christian Faiths' P. Chenchiah made their position very clear in the following words: "In Europe and other Christian countries, Christians see Jesus only. In the unique situation in India which determines the status and influence of Christianity, we see Jesus in the company of other founders of religions or saviours of men – Buddha, Rama, and Krishna (here we may add 'Nanak'

---

[7] Devanandan, P.D.: *Selections from the Books of P.D. Devanandan*, Bangalore, 1983, 3-6.

[8] Massey, James: "Christianity and Culture: their relationship in the 19th and 20th Centuries in Punjab", in *Religion and Society*, Vol. XXXVI, No. 4, December 1989, 27-28.

[9] Rao, CH. G.S.S. Sreenivasa (Editor): *Inter-faith Dialogue and Worlds Community*, Madras, 1991, XVII-XXIII (prelims).

as well). Christianity moves and has its being in the midst of life and active religions commanding the homage of millions and claiming, if human testimony counts for anything, to minister and sustain its followers in the struggle of life, giving them the faith to live and courage to die with hope for the future. In India these religions are in numbers and influence such as to compel mutual attention and respect. The life and destiny of Christians has to be studied in this vital context." [10] Similar points of view were also expressed in the Edinburgh 1910 Document, as we have seen in our discussion.

By looking closely at the these opposing views, it is correct to conclude that the conflict between the liberal and neo-Orthodox theologians gave birth to inter-religious dialogue during the second half of the 20th century.[11]

One outcome of various ecumenical conferences and councils was the formation of the World Council of Churches in 1948, which continues to help and encourage various member churches and councils all over the world, including India, to enter into the process of inter-religious dialogue. In January 1971 the W.C.C. opened a new sub-unit 'Dialogue with Men of Living Faiths and Ideologies', which became a guiding force in the area of inter-religious dialogue.[12] This sub-unit later provided 'Guidelines on Dialogue with People of Living Faiths and Ideologies"[13] in 1979, which is now available in its 1990 revised form. The WCC sub-unit indeed had played a definite role in developing the Sikh-Christian dialogue. Besides Dr Samartha (who was the first Director of this Sub-unit) coming to Punjab, a number of times the author of this paper was involved in various inter-faith dialogues, and conferences to present the concerns of Sikh-Christian dialogue.

Sikh-Christian Dialogue

CHRISTIAN INITIATIVE

The first ecumenical institute which worked in the area of Sikh-Christian Dialogue was the Christian Institute for the Study of Religion and Study (C.I.S.R.S.). The Institute came into existence in its final form in October 1957. Besides promoting and supporting the concern of inter-religious

---

[10] Job, G.V. & Others: *Rethinking Christianity in India*, 1938, Madras, 47.

[11] Rao, CH. G.S.S. Sreenivasa (Editor): op. cit., XXIII.

[12] Hallencreutz, Carl F.: *A Long-Standing Concern: Dialogue in Ecumenical History 1910-1971, in 'Living Faiths and the Ecumenical Movement'* edited by S.J. Samartha, Geneva 1971, 57-71.

[13] *Guidelines on People of Living Faiths and Ideologies,* WCC Publications, Geneva, 1990. (in the successive references only as 'WCC Guidelines' are referred).

dialogue through its journal and research based publications on dialogue,[14] C.I.S.R.S. has also helped in developing and establishing the work of dialogue by organizing various seminars and lectures. For example in December 1962, it organized a seminar on 'Sikhism and Christianity in the Punjab' which laid the future basis for Sikh-Christian dialogue in the country. (The author of this paper at that time was a B.A. second year student at Baring Union Christian College, Batala, Punjab, where this seminar took place and he had the privilege of attending some of the sessions). The report and papers presented in the seminar were published in **Religion and Society**.[15] With regard to the general basis of this first Sikh-Christian meeting, the former Director of C.I.S.R.S the late Dr. M.M. Thomas stated: "Sikh and Christian scholars are meeting together in this Conference for a conversation on the deepest things of religion, in which they are different. But we meet as men sharing a common humanity. There will no doubt be differences even in the way Sikhism and Christianity define this community of humanness. But I suppose we can all affirm two aspects of this community. First is that we all faced with the challenge to respond to ultimate meaning and destiny of our living. Second is that we have a common task of building a society and a nation in which all men realize their dignity as human persons called to love and serve one another."[16]

The next example of an ecumenical institute involved in inter-faith dialogue is from North India, namely, the Christian Institute for Religious Studies (C.I.R.S.), Batala, Punjab. This institute during the 70s and the 80s organized a number of seminars; for example, it held the first major inter-religious seminar from December 7-9, 1973 at Batala on the theme 'Popular Religion in the Punjab To-day.' The purpose of the seminar was to find out what was happening in the religious life of the Punjab at that time.[17] Participants came from Sikh, Hindu, Muslim, Jain and Christian backgrounds. The other major seminar that the Institute organized was on "The Nature of Guruship" and the purpose of this was to arrive at a fuller and more comprehensive understanding of Guruship according to different religions and religious traditions.[18] The participants included Hindus Sikhs, Christians (both Roman Catholics and Protestants), Muslims, and popular

---

[14] Examples of C.I.S.R.S. Inter-Religious dialogue related publication: Devanandan, P.D.: *Preparation for Dialogue*, Bangalore, 1964.

b) Singh, Herbert Jai: *My Neighbours (Men of Different Faiths*), Bangalore, first impression in 1994 and
second in 1966.

c) Singh, Herbert Jai (Editor): *Inter-Religious Dialogue*, Bangalore, 1967.

[15] See in *Religion and Society*, vol. XI, no.1, March 1964, Bangalore.

[16] Ibid., 4.

[17] Webster, John C.B. (Editor): *Popular Religion in the Punjab Today*, Delhi, 1974, 1.

[18] McMullen, Clarence O. (Editor): *The Nature of Guruship*, Delhi 1976, 1.

Hindu and Muslim sects such as the Ahmadiyya Movement and the Radhaswami Sat Sang. (Again the author was present in all these inter-faith dialogue meets).

The Sikh Initiative

In recent years the response to the concern of inter-religious dialogue has been strong from the followers of the Sikh religion. Two of the major Universities in Punjab have given a lead in this area, namely Punjab University, Patiala and Guru Nanak Dev University, Amritsar. The Sikh professors and others academicians from these universities have actively responded to the invitations extended to them by various Christian institutions. Punjabi University has a Department of Religious Study, where all religions are taught by professors belonging to different religions. It also organizes lectures and seminars on different themes relating to religions in India. For example in March 1985 it organized a three-day seminar on the theme 'Religious Pluralism and Co-Existence'. About 27 scholars belonging to Hinduism, Christianity, Sikhism and Islam participated in this seminar and all through the seminar the need for religious co-existence was felt by everyone.[19] During February 2007 Punjabi University held a seminar on the theme "Towards Building a Peaceful Role of Religion", which was organized by its Department of Encyclopedia of Sikhism.

The Guru Nanak Dev University has a department of Guru Nanak Studies, under which it has been organizing inter-religious dialogue meetings and seminars. One of the earliest major seminars was held in March 1973 on the 'Sikh Concept of the Divine' where papers from Christians and Hindus were also invited; as a result, the seminar took the form of comparative studies.[20] A major seminar also was organized by Guru Nanak Dev University in March 1991 on the theme 'Co-Existence in Pluralistic Society: Punjab's Problems and Prospects'. Here too the participants were from Hindu, Christian, Muslim and Sikh backgrounds.[21]

Besides the above two Universities in the Punjab, there are a number of research institutes namely the Guru Nanak Foundation, New Delhi, the Institute of Sikh Studies, Chandigarh, the Gobind Sadan Institute of Advanced Studies in Comparative Religion, New Delhi, and the International Institute of Gurmat Studies, Ludhiana that regularly conduct inter-religious dialogue also on different themes by organizing meetings and lectures. There are some official committees of Sikh temples like the

---

[19] Proceedings of the seminar are published under the title *'Religious Pluralism and Co-Existence'* edited by Wazir Singh, Patiala, 1986.

[20] Proceedings of the seminar are published under the title *'Sikh Concept of the Divine'* edited by Pritan Singh, Amritsar, 1985.

[21] Proceedings of the seminar are published under the title *'Co-Existence in Pluralistic Society: Punjab issues and Prophets'*, edited by Madanjit Kaur, Amritsar, 1991.

Delhi Gurdwara Management Committee, which also often organizes inter-faith meetings. For example the Delhi Committee had a 'National Seminar on Guru Nanak Dev and Composite Indian Culture' on November 10, 1991, to which Hindu, Christian and Muslim scholars were invited to make presentations on the main theme from their religious backgrounds and perspectives. I was also asked to make presentation on "Guru Nanak Devji's Teachings in the Context of Inter-Faith Dialogue" in this seminar.

The most recent examples of these efforts are the four national seminars on inter-faith dialogue organized mainly by various Sikh Academies. Again I was privileged to take part in all these seminars to present my point of view as a Christian. These seminars were held as part of the celebration on the occasion of 300 years Guruship of Sri Guru Granth Sahib. The first of these was organized by the department of Guru Nanak Studies, Madurai Kamraj University in December 2008 in which I was asked to present a paper on 'The Social Question in Sri Guru Granth Sahib'. The second was organized by Sri Guru Gobind Singh College of Commerce (University of Delhi) on 29th January 2009, at which I was asked to deliver the key note address on the theme 'Sri Guru Gobind Singh: Apostle of Universal Brotherhood'. The third seminar was organized by Mata Sundri College for Women (University of Delhi), in which I was asked to present paper on the theme 'Sri Guru Granth Sahib: A Unique Scripture' and the fourth was organized by the University Grant Commission, Guru Nanak Studies Centre of Shyama Prasad Mukherji College (University of Delhi) on 29th February, 2009 where I was invited to deliver the inaugural address on the theme 'Universal Message of Sri Guru Granth Sahib'. Having seen some of these representative examples of Sikh initiative in the whole process of inter-faith dialogue, which also show equally active Christian participation in these efforts, let us turn our attention to what the future holds for us.

Looking Beyond Edinburgh 1910

Edinburgh II is due next year, in 2010. While discussing its agenda Prof. James A. Scherer recalled the previous conference saying, "The watchword or motto of Edinburgh I was the evangelization of the world 'in this generation".[22] The famous Dutch professor Hendrik Kraemer had also made a similar observation in 1938, when he said, "The Conference of Edinburgh 1910 focused its chief attention on a strategic review of the whole mission field throughout the world."[23] Edinburgh 1910 was in this way dedicated to how the western missionary movement understood the completion of what Prof. Scherer calls the "unfinished task". On the other

---

[22] Scherer, James A.: "Edinburgh II – A New Springtime for Ecumenical Mission" in *International Bulletin of Missionary Research*, Vol. 31, No. 4, October 2007, Connecticut, USA, 196. (left column).

[23] Kramemer, H.: *The Christian Message in a Non Christian World*, The Edinburgh Home Press, London, 1938, 36.

hand Prof Scherer says that this unfinished task 'had been substantially completed by the end of the twentieth century'. However he observes that "the percentage of Christians worldwide is today no greater than it was in 1910". The question he raised for reflection is one which I too want to make some observations on, at the end of my paper, because it concerns the inter-religious dialogue in India in general, and Sikh-Christian dialogue in particular. The question raised by Prof Scherer is, "What went wrong with the evangelization efforts?[24]

Here it may be appropriate to take a look at the ground realities of the Indian situation, or rather of the situation as it stands in North-India because it includes the birthplace of the Sikh religion -the Punjab, with which we are mainly concerned in this paper. Based on the Census of 1981, I did an analysis of Christians in North India with a special reference to Christians in the Punjab. I shall quote a part from that analysis in order to make my point clear. The total number of Christians, excluding the state of Assam, during 1981 was 665,287,849 out of which "65% of the total Christian population live in the four southern states of India, and about 14% of all Christian live in North-East India and the remaining 21% live in North India; they number 3,348,153. These figures can also be seen according to the geographical areas. The total area of all the Indian states and Union Territories is 3,280,483 sq. kms, out of which Southern states and Union territories cover 6,42,283 sq. Kms. or about 20%, where 65% of Christian live. North-Eastern states and Union Territories cover 176, 576 sq. Kms. or about 6% where 14% of Christian are living and Northern states including Central, Western, Eastern and Union Territories cover 2,461,621 sq. Kms. about 74% of the country, where only 21% of Christian live" [25]

In our review of the Report of Edinburgh 1910 a point was made about "the way missionary work was carried on with variation, especially with less emphasis on North as compared to South India."[26] This can to some extent explain the above statistics. Still a more serious reason behind the lukewarm response to Christian missions in North India (including the Punjab) can be found in the prevalent national and spiritual movements in India. The missionaries were not fully equipped with knowledge about the local situation and their methodology of work was also quite myopic. In fact their understanding of their mission as a whole was based on their narrow views, which they tried to carry out in the hope of conquering the 'non-Christian world' as "representatives of the Church Militant".[27] However, a very positive outcome of the Conference was in its appeal for

---

[24] Scherer, James A.: op. cit., 196. (right column).

[25] Massey, James: "Christianity in North India: Historical Perspective with special reference to Christian in Punjab", in *Religion and Society,* Vol. XXXIV, 403, September 1987, Bangalore, 89.

[26] Gairdner, W.H.T.: op. cit., 81, 82.

[27] Ibid., 16.

'real sympathy and respect' with which the missionaries were required to equip themselves in order to view and study the non-Christian religions. In time this appeal proved "most profound in significance and importance not only for the missionaries but even for the church itself".[28] This point brings us directly to another important question with regards to the 'interfaith dialogue': ***can this process of inter-faith dialogue be taken as a part of the Christian mission?***

Both the scope and size of this paper will not allow us to deal with the whole issue of the nature and goal of the Christian mission, except to say that 'the Church's authentic mission is to struggle against such structures and systems which oppress human beings'.[29] As we know the main purpose behind the two divine interventions in human history was to deal with such situations (Exodus 3:7, 8 and Luke 4:18, 14). This has now been entrusted to the Christian community or the Church to carry on the mission in this world. One of Jesus' own method was 'dialogue', which he used to communicate his Gospel to different groups (John 4:7-9; Matthew 20:1-16). In the context of 'dialogue and collaboration' it is also a well accepted principle of Christian mission today. For example a famous Roman Catholic theologian, Fr. Michael Amaladoss SJ, while reflecting on the theme 'Towards a New Heaven and a New Earth' in support of the 'dialogue process' as part of Christian mission, says: "We need to liberate the Church from the seemingly exclusive focus on building itself up rather than promoting the Kingdom".[30] In order to transform the whole of society, Fr. Amaladoss suggests that "in a multi-religious society religion can do this together in dialogue. They can try to forge a consensus on shared values, supporting them in term of their religious beliefs. Their common impact on society will depend on such consensus".[31] This brings us to our final assertion which is directly related to the 'Sikh-Christian dialogue'.

Unfortunately the younger religious movements including the Sikh faith have not been on the priority list of the Christian world. We have already seen that even in Edinburgh 1910 Indian religious traditions were limited to Hinduism and in a limited way to the religion of the adivasis, which was called 'animism'. With such an understanding the missionaries came to North West region of India, where even today the Christians number-wise are even less than 1%, which according to the 1981 census reads in the following manner: J&K (8,481), Punjab (1,84,934), Chandigarh (4,470), Haryana (12,213), Himachal Pradesh (3,954).[32] Incidentally, more than

[28] Ibid., 228.

[29] Massey, James: *Current Challenges and Church Response*, North India Church Review Publication, 1998, New Delhi, 64.

[30] Amaladoss, Michael SJ: "Towards a New Heaven and a New Earth – Some Reflection on Mission To-day" in '*Vidyajyoti Journal of Theological Reflection*', Vol. 73, No. 6, June 2009, New Delhi, 409.

[31] Ibid., 412.

[32] Massey, James: op. cit., 89.

95% Christians in these areas are from Scheduled Castes origin or are Dalits. It is this situation, which calls us to 'look beyond Edinburgh 1910' and go for an alternative 'paradigm of mission'. In this effort Sikh-Christian dialogue is bound to play an extremely important and positive role. We have seen that in the beginning more active initiative in this area came from the Christian side, but over a period of time, the Sikhs have overtaken them leaving the Christians behind. Why this is so, is the point we need to ponder.

Dialogue with Sikhism in the Diaspora

John Parry

Taxi, Sahib?

There was a joke recounted around the Sikh community when Neil Armstrong first set foot on the moon. It was said that after he had walked around a little he stopped to admire what he saw and contemplate his being the first person to walk on the moon. However, he felt a tap on the shoulder only to turn around to find a Sikh taxi driver asking, 'Taxi, Sahib?' Sikhs get about. They are to be found in many places throughout the world. I met a Sikh tailor in Singapore who told me of his brother whose shop was on the Royal Mile in Edinburgh. During the days of the British 'Raj' many Sikhs sought employment in the British Indian Army and later were posted to many parts of the then Empire often staying on as police officers and the like. Here is a martial race which suited this employment. But their nature was not in terms of fighting for the sake of battle, but fighting as part of the struggle for justice.

The Scattered Sikh Diaspora

In the United Kingdom many Sikhs went to England after the Second World War. There was a push-pull factor. Because of the partition of the Punjab in 1947 many Sikh families lost their lands in what was to become West Pakistan, made their way to work in factories then short of male workers who had lost their lives in the war. Later they were joined in the late 60s and early 70s by Ramgharia Sikhs from East Africa, many of whom had been thrown out by Idi Amin. Their forebears had moved there at the end of the Nineteenth Century to help build the railways. They stayed to service the railways they had built and subsequently brought over their families. Educated in British style schools and gaining British qualifications, their move to the U.K. was eased by access to better work and often into the professions and often better paid than their Jat counterparts.

Similar to the move to East Africa many Sikhs also went to Canada to help build the Canadian Pacific Railroad. They were skilled craftsmen who later settled and eventually brought up families. Some, however, made their way down the west coast into Washington State and further into California, encouraged by members of the Chinese community with whom they had worked in Canada. In California many settled in the Central Valley near Sacramento. There they found an environment not dissimilar to the Punjab where soft fruit could be grown. Their natural farming skills enabled them to develop soft-fruit growing businesses. The down-side, however, is that they were refused permission to bring their families. Many settled with Mexican Roman Catholic partners. Later *gurdwaras* were built and a thriving Sikh community established.

Smaller such communities are now to be found elsewhere in Malaysia, Singapore, Hong Kong, dotted around mainland Europe and in other parts of the USA.

One of the largest Sikh communities outside India is to be found in Southall, West London. Employment was offered there after the Second World War essentially in two factories. One was Wolf's Rubber factory, an occupation which did not find favour amongst white British males. The other was the Abbess office furniture factory where the production of wooden furniture suited the skills of the Ramgharia Tarkhans – carpenters. In the late 40s and early 50s Sikh males, along with Hindu and Muslim counterparts were the dominant foreign workers living in the town. Before immigration restrictions increased many Sikhs brought over their families from the Punjab. By the 60s Sikh *gurdwaras*, often converted houses, had been established and the community began to take shape. Some of the smaller groups, Namdhari Sikhs, for instance, worshipped in hired Church Halls and thus began the first encounters of Sikhs and Christians in the United Kingdom.

Encounters with Christians

Such encounters were nothing new. It seems that the first recorded indication of such encounters was through the *Deen Ilahi* of the Emperor Akbar. Bhai Gurdas met two or three Jesuit priests. He was not impressed. In his eyes they were 'self-centred and confused'! Later, by the mid 1830s American Presbyterians made their way to Ludhiana, mainly at the invitation of Col. Wade, the British Agent who saw great potential in the Sikhs and recognised in them people who 'bucked the trend', asking questions of Hinduism and Islam which demonstrated them to be a group searching for the answers to spiritual questions to which the Christians believed they had the answers. The Americans were followed by the Church Missionary Society who settled in Amritsar and founded work which continues to this day.

The Sikhs treated the Christians with both interest and suspicion. Why was Christianity thought to be any better than their own faith? Weren't these people actually agents of colonial rule? The Americans, like the British saw few converts from Sikhism for their efforts. Between 1835 and 1880 there were only about 24 converts from Sikhism, their target group. By 1880 the conversion of a Dalit man called Ditt brought large numbers of people of his community into the Christian camp and from then on missionaries concentrated mainly on that group.

However, the threat of the conversion of four schoolboys in 1873 opened the minds of Sikhs to the potential loss of young people to Western Christianity. Thus were formed the Singh *Sabhas* in an attempt to regain potential Sikh backsliders.

Sikh attitudes to Christianity ranged from hope in the early days – Christianity could provide Western education and, therefore, work; to competition for the hearts and minds of young people; to cooperation by the 1950s/60s when thanks to an American Presbyterian missionary by the name of Clinton Loehlin there was greater understanding amongst the Sikh and Christian intellectuals; to apathy during the 1980s when Sikhs were fighting for their lives; to renewed cooperation through organisations like *Manov Manch* established by Sikhs and Christians together to give hope, encouragement and affirmation to the poorer classes of Punjabi society.

Meanwhile in the U.K. and elsewhere Diaspora Sikhs were building their *gurdwaras*, but more than that they were establishing social centres where Sikhs could meet unselfconsciously.

In California one Christian who was to encourage and support such community building was Clinton Loehlin who by now had returned to the USA and deliberately settled down in California in retirement. A clergyman with a PhD in Sikh studies, he supported the establishment of a *gurdwara* in Marysville near Yuba City. Regularly he broadcast on one of the local radio stations enabling local residents to understand the nature and significance of Sikh festivals, a fitting occupation for someone who, in his final years as a missionary, was invited to speak at a major function at the 'Golden Temple' – probably the first such person to do so.

In the U.K. another 'returned' missionary, Roger Hooker, together with Pat his wife, acted as a quite remarkable bridge between the faiths in the West Midlands. After Roger's death Pat went on to write two basic introductions to the Sikh faith for British Christians. Similarly Ruth Lambert who had worked in Coventry and Leicester wrote her M.Phil. thesis on 'What might Christians learn, theologically and spiritually, from the Christian-Sikh encounter?' Moved by the generous hospitality of Sikhs in their *gurdwaras* she wrote of the concept of *seva*, service, which challenges church congregations to consider further ways in which their church buildings could be thrown open to wider use.

Further to that were theological challenges: How does one communicate Christ's kingdom values in the world? She sees the way in which the Sikhs' example also challenges Christians to become active communicators of the grace and gifts of God received through Scripture.

Dr Joy Barrow, now British Methodism's interfaith secretary, has also edited a similar compendium in which Sikh and Christians alike write of their experience together and of the nature of the practice of faith in the U.K.

Meetings for Bilateral Dialogue with the Sikh Community

During the 1980s the United Reformed Church sponsored a series of meetings with the Sikh community. These were not confined to members of particular denomination or Sikh group but open to interested parties. Thus, at a time when the Sikh community in India was facing rejection and antipathy by the majority community thanks to the tensions in the Punjab and the assassination of Mrs Gandhi, in the U.K. there was an albeit small example of genuine interest in Sikhism and the nature of the practice of its faith.

Our first weekend meeting was spent looking at the basics of our faiths with a view to finding topics of mutual interest for discussion. In later meetings we were to consider the nature of Liberation Theology, then, for us Christians a fairly novel issue, but for Sikhs an inherent part of their theological stance – 'What is the use of your spirituality if my stomach is still empty?' was a question posed by the Guru and a major challenge to some Christian's preoccupation with personal salvation.

We looked at the matter of communicating the faith to the coming generation. This was, and still is, a major matter for the Sikh community in exile. Owen Cole once memorably remarked that in the Punjab you imbibe your Sikhism with your mother's milk, in the U.K. you have to learn it. But how do you learn your faith without the ethos of Sikhism consciously, but more often unconsciously and unselfconsciously, present in a predominantly Sikh town or village. We looked at materials Christians had used in a century of Sunday School work and heard of Sikh efforts to establish similar bodies. How did children learn the faith when both parents were out working to meet mortgage payments and grandparents, often the ones who told the stories of the Gurus, were thousands of miles away in the Punjab?

Most memorable were the scripture studies we shared together. It is the practice in Christian meetings to start with devotions – prayers, a scripture reading and perhaps a hymn or two. In the early days of dialogue when any notion of interfaith worship was frowned upon by many Christians, we sought an alternative expression of our common faith and trust in God. This we did through scripture study. We prepared two passages, one from the Guru Granth Sahib and the other from the Bible. A Christian introduced the passage from the Guru Granth Sahib and a Sikh from the Bible. What emerged was the most wonderful gift of fresh understanding of often familiar passages as they were explored with new insights. We used this technique lest we be confined to 'standard' interpretations which may have been the case if Christians had introduced the Bible passage first or Sikhs the *bani* from the Granth. Often discussion went on far longer than was planned and people spoke of the deeper things of faith often preceded by the words, 'I've never said this to anyone before…' Such was the depth of trust and mutual respect found at the meetings.

Perhaps most memorable was an exploration of the words of Jesus that if one wanted to follow him one must take up the Cross daily. What followed was a fascinating discussion which took in issues of both vulnerability and the willingness to give one's life in fighting for a cause. But then a Sikh colleague noticed the words that followed Jesus' dictum, that whoever lost his or her life would gain it and whoever tried to gain it would lose it. This was something Sikh colleagues warmly related to. It was about *haumai* – self-centredness – and the need to eliminate egotistic behaviour, for if one was self-centred one would never be God-centred.

The exploration of scripture together was further continued on a fairly regular basis through meetings of a Methodist congregation with Sikh colleagues in Southall, a predominantly Sikh town in West London. These were normally in our own home and attended by 15 -20 people. We used exactly the same pattern and experienced the same sense of belonging. But what insights did we gain?

At a time in the U.K. when Biblical languages do not have the same place in theological education than was once the case, one was confronted with the recognition of how their knowledge enhances the study of scripture. By the same token it was also worth learning sixteenth century Punjabi to understand the Guru Granth Sahib all the better. Sikh children of coming generations may lose out, as will future generations of Christian theological students, if only translations are used. That said, we became aware of the two fold alienation of young Sikhs from their scriptures. Some speak but do not read Punjabi, but the Punjabi they speak is not the Punjabi of the scriptures. If they don't learn the ancient language, and to read it, then their scriptures remain a closed book. The debate about the use of translations continues and for some it will be the only way they learn of their heritage. It's a dilemma for many.

Of those Christians who were involved in the studies many found that their own faith was considerably enhanced by dialogue. This can happen in a number of ways. One is challenged to think about what one actually believes, not just about what one is 'supposed' to believe. Honesty was the issue. There was often a sense of 'Help my unbelief!' But something else occurred. That was we were challenged to find ways of expressing our faith in a manner which people of the other faith understood. Jargon and clichés were out, straightforward, daily language was the order of the day.

We became increasingly aware of the depth of spirituality of our Sikh colleagues. Their faith was not compartmentalised. It was about life, the totality of life, lived under the *hukum* – the will – of God. It was measured not by pious words but by service – *seva* – unstintingly given and without fuss.

We learnt that if dialogue is to be worthwhile then mutual understanding is of the essence. It calls for careful, specific and non-polemical articulation of the Christian faith, but the questions the Sikhs asked made us realise that there are issues which require further exploration in the articulation of a Christian apologetic to Sikhs.

First is the nature of the atonement. What is the difference we were asked between the deaths of our Gurus, Arjan and Tegh Bahadur and that of Jesus? Why does the death of Jesus have such cosmic implications? All died on behalf of others. Thus there were questions about vicarious suffering. We recognised that any martyrdom that portrays the death of a passive victim will not find Sikh sympathy. Death must be for a purpose and to this extent the model of '*Christus Victor*' may be worthy of exploration. The Cross cannot be portrayed as a mechanical transaction freeing the believer but that which enables the believer to go through the process of dying to self-centredness to find the power of God in self-renewal.

The second issue that requires further work is that of the analysis of humanity and the consequent nature of enlightenment or redemption, since the Sikh faith will be more concerned about overcoming ignorance of humanity's inherent relationship with the divine rather than what is seen as the Christian preoccupation with sin – often individual and not corporate sin.

Thirdly, we are obliged to consider how we present the incarnation since Sikhs are inclined to recognise the presence of God amongst God's gathered people rather than an individual such as Jesus Christ. There is that of God within each of us, so it would be worthwhile exploring the concept of the Body of Christ especially in terms of self-giving service to humanity as a manifestation of God's nature and continuing sustaining concern.

The fourth matter is the need for the continuing reflection on the Word/*logos*/*shabad* in both faiths since this would provide insight into the nature of God's relationship to 'his' creation and into God's desire to communicate.

It would also do us well to consider the nature of discipleship, both in terms of the deeper understanding of faith and the cost of discipleship in the living out of our faith.

The sixth matter for reflection would be in terms of considering the nature of the mystery of faith and its not being divorced from the harsh realities of life since withdrawal from the world, in Sikh eyes, is seen as an abrogation of the search for God's justice in creation.

Those of us from the Reformed traditions discovered to our delight something of the Sikhs' understanding that humanity can only find its liberation or salvation through the grace of God. The term *gur prasadi* – by/through God's grace, so dominates the Sikh understanding of God's gracious support of our search for faith and liberation. But we are confronted by a major difference of opinion – who takes the first step?

The eighth matter is the consideration of witness and identity. Unlike *Keshdari* Sikhs who are clearly identified by their wearing the 5Ks, Christians are less readily distinctive. If service to the community is a manifestation of faithful living, how does one distinguish between the two faiths, or is such identification really necessary?

We were further challenged by the matter of exclusiveness. A Sikh text which challenged was 'O God, this world is burning, save it by whatever means you can.' It challenged us to recognise the question of the sustainability of the environment. It challenged us once again to recognise the way in which God uses other people, or peoples, to fulfil 'his' purposes. It also could take us on to the question of who are our partners in mission, if the goal of mission is the reign of God.

The tenth, and perhaps most significant, matter for consideration is with regard to our understanding of the nature and being of God. 'The more you say about God, the more you need to say about God', said the Guru. God is always beyond our understanding. Finite human beings cannot understand the totality of an infinite God.

The agenda for discussion is actually quite enormous. I believe these are no questions of difference but questions in which mutual discussion can open up fresh understanding. Dialogue becomes a matter, not of exploring faiths, but exploring faith and deepening faith. Whilst some of my Christian friends talk of bringing people to Jesus, I want to suggest that Jesus actually pointed beyond himself to God's reign, God's commonwealth – however we translate that Greek word *basilea*. My Sikh colleagues talk in terms of following the *hukum* of God – God's will. Is this the same will that Jesus taught us in prayer to seek so that God's 'kingdom' could come?

Dominant in the many questions is one final challenge. Have we failed to recognise that Jesus, along with other founders, may have had a vision and an insight into something far greater than we have recognised? We use the term 'kingdom', sometimes it has almost been presented as co-terminus with the church. Even if we now recognise that we no longer live in a Christendom situation, is this still too narrow a vision? We have failed to point to that which is beyond. We have presented our domesticated, inadequate, parameter fixated view and I do not think it matches the height, depth and breadth of Jesus' vision. Like our understanding of God it is inadequate and insufficient. God grant us grace and point us to a fuller understanding.

Section IV

Interfaith Relations from Subaltern Perspectives

Subaltern Movements Before and After the Independence of India and the Impact of the Roman Catholic Mission (From 1910 to 2009)

A. Alamgaram

In this essay, the meaning of '*Subaltern Movements*' is restricted to the understanding of conversion movements of the oppressed castes and classes of people in Tamilnadu, India, from Hinduism to the Roman Catholic Church. I try to present here some concrete historical moments of conversions of subalterns to the Roman Catholic Church before the independence of India and the prevention of such movements and their growth after Independence. I will also try to explain the reasons, the cultural impacts of conversion including opposition to conversion and finally point out some movements towards revolutionary change. The conversion in one place influences the conversion of the same caste people in another village and spreads slowly in different villages, becoming conversion movements. Such conversion movements flourished in Tamilnadu only before the independence of India. Thinking of the prospects of conversion in 1928, in his parish Periyakulam, Tamilnadu, Fr. Munch said the following: "…the three requisites for conversion: (are) grace, good will, and money, the first is beyond our calculation, the second is so far not much in evidence and the absence of the third is, alas! only too evident. Let us, then, be toiling patient and patiently toiling and trust that God will do the rest in His wisely appointed time"[1]. Indeed the sweat and toil of the Catholic Missionaries did bring abundant fruits in different parts of India particularly in South India. Such was the situation before the independence of India.

After Independence conversion among the Indian masses totally changed. Conversion was not any more reported as movements in Tamilnadu. There had been reports of only a few conversion of individuals here and there. Mahatma Gandhi was not in favour of conversion, especially the conversion of the oppressed castes whom he called Harijans. He was even in favour of legislation to stop it[2]. Though the Indian

[1] Fr. Munch, S. J., "The Mission ad Paganos of Periyakulam" *Caritas* I (January 1928), 5.

[2] Fr. Julian Saldanha, S. J., *Conversion and Indian Civil Law* (Bangalor: Theological Publications in India, 1981), 144-45.

Constitution, art. 25. allows every person freely to profess, practise and propagate religion, Christians are often accused of converting people by force and inducement. In addition to all these, there was strong opposition from the Hindu religious leaders that made the whole process of conversion to dwindle in Tamilnadu and India.

Here I must confess that it was not easy for me to find relevant material for the past one hundred years of the mass conversion movements. Whatever material I could get for this essay, I am greatful to Frs. Joseph Antony Samy, S.J., and Edward Jeganathan Anthony, S. J., who are the Director and Assistant Director respectively of the Madurai Jesuit Province Archives at Schembaganur, Kodaikanal. I thank them immensely for all their help.

Conversion and Ongoing Formation

When we read back into the history, we understand that the missionaries of different churches not only converted people to Christianity but also constructed church-buildings for the Christians to come together, to pray together and participate in the Eucharist. They established a number of educational institutions to educate them, constructed boarding houses, orphanages and hostels to feed the Christian students, organised binding workshops to provide opportunities for works[3], appointed catechists to take care of the catechumenates and the flock with an on going faith formation. Sometimes Christians expected the priests to settle their disputes, and helped them to form a cooperative credit society among themselves that would help them financially[4]. Retreats were organized both for men and women separately. For the first time, the feast of the Blessed Sacrament with the solemn procession around the church of Suranam (which is a parish today in the diocese of Sivagangai) was held[5].

Although the western missionaries baptized people in the name of one God who is the Father and the Mother of all, they had not confronted the fact of caste that remains a "diabolic" factor of division, separation, hatred and oppression among people even today. After converting them they had also registered their names according to their castes[6]. Till recently the

---

[3] Fr. Augustine Saulier, S. J., "Central District" Vol II, Rewritten in May 2000, this record is kept in the Jesuit Madurai Province Archives, Shembaganoor, Kadaikanal, Tamilnadu, India, 271.

[4] Fr. Agniswami, "Kalugumalai" *Caritas*, II (March 1926), 5.

[5] Saulier., 410.

[6] Ibid., 411: "Fr. Vincent Vignon is the first panguswami in charge of Salaigramam. There are 3841, Christians in the pangu, divided as follows:

Agambadiars	150	Pariahs	40	Uddayars	2150	Vellalas	30
Pallers	720	Idayars	30	Sanars	480	Mudalis	20
Kammalars	110	Nayakars	13	Paravers	60	Vanniers	3
Maravars	45						

baptismal registers included the caste of the baptized Christians. It appears that in the area of ongoing formation of Christians, that the missionaries did not organise either programmes of critical consciousness against the caste system and its dehumanising factors or to unite people in Christian churches beyond castes. Some efforts had been made to bring the Christians of different castes into the same church building. But there had been the practice of taking the unsolved caste-problems of the churches to court in order to find an amicable solution.[7]

Having listened to the Gospel preached by the missionaries, people of different castes embraced Christianity. But what is conspicuous is that the majority of the converts came from the oppressed castes of the subaltern movements (the Dalits, the Shanars). Just to give two examples from the letter of Fr. Keller to his Bishop and Superior in 1925: "There are now 29 Christians (at Avudeiapuram) and over 60 Pariah catechumens (Dalits),. Moreover two families of Maravers and one of Nadars and five families of Pallers (Dalits) have just come to give me their names. … (moreover) the 92 Catholic Pallers (Dalits) of Kunjumpatti who wish me to build them a chapel in stone and mortar instead of the mud-walled chapel which goes to ruin"[8]. Fr. Keller had remembered to mention that the Dalits at Kunjumpatti borrowed Rs. 100 from one Nayakker and gave it to him for the same purpose.

On February1926, the writer to Caritas explains how the ongoing pastoral visit of the Bishop helps people to grow in faith, piety and attachment to the hierarchy. The Bishop himself administered 879 confirmations in Kamanayakenpatti and Pannikulam and another 700 confirmations, 100 solemn first communions and over 3000 communions at Avur. Moreover he listened to the problems, difficulties and disputes that arose from different caste-Christians and brought amicable solutions and peace among them. To cite an example, the old centre of Cayetar, which St. John de Britto and Fr. Beschi had visited, had two churches, one for the Vellalers and the other for the Nadars. During the visit of the Bishop, he stayed one day in the Vellalers' church and on the following day in the Nadars' church. By the teaching and guidance of the Bishop, both the castes agreed upon the construction of a common church[9]. It was truely a miracle.

Collaboration with Other Religious Congregations and Other Religions

Although missionaries opened boarding houses for the Christians, they were always open to accommodating students of other churches and other

[7] ----------, *Caritas*, II, (May 1922), 5.

[8] Fr. Keller, S. J., "Kalugumalai. – From Fr. Keller to His Lordship and to the Superior" *Caritas*, VI (November 1925), 17-18.

[9] ……, "His Lordship's Pastoral Visitation" *Caritas*, III (May 1926), 6-7.

religions in their schools and colleges. For example in 1911, the total number of boarding boys residing in St. Mary's Madurai were 241 and among them only 100 were Christians. Similarly, a school for girls that was started by the Sisters of *Viagulamada* had 112 girls, 80 of them being Christians and the other 32 Hindus belonging to the families of weavers (*Pattunulkarars*) [10]. This practice is maintained even today in almost all the institutions run by the members of the Roman Catholic Church, in admitting students of other religions and other churches into their schools and colleges as well providing them rooms in hostels. Thus we see that the missionaries were open to other religions and people and helped them in educating their children.

The Challenges of Mission

First and foremost, the missionaries met the challenges of adjusting themselves to a new climate, food, clothes and cultures. They did not have good and well organised medical and health facilities. In 1911, two sisters belonging to the order of St. Joseph of Lyons died of cholera, and two others left for France and a quite a number of them were seriously affected by the disease[11]. To cover such a vast area and population of the mission, to construct schools, chapels and churches, the missionaries needed a lot of financial support from Europe and the USA. Such financial dependancy on others both locally and abroad was another challenge that controlled the works and expansion of the mission[12].

Moreover the missionaries had no proper rooms and housing facilities to stay, no proper roads laid to reach the villages and no proper conveyance to travel. Fr. Mahé, for example explained how the residence was built at Sarugani: "Narrow rooms badly ventilated, dark, hardly sufficient for one inmate each and where, however, two and even three had to be lodged." Further they undertook many difficult journeys to reach out to people, to celebrate the holy mass, to administer sacraments and to serve them in many other ways. To illustrate this we have an example from the writings of Fr. Mahé in 1925: "As we begin our journey, we have to cross a river; the horse refuses to move, and the (people) have to push both coach and horse across it. But even on the road, the horse takes its time; we spend five hours for going over eight miles. What a journey under the scorching sun of July! We reach at last, when it is already pitch dark.[13]"

The association of the missionaries with the high castes in the society brought them respect and honour, and with the downtrodden and the oppressed, illtreatment and humiliation. Once the bishop was accompanied

---

[10] Fr. Augustine Saulier, S.J., 261.
[11] Ibid., 270.
[12] Fr. Keller, S.J., "Kalugumalai. – From Fr. Keller to Rev. Fr. Superior" *Caritas,* V (September 1925), 7.
[13] Fr. J. Mahé, S.J., "Correspondence" *Caritas,* VI (November 1925), 4.

by Pallers (Dalits) and had to travel through a village called Rajasingamangalam in Tamilnadu, where the majority in the village who were Muslims stopped him. The following year the same bishop was accompanied by a group of high caste people and this time the same Muslims showed great interest and respect to the bishop. It looked thus that even the Muslims of that time were not free from the caste culture and the missionaries had to face such challenges because of caste discrimination.[14]

Most of the Christian communities were made up of landless labourers or persons with small land holdings. They lived in huts[15] and houses with thatched roofs which were at times destroyed by fire[16]. The new converts were so poor that the missionaries had to help them financially to construct churches, schools, hospitals and other such infrastructure to improve their living conditions. It was the missionaries who had to travel for miles to save people from epidemics like cholera. Fr. Revilla writes about cholera at Illupur near Avur: "Before my arrival, 23 persons had died; after my coming only two old women, already much weakened by the epidemic, succumbed and the other 37 patients were now all doing well."

Another challenge of the Catholic missionaries was the day-to-day encounter with the missionaries of other churches and the Hindus. For example when we read the mission work in the Kallanadu, there were 25 Catholic schools in the taluk of Tirumangalam. But then almost in all the areas of the mission, the other churches such as the American Mission and Swedish Lutherans had also started schools and boarding houses both for the boys and girls. Moreover in Usilampatti, the Kallar Police department had built its own school and with its influence had started a high school by the local board. In the presence of other schools, the Catholic missionaries had a number of challenges such as getting the needed strength of pupils, good food in the boardings and quality education in the school[17].

Christians could not easilt take out a religious procession where already there was a Hindu Temple. The Hindus protested such efforts by throwing stones at the Christians. Sometimes the missionaries organised such processions with the help of the police and the Sub-Magistrate of the place [18].

Conversions from One Church to Another

During and after the First World War many non-Catholics became Catholics. This was true especially in France where many British soldiers

---

[14] Ibid., 8.

[15] ….., "Cholera at Illupur" *Caritas,* V (September 1926), 5.

[16] ….., "His Lordship's Pastoral Visitation" *Caritas*, III (May 1926), 9.

[17] Fr. Prince, S. J., "Centre-The Mission work in the Kallanadu" *Caritas*, I (January 1928), 9-13.

[18] Fr. Keller, "Kalugumalai. – From Fr. Keller to His Lordship" *Caritas*, VI (November 1925), 14-16.

loved to visit Catholic churches and participate in the services being held there. Such movements were echoed in India and other places. For example, in 1914 an Anglican clergyman was received into the Catholic Church and in his turn he baptized his mother and father Mrs. and Mr. Dudley of Redhill and gave them their first communion[19].

There had been innumerable cases of conversions from one church to the other when the faithful were not happy with their pastors or when they had problems and resentments against them. There had also been instances when Catholics decided to become members of other churches and vice versa. The case of Vadakenkulam is an example for this[20]. A magnificiant Church was built by the Jesuit priests at Vadakenkulam. The congregation consisted mainly of two caste groups. Although Shanars (the oppressed) were the majority, they were not respected and treated as fellow Christians by the Vellalas (the high caste). Hence a wall was built in the church dividing the two communities. As the Shanars flourished, they found the wall becoming an inconvenience to them. Being aware of this, Fr. Caussanel. S.J., broke it. There was a prolonged litigation over it. Initially the Vellalas got a judgement favourable to them from the Sub Court that the partition was to be maintained. But the case was taken to the District Court and the court then decided in favour of Fr. Caussanel and the Shanars, stating that the priests were at liberty to make reformation in connection with religion, suppressing former customs. That decision was further upheld by the High Court as well. But what happened afterwards was that nearly 300 Vellalas left the Catholic Church and Rev. Lutz of Nagercoil admitted them all into the American Mission Church. Moreover the Vellalas built another Church for themselves and started a separate school for their children[21].

At Vagaikulam which was the central place of the Lutheran Pastor, Fr. Keller wrote to his Jesuit Superior, that there were ten Lutheran families who had joined the Catholic Church and they expected some financial help to construct a new chapel for them[22]. He also mentioned to his Superior on

---

[19] ---------, *Caritas*, V (September 1917), A bimonthly family record for the use of The Madura Missionaries. (English Supplement to "La Gerbe du Madure."): In this issue, it is pointed out that many non-Catholics loved to join the Catholic Church and had the desire to know her faith and practices, 23-24.

[20] Leon BESSe, S. J, *LA MISSION DU MADURE – HISTORIQUE DE SES PANGOUS,* Vol. 1. Trichy, 1914. Also refer *THE MADURAI MISSION – HISTORICAL ACCOUNT OF ITS PANGUS,* Translated by Fr. L. Moumas. S.J. (It is kept in the Jesuit Madurai Province Archives, Shembaganoor, Kadaikanal, Tamilnadu, India, 478 – 90: (a) Read the extract from the Indian Review (October 1915) viewed from a non-missionary standpoint by J. Chartres Molony, I.C.S. (b) Read the extract from the Madras Times, Sunday January, 21st 1917, by Bede. (c) Read the extract from the Hindu paper of Madras – no date or year mentioned.

[21] Ibid.

[22] Fr. Keller, "Kalugumalai. – From Fr. Keller to Rev. Fr. Superior" *Caritas*, V (September 1925), 7.

08. 10. 1925 that at Pandavaramangalam two 'Protestant' families have given their names to join the Catholic Church and "during the last quarter we have baptized sixty pagans and four Protestants".[23] In January 1926, Frs. Keller and Agniswamy visited seven villages in 17 days and baptized 102 persons, of which 46 were Hindus, 26 were Protestants and 30 were children of Catholic parents. And as they had just passed through a village called Rajaramapuram, eight Paller families (Dalits) wanted to embrace Christianity[24].

In November 1928, Fr. Kueny wrote from the parish of Hanumandampatti that 29 Protestant Pariahs of Thevaram had moved out of their mission and had been baptized in the Catholic Church. On the same day about 20 apostates were also reconciled to the Catholic Church. He further wrote that even the caste pagans and the local zamindar had encouraged such a movement of Pariahs joining the Catholic Church[25]. In the last thirty years (1979-2009) there are Catholics who had joined many other churches. This is because their pastors did not visit them for a long time or did not care for them. Such a pathetic situation of the *sheep without shepherd* paved the way for the pastors of other churches to visit them and to admit them into their churches.

Reasons for Conversion

Although some Hindus accused the Christian missionaries of converting Hindus forcibly through various inducements, there are many reasons for conversion from Hinduism to Christianity. One of the reasons for conversion of the depressed classes was the oppression, hatred and ill treatment they received from the high caste Hindus. Another reason for conversion was that the children of Pallars, Parayars and Nadars were denied admission to the schools run by Hindus. Yet another reason for conversion was the charitable works undertaken by the Jesuit missionaries. In general, for other castes besides the oppressed classes, conversion to Christianity meant an upward mobility through education and other socio-economic help. Many such reasons account for the conversion from Hinduism to Christianity[26]. In 1925 cholera raged in many villages in the southern part of Tamilnadu. Fr. Dhür from Michaelpatnam in Madura district wrote that out of 1, 175 Christians, 66 died of cholera[27]. Another priest wrote from Avur that the people of two villages near to it suffered from cholera and he had set up his tent in their midst and had visited house

---

[23] Fr. Keller, "Kalugumalai. – From Fr. Keller to Rev. Fr. Superior" *Caritas*, VI (November 1925), 17-18.

[24] Fr. Agniswami, "Kalugumalai" *Caritas*, II (March 1926), 5-6.

[25] Fr. Kueny, S. J., „Trichy. – Movement of conversions" *Caritas*, VI (November 1928), 2-3.

[26] Leon BESSe, S. J., 481.

[27] Fr. Dhür. S.J., "Michaelpatnam, Madura Dt." *Caritas*, II (March, 1925), 12.

after house distributing medicine. All the patients recovered. Finally the priest concluded his letter to his Superior that St. Joseph might lead the people a step further to the conversion of the whole village[28].

When Fr. Agniswami visited Elavendoor, he was informed that there were 30 C.M.S Protestants families who wanted to become Catholics. When asked why they wanted to become Catholics, they replied: "… The Padre had no sense of justice and that the Protestant religion did not satisfy them.[29]" The Christian school or college environment at times provided the opportunity for the students to become Christians. Fr. Pappayah, S. J., wrote from Tinnevelly Tenkasi, that a boy named Selvam studying at Vaikalipatti School, wanted to become a Christian. He was from a well-to-do Hindu family and was a serious and good student. He was drawn to the Catholic manner of praying and worship. After baptizing him, Fr. Pappayah hoped that he would bring about the conversion of his family in the future[30].

Family quarrels among brothers and sisters at times was one of the reasons for conversion. A story by Fr. Prince from the Center of Kallanadu illustrates this. There were two Kallar brothers at Chockathevenpatti. The younger brother fought with his elder brother and took over the family property. The elder brother who felt cheated, with his entire family and several of his relatives became Christians in protest[31].

Conversion Accounts in the Catholic Church

The Jesuit Major Superiors asked the Jesuit missionaries periodically to submit the accounts of conversion in their respective parishes or mission stations. One can understand this from reading the following details submitted by Fr. Keller to his Major Superior in 1925: "Lastly, while I was on the hills, Your Reverence asked me for some details regarding the conversions made in this Pangoo (Kalugumalai),

Conversion of Pagans	Adults	Children
1922	55	10
1923	288	123
1924	102	41
1925 (to July 1st)	67	21
	------------	------------
Total	512	195

(and) Catechumens: 300. – Conversions of Protestants: 12. I must soon go to visit Avudeiapuram, where there are some 30 families of

---

28 --------, (then Parish Priest of Avur) "CHOLERA" ***Caritas,*** V (September 1925), 6.

29 Fr. Agniswami, S.J., "Kalugumalai" *Caritas*, II (March 1926), 6.

30 Fr. Pappayah, S.J., "Tinnevelly.-Tenkasi" *Caritas* I (January 1928), 7-8.

31 Fr. Prince, S.J., "Centre – The Mission work in the Kallanadu" *Caritas* I (January 1928), 11.

catechumens, whom I have not seen for six months.[32]" Sometimes a parish priest wrote to his Bishop giving the details of conversion in his parish.

In 1930 there was a new wave of conversions. For example Fr. David. S.J., wrote from the parish of Rayappanpatti saying that there was a village called Kamatchipuram where 150 families of Nadars (900 persons) and 50 families of Panchamas (250 Dalits) were ready for baptism. These were subaltern people of Tamilnadu. Fr. David gave them their first catechism books to study and prayers to learn by heart. Later when the people were ready, they were all baptized. It was also hoped that all the Subaltern people of the neighbouring villages would also follow their example soon[33].

The Effects of Conversion

The people who belonged to the so called depressed classes such as the Christian Pariahs, Pallers and Shanars, lost all the benefits and scholarship from the Government as a result of embracing Christianity. Further the then Government planned to suppress the grants to private schools gradually and absorb them all within the school system of the state. That was the way they planned to control the various activities of Christian missionaries who were busy in promoting education among different people especially among the oppressed and depressed castes[34].

The Jesuit missionaries then did not have a clear cut option for the subaltern people as the Jesuits of today. Therefore people of different castes including the Subaltern came under the category of '*Catholic students*'. The statistics of Jesuit Colleges and High schools in 1930:

	Catholics	Others	Total
St. Joseph's College, Trichy	210	783	993
St. Joseph's High School, Trichy	464	727	1191
Loyola College, Madras	52	663	715
St. Xavier's College, Palamcottah	44	232	276
St. Xavier's High School, Palamcottach	258	619	877
St. Mary's High School, Madura (Apos. 42/Orps. 64 in 560)	260	560	820
St. Mary's High School, Dindigul	152	461	613
St. Francis Xavier's High School, Tuticorin	202	132	334

From the above statistics of the educational institutions run by the Jesuit Missionaries in 1930, we can see that the Catholic students are more in comparison to the others only in Tuticorin and in all other cases the others are more in number than the Catholic students. Moreover it is not stated

---

[32] Fr. Keller, "Kalugumalai. – From Fr. Keller to Rev. Fr. Superior" *Caritas*, V (September 1925), 7-8.

[33] Fr. David. S.J, "Rayappanpatti – A new Vein for Conversions" *Caritas*, V (September 1930), 5-9.

[34] --------, *Caritas*, II (May 1922), 7.

clearly how many Catholic Subaltern students were educated in the high schools and colleges. Exceptionally among the 560 other students studying at St. Mary's Madura, 64 of them were orphans. One thing is clear that other than the Catholics and the Subalterns in general, people of other castes and religions made use of the educational facilities offered by the Jesuit Missionaries of that time[35].

The Cultural Impacts on Conversion

The missionaries had converted people of different castes from Hinduism to Christianity but for a long time were not critical about the oppressive caste-structures in India. Without ignoring the good elements in Indian culture, one cannot deny the diabolical face of the caste-structures pervading every walk of Indian cultural life, ruining human dignity and freedom and destroying an equality based on sisterly and brotherly love and peace based on justice. The missionaries were aware of scriptural passages such as: "You are all children of God through faith in Christ Jesus, for all of you who were baptized into Christ have clothed yourselves with Christ. There is neither Jew nor Greek, slave nor free, male nor female, for you are all one in Christ Jesus" (Gal 3, 26-27). But due to various circumstances of the time, they failed to bring about a counter culture against caste structures. However one should make mention of persons like Fr. Caussanel, S.J. who had consistently fought against caste oppression in his parish and had tried to bring justice to the Christian Shanars (Nadars) oppressed by the Vellala Christians in Vadakenkulam. Mention must also be made of Arch Bishops Leonard, S.J. and Casimir, S.J, who during their pastoral visits and through pastoral letters spoke against caste oppression and showed the way to practise equality among Christians.

There had been innumerable conversions from the subaltern masses. However a section of high caste Christians had wished the subaltern people to remain pagans so that they could successfully exploit them for their own economic development. The high caste Catholics built their own churches and refused entry to the subalterns when they were converted. Therefore the missionaries were forced to build separate churches for the subaltern people[36]. At times the high caste Catholicswould give the excuse that there

---

[35] J. Castets, S.J., "Statistics of Our Colleges and High Schools" *Caritas*, V (September 1930), 1-2.

[36] Fr. J. Mahé, S.J., "Correspondence" *Caritas,* VI (November 1925), 7: Fr. Mahé writes that somewhere in Irudeyaburam parish, "This church has been built and the centre chosen for the sake of Pallers, very numerous all round, who are not very welcome in the churches of the Udeyars." Moreover he explains that "... these Catholic Udeyars have generally pagan Pallers or Pariahs as their servants; but though often a single word from them would suffice to bring about their conversion, that word their Udeyar masters will never even think of uttering. They rather prefer

was not sufficient place to accommodate the oppressed castes. To cite an example, in Agilandapuram near Pannikulam Parish, during the pastoral visit of the Bishop, it was found that the Christian Reddys did not allow the Christian Nadars to enter their church, although there was sufficient place to accommodate the subalterns[37]. There had been cases of fightings and oppression between the subalterns like the Pallers and Nadars. To cite an example, there were 300 Pallers (Dalits), in one of the substations of the parish Pannikulam, who had organized a reception for the Bishop. But the Christian Nadars did not allow the band to go there. Later on the parish priest asked the Nadars to beg pardon and forgiveness both from the Bishop and the Pallars[38] and brought peace and reconciliation among the subalterns.

Though the new converts tried their best to follow the new religion that they had embraced, they were forced to fall back to the old religion at times especially when it came to marriage. In 1926, Fr. Münch wrote from Periyakulam: "The great obstacle to conversion … is that the Hindu Pallars (Dalits) refuse to give their daughters to Catholics, and as a sufficient number of Catholic girls are not available, even young Catholics return to Hinduism for the sake of their marriage.[39]" In the same way and in the same year, during the pastoral visit of the Bishop, Fr. Mahé wrote: "Around Satarasampatti are found several villages of Kallars, descendants of those who received and harboured in their woods Bl. John De Britto. Alas! every year sees the number of those Christian Kallars dwindle away, through the pest of pagan marriages.[40]"

Unfortunately, even today in the Catholic Church in India one can see caste oppression and discrimination being practised among the Catholics, especially during the time of marriage in choosing the partner of the same caste and in some places discriminations are imposed even in the places of burial. All over India, caste based settlements exist in almost all villages.

Opposition to Conversion

During the twentieth century one can observe that the conversion to the Roman Catholic Church in India was more in the first 30 to 40 years than in the later years. The reasons were on the one hand, a strong protest during the Indian Independence movement all over India against the British which

---

those poor people to remain pagans, because they can thus manage them more easily."

[37] ……, "His Lordship's Pastoral Visitation" *Caritas*, III (May 1926), 5-6.

[38] -------, "His Lordshp's pastoral Visitation" *Caritas*, III (May 1926), 3-9.

[39] Fr. Münch, "A first stock-taking of a *pangoo ad paganos*" *Caritas* V (September 1926). 8.

[40] Fr. Mahé, "His Lordship's pastoral visit in the Marava" *Caritas* V (September 1926). 15.

happened to be Christian and on the other hand, the opposition from Hindu religious leaders. After Independence the number of conversions from Hinduism to the Roman Catholic Church has considerably dwindled.

The effective missionary work of Mother Teresa expanded in the 1950's and 60's in Calcutta and in different parts of India. But it did not lead to mass conversion. The reason was conversion by that time, had become a political issue. The good works that she did along with her sisters, for the poor, the needy and the dying, fetched her the Nobel prize in 1979, and India's highest civilion honour, the Bharat Ratna in 1980.

In 1958 the Madhya Pradesh Prevention of Religious Conversion Bill was introduced in the Legislative Assembly but was rejected by the Assembly. Later many State Governments passed anti conversion laws, making conversion very difficult. In 1968 Orissa was the first State to enact legislation to control conversions[41] and that became "a model for many States, namely Madhya Pradesh (1968) Arunachal Pradesh (1978) Gujarat (2003) Chhattisgarh (2003) Rajasthan (2005) Himachal Pradesh (2006) and in Tamil Nadu a law was enacted in 2002 but was repealed in 2004.[42]" In October, 2008 Mr. Advani called for a national debate on conversion.

However the Dalits in India have openly come forward and protested against such laws saying that these are planned to keep them untouchables and to block their growth, freedom and independence. Bishop Devasahayam commented on the Tamilnadu Ordinance saying that it 'scuttled the hopes of the Dalits for social liberation and justice and it justified untouchability by denying them (Dalits) religious freedom'[43].

In 1981 there was a mass conversion of the Pallars (Dalits) to Islam at Meenakshipuram in Tamilnadu that drew the attention of the whole nation. Later the RSS, the entire Sang Parivar with its polical party called the BJP, systematically organised their attacks first on Muslims and then on Christians in different places in different states of India. They accused Christians of converting Hindus by force or fraud or inducement but Christians deny it. The RSS continues to propagate "hate Muslims and hate Christian politics" all over India and also call them outsiders. One of the recent attacks of the Sangh Parivar against Christians was in Orissa. The violence that started on August 23, 2008 continued unabated for more than two months. It was very unfortunate and unjust that the Central and State Governments were only onlookers. What is important to note here is that most of the Christians in Kandhamal happen to be Dalits.

---

[41] Ibid., 146.

[42] http://www.hinduonnet.com/fline/fl2519/stories/20080926/251902600.htm

[43] http://www.rediff.com/news2002/oct/30tn2.htm

Revolutionary Changes Now

Knowing fully well the plight of the oppressed Christians in the Catholic Church, the Dalit Christians started a few peoples' movements in the late 1980s, to fight for their rights and human dignity in the Catholic Church. Moreover, a few religious congregations like St. Ann's of Madavaram (for women) and the Jesuits of Madurai Province (for Men) have taken up since late 1980's, the option to include the poor, especially the the Dalits in all their mission-activities. I wish such a spirit spreads to all our congregations and dioceses in Tamilnadu and India. As the Dalit Christians are the majority in Tamilnadu, it is right and just that they have their share in different areas of management and administration of the dioceses and congregations. Such a step will be a sign of the Reign of God in our midst (Lk 6, 20). Such a consciousness is something new in the Indian Church. For example in Tamilnadu, now we have three Bishops and one Arch Bishop from the Dalit community to lead four Catholic dioceses in Tamilnadu. Although one may expect more Bishops from the Dalit community to lead the Catholic Church in Tamilnadu, it is undeniably a work of God in our midst.

We have witnessed in the past few years as well as this year (2009), increasing attacks on Christians. The main reason is that the tribals and the subaltern people are being educated by the Christian institutions and as a result, more and more subaltern people come up in life all over India. This is not welcome or acceptable to the Hindu fundamentalist groups. But being fully aware of the special option that Jesus took in his life for the poor, the needy, the widows, the lame, the blind, the crippled, the daily wage earners and the Samaritans of his time, we too as the true followers of Jesus Christ, in a context of threats, attacks, blood shed, suffering, loss of life and property and even persecution, need to continue more prophetically, vigorously and courageously our mission of helping, educating, liberating and saving the tribals and the people of the subaltern groups in Tamilnadu and in India.

Christianity and Tribal Religion in Jharkhand (India): Proclamation, Self-Definition and Transformation

Jhakmak Neeraj Ekka

Introduction

On September 22, 2008, the local newspapers in Ranchi, the capital city of Jharkhand state in India, printed the news of vehement opposition of the Non-Christian tribals (*sarna*[1] tribals) to the words of the *Nemha* Bible, a translation of the Bible into the Oraon indigenous tribal language of Jharkhand area. In the cover page news, the *sarna* community (non-Christian indigenous tribal people) not only denounced the lapse in translation but announced that they would burn copies of the translated Bible. The controversy was occasioned by the use of the word '*sama*' in the Bible.[2] The matter was also raised in the state assembly. The *sarna* community accused the Church of a conspiracy against the tribal religion. The events that unfolded in the following weeks showed their deep resentment against the Church. They burnt effigies of the Roman Catholic cardinal[3] and the copies of the *Nemha* Bible several times in different locations. They even demanded the death penalty for the translators.

This incident brings to the fore the issues and dynamics involved in any discussion on Christianity and tribal religions in general and particularly in Jharkhand today. This incident in Ranchi shows that the topic is not merely an academic issue but it is, in fact, an existential challenge for indigenous

---

[1] *Sarna* is a generic name for non-Christian tribal people belonging to the Oroan, Munda, Kharia, Santali and other tribes of Jharkhand.

[2] In 2000, the North-Western Gossner Evangelical Lutheran Church in Chotanagpur and Assam, headquartered in Ranchi, translated the Bible into Kurukh (Oraon) and called it the *Nemha* Bible which was published by the Bible Society of India on the occasion of the 150-year jubilee of the existence of the Church in Chotanagpur. The word 'sarna' is used for green trees and oak trees in the *Nemha* Bible. The use of the word 'sarna' in Deuteronomy 12:2 became controversial as the non-Christian tribal people thought the verse referred to their sarna religion.

[3] Telesphore P. Toppo is the Cardinal who resides in Ranchi and who is also from the Oraon indigenous tribal community.

tribal Christians.[4] There are some scholars who have dealt with this subject matter from different perspectives. For example, Joseph Marianus Kujur, a Jesuit scholar, has studied Christian faith and tribal culture from the perspective of crisis, negotiations and convergence.[5] He has also published an essay titled "Tribal and Christianity: An Indian Experience".[6] Joseph Bara also reflects on the subject of Christianity and tribal community in Jharkhand from the perspective of the colonial-missionary relationship, the process of contact and proselytization and conversion and its impact on the tribal community in Jharkhand.[7] Agapit Tirkey, another Jesuit, discusses the various points of convergence and divergence between these two religions.[8]

In a majority of these studies, the Christian faith and the tribal religions of Jharkhand are shown, for right reasons, to be compatible. Accordingly, many aspects of both faith traditions are underlined as parallel and complimentary. Many points of convergence are emphasized to underline the fact of continuity. Notwithstanding some remarkable strands of continuity and many similar valuable insights and parallels between Christianity and tribal religions in Chotanagpur, taking these two religious traditions as fully compatible may amount to superficial and even an ignorant understanding of the two. It is evident that they are two different and distinct faith traditions. In spite of all the similarities and convergences between the two, both religious traditions cannot be equated nor can they, in the ultimate analysis, be said to be fully compatible in all respects of

---

[4] I have tried to use the term 'indigenous tribal Christians to designate tribal Christians in Jharkhand. The reasons and rationale are discussed in the third section of the essay. I have used 'indigenous' in addition to 'tribal' to avoid socio-political categorization by the government and to emphasize the people in terms of first settlers of the land.

[5] Joseph Marianus Kujur, "Christian Faith and Tribal Culture: Crisis, Negotiations and Convergence" in *Seeking New Horizons*, ed.Leonardo Fernando (Delhi: Vidyajyoti Education and Welfare Society and ISPCK, 2002), 161-181.

[6] See, Joseph Marianus Kujur, "Christianity and Tribals: An Indian Experience", in *Indigenous People of India Problems and Prospects,* eds., Joseph Marianus Kujur and Sonajharia Minz (New Delhi: Indian Social Institute, 2007), 299-322.

[7] Joseph Bara, "Colonialism, Christianity and the Tribes of Chotagpur in East India, 1845-1890" *South Asia: Journal of South Asian Studies*, XXX,No.2(Agust 2007),195-222.

[8] Agapit Tirkey, "Christianity Meets Tribals in Chotanagpur" *Sevartham* 23 (1998). Other studies would include Nirmal Minz, "Mission in the Context of Diversity – Mission in Tribal Context" in *Pearls of Indigenous Wisdom* eds. Joseph Marianus Kujur and Sonajharia Minz (New Delhi: Indian Social Institute; Bangalore: Christian Institute for the Study of Religion and Society, 2007) 155-172, "Christianity Among the Mundas, Oraons, and Kharia of Chotanagpur", in *Christianity In India* ed. E. Hrangkhuma (Delhi: CMS/ISPCK, 1998), 14-38; A. Bruggemann, "Worship: Sarna and Christian:Theological Reflections on the Munda Ba-parab," *Sewartham* 7 (1982);

faith traditions and rituals. Stating this categorically might seem to jeopardize the very purpose of a meaningful discussion on Christianity and tribal religions in the region, one of the intents of the discussion. Yet, the fact of divergence should be underlined at the very beginning for the sake of both integrity and uniqueness of both faith traditions. Thus, it is in this context of both divergence and convergence that we propose to do the following in this discussion:

Firstly, while reviewing the relationship of Christianity with the tribal religions of Jharkhand from the earliest times the paper seeks to affirm the indigenous tribal receptivity of the gospel of Jesus Christ as God's gift of truth and empowerment. Secondly, the paper will attempt to assess the Christian engagement in Jharkhand from the perspective of the tribal religion and community to evaluate the extent to which the Church has become the Church *of* Jharkhand. Thirdly, since the encounter between Christianity and tribal culture created a new community namely the indigenous tribal Christian community, this paper will attempt to argue that a healthy, robust and transforming relation between Christianity and tribal religion is to be located precisely in this new creation. Given the nature of the subject the paper does not claim to be exhaustive in any way. However, in this discussion, theological reflection and missional implications may only be avoided at the expense of comprehensive reflection.

Indigenous Tribal Receptivity of the Gospel

Proclamation Not Intended

When the four German missionaries reached Jharkhand in 1845 it was not the place they had intended to go when they left the shores of Germany. A few years before they arrived, Evangelista Gossner of Berlin had received a request from a German widow whose husband had been killed while working among the Karen people of Burma. The widow had hoped that if people in Burma heard the gospel of Jesus Christ they would come to know about the Saviour of the world and a life of love, compassion and generosity. In response to her request, Father Evangelista Gossner sent four young missionaries to Burma but when they arrived in Calcutta they found out that a group of missionaries had already started working there. Thus, they waited for further instructions from Father Gossner, the man who had sent them and God's guidance while staying with Dr. Hoeberlin in Calcutta, the then secretary of the Bible Society of India. It is important to note that God's guidance and intervention came in their lives one day when they saw labourers working in the street of Calcutta. The missionaries were struck by the simplicity, hard working nature and poor condition of these labourers.

They felt compassion for them.[9] Upon inquiry they found out that these labourers were indigenous tribal people of Chotanagpur in Jharkhand. In the meantime, Dr. Hoeberlin received a letter from the Deputy Commissioner of Ranchi, seeking missionaries to work among the tribal people in the Ranchi area. The letter confirmed that missionaries' growing intent to go to Ranchi.[10] Thus, the first missionaries to Jharkhand came to preach the gospel to the indigenous tribal people not by careful planning but by their encounter with the exploited and runaway indigenous tribal labourers. It would seem God's providence for both the people of Chotanagpur and the missionaries of Germany.

Faithful Proclamation and Not Conversion Reason for Mission

Four young and energetic German Lutheran missionaries went to work as soon as they reached Ranchi but their enthusiasm and hope began to dwindle as their hard work and sacrifice in genuinely proclaiming the good news of Jesus Christ did not produce any converts in almost five years. In their self-doubt about the place and their frustration about the people, they wrote a letter to Father Gossner in Germany seeking permission to go somewhere else for sharing the good news as they accused the people of Chotanagpur of being very rigid, hard hearted and unconvinced.[11] Contrary to their expectations Father Gossner reminded them that their task was to preach the gospel with hope and sincerity and leave the rest on God. Thus, the missionaries persevered in obedience and shared Jesus with those who were willing to listen. However, to deny that the missionaries sought converts would mean denying history. Nonetheless, the focus was proclamation of the Gospel with complete trust in God's power to move people's heart.

Vision the Basis of First Acceptance

At last, four Oraon indigenous tribal people became genuinely interested in what the missionaries had to say about Jesus Christ. The missionaries' claim that Jesus was the Lord and that He was alive stirred the inquirers'

---

[9] Nirmal Minz, "Christianity among the Mundas, Oroans and Kharias of Chotanagpur," in *Christianity in India*, ed. E. Hrangkhuma (Delhi:CMS/ISPCK, 1998) , 23.

[10] In this regard Joseph Maranus Kujur's assertion that "Christianity came to Jharkhand along with colonization" is not beyond contention. It is obvious that the poor and helpless labourers had more to do with missionaries coming to Jharkhand then any well thought out missionary plan by the British colonizers. For Kujur's opinion, see, "Christian Faith and Tribal Culture" 163.

[11] See, E. Viste, *Chotanagpur Ki Masihi Mandiliyon ka Itihaas (History of Christian Congregations in Chotanagpur),* (Ranchi, Jharkhand: GEL Church, 2007), 15.

curiosity. The four inquirers, Navin Doman Tirkey, Kesho, Bandhu, and Ghuran came to the missionaries seeking answers to their many questions about the new faith the missionaries were preaching. One of their fundamental questions was about the living Lord Jesus Christ as claimed by the missionaries. Their innermost desire was to see Jesus before they would commit themselves to the baptism sought by missionaries. Thus, their repeated requests to be allowed to see this Jesus became a challenge to the missionaries.

As the tradition has it, after many meetings when the inquirers were not satisfied with the explanations of the missionaries they felt let down and felt that the missionaries' claim was proving empty. And as a result, they wanted to quit. Upon the request of missionaries they all knelt down to pray as a prayer of departure and God's intervention. Something happened in this prayer. The four Oraon indigenous tribal people of Ranchi area had a vision of Jesus which convinced them about the truth of Jesus Christ.[12] They were baptized on 9th June 1850. This was the beginning of the Church in Jharkhand. Some writers have argued that it was primarily their concern to safeguard their land rights that the indigenous tribal people became Christians.[13]

The land was a prominent issue for the indigenous tribal community at that time and it did have a lot to do with conversion later on. Yet the first Christians were converted because they were the seekers after the truth. The fact that the first Christians had embraced *Kabir panth* indicates that they were spiritually sensible and hungry. Joseph Bara himself provides clues for the spiritual reason for the first conversion. He reports that the first four converts were "religiously inquisitive, they bombarded the missionaries with questions."[14] Their many questions about this new faith were religious and spiritual questions. One among them was a very difficult question of being allowed to see Jesus with their naked eyes. It is clear that they were spiritually hungry people. Again what Bara says is indicative of the spiritual need of the first Christians over their material need. "...the Mundas and Uraons, like other Indian tribals in the mid nineteenth century,

---

[12] Nirmal Minz, "Christianity Among the Mundas, Oraons...", 23.

[13] For example, See, Joseph Bara, "Colonialism, Christianity and the Tribes of Chotanagpur in East India, 1845-1890", *Journal of South Asian Studies* Vol. XXX No.2 (August 2007),205 ff. However, by his own account Bara establishes the fact that as early as 1853 "Western' missionary enterprise evolved into 'spontaneous activity' of the tribals who carried the work in the field. This shows that those spreading the Gospel had a holistic message of well being instead of just material benefits regarding land rights. See pg. 206-207.

[14] Joseph Bara, "Colonialism, Christianity and the Tribes of Chotanagpur in East India, 1845-1890", *Journal of South Asian Studies* Vol. XXX No.2 (August 2007), 204.

craved spiritual solace."[15] The social status of the first Christians as educated and comparatively economically well off people also suggests more of their inner spiritual need as the decisive reason for conversion.

It took five long and hard years for the first conversion to establish the Church in Jharkhand. But once the indigenous tribal opened up to the Gospel it spread like wild fire. Soon people belonging to other indigenous tribal communities notably the Munda and the Kharia tribes joined the new movement of faith in Jesus Christ. The Jesus movement received further impetus and depth in witness and service with the establishment of the S.P.G. Mission in 1869 as well as the Jesuit Mission in the same year.

Reward of the New Faith: Persecution

Contrary to the idea of the mission-compound Christians of the later era, the four first adult converts went back to their families and villages. Filled with the joy of receiving Jesus Christ as God's gift for salvation they began to share about Jesus with their fellow villagers. It elicited two responses. The family members and fellow villagers became curious about the promise and power of the new faith but on the other hand, the powers that be of the time became furious about the power of the conversion. Zamindars (Landlords), Jagirdars (People appointed by the kings) and other influential and rich non-tribals began to persecute the new Christians and their families. So great was the pressure and persecution that with the exception of Navin Doman Tirkey the three other first converts may have gone back to their earlier faith or fled the place. History does not tell us much about them with certainty. However, Navin Doman 'stood the test of time' and because of his faithfulness to Jesus Christ he is called "the father of faith for the Christians in Jharkhand."[16]

The first wave of persecutions did not stop indigenous tribal people from accepting Jesus. Many found Jesus to be the Truth, the Way and the Life. But soon the historical turn of events in the form of the Sepoy Mutiny of 1857 (now understood as the first War of Independence) presented an opportunity for the anti-Christian forces for a second and more intense wave of persecutions. The revolt of 1857, aimed at overthrowing the British rule also included vehement and violent opposition to the missionaries. Missionaries could escape by fleeing the place but the new Christians had no choice but to face the consequences for their faith. Though the violence and opposition this time around was intense and more widespread, none of the new believers succumbed to the demands of the persecutors to abandon their faith. Instead, their confident and calm tolerance of the persecution

[15] Joseph Bara, "Colonialism, Christianity and the Tribes of Chotanagpur in East India, 1845-1890", *Journal of South Asian Studies* Vol. XXX No.2 (August 2007), 206.

[16] Nirmal Minz, "Christianity Among the Mundas, Oraons, and Kharias of Chotanagpur" 23.

became testimony of a divine power in their lives. It is important to note that these indigenous tribal Christians converted from tribal religions to Christianity yet the opposition and persecution came from those who were not even tribals.

The acceptance of the Christian faith probably meant two things for the people who had been exploiting the indigenous tribals for centuries by looting the land and forcing them for *beth-bagari* (forced labour) etc. The conversion, in the first instance, was a rebellion against the powers that were. The step towards accepting the Christian faith was a step against the faith of the exploiters also. Next, it was also a statement that was bold and clear that though exploited for generations, the indigenôus tribal people, contrary to what the exploiters thought, were not completely under their whip. They probably perceived a new source of empowerment in their new faith.

Gospel Proclaimed and Practiced

In the course of their preaching, the missionaries also became closely associated with the indigenous tribal society. They not only learnt the tribal languages but became pioneers in producing dictionaries, anthologies, and grammars etc., which are, till this day, considered standard for reference. J.B. Hoffman and A.V. Emlen co-authored the brilliant Encyclopedia Mundarica in fifteen volumes. Likewise, Nottrott, Hahn, Grignard, Bodding and Archer have left resources of immense value for tribal languages. The missionary proclamation was also accompanied by the establishment of schools and hospitals to meet the urgent needs of the local population.

In the course of time, the missionaries realized the great extent to which the tribals were subjected to terrible injustices by landlords and Jagirdars and business people. One of the serious threats to their very survival as a people was the continuing usurpation of tribal land by the non-tribal people. The issue of land right became an integral part of witnessing for the missionaries. Among missionaries a Jesuit, C. Lievens earned for himself the title "the Apostle to Chotanapur" because of the brilliant support he provided to the tribal population regarding their right over land. The whole indigenous tribal community would remain forever grateful to J.B. Hoffman who drafted the *Chotanagpur Tenancy Act (1908)*, which has proved to be the corner stone in the preservation of the land in Chotanagpur till the present time.[17] That the land is life for indigenous tribal people is an undeniable fact as is also is the fact of the Chotanagpur Tenancy Act in safeguarding this life-line of the indigenous tribal people. Though, at the present a vast majority of the indigenous tribal people are not sure who

---

[17] Agapit Tirkey, "Christianity Meets Tribals in Chotanagpur", *Sevartham* 23 (1998), 31.

helped craft this community 'life-line', both indigenous tribal Christians and non-Christian tribals alike are most grateful for it.

From the outset the missionaries understood witness both as preaching about the salvation in Jesus Christ and witnessing the abundant life in Jesus Christ in imparting education and in the ministry to the sick through clinics and hospitals. This is how they undertook God's work in Jharkhand.[18] The Gospel which the missionaries preached and its imperatives for abundant life may be said to be largely responsible for the present well being and somewhat enlightened status of a large majority of the tribal people today.

Empowered by the Gospel

By the beginning of the 19th century, land alienation and injustices against the local people were acquiring critical proportions. A glimpse of the exploitation suffered by the local population is seen in the following report posted by a writer in the Calcutta Review of July 1869:

> When the oppressor wants a horse, the Kol must pay; when he desires a palki, the Kols have to pay, and afterwards to hear him therein. They must pay for his musicians...Does someone die in his house? He taxes them; is a child born? Again a tax...And this plundering, punishing, robbing system goes on till the Kols run away. These unjust people not only take away everything in the house, but even force the Kols to borrow, that they may obtain what they want, reminding one of Sidney Smith's account of the poor man taxed from birth to his coffin. Again, whenever, the Thikadar has to go to Cutchary or to the King, to a marriage, on a pilgrimage, however, distant the place, the Kols must accompany him and render service without payment.[19]

That indigenous tribal people protested against injustice and exploitation is borne by many uprisings and revolts against both the colonial rulers and their associates namely, land lords, thikadars etc. Prominent among them are 'Kol Insurrection of 1832, Bhumij revolt, Santal Hul of 1855, Munda Ulgulan (1860-1900) and Birsa Andolan (1895).[20] However, on their own it was not easy for the indigenous tribals to successfully struggle for their genuine rights without an ally. In Christianity they found this new ally, "the religion of the Cross."[21] What the new faith did to the converts and the

---

[18] E. Viste, *Chotanagpur Ki Masihi Mandiliyon ka Itihaas (History of Christian Congregations in Chotanagpur)*, (Ranchi, Jharkhand: GEL Church, 2007) , 12.

[19] Quoted by S.C. Roy, *The Mundas and Their County* (Ranchi, Jharkhand: Catholic Press, 1995, reprint), 140. (Many writers use the term Kols to refer to the indigenous tribal people of Jharkhand. For people themselves it is a derogatory term and hence, is not used anymore.

[20] See, N. Minz, Adivaasi "Struggles and Movements", in *Pearls of Indigenous Wisdom* (New Delhi: Indian Social Institute; Bangalore:CISRS, 2007) ,100-111.

[21] S.C. Roy, *The Mundas and Their Country* (Ranchi, Jharkhand: Catholic Press, reprint 1995), 145.

exploiters is powerfully presented by Captain Davies, the then Senior Assistant Commissioner in 1859:

> With Christianity has naturally come an appreciation of their rights as original clearers of the soil which rights in many instances they have asserted and established; – this, independent of other causes which induce the higher castes of natives to view with displeasure the spread of Christianity, caused great alarm amongst the land-holders and farmers, who were not slow to use against these converts every means of persecution they could safely venture on, but no other effect than the spread of conversion.[22]

The empowerment process and the total impact of the Gospel intervention are to be noted in the following: education that produced teachers; health care that showed the depth of missionary compassion especially in hospitals for leprosy patients; missionaries' respect for indigenous tribal people which increased self-esteem of the people and missionaries' genuine commitment to the people as friends in providing moral and legal support. Joseph Marianus Kujur speaks of this empowerment in terms of social justice, philanthropic activities and political consciousness.[23]

Many have argued for the secular reasons for accepting the Gospel of Jesus Christ by the indigenous tribals in Jharkhand.[24] While economic reasons of strategy and agrarian rights are part of the total perception of how the tribals understood the message of Christianity, yet to completely discredit the spiritual factor is to disregard an important part of history. In this regard, K.N. Sahay's conclusion that missionaries changed their "approach to include temporal concerns" because purely evangelical work did not produce converts and his evidence for this is that only four families were converted in five years,[25] should be put to historical test.

It is true that it took five years for missionaries to baptize four people and their families, yet, by this, it cannot be proved that the missionaries spent all these years convincing these four families. When the four people came into contact with the missionaries, their engagement with them was intense, forceful and without undue delay. As the followers of *Kabir panth*, the first converts desired peace of soul by seeking after the truth and when they learnt that missionaries preached about a God who is the lord and He is living, they engaged seriously with the missionaries. We have indicated

---

[22] Quoted by S.C. Roy, *The Mundas and Their Country* (Ranchi, Jharkhand: Catholic Press, reprint 1995), 145.

[23] See, Joseph Marianus Kujur, "Christianity and Tribals: An Indian Experience", in *Indigenous People of India Problems and Prospects,* eds., Joseph Marianus Kujur and Sonajharia Minz (New Delhi: Indian Social Institute, 2007), 306ff.

[24] For example. See, Joseph Bara, "Colonialism, Christianity and the Tribes of Chotanagpur in East India, 1845-1890", *Journal of South Asian Studies* Vol. XXX No.2 (August 2007), 205ff.

[25] Kishari N. Sahay, *Under the Shadow of the Cross* (Calcutta: Institute of Social Research and Applied Anthropology, 1976)

how they bombarded the missionaries with questions and one may surmise they must have had spiritual questions about Jesus' lordship and livingness. Since the missionaries claimed Jesus to be alive, the simple but straightforward Oraon indigenous tribal people wanted to see Jesus.[26] More than anything their demand to see Jesus speaks of their deep spiritual search. It is only when they were satisfied with the missionaries' answers and their own experience of the living lord that they were willing to be baptized. Thus, for the first four courageous people who had taken a radical spiritual step in accepting *Kabir panth* (indicative of their spiritual search), the decisive nature of spiritual factors cannot be easily discredited especially in the light of the fact that they came many times to the missionaries and sought answers to many of their religious and spiritual questions and their own experience of religious truth of the Christian faith. Moreover, along with the promise, people experienced miraculous healing which also helped in people's acceptance of the new faith.[27] It must, however, be said that that missionaries' five year stay and involvement in and with the indigenous tribal community gave them insights into the injustices and exploitation perpetrated on the tribal community. And as a result, they approached their witness by contextualizing their message which also included standing with the oppressed and the exploited people for justice.

One of the consequences of the Gospel was that the new believers developed a new understanding of reality about themselves and their condition. The acceptance of the Gospel changed their views about themselves as God's people and hence felt empowered to overcome man perpetrated injustice of their lives. Of course, there were other constituent factors of this new sense of empowerment.[28]

Truth Defined and Incarnated in the Tribal Religious World

As noted at the beginning, many indigenous tribal authors and researchers have underlined the compatibility between tribal religions and Christianity. Given the similarities in the values of community, and creation and "human-natural-supernatural complex" acceptable to Christianity and tribal

---

[26] E. Viste, *Chotanagpur Ki Masihi Mandiliyon ka Itihaas (History of Christian Congregations in Chotanagpur),* (Ranchi, Jharkhand: GEL Church, 2007) ,16-17; also P. Minz, *Father Yohannes Evagelist Gossner and Gossner Mission Ka Prarambhik Itihaas (Father Yohannes Evangelists Gossner and the Early History of Gossner Mission),* (Ranchi, Jharkhand: G E L Press, 1986), 16-17.

[27] Philip Ekka, *Tribal Movements* (Pathalgaon, Cahhatisgarh: Tribal Research and Documentation Center, 2003), 109.

[28] Joseph Bara, "Colonialism, Christianity and the Tribes of Chotanagpur in East India, 1845-1890", *Journal of South Asian Studies* Vol. XXX No.2 (August 2007) 205ff.

religions[29] such a conclusion is valid and helpful as far as the possibilities of cultural and theological incarnation of the Jesus-faith is concerned. However, in the final analysis a neat, smooth and complete compatibility of these two faith traditions tantamount to an injustice to inner framework and plausibility of these religious traditions. To insist on a complete compatibility is to prove the Christian faith as a superfluous and unnecessary appendage to the tribal religions.

It is only when both compatibility and incompatibility of the tribal religions of Jharkhand with the Christian faith is taken, can a greater understanding of the missionary intervention and its message be appreciated. The fact of compatibility facilitated continuity with the tribal culture and the reality of incompatibility provided discontinuity with the tribal religion.

The four major tribes of Jharkhand, namely the Santhal, Oraon, Munda and Kharia have their own tribal religions. Though there are variations in rituals, practices, festivals, symbols and traditions and others, yet, all these religions share some major characteristics with regard to the concept of God, benevolent and mal-violent spirits, ancestor worship, the centrality of nature etc. In recent history since the intermingling of these tribes, the generic name 'sarna' has been used for the religions of the tribes in Jharkhand.[30] Again the cultural differences in terms of music, social customs, languages, are quite clear, though the theme of nature, hospitality, clan system, the use of the same musical instruments and the centrality of community unite them in one entity of tribes of Jharkhand. Nonetheless, the social, religious and cultural world of the tribes of Jharkhand may rightly be referred to as one entity for the purpose of our present study of Christianity and tribal religions. It is in this broad understanding of the tribal religions, Joseph Marianus Kujur has studied Christianity and tribal religions of Jharkhand in terms of 'revealed and natural religion', 'animism and Christianity', 'tribal polytheism and Christian monotheism', 'tribal-Christian spirituality' etc.[31] In considering these aspects of both the religions, the author rightly demonstrates continuity between the two. For example, the belief in the one Supreme Being, community centered living, life after death, belief, human-natural and supernatural complex etc.

These convergence /continuity of the tribal religions with Christianity played an important role in internalizing what Christianity had to preach and practice. Nonetheless, the aspects of discontinuity also acted in no less a decisive way. In fact, the discontinuity with the old religion may have

[29] Joseph Marianus Kujur, "Christian Faith and Tribal Culture", 173.

[30] Originally the word 'sarna' referred to a grove of sal trees where the tribals worshiped on certain occasion but this word has, over the years acquired additional meanings too. Now this refers to their deity and it is also used to refer to the people who are non-Christian tribals. In addition, it has acquired political overtones too in the context of Jharkhand.

[31] Joseph Marianus Kujur, "Christian Faith and Tribal Culture", 170 ff.

given the courage to accept the new and novel faith. The new faith showed new possibilities; it spoke of new promises; it also gave new community and identity. This discontinuity gave rise to a new community to which we will turn in the third section but let's now turn to consider how the Christian engagement with the tribal community has been perceived by the non-Christian tribal community.

Church of Jharkhand or Church in Jharkhand

In this section our attempt is to evaluate Christianity (the Church) from the indigenous tribal perspective. To a certain degree, this effort may be supposed to be artificial, because it is undertaken by an indigenous tribal Christian and not by a *sarna* tribal, yet, it would afford a vantage point to evaluate the Church's promises and practices over the years.

History of Tension Between Christianity and Tribal Religion

TENSION AND CONFLICT EARNED OR IMPOSED?

The *Nemha* Bible (the Oraon Bible) episode, referred to at the beginning of this paper, illustrates vehement opposition and accusation by the tribal community against the Church. Accumulated feelings of dissatisfaction against the Church found the Bible translation event merely an opportunity to give vent to their anger and frustration. More than simply registering their antagonism, the community resorted to burning effigies, demonstration on the streets and burning the copies of the *Nemha* Bible in public. The lapse in the translation was interpreted as an attack on the tribal religion and also a conspiracy to annihilate the indigenous tribal community itself.[32] It is obvious the indigenous tribal community is harbouring animosity against Christianity.

Many Christians today wonder as to what the Church has done to earn such animosity expressed in such a violent way. In other words, what are the reasons for the conflict between the indigenous tribal religion and Christianity? How and why is the Church, established by "the true friends of the tribals"[33] opposed and accused?

Before we analyze the reasons, events and process which led to the present day conflict between the two faith traditions, we should remember that such an attitude included both reality as well as perception of the

[32] After September 22, 2008 the local newspaper in Ranchi regularly reported the indigenous tribal community's opposition expressed through the burning of effigies of the cardinal, street demonstration and rallies, burning of the copies of Nemha Bible etc.

[33] Nirmal Minz, :Mission in the Context of Diversity: Mission in the Tribal Context," in *Pearls of Indigenous Wisdom,* eds. Joseph Marianus Kujur and Sonajharia Minz (New Delhi: Indian Social Institute, 2007), 164-165.

indigenous tribal community over a very long time. As true friends of the indigenous tribal community the first missionaries not only preached the gospel but they also made social service an integral part of the early mission activities. Socio-economic issues such as forced labour, land litigations and alienation etc., were taken up boldly both by the Lutheran and Jesuit missionaries.[34] Such was the genuine commitment of the missionaries to the cause of the tribal community that their otherwise pragmatic and cordial relations with the colonial power experienced clashes and strains, especially because of the missionaries' support to the anti-zamindar posture of the tribals.[35] Thus, the engagement of the gospel thus preached and lived, created confidence in the indigenous tribal people's mind and heart about what the missionaries preached and invited to. It made following their religion not so difficult.

The brilliant leadership of missionaries in advocating the agrarian rights of the indigenous tribals and genuine commitment in providing legal and technical support to win litigations in the courts convinced the tribal people of their generosity and good will. However, this is not to deny many misconceptions, misunderstandings and even mistakes of the missionaries regarding tribal culture and religion and their negative impact on the unity and integrity of the community. There were times when missionaries hesitated to give all out support to the villagers. In one such event, the Lutheran missionaries had, on behalf of the tribals, submitted a petition to the government "but the pastors were told to keep their hands off the prevailing agrarian unrest in the region."[36] And when pastors obeyed such instructions many Christians felt betrayed by their pastors and in protest joined the struggle of the tribal chiefs against landlords called *Sardar Larai,* . The village leaders of many villages opposed the landlords, the government and even the pastors for the injustices inflicted upon them. Incidents like this, early on in the history of the Church sowed seeds of mistrust in the minds of the tribal community.

As we had mentioned earlier, the missionary engagement in Jharkhand also included the establishment of many educational institutions wherever the different missions opened mission stations. Because of educated, committed and trained teachers and leaders, these educational institutions achieved fairly good standards of education and discipline which reflected in the results of those students sitting in the public examinations. However the missions developed institutionalization, denominationalism and an

---

[34] Nirmal Minz, :Mission in the Context of Diversity: Mission in the Tribal Context," in *Pearls of Indigenous Wisdom,* eds. Joseph Marianus Kujur and Sonajharia Minz (New Delhi: Indian Social Institute, 2007) ,165.

[35] Joseph Bara, "Colonialism, Christianity and the Tribes of Chotanagpur in East India, 1845-1890", *Journal of South Asian Studies* Vol. XXX No.2 (August 2007), 211.

[36] Agapit Tirkey, "Christianity Meets Tribals in Chotanagpur", *Sevartham* 23 (1998), 31.

attitude of competition among themselves which turned them inward looking. As a result, they adopted a policy of preference for the students of their own denomination. In this calculation the non-Christian tribals were not counted as they did not belong to any of the missions. Hence, they received treatment other than preferred. Because of the importance of good education for all including the tribal people, this attitude of the missions led to a feeling of discrimination and even animosity against the Church.

Even the desirable practice of adopting indigenous tribal heritage in the Church has also become a bone of contention between the indigenous tribal church and the non-Christian tribal community. The example of celebrating *Karam,* a tribal festival, observed in the Roman Catholic Church attracted criticism and opposition.[37] However, on the other hand, the discontinuity with the older religio-cultural traditions of the indigenous tribal community is also cited to accuse Christians of destroying the tribal traditions and customs. The grievances of the indigenous tribal community against the Church came to the fore during the negotiations over the *Nemha Bible* controversy. In the meeting of 11th October 2008, the leaders and representatives of the tribal community put forth many demands before the leaders of the Church which included the cardinal Teleshphore Toppo and many Bishops and leaders of mainline churches of Jharkhand. Among other things the prominent demands of the tribal community were that the tribal festivals of *Karam* and *Sarhul* shall not be observed by the Church; that the Church shall prefer the *sarna* students in their institutions; the Church school shall not force the *sarna* students to write their surnames; that the Church shall support the tribal demand for separate *sarna* code in the Census form of the government of India.[38]

CHURCH SEEN FROM NON-CHRISTIAN INDIGENOUS TRIBAL EYES

Aloysius Pieris speaks of Church in Asia and Church of Asia. For him, the Asian Church is *in* Asia and not the Church *of* Asia.[39] The statement is both a condemnation of the Church and a challenge for her authentic existence. This is what the indigenous tribal community perceives when she looks at the Church. The material culture of the Church such as church structures, dress of the religious personnel, eating habits, music and musical instruments, liturgy, songs, worship, church hierarchy, etc and non-material culture which includes the attitude of competition, individualism, and

[37] Joseph Marianus Kujur cites an example of how a prominent indigenous tribal university professor who was invited as the chief guest, was extremely critical of the way the *karam* branches were used in the celebration of *Karam* festival in a Christian institution in Ranchi. See, Joseph Marianus Kujur, "Christian Faith and Tribal Culture".

[38] Prabhat Khabar (Hindi), Ranchi Edition, 12th October 2008, 5.

[39] Aloysius Pieris, *An Asian Theology of Liberation (*Maryknoll, N.Y.: Orbis Books, 1988.

western ethos make the Church an island in the tribal eye where only the initiated ones are welcome.

In their efforts to revive the tribal religions, the political, religious and intellectual non-Christian tribal leaders have been vocal and aggressive in condemning the Christians as betrayers of their religion. More than this, their perception that the converted indigenous tribal people are anti-tribal community is the basis for suspicion and mistrust of even genuine Christian gestures and initiatives for indigenous tribal solidarity. In addition, the right wing Hindu fundamentalist organizations like the R.S.S.'s slogan that all tribal are Hindus and the Sangh Parivar's agenda of instigating the non-Christian tribal against the indigenous tribal Christians have further coloured the understanding of the tribal community. Such divisive agendas prove effective when the tribal people realize that the Church virtually ignored the traditional social and cultural institutions like *Dhumkuria*, *Parha* etc. For a very long time the tribal dance was also prohibited in the Church. The *sarna* tribals are appalled to see Christian marriage among the same clan without any qualms even though this is a *sin* against one of the community's fundamental laws. Thus, for *sarna* tribal people, the Church may be located *in* Jharkhand but it is yet to become a church *of* Jharkhand.

The Reality of Indigneous Tribal Christianity

In this section we will argue that a healthy and robust relationship between Christianity and tribal religions is to be located in the recognition, acceptance and promotion of the creation of indigenous tribal Christians and also in the recognition of the indigenous tribal community as integral to meaningful existence of the Church in Jharkhand. The reality of indigenous tribal Christianity is an outcome of the inevitable process of self-definition sought by the people group that accepts the Lordship of Jesus in their socio-cultural milieu.

Generally speaking the mission understanding is that the proclamation of the gospel results in conversion. Though this is true the greater truth in this regard is the creation of a new community. In the case of an indigenous tribal context this new community is the community of Indigenous Tribal Christians. Historically, mission encounters and gospel proclamation necessarily entail shifts in self-definition of the new believers. It has been no different in Jharkhand. The mission encounter affected the same shift in the self-definition of the people of this place. It was true also when the Jesus movement reached the Greek world in the earliest times. Thus, Ben F. Meyer speaks of the impact of the Gospel's mission encounter in Greek World. He concludes that mission encounters also "generated a change in Christianity itself from its first self-understanding as the vanguard of Israel to its second self-understanding as humanity reborn of the last Adam-a new mankind."[40] Again the same idea of changing self-definition is underlined in what R.A. Markus says, "In one sense the whole of the Church's history is growth in self awareness; every important encounter with a new society, a new culture, with shifts in men's assumptions about their world, themselves, or God, with upheavals in the values by which they try to live, brings with new discovery."[41] The Gospel encounter helped develop a new awareness of themselves and their world and found in the Gospel of Jesus Christ that which transformed them as people. Regarding the indigenous tribal people of Jharkhand, Joseph Bara opines that "the tribals acculturated only partially in the ways that Europeans had not anticipated. Mundas and Uraons took elements from Western and Christian cultures selectively and internalized them in their tribal culture in order to empower themselves."[42] Though, Bara speaks of this in the context of empowerment against the exploiters, it is also indicative of a sense of their new identity.

Joseph Marianus Kujur is one of the few who has rightly spoken of the emergence of a new religious community called 'Tribal Christians'[43] as a result of the proclamation of the Gospel of Jesus Christ. He underlines a change in the indigenous tribal Christian identity. He speaks of a double identity as Christian and tribal.[44] However, this unique identity is not discussed further and hence its logical and inevitable theological and cultural implications remain undeveloped. Instead, he speaks of identity and loyalty in terms of denomination and mother mission and daughter church.

However, the claim for double identity and its corresponding loyalty is still valid to underline the issue of indigenous tribal identity. Almost all scholars and authors recognize the twin aspects of 'tribal' and 'Christian' to argue that both Christian faith and tribal culture are essential for an authentic existence of the Church in Jharkhand. Nonetheless, it seems many of them fail to recognize the theological significance of this inevitable double edged identity. It is true that in common parlance and even scholarly literature, the Church in Jharkhand has been referred to as an "*Adivasi* Church" and "Tribal Church." It seems, however, in such terms only the sociological reality of the people and place is recognized without adequately understanding the theological significance and implications. The name of indigenous tribal Christians is most appropriate as this

---

[40] Ben F. Meyer, *The Early Christians* (Wilmington, Delaware: Michael Glazier Inc. 1986), 13.

[41] R.A. Markus, "The Problem of Self-Definition: From Sect to Church in *Jewish and Christian Self-Definition*, ed. E.P. Sanders (London: SCM, 1980), 3.

[42] Joseph Bara, "Colonialism, Christianity and the Tribes of Chotanagpur in East India, 1845-1890", 221.

[43] Joseph Marianus Kujur, "Christian Faith and Tribal Culture", 165.

[44] Joseph Maranus Kujur, "Christian Faith and Tribal Culture", 165.

establishes both their *indigenousness* and *Christian-ness* at the same time. It incorporates both an act of affirmation and an act of transformation.[45]

Regrettably, the inevitable process of self-definition accompanying the preaching of the Gospel in Jharkhand seems to have been understood as complete and closed. The indigenous tribal Christian community understood as complete and closed is contradictory to the Gospel of Jesus Christ which is open and dynamic. If what has been accepted thus far is understood to be final then this position advocates a Christian faith of the past that lays undue emphasis on discontinuity with the indigenous tribal culture and perhaps also spurns any continuity as pagan and thus unchristian. The living and dynamic gospel of Jesus Christ that pervaded the gentile world which defined Christian faith should continue the process of mutual impregnation: a process whereby will emerge a more thorough and mature Jesus *Panth* in Jharkhand. That the process of self determination is yet to be developed fully is evident in how Christians are identified in the region.

For example, Agapit Tirkey uses two categories of Christianity and tribal religion to show many points convergence and a few divergences.[46] However, while using the term 'tribal new Christians' once without any discussion[47] he generally speaks of 'Christians', 'Christianity' and 'tribal'. In the other category belongs scholar like Joseph Bara who use the term 'tribal' in relation to Christianity and Christian mission.[48] There is yet another group of authors who designate the tribal Christians of Jharkhand by the term 'Christian tribal.'[49] Though the term 'Christian tribal' combines both the essential aspects of being Jesus-follower in the Jharkhand context, the word order is still less than appropriate. To call believers only Christians in the context of Jharkhand is to underline the discontinuity with the indigenous tribal community to the neglect of essential cultural continuity. Likewise, to call them Christian tribals is to still deny the cultural priority that accords uniqueness to them.

Thus, the designation for Jesus-followers in Jharkhand should be *indigenous tribal Christians* because it maintains essential priority of

---

45 For a discussion on indigenous Christians from a theological perspective see, Jhakmak Neeraj Ekka, "Indigenous Christian Theology: Questions and Directions in the Making", *Bangalore Theological Forum* Vol. XXXIX, No. 1 (June 2007), 102-125.

46 Agapit Tirkey, "Christianity Meets Tribals in Chotanagpur", *Sevartham* 23 (1998)

47 Agapit Tirkey, "Christianity Meets Tribals in Chotanagpur", *Sevartham* 23 (1998) 31; he also uses the term Roman Catholic Christians on 32.

48 Joseph Bara, "Colonialism, Christianity and the Tribes of Chhotanagpur in East India, 1845-1890"

49 For example, see, Joseph Marianus Kujur, "Christian Faith and Tribal Culture" 164, 165;Nirmal Minz uses the terms both 'Christian' and 'Adivaasi christian', see, Nirmal Minz, "Christianity Among the Mundas, Oraons…"

indigenousness in which and because of which the process of self-definition is effected. This is a contextual priority for a new theological reality. As a new theological creation it is grounded in the cultural particularity. The indigenous tribal Christian is a new creation which includes both affirmation and transformation. "In a single act of acceptance of the gospel and acknowledgement of the Lordship of Jesus Christ, the two events take place: an act of both affirmation and transformation. This is a divine event of affirmation of who they are and a divine event of transformation to what they have become."[50] Such theological understanding would remain ineffectual if we fail to consider still important question in this respect. For example, what does it mean to have a unique identity of indigenous Christians vis a vis the non-Christian tribal community? What impact would such self-understanding have in its relation with tribal religions?

The new creation of indigenous tribal Christian exists for the sake of the whole community. One the one hand, the newness of the Christ follower underlines discontinuity with the old in one level. Yet, on the other hand the same newness of the person calls for being greater gifts to the whole community. Thus, a new creation of which we spoke of earlier is a new creation for the sake of newness of the whole community in terms of wholeness and abundant living, newness in terms of community living free of exploitation, injustice and discrimination. In this newness of life the tribal religions in Jharkhand would not be something to compete against but an essential aspect of the root and heritage from which vision of new creation is possible.

For a desirable, healthy and authentic relationship between Christianity and tribal religions in Jharkhand, it seems common acceptance, self-recognition, community and individual promotion of the tribal believers as indigenous tribal Christians is helpful. A conscious and common insistence on the designation of the indigenous tribal Christians or the indigenous tribal Church in Jharkhand will greatly help in two important and desirable objectives. First, in the accentuated and conscious process towards the realization of the increasingly mature theological creation of 'indigenous tribal Christian' with the two pronged heritage of one identity. Based on the foregoing discussion of the inevitable process of self-definition, the new creation is somewhat achieved as a new term for a general categorization but what is still needed is the Church's serious commitment to the power of the Gospel grounded and manifested in the theological and cultural reality of the people. Such a decisive course would help keep the heritage of Biblical faith and cultural richness in creative interaction for a unique experience of God's promise in Jesus Christ. While protecting the

---

[50] Jhakmak Neeraj Ekka, "Towards an Indigenous Christian Theology: Questions and Directions in
Making" in *Indigenous People of India.* Eds. Joseph Marianus Kujur and Sonajharia Minz (ISI:New Delhi, 2007), 366.

indigenous tribal Christians by separating them from *sarna* tribals, it will speak of tribalization of what newness they have received.

Second, is the corollary of the first as it may lead to the realization of an increasingly cordial and complementary relationship with the *Sarna* tribal religion and society. By understanding themselves as and only as 'indigenous tribal Christians' the Christ followers would realize the value of the cultural soil for the tree of their Christian faith. It is in this, the Christian identity is affirmed and cultural identity is transformed and also cultural identity is affirmed and Christian identity is transformed. For many it may be a challenge of a dilemma or confusion of the two realities but it is, in fact, a theological mandate of the Gospel of Jesus Christ which is expressed in oneness and distinction at the same time.

We believe that the above mentioned conceptual understanding of the existence of the Church and Christ followers would leads to the transformation of faith which is to be understood in the solidarity and continuity credentials of Christianity with the people of a same culture. One critical question in this regard is the question of the manifestation and credibility of the transformation. Though it is artificial and somewhat contrary to our arguments to highlight the areas a Church in transformation to be located, yet it is helpful at least for a direction to be charted. The area of language in which missionary contribution is gratefully acknowledged can further be bolstered by leadership and genuine commitment. Likewise, the sphere of socio-economic and politics in which the Church has been less than sure and forthright would require the Church to throw her lot with the greater indigenous tribal community. Moreover, any serious transformation of Christianity would entail negotiation and adoption of three indigenous rites in the practice of Christian faith in Jharkhand, namely, birth, marriage and burial.

The significance of the term is of considerable consequence as it speaks of identity in relation to those in community who are not Christians. As we have said, the acceptance of the Gospel by the indigenous tribal person creates a new reality i.e. the *indigenous tribal Christian*. The person is both an indigenous tribal and a Christian at the same time. To many, the term for those who accept the Jesus '*Panth*' (Way) is barely of any consequence but, in fact, in this seemingly unimportant term lies the authenticity of the inevitable process of self-definition. Thus, how people of the Jesus *Panth* are identified as community as well as individuals has immediate implications for their self-definition. Moreover, indigenous the tribal Christian as the Jesus *Panthi* may well find an acceptable place in non-Christian tribal understanding. Non-Christian tribal scholars like Karma Oraon have argued that there are many *panths* in Oraon tribal community and those following Jesus could be accepted as Jesus *panthis*. Such understanding should be promoted by the Church so that acceptable terms such as these could be universalized without compromising historical and theological truth claim.

As we have indicated earlier that a self-definition of this community would have an immediate impact on the relevance of the existence of the Christian community in a particular cultural context. In relation to the tribal cultural milieu, the process of the determination of self-definition has been provided less than adequate reflection and regard. The 19th century phenomenon of competition among various missions may have replaced the key aspect of cultural identity with denominational identity.[51] Therefore, the Christians of Jharkhand till recent years referred to one another by mission i.e. German Christians, Roman Christians etc. Even today, 'denominational reference' has given way to 'indigenous tribal preference' is not beyond doubt.

Conclusion

The lesson for the Church in Jharkhand is serious self-retrospection in the light of the historical vision of the Gospel proclaimed and lived in response to the plight of the people. What began as a result of a few people's conversion the Church soon became a people's movement that demonstrated the inevitable commitment of the Gospel to truth and justice. The Gospel march was marked by the sincere thirst and hunger for the God given life of freedom and justice. Accordingly the Church was mostly found to be on the side of the people. Free from institutional interests and barriers, the power which inspired the first missionaries was the power of the Gospel-truth and the power of the Gospel-life for the sake of the people. In order to reorient itself as a people's movement, the Church in Jharkhand, once again, must seek people as the focus of its witness. In fact, the present Church in Jharkhand should reclaim its heritage of witnessing the Good News of Jesus Christ both in word and deed at the same time. It must allow her theology and the history of the Gospel to redefine itself in the cultural milieu of the people and the place.

A decisive cultural and theological self-understanding keeping in mind the larger context of the people would underline the solidarity and continuity credentials of Christianity. Many important areas of concerns for the indigenous tribal society such as the preservation of the tribal languages, socio-economic development, political conscientization to name a few, may acquire equal importance as other ecclesiastical matters and hence, may command the Church's urgent and honest commitment for the sake of the whole community. In this approach indigenous tribal

[51] This competition was quite intense in Chotanagpur as is obvious from the statement of Peter Tete regarding the Jesuit Mission in Chotanagpur. Tete says that "The young Jesuit, Constant Lievens had been picked up by his foresighted and inspiring Superior, Sylvanus Gosjean and his Bishop, Msgr Paul Goethals, *to halt the progress of the Lutherans and Anglicans in the tribal land.* (Emphasis added) see, "History of the Mission of Chotanagpur: Facts and Challenges Today", *Sevartham* No. 21 (1996), 48.

Christianity is likely to be accepted as one of the many *panths* within the tribal community which would remove prejudices and ill-feelings against it. In an ideal relationship, both indigenous tribal Christianity and non-Christian indigenous tribal religions would accord each other validity without compromising their respective uniqueness and also accept their diversity without disregarding cultural unity.

Christian Mission and Primal Faith: The Need for an Inter-Faith Relation in the Khasi Jaintia Context

Bolinkar Sohkhlet

Initial Remarks

It is worthwhile to state at the outset that the Pre-Edinburg Centenary Celebration Consultation would facilitate among different churches around the globe, better understanding of and further consideration on mission. The theme "Christian Mission Among Other Faiths" which has been consequently developed to "Witnessing to Christ in the Company of Other Faiths", opens the door for bringing in the valuable essential elements found in other faiths that may be useful for healthier enhancement and enrichment of mission in the contemporary world. Undertaking mission by articulating such elements of other faiths is an endeavor that would surely generate the more meaningful and successful mission without possessing negative attitude to other faiths, the trend that is globally needed today. There is, therefore, hope that the celebration with a variety of programs will enlighten the churches all over the world concerning the right understanding of mission with its several required methods and approaches amidst many complex problems and challenges. So the writer prays and wishes for the smooth functioning and success of the celebrations.

Introduction

It is quite evident that the central mission enterprise of the 1910 Edinburg Conference was basically understood in terms of planting and organizing the Christian Church among non Christians along with which some other unappreciable concerns were adopted; for instance, it was arrogantly felt that colonial powers and strategies inter alia, were factors that could help the Church to conquer people of other faiths, the mission understanding and ideology of the churches that time. Such an attitude has to be no more acknowledged or given space in the mission process of the Church today.

As per the topic, this paper discusses the Christian mission requiring the company of Primal faith in the Khasi Jaintia (Meghalaya) context. It begins with a short introduction on the land and the people (Khasi Pnars) and describes their religious faith before the advent of Christianity; in so doing, it highlights the essential features of the Khasi Pnar primal religion/faith in which traditional moral-ethical values were embedded. It further highlights briefly the history of Christian Mission and analyzes its condition and weaknesses in which a critique is made regarding the Church's position in connection with inter-faith relations (i.e. specifically between Christianity and the Primal religion), marking its laxity of perception of theological significances and values of indigenous religion, ignoring thus the theological reflection on and interpretation of them, consequently leading to the development of problems and challenges (social and religious). Finally, the paper brings out some proposals needed for the Church not only of the Khasi and Jaintia Hills but also of other places, to take into consideration and start constructing a more meaningful and successful mission in the contemporary era.

The Khasi Pnars

The Khasi Pnars are the original inhabitants of the present four Districts (West and East Khasi Hills, Ri Bhoi and Jaintia Hills) of Meghalaya in North East India. There is no consensus of opinion regarding their origin even though many researchers are of the view that they migrated from East or South-East Asia. The most common scholarly argument asserts that they belong to the Austro-Asiatic and Mon-Khmer race. According to the Indian constitution, they, along with many backward groups, are classed under the category of Scheduled Tribes (even though they may not call themselves "Tribes")[1]. One of the socio-cultural structures that they observe, but seldom followed by other communities, is the matrilineal system. Concerning religion, the majority of them has embraced Christianity, although large numbers (even if a minority) still adhere to their indigenous/traditional/primal faith.[2] For certain reasons, it can be asserted that the attitude between the followers of one-another tradition in terms of religion is internally not noble. This reduces the inter-religious relation, the fact that, to some extent, disturbs the decent honesty of social relation among members of the community, which if held fast and observed well, would contribute to challenging the ill-fated problems and challenges faced by the people.

---

[1] See A Wati Longchar, "Tribal Theology – Issues, Methods and Perspective", in *In Search of Identity and Tribal Theology*, ed. by A. Wati Longchar, Jorhat: Tribal Study Centre ETC, 2001, 45.

[2] It should be noted that the term "indigenous" and "traditional" (religion) which are frequently used in this paper are not considered as different from the term "primal" (religion).

The Khasi Pnar Primal Faith

Before the coming of Christianity, the Khasi Pnars like many other tribes continued to adhere to their indigenous faith (Traditional/Primal religion). Undoubtedly, they had been the *homoreligious* community. Their religion though observed and practiced within families, clans, villages and chiefdoms (*hima*) respectively,[3] has the theology unique among the whole community which, nonetheless, could be hardly understood or explained except if explored from the perspective of the theology, phenomenology and other methodological disciplines of religious study. Otherwise, mere looking at peripheral phenomena would lead to misunderstanding and misleading or misrepresenting of the true theological nature and significance of primal faith. It would rather be worse when one tries to explain so with prejudicial and judgmental outlook as was the case with the missionaries and many early writers of the Khasi Pnar Primal religion.[4]

God – the Core of Primal/Indigenous Faith

Theologically, the core of the Khasi Pnar faith is no other than the concept or experience of God (the *Theos*) known as *Blei.*[5] Perhaps God was seldom mentioned in name, yet the concept and understanding of God exists as the core of primal faith being articulated in the traditional speeches/stories, practices and experiences of the people. God, according to Khasi Pnar primal faith, can be both personal and impersonal, but at the same time is supernatural.[6] So also God is beyond human gender but is also occasionally attributed to both the sexes as God is the be-all and end-all. God is the Creator (*Nongthaw*), the Dispenser (*Nongbuh*) and the Designer (*Nongpynlong*); God is all-powerful or omnipotent and omniscient (*balah-baiai*); As God is the Creator, so all of creation belong to God and for that reason, God is also called *Blei Trai Kynrad* (literally "God the Lord and Master"). Moreover, God rules over all and has His/Her role in every human activity. Thus God is addressed in many names as to signify His/Her attributes in relation with different human acts; for instance, God is

[3] It is on the basis of looking at such observation, that many writers wrongly asserted that the Khasi Pnar primal religion/faith is limited within certain groups or areas.

[4] Cf. J.D. Hooker, as quoted in J.N. Choudhury, *The Khasi Canvas*, Shillong: Smt. Jaya Choudhury, 1998, 183.

[5] The author (B. Sohkhlet) had an opportunity to do research on Traditional Religion of the Khasi Pnars during 2004 – 2008 and submitted a thesis to the Senate of Serampore College/University for the partial fulfillment of the degree of Doctor of Theology (D.Th). Refer for details, B. Sohkhlet, "A Phenomenological Study of the Understanding of God as Emerging from Selected Myths and Rituals in the traditional Religion of the Khasi Pnars", Unpublished D.Th. Thesis, Senate of Serampore, 2008.

[6] Ibid., 93 (The point is based on the research finding).

called *Blei longspah* in relation with His/her role in the people's economy, *Blei synshar* for His/Her role in polity, etc. Attributes of God are also expressed in various Khasi Pnar religious features like myths and rituals, symbolizing the pervading role of religion in every aspect of life. So, in fact, primal religious elements like myths, rituals, symbols, etc, are the data that can convey the insight of the experience, understanding or concept of God and it is here that theology of the Khasi Pnar primal faith has its basic tenet.

The Breakdown of God-Human Relation

The Khasi Pnar religion has the conception of the breakdown of God-human relationship being expressed in the form of myth. As per the narration, the exact cause of the breakdown is not clear but it was the human being who was the root cause.[7] The version of the myth says that at the beginning God, who created everything including human beings of sixteen huts (families), made heaven their (humans) settled home place and the earth their working field. They walked between heaven and earth through the golden ladder that joined heaven and earth through the hill called *lum sohpetbneng* (the hill of the naval of heaven). Everything was excellent as all things are under God's control and God's blessing. So was the relationship, unique and undisturbed. Such an age was known as the golden age. Once it happened that when seven of the sixteen families toiled on earth, the ladder was removed or fell down. The seven huts since then were made to settle forever on earth and the relationship with God was thus affected. Yet God did not forsake the seven huts (humans) but continued to help them whenever they approached Him/Her, but the unique relationship was no more restored.[8] Ever since, God can no more be contacted directly but only through nature and other parts of creation. So also God would continue to reveal or manifest His/Her act of response to humans.

Religious Acts as a Means to Approach God

As time went on, human life often going underwent tests and so was affected by several calamities. Evil forces continued to endanger and attack from time to time. So also human nature and behavior became worse. Another oral tradition (myth) tells that once in a big festival, different creatures were invited and they performed dances. Among many, were a sister and brother – the sun and the moon. They performed together a dance

[7] There has been an expression and interpretation of the myth related to the breakdown of the relationship pointing to *u thlen* (comparable with Satan in Christian belief) as the root cause. However, it seems to be a kind of later transposed version so as to suit with Christian understanding of original sin.

[8] B. Sohkhlet, op.cit., 142 ff.

that looked peculiar to other creatures especially humans who ridiculed and mocked at them. The sun felt so embarrassed and was let down by such mockery. She went away and hid herself in the cave located inside the thick bushes (*ka krem lamet latang*). The whole world was then covered with darkness and all creatures were in the state of chaos. As they tried to find out the reason, they, at last realized their own mischief. Humans then tried to search for someone who could go to plead for the sun's forgiveness but no one dared to take the responsibility as they all felt guilty. Amidst such despondence, one bird came forward and expressed his eagerness. He was then entrusted with the task. However, when he reached near the sun he disclosed his arrogance and pride, an act that angered the sun. The sun chased him away. At last, there was only one creature who never came out of his dwelling place as he was too poor, having not even a simple cover over his body. That was the cock living inside the bushes in a sacred grove. He had been always submissive and obeyed to whatever was asked by the Creator God. As he learned about the commotion, in a spirit of humility he decided to come out and expressed his concern to humans with a request to the latter to offer him only something to cover his body. The humans then agreed and thus the cock went to the sun. With all humility and modesty, he prayed before the sun requesting for her forgiveness and at last could convince the sun. Forgiving the guilt of the humans and other creatures, the sun came out of her hiding place to give light to the world once again and so the whole problem was solved.[9]

As humans approached God and the sun for thankfulness, God explained to them about their weak human capacity and inability as they lived in this world. God also showed His/Her concern for the problems they would continuously face. So humans prayed to God, requesting for God's mercy. In response, God instituted the religion by which humans can live a life and approach to God, with the cock or hen, besides other animals, as the main instrument of sacrificial acts. However, as stated earlier humans could never contact God directly but only through nature; hence nature and other parts of creation became the channel through which humans could communicate with God. It is also in and through nature that signs of God's responses can be observed.

Together with religion, three major moral-ethical principles were juxtaposed.[10] In short, they are (1) *Tip briew-tip Blei* (literally, knowing humans and knowing god), (2) *tipkur-tipkha* (knowing maternal and paternal kin) and (3) *kamai ia ka hok* (earn in and for righteousness). In every part of life, these principles should be kept in mind and followed, failing which would lead to several disasters. In case of accidental violation, humans should approach God for forgiveness and for showing the way by means of religious rites. More so, God should be approached

[9] Ibid., 145 ff.

[10] H.O. Mawrie, *U Khasi bad la ka Niam*, Shillong: H.O. Mawrie, 1973, 12.

for blessings and help in different spheres of life; for this, rituals should be performed with a cock, hen or egg as the main sacrificial elements besides which other animals can be used. Alongside, praises and thanksgivings are also needed as a mark of expressing gratefulness to God for the blessings that He/She bestows, through the performance of related rituals.[11]

From the above discussion, it is therefore clear that all sets of religious beliefs, observances and practices are based on people's experience and understanding of and relationship with God. Nature and other creatures are part and parcel of such a relationship, signifying their sacredness. The said principles are also meant for right and good conduct in every aspect of day to day life, be it individual or social. The following brief elaboration of each of them would throw some light on their meaning;

1. Tipbriew-Tipblei: The word *tipbriew* denotes commitment to social concerns. It involves the use of benevolent words and the performance of beneficial actions towards other fellow humans for constructing a just, liberative, humanitarian and communitarian society. The expression is joined with the word *tipblei* which implies a relational and cognitive understanding of God who one experiences as one involves himself or herself in social concerns. While *tipbriew* focuses on social commitment, *tipblei* emphasizes the knowledge of God. Therefore the compound *tipbriew-tipblei* underlines the view that social commitment is a godly concern. Social involvement leads to deeper knowledge of God. So also the understanding of God leads to social commitment.[12]

2. Tipkur-Tipkha: The word *tipkur* literally means "knowing one's clan". In fact, it denotes the acknowledgement of the existence of a maternal relationship between members of the same clan, expressed through mutual respect. The word *tipkha* on the other hand, signifies the acknowledgement of the existence of relationships with the clan of one's paternal kin, expressed once again through mutual respect. In other words, according to the *tipkha* principle, the father or the husband and his family are respected by the mother or wife and her family, and vice versa. So, when the two terms *tipkur-tipkha* are joined together, it articulates a principle of respectful mutual relationships among the different clans of the Khasi Pnar society. In other words, it emphasizes the importance of communitarian respect and togetherness.[13]

3. Kamai ia ka Hok: The principle means "for righteous earning". It implies that one must be sincere and righteous in one's work. It also means that one must not harbor selfish or greedy motives in performing any task

---

[11] R.T. Rymbai, "Some Aspects of Khasi Religion", in *Khasi Heritage*, ed. by H.R. Kharshiing, Shillong: Seng Khasi, 1989, 112ff.

[12] Ibid., 110ff.

[13] S. Sawian, "Shaphang ka Shongkha Shongman", A lecture at the meeting of *Seng Khasi* (women wing) at Shillong on 18.10. 1995.

or job, so as to cause danger to other beings or to the society. In such labor, there is no place for stealing, deception, corruption, etc.[14]

Altogether, the basic feature of the primal/indigenous religion of the Khasi Pnars has been highlighted in common. It can be seen that the central core of religion is God i.e. the experience and understanding of and relationship with God. Therefore, as stated earlier, various religious elements are, but based on this experience, understanding and relationship. Moreover, religion permeates the different aspects of life as life also belongs to God. Even relation with other parts of creation has its significance in the primal faith and belief in the sense that all are created by God and also are the channel through which humans can contact God and in which God manifests His/Her acts of response to humans. Thus, the theology of the Khasi Pnar religion is wholistic in nature.

Christian Mission among the Khasi Pnars

Christian Mission as understood from an academic viewpoint may be multi-dimensional in character, the fact which indicates that it is required for any church to enter into careful comprehensive understanding in doing its mission. For that, theological understanding of mission has to be properly taken care of, for it has to be engaged in interaction with other faiths; hence, it is the faith or religious matter that it has to primarily deal with. Thus, as L. Pachuau rightly asserted, "In essence a theology of mission is also a theology of religions".[15] Here, appropriate methods, though some may feel unnecessary, are important to be employed for the relevant and satisfactory success of mission especially in connection with inter-faith relation. On the basis of this concept then, we need to critically analyze the process of Christian mission in the Khasi Jaintia context.

Talking about the Church's mission among the Khasi pnars, one cannot do so without looking at its history. The advent of Christianity or Christian mission among the Khasi Pnars[16] started in 19th century A.D. when the Serampore Mission made its attempted to start its mission works in 1813 A.D., in the South Khasi Hills but without bearing much fruit. It was only until Thomas Jones arrived from Wales in 1821 A.D. and settled at Sohra (Cherrapunji) to set up his mission that Christianity started to take root.

---

[14] H.K. Synrem, "Religion of the Khasis", in *Seng Khasi Shispah Snem, 1899-1999, Ka Thup buh Jingkynmaw*, 109-110.

[15] See L. Pachuau, "Trends and Issues in Missiological Methodology", in *Methodological Issues in Theological Disciplines*, ed. by S. Prabhakar, Bangalore: SATHRI, 2002, 104.

[16] For detailed information on the advent and development of Christianity and its mission among the Khasi Pnars, see O.L. Snaitang, *Christianity and Social Change in North East India*, Shillong: Vendrame Institute and Calcutta: Firma KLM Private Ltd., 1993; see also Nalini Natarajan, *The Missionary Among the Khasis*, New Delhi: Sterling Publishers Pvt. Ltd., 1977.

Thomas Jones and his successors launched the Christian mission at Cherrapunji and its surrounding areas where they established preliminary educational centres and institutions, in which members of the community especially the children received education. This missionary venture in terms of education has been of great contribution to the people at large, as many such and other types of institutions were founded subsequently, serving for enhancement of people's education; however, the paper sidelines this, as the focus of discussion is on mission and inter-faith relations, the issue that the missionaries and the Church seemed to have been less concerned with. Alongside education, Christian teachings and principles were incited among native people, the efforts that gained success as some villagers were converted to Christianity. The process of religious conversion thus continues thenceforth. Nevertheless, in striving to win the people to Christianity, the missionaries were totally against the traditional/indigenous faith and inculcated the same mind-set upon the converts, the objective that continues to remain till now. It is on the basis of this purview that we can now discuss for re-evaluation, reformulation and renovation of the condition and task of Christian mission in connection with interfaith relations.

It could be said for sure that the missionaries operated the mission on the ground of normative theology that seemed to have been in line with Western imperialistic orientation upholding and developing an exclusive attitude towards the traditional/indigenous faith/religion.[17] With such an outlook, the missionaries with their exclusive theological perspectives, considered the traditional and religious faith of the Khasi Pnars as false, superstitious, irrational, contaminating, etc. The God in whom they believe was not the true God and all their religious sets and practices were false and sinful. Thus, no proper study or analysis of indigenous faith was necessary to be undertaken nor would any concept or practice related to traditional faith be incorporated for it was feared that the Christians would be contaminated. For the Khasi Pnars, to attain salvation they would have to completely abandon their religious beliefs and practices even renounce their traditional value principles but embrace Christianity.[18] Such a negative understanding and endeavor if analyzed from the viewpoint of theology of religions, brought about a different cropped up theological paradigm, in which God was conceived more as a person living in heaven and is concerned about salvation of the individual human being. God seems

[17] Though some pro-missionaries scholars defended the missionaries as being free from the British Gevernment direction (Cf. O.L. Snaitang, Ibid, 50), some other writers claim that the missionaries were not free from the spirit of imperialism as they operated their mission for the purpose of religious transformation (Cf. P. Tariang, *The Inter Faith Dialogue Between Christianity and Khasi Indigenous Religion*, Shillong: Banshai and Badapbiang, 2003, 3).

[18] Cf. Shobhan Lamare, *Resistant Movement in North East India: The Jaintias of Meghalaya 1860-1863*, New Delhi: Regency Publications, 2001, 50.

to be a conservative divine being who rejects the significant and valuable elements of all other faiths except those of conservative Christian theology. It was such a theological perspective that, erroneously though effectively, distorted and degenerated the nature of the primal faith and alienated all of its values from people's consciousness. It is on this factor that the polarization of religious relations between the Christians and the adherents of the indigenous faith has its background. Hence, sharing for building up a living community and a healthy society from the perspective of common religious principles has been hardly possible; instead, division among members of the community has widened in terms of religious faith.

Moreover, traditionally among the Khasi Pnars, religion as already mentioned, permeates other aspects of life. Therefore, different aspects of life are linked with religious faith. Hence, as in other tribal societies, dichotomy between body and spirit, spiritual and material, etc is impossible.[19] Therefore the value principles, social and cultural practices are associated with religious faith and thus are considered as sacred which should not be taken lightly or irresponsibly. Various parts of life be they individual or social, should be taken care of in accordance with directions of religious faith and principles. This is the reason that made the adherents of traditional religion to be more honest, in some cases, than the converts. So once the religion is ignored or not emphasized, those religious principles and values set forth for various parts of life become loosened. In addition, in contrast to traditional/primal understanding and belief, were the normative and conservative theological and philosophical principles that divide and dichotomize the soul and the body, the spiritual and the material, etc., which the missionaries and the Christians seem to have emphasized more. In this, the converts were led to be more consciously careful and inclined towards the soul or the spiritual aspect without having much concern of other physical or material facets. Such a confrontation between the western based theological principles and the traditional beliefs and practices resulted in the creation of confusion of moral-ethical principles among the Khasi Pnars. It is this kind of implanted understanding and confusion that has caused many problems and challenges in the society as time goes on. Problems that have become hazardous can be mentioned like – threat to identity; social, cultural, political and economic oppressions, injustices and evils; corruption, poverty, degradation of nature, etc., the problems and issues that are at the brink of catastrophe endangering so much the life of the community and of the society as well.[20] As of now, when people, on the one hand are passively attentive to and concerned of their so called spiritual life, on the other hand, they are so carefree in duties

[19] See S. Miri, "Holism in Khasi Religion", in *The Tribes of North East India*, ed. by S. Karotemprel, Calcutta: Firma KLM Private Limited, 1984, 346; See also A .Wati Longchar, *The Traditional Tribal Worldview and Modernity*, Jorhat: ETC, 1995, 6, 27.

[20] B. Sohkhlet, 225 ff.

and behavior of other aspects of life. This in fact, affects generally the quality of life as a whole, subverting the stability of moral-ethical values in the society.

Besides distorting the valuable theological concepts of primal faith, the missionaries and the subsequently established churches created a big gap between the Christians and the traditional believers; they also thwarted the vital implying significance of traditional religious principles worth preserving for sustenance of moral-ethical values relevant for endowing and establishing a better quality of various aspects of life. This phenomenon became the factor that makes the Church to be less concerned about the rise of endangering socio-cultural and moral-ethical problems faced by the community and the society.[21] It is also the same reason that brought about revival movements among the adherents of the primal religion under the umbrella of the organization called *Seng Khasi* and *Seinraij*. Through the works of these organizations the members are taught to revive their traditional beliefs and practices as against the teachings of the missionaries and the Christian churches. Several regular programs have been organized by the organizations where traditional beliefs and practices are lauded but the Christian teachings and churches are spoken against.[22] Thus it worsens the inter-faith relationship.

As highlighted above, if one considers mission from the primal perspectives of the Khasi Jaintia context, one may critically make a statement that the missionaries and the Church initiated the process of mission without taking into consideration the primal theology of religion/faith, a process that did not create a satisfactory concern of establishing the kingdom of God here and now, the kingdom in which the people can live a life of happiness, justice and peace, free from the perilous problems and challenges mentioned above.

---

[21] It is difficult to bring out for discussion each of the problems and challenges in this limited article. It can be mentioned, however, that while the Church has taken the subject of conversion as the main agenda for mission, it does not bother much about checking the rise of evil practices such as corruption, unjust political motivation in different departmental functions of the government, etc. More so, the church is not keen in taking an initiative of addressing awareness of other burning issues like the problem of ecology, a threat to identity, the economic rights of the indigenous people, etc. What it stresses more is the way to heaven assumed to be the eternal home of everyone which an individual is urged to strive for by means of spiritual living in which concern for other aspects of life is less emphasized.

[22] See H.K. Synrem, *Revivalism in Khasi Society*, New Delhi: Sterling Publishers Pvt. Ltd., 1992. 44 ff.

The Need for Inter-Faith Relations – The New Course of Action for Better Mission

In a worsening and deteriorating situation, if Christians and the Church aim to improve their mission, they need to do away with the conservative and negative attitude towards primal faith and start thinking of mission afresh. For the Church in the Khasi and Jaintia Hills, it has to initiate and carry out a number of new ideas and activities. Some of the many primary tasks of mission that can be considered are: firstly, helping people safeguard the identity of the community which seems to has been endangered due to lack of awareness and a negligence of the issue and rapid influx;[23] Perhaps it has to be undertaken rightly and carefully from the right perspective and within the framework of the Indian constitution. Secondly: the need to tackle social and political injustices and many such evils in society. Wrestling with such injustices is a big challenge. Thirdly: Mission service has to be pragmatic to help all those holding responsibility for the enhancement of economic enterprises; this requires proclamation as well as action against corruption and bribery. Fourthly: the task is also to conscientize the people regarding the preservation of nature. It entails creating a sense of awareness of the danger to life if nature is continuously destroyed; in this, knowledge of the sanctity of nature should be imparted among people.

Such a mission would require the interaction with and the assistance of primal faith. Therefore interfaith relations must be prioritized. It should be understood that interfaith relations is the meeting place of both the Christian and Primal faiths from which a theological-spiritual renaissance and a kind of community that is struggling to be born would be consequently produced. Interfaith relations is an issue that needs to be importantly considered, for it is the factor that can ensure reestablishment of unity among members of the community, so as to be able to reciprocally, unanimously and wisely safeguard identity.

The churches in the Khasi and Jaintia hills have never taken interfaith relations into consideration. The issue has never been the concern of the Church. So far, if one talks about interfaith relations as an issue needed for discussion, it would certainly sound as a new unrelated or even an unacceptable issue. The main reason is the understanding that Christianity is always the super-incomparable religion set forth to conquer over others.

---

[23] In one of the sessions of the pre-Edinburg Centenary Celebration consultation held at UTC Bangalore (July, 17-19, 2009), a unanimous understanding is that the tribals, dalits, adivasis or the so called subaltern groups are people struggling to affirm their identity. In the case of the Khasi Pnar community, the issue is more of safeguarding the identity and unifying the community. Nevertheless, this seems to be not the part of mission of the Church in so far as the Church has not taken it into concern. Part of it appears only in one or two theological seminars (for instance, see J.F. Jyrwa, "Theological Education in North East India: Challenges and Prospects", in *Theological Education in North East India, Problems and Prospects*, ed. by B.L. Nongbri, Shillong: JRTS, 2008, 14-16.

Moreover, there is fear that an inter-religious relationship may lead to syncretism, a misunderstanding and decline of evangelism, the reasons that one should not preponderate as one would not be forced to fall into.[24]

So if the Church or the Christians in the Khasi and Jaintia hills are to take up the issue of interfaith relations as a step for better mission, they should first reexamine their attitude in relation to primal religious beliefs, practices and principles. They may also need to review their exclusive claims on behalf of Christ.[25] While living in a society where people of other faiths are our fellow neighbors, it is required for the Church to recognize their rights of belief, and then re-construct a mission theology which has its base on an understanding of how God through and in Jesus Christ relates Him/Herself with the world which is different from God's distinctive divine nature. On these grounds, theological reflection on the same issue can be estimated. Then only can inter-religious relation be progressive so as to draw other faiths into mission. In the Khasi Jaintia context, it does not necessarily mean that the adherents of primal religion should externally or physically be involved in service for mission; it rather means that they share the common religious insights, issues and agendas relevant for the augmentation of mission.

Making interfaith relations possible for the process of the company of other faiths in mission would require interfaith dialogue for it is through dialogue that differences could be resolved by peaceful means.[26] It is also in and through dialogue that sharing of faith experiences and faith values is possible. Dialogue is the relevant factor that can build up mutual understanding where realization of one's weakness and one's problem can be highlighted and bring about a solution. It is also in and through dialogue that religious issues and insights of both the traditions applicable for developing a just and peaceful society can be discerned, discussed and put into practice together. In fact, "dialogue" has been the subject that has enchanted contemporary religious leaders for building interfaith relations. One can note the WCC declaration on dialogue as follows: "We feel able with integrity to assure our partners in dialogue that we come not as manipulators but as genuine fellow pilgrims, to speak with them of what we believe God to have done in Jesus Christ who has gone before us, but whom we seek to meet anew in dialogue."[27] For the Church in this

---

[24] Cf. Vinay Samuel and Chris Sugden, "Dialogue with Other Religions – A Evangelical View", in *The Bible and Theology in Asian Contexts – An Evangelical Perspective on Asian Theology*, ed. by Bong Rin Ro and Ruth Eshenaur, Bangalore: ATA , 1984, 276-281.

[25] Cf. S.J. Smartha, "The Cross and the Rainbow: Christ in a Multi-Religious Culture", in *Christian Faith and Multiform Culture in India*, ed. by Somen Das, Bangalore: United Theological College, 1987, 15.

[26] Srinivas Rao, Preface to Sreenivas Rao, ed. *Interfaith Dialogue and World Community*, Madras: CLS, 1991, iii.

[27] WCC Guidelines on Dialogue, Geneva: WCC, 1979, 11.

conception, dialogue can also lead to an increased understanding of the Universality of Christ by understanding his activity in other religions.[28] The imperatives of dialogue that should be realized in the Khasi Jaintia context may include (1) to understand our neighbors and to know what and why they believe, (2) To enlarge and enliven our own faith, to bring new dimensions and meaning to it as it searches to understand new ways of speaking about truth and relating to reality, (3) it helps us in mutual correction, it breaks down the dividing walls of hostility and helps in enhancing moral-ethical values in the society, enabling both the groups to identify and discuss issues, problems and challenges and to come together for their solution and so help people to become aware of the primary concerns and ensure stability to the community's identity.[29]

To proceed in inter religious dialogue, some of the mentioned religious concepts of primal faith which are similar to Christian teachings can be taken as common insights. For instance, the view of God as one, a God who is the Creator, the All-Powerful, the Omniscient, the Helper, etc, is not different from the Christian theological concept of God. Many other different given titles of God connoting God's attributes are authentic if taken as common theological agenda in dialogue for the purpose of mission. So also is the understanding of the breakdown of the God-human relationship which looks similar to the Christian concept of the human fall, though slight differences may be found. The moral-ethical principles can also be used appropriately as points for dialogue. The three mentioned principles of *Tipbriew-tipblei*, *Tipkur-tipkha* and *kamai ia ka hok* can be considered as divine commandments, the import of which is relevant for good social structure of the Khasi Pnar indigenous faith relevant for constructing a peace and just society. The principles point to an integral relationship between God, humans and even with other creatures; they address the knowledge of one's own life and family which should be just and righteous; hence, they signify the holistic vision of human life and affirm the positive relationship of God, humanity and even nature. Moreover, the ever proneness to observe and follow God's will and God's directions as per the understanding in primal faith serves for correcting the ways of living individually and socially as members of community. The significance of nature is another important facet entrenched in the primal faith worth integrating for missionary venture. As stated earlier, it is vital to have a relationship with nature which stands as viaduct of connection and relationship between God and humans.[30] Such a precious religious insight

---

[28] Vinay Samuel and Chris Sugden, op.cit., 285.

[29] Cf. S.W. Ariarajah, "The Understanding and Practice of Dialogue, Its Nature, Purpose and Variation", in *Faith in the Midst of Faith*, ed. by S.J. Samartha, Geneva:WCC, 1977, 56.

[30] Cf. Wati Longchar., op.cit., 6 (Though Wati Longchar's assertion is generally meant for religious tradition of all the tribes, it is rightly suited with the

should be made known and conscientized to the community as a whole so as to reduce the continuous degradation and exploitation of nature.

In conclusion, it may be reminded again that the Khasi Pnar context as discussed is one where religious negation between one (religious) tradition and another exists psychologically and socially. It is a phenomenon, as simple as it seems to be (in fact not), positing as blockade to development of reciprocal understanding among members of the Khasi Pnar community, hence hindering better progress of mission. If Christianity as claimed by many Christians is the sole religion which can bring unity to the Khasi community and which can make a promise for justice peace and harmony, the question may arise, whether it (Christianity) is aware of the rise of such conflicts caused by its intolerance of and negative attitude towards indigenous/primal religious beliefs? Is it ready to come forward with an inclusive stance and share in dialogue for creating opportunities for mutual understanding and a new relationship with the followers of the primal religion? Is it willing to include and make use of the valuable religious principles and facets of primal faith resources? And isit ready to venture in its mission in the company of other faiths?

---

characteristic of the Khasi Pnar Primal religion too. See also B. Sohkhlet, op.cit., 52-56, 109-119.

Rethinking Mission: Looking from Tribal People's Experience

Wati Longchar

Jubilee is an occasion to thank God for what he has done to us. It is also a *kairos* for the churches and theological communities to look back critically, to discern the prophetic task of the future for greater unity, witness and service. The Jubilee celebration of UTC and Edinburgh – 2010 comes at a moment in history when the whole world is bleeding and life – both human and of nature – is under constant threat from the global market and the Empire. This has led to a situation of unrest and fear/terror across the world leading to the undermining and denial of the principles of self-assertion, self-reliance and mutual co-operation. Hence, Jubilee is an occasion to revision of our participation in God's mission.

Looking Back the Past

> The modern colonizer … believed in the superiority of his religion, race, economy and culture. This superiority called upon the colonizer to bear the vocation of converting and ordering the world toward his own identity. Such an ideology was grounded in the belief of modernity, Christianity, and industrial advancement. The colonized… on the other hand, were imbued with the belief that their own religion, race, economy, and culture were backward.
>
> Musa Dube

Edinburgh 1910 was convened to challenge and correct the denominational oriented mission. However, the expansionist missiological motif was reiterated. Mission was perceived as proclamation of "the gospel to all creatures, to gather the ignorant and godless from every corner to the earth, and to lead those in deplorable error to the flock of Christ and to the recognition of the shepherd and Lord of the flock."[1] The whole mission enterprise was understood in terms of planting and the organization of the Christian Church among non-Christians. The conference also lauded the achievements of science and technology as evidence of God's providence for the furtherance of mission. Improved means of communication and

[1] Karl Muller, *Mission Theology: An Introduction* (Netherlands: Stely Press, 1987), 30.

transport was lauded for reaching the `unevangelized world'.[2] M.P. Joseph recalled that the majority of the missionary enterprises at that time was undertaken with the zeal of promoting the western scientific rationality informed by the European Enlightenment.[3] Such a campaign of the new rationality against the traditional wisdom of the natives was conceived as a civilizational imperative and thus it was carried out with utmost earnestness.[4] M.P. Joseph further moves on to argue that "the new scientific rationality was presented as the only panacea for growth and prosperity."[5] The conference reiterated that the colonial expansion was the providence of God to take the good news to heathen lands.

The Edinburgh 1910 conference was held under the patronage of colonial powers. Some generals of the colonial administration were present in the conference signifying the mutual importance of the mission agenda and the colonial project. In the Edinburgh conference, from among the 1200 participants, only three came from the people in the periphery. The people who sent greetings to the Edinburgh conference included the King of England, the President of the US and other colonial heads. *Oikoumene* in Edinburgh pretended that Christian unity is possible even without removing and transforming the structures of oppression and the exploitation by the colonial regime. In fact, the Edinburgh conference co-opted the poor and marginalized such as the tribal people into the larger scheme of the western empire. As we celebrate 100 years of the Mission Conference, we need to challenge and repent of our past prejudices and partiality, and dream for a wider unity, witness and service.

Christian Mission, Colonialism and Disorientation of Tribal People

The spread of Christianity coincided with colonial expansion. This resulted in suspicion, disorientation and an identity crisis. We have evidence that the colonial powers such as the Portuguese, the Dutch and the British not only abused power but that the churches among others, benefited immensely from such abuse of power. Possession of lands in prime locations in Indian cities speaks of the privileged status of the Church with colonial powers.[6] Speaking about the relationship between colonial power and Christian missionaries, Arthur Jeyakumar, a noted historian, writes,

> In obedience to the command of the Pope, the Portuguese colonizers got engaged in missionizing their territories in India by a diverse way.... The

[2] J.P. Joseph, "Revisiting the Edinburgh Conference in the Context of Globalization" in *Witness in Context: Essays in Honor of Eardley Mendis*, ed. by Monica J. Melanchthon and George Zachariah (Tiruvalla: Chrisitave Shitya Samith)

[3] Ibid., 156.

[4] Ibid., 157.

[5] Ibid., 157.

[6] Rienzie Perera, "Christian Identity in a Multi-Religious Context" in *CTC Bulletin*, Vo. XXIV, Nos. 1-2, April-August 2008, 51.

> Portuguese administration in Goa offered jobs to Christians only. It was decreed that public offices could be held by Christians alone. So, some of the Indians in those territories embraced Christianity for the sake of government jobs. Christian faith was spread by direct evangelism too. At the same time there was forced conversion too. The Portuguese government prohibited in its territories the public worship of Hindu and Muslims. Moreover only Christians were given the power to own lands and possessions. Others were asked to leave the area or to embrace Christianity. Those who had their ancestral property, preferred to join the Church rather than leave the place....[7]

This speaks clearly of the use and misuse of power.

Though in some contexts, missionaries opposed some of the colonial government's policies, we have clear evidence that missionaries also functioned as colonial agents. In some places, missionaries were paid by the colonial government.[8] The military was obliged to protect the missionaries from any hostile people's resistance to evangelization, and the missions were to produce part of the sustenance for the regional military government. As a result, some scholars have even pointed out critically that, "missionaries were there not for advocating a faith but for keeping imperialism alive."[9] This is the reason why the Church is identified even today as an arm of western imperialism.

The colonial power and Christian missions (irrespective of the denominations or missionary societies they came from) considered themselves "superior" in terms of religion, race, economy and culture and they consistently maintained an exclusive and negative attitude towards the traditional religions and cultures. They considered the `others' as primitive, uncultured, uncivilized and savages. "Their description of the people ranges from people with no culture to those of an inferior culture, life style and way of life. Their religion was derided as demonic, superstitious and evil."[10] The people's characters and virtues also viewed negatively and

---

[7] D. Arthur Jeyakumar, *History of Christianity in India: Selected Themes* (Revised and Enlarged) (Madurai: Author, 2007), 20.

[8] For example, William Pettigrew's was a government appointed school inspector while at the same time working as a missionary in Manipur state. Recognizing Pettigrew's reputation among the hill people, the colonial government sought for his help in the recruitment process and he did oblige with the request. Pettigrew was instrumental in recruiting many hill people to serve in the Labor Crops for the Allied forces during the First World War. See to further details, Yangkahao Vashum, "Colonialism, Missionaries and Indigenous: A Critical Apprisal' in *Journal of Tribal Studies,* Vol. XII, No. 2, July-December 2007, 1-22.

[9] Quoted in K. Suresh Singh, ed., *The Tribal Situation in India* (Simla: Indian Institute of Advanced Study, 1972), 620.

[10] Yangkahao Vashum, "Revisiting Tribal/Indigenous Theology and Its Theological Methodology", a paper presented at consultation on "Revisiting Tribal and Dalit Theologies and Their Theological Methodologies" Centre for Dalit/Subaltern Studies, New Delhi, from 14-16 March, 2008, 8.

were held in the lowest esteem.[11] This superiority complex justified the slavery system, exploitation, war, domination and replacement of the native culture with the white culture and saw cultural conversion as a prerequisite to conversion to Christianity. Such an ideology was grounded in the beliefs of modernity, Christianity and rapid industrial advancement. The colonized people, like the tribals and dalits, who have been suffering under the caste system further led to an internalization of native inferiority and the idealization of the white culture and religion. Even today many people (including tribal people) think that their own religion, economy and culture are inferior and backward. Hence, "Conversion" was justified., George Tinker[12] noted four cultural disorientations in the process of conversion:

First, the converts were separated from their native village and relatives in new communal enclosures; that is, the native persons were removed from their former mode of existence.

Second, once converted and relocated in the mission compound or in a new village, the converts were permanently proscribed from rethinking their conversion and returning to their own homes. In some contexts, the missionaries had military assistance at hand to hunt down fugitives and return them to their missions for discipline.

Third, converts were committed to a rigorous regimen of work to support the mission, the missionaries and their obligation to the military government.

Fourth, converts gave up all aspects of self-governance to live under the strict and authoritarian governance of the missionary priests.

Furthermore, the perception of cultural and intellectual superiority motivated missionaries to promote western scientific rationality informed by the European enlightenment. This campaign for a new rationality against the traditional wisdom of the natives was conceived as a civilizational imperative and carried out with utmost earnestness. The new scientific rationality was presented as the only norm for growth and prosperity.[13]

The educational ministry of the missionaries had the most significant impact on the life of the people. Arthur Jeyakumer writes:

> It not only enabled them to read and write, it also sowed the seed of nationalism. It started a renaissance. It paved the way for reforms in the society. Missionaries by opening their educational institutions for everybody irrespective of caste, creed, colour, or status began to revolutionize in more than one sense.[14]

---

[11] Ibid.

[12] George E. Tinker, *Missionary Conquest: The Gospel and Native American Cultural Genocide* (Minneapolis: Fortress Press, 1993), 48-49.

[13] M.P. Joseph, "Be Witness to Life: Towards a People's Concept of Mission" in *Re-routing Mission: Towards a People's Concept of Mission and Diakonia* (Tiruvalla: CCA-URM, 2004), 11.

[14] *History of Christianity in India,* 30-31.

Mission schools were used as instrument for civilizing local people, a process which systematically integrated the tribal people into imperial/colonial structures.[15] Gangmumei Kamei observed that modern education was "designed to inculcate European liberal ideas, literature, and science in the Indian mind, and to produce educated persons who could be conveniently employed to run the colonial administration."[16] Even if the missionaries did not consider themselves agents of colonial powers, they participated, wittingly or not, in advancing the colonial project.

The education process, medical practice, reduction of languages into written form and the production of first literary texts, the introduction of new housing, hygiene, clothing, time, and history led to a complete disorientation of traditional cultural structures of existence that had given a people a sense of holistic and communal integrity. No longer did the life of the people revolve around the soil-centered culture, but revolved around church services, prayer meetings, revival camps, Christian Endeavor, etc. This process had contributed to the loss of identity and spirituality rooted in the soil. To conclude, I quote the statement of Indigenous People Conference met in Bagiuo,

> In our history, we recognize that some of Christian missionaries have done immense work for the liberation of indigenous people. They were the first to open mission school, printing press, hospital, translation work and many others. Recognizing their genuine interest in the well-being of the oppressed people and commitment to bring the people to the gospel message of salvation, many oppressed people converted to Christian faith searching for a more dignified life. While acknowledging many dedicated and selfless works rendered by the missionaries, we are recognized that the church has been an ally of empires in the marginalization, oppression, exploitation and even obliteration of indigenous peoples' communities. In the name of God, Christian missionaries have demonized indigenous cultures and traditions forcing it to hide and, consequently, robbing the younger generations of its own heritance. Christian faith and churches became the Trojan horse of empires, and to this day continues to be an instrument of subjugation of indigenous people's communities. The church has consistently played her role as the cultural partisan in our colonization, consistently breaking our will to resist subjugation and domination, and tragically standing in silence in the face of the destruction of our habitat, our livelihood and culture.[17]

---

[15] Ward Churchill observed that "since schooling was brought to non-Europeans as part of empire … it was integrated into the effort to bring indigenous peoples into imperial/colonial structures." See his book *Since Predator Came* (Colorado: Aigis Publications, 1995), 245.

[16] *Ethnicity and Social Change: An Anthology of Essays* (Shillong: Pounglau Gangmei, 2002), 138.

[17] Statement of "Ecclesial and Social Vision of Indigenous Peoples", 21-26 October, 2008, Baguio, Philippines.

Approaches to Mission

Huang Poho, a Taiwanese theologian, writes;

> The traditional views of mission history that centered on ecclesiology saw mission as a strategy to expand a church's territory and made people into objects of missionary activity. Human beings were "commodified" for the sake of mission programs. Christian mission derived from this historical view expresses the mentality of conquest. More precisely, it is in view shaped by a religious colonization history.[18]

The perception of cultural and intellectual superiority of the white led to engagement through three types of mission practices. Such approaches make it impossible to engage in meaningful dialogue with other faiths.

a) *Civilizing mission:* The issues have already been noted above. During the colonial era, Christian mission was primarily understood as "civilizing people". The language was absolute and exclusivist. The task of the Christian mission was seen in terms of demolishing native cultures and establishing Christianity. Often military and warfare terms such as "army", "advance", "attack". "battle", "campaign, "crusade", etc.,were used as motivational means for missions. Even words such as "pagan", "darkness" and "heathen" have been used to refer to our friends, relatives, neighbours and other faiths. In the process of aggressive evangelization "local people abandoned their own cultures and betrayed their countries in order to follow a foreign mission. Following Christ in practice meant "accepting the existence of colonialism and the abolition of local cultures and languages."[19] The civilizing mission approach led many tribal people to lose their land, their mother tongue, cultural and social structure. Today the Euchee language is spoken only by 3 persons worldwide. More than 500 languages in Australia disappeared due to colonial policies. This attitude contributed to carrying out mission in an exclusive way, refusing dialogue with people of other faiths, and of obsessing with the expansion of the community in a kind of militant evangelistic approach.[20] The aggressive attitude had kept and continues to keep the Indian churches away from the mainstream of Indian culture and political life as a community. The church is seen as a stranger by many people.

b) *Charity mission:* The charity mission is an empire model of doing mission. It is seen in the form of gifts of food and clothes for the poor, consolation to the sick and other humanitarian services. Charity oriented mission was the product and extension of industrialization in Europe and North America during the 19th century. Charitable mission creates subject-

---

[18] Huang Poho, "From Galilee to Tainan", in *ATESEA Occasional Paper No 15* (Tainan: ATESEA, 2005), 29.

[19] Josef P. Widyatmadja, *Rerouting Mission: Towards a People's Concept of Mission and Diakonia* (Tiruvalla: CCA, 2004), 23.

[20] Huang Po-ho, *A Theology of Self-Determination* (Tainan: Tainan Theological Seminary, 1996), 28.

object relationship between the giver and the recipients and helps to maintain the status quo based on unjust power relations. It is seen as "reproducing dependency relationships and failing to account for the subjectivity of the poor and needy."[21] It also fails to restore and recreate the identity of the people with justice and dignity.[22] The people of other faiths see it as a ploy to attract the poor and needy into the church and eventually to baptize them. Poho is critical of charity approach mission.

c) *Development mission*: Mission was/is understood as developing the underdeveloped people, a dominant model till today. It identified the problem as one of poverty and malnutrition, and even that diseases such as HIV and AIDS were the result of `underdevelopment', lack of skills and resources and therefore it is a mission imperative for the churches to help the poor communities around the world to `develop'. Development hence assumed the nature of a missiological witness of the charity and compassion of Christ expressed through the Body of the Church. Even the communities and nations who were critical of the development paradigm were brought under the grand design of the capitalist development ideology through the committed and uncritical work of the church bodies.[23] Theological assumptions regarding unity, freedom, humanization informed by the values of self-hood, democracy and more directly development were symbolic of the trapping in the project of modernity.[24] The understanding of mission as "developing" slowly reduced the churches to NGOs who function as an implementing agency of the projects designed by those who hold the capital. Many churches have reduced themselves to local agents or sub-contractors for development assistance from western economies, banks and governments, to the communities of the poor.

Are they not mere replicas of the mission agencies of the colonial period? The churches have not moved away from such mission priorities. We need a paradigm shift in our mission.

Mission in Context

The CCA Jubilee declaration underlines the reality of Asia, thus;

> The defining reality of the socio-political milieu is globalization, a political construct of the predominance of the market and speculative portfolio-capital. This reality coupled with the *war on/of terror* leads to the escalation of violence resulting in militarization, plundering of earth's resources, and oppression of marginalized sections within communities such as the women, children, indigenous peoples and the poor in each nation. This hegemony of the Empire that creates a collusion of the Market, State and Religion breaks

[21] Josef P. Widyatmadja, op.cit. 99.
[22] Ibid., 99
[23] M.P. Joseph, *They Left by another Road: Rerouting Mission and Ecumenism* (Chiangmai: CCA, 2007), 215.
[24] Ibid., 214.

> down relationship between individuals, groups, communities, countries, and amongst all of God's creation – humanity and nature alike.[25]

Further, it elaborates on the current situation of ecumenical movement, thus:

> Churches and ecumenical bodies have often departed from being a movement of ordinary people and from siding with the poor. Such a position has rendered churches and ecumenical bodies to being mere associations creating self-justifying structures that ease the process of being co-opted as the agencies of the Empire. Self-dependence, Resource sharing, and Resource Management, as much as the spirit of peoples' sovereignty and moral sensitivity have become euphemistic clichés, or at best the dream and not reality that it defines.[26]

How can people celebrate life in a situation of economic depravity, corruption and the misuse and abuse of political power? How can God's mission be done in a situation where the rich and powerful decide who is to live and who is to die?

Today we realize that peace and justice have remained distant hopes and dreams. The situation of the poor has turned from bad to worse. The violence of cultural nationalism against the tribal people is on the increase. The attack of Christian in Orissa during Christmas celebration in 2007 and continuing attacks of tribal Christians in Kandhamal and other part of India are concrete examples. The anti-conversion ordinance in some of the states in India are examples of institutional forms of violence, inflicted by evangelists of the gospel of cultural nationalism, genocide and ethnic cleansing of certain communities of India today and are expressions of direct forms of violence of cultural nationalism.[27]

The global market turns human beings and their cultural activities and earth's resources into commodities for profit. The weak, namely the migrant workers, farmers, consumers, small entrepreneurs and the whole eco-system are the victims of globalization. The poor and their resources have become mere sources of raw materials, cheap labor, and food needs. The unjust financial system, ever increasing ideology of consumerism, materialism, individualism, competition and greed erode life-affirming values, fragment communities and increase poverty. The poor are deprived of their rights to celebrate life in the midst of all those problems.

We need to discern God's mission amidst all those problems and challenges. To be relevant to the context, mission priorities in India have to be life-centered, seeking ways to establish peace and justice, overcome violence while affirming the rich contributions of pluralistic communities

---

[25] "Jubilee Declaration on "Rerouting Mission and Ecumenism in Asia", The Christian Conference of Asia, March 4-8, 2007, Parapat, Indonesia, 1.

[26] Ibid., 2

[27] George Mathew Nalunnakkal, "Mission as if People Mattered: An Indian Perspective" in *Re-routing Mission: Towards a People's Concept of Mission* (Tiruvalla: CCA, 2004), 98.

and traditions. Therefore, the future of the Church in India lies in its ability to create counter movements against all these oppressive powers and structures. This counter movement is possible through strengthening and building grassroots or local social movements.

Discerning from the Past

John England has pointed out that the Christian presence in Asia goes back to the 2nd century and mission was understood as a common sharing and respect of one another[28]. He further argues that during the first 15 centuries of Christianity in Asia, there are clear signposts of Christian's engagement in various secular vocations. Although they were not critical of caste oppression and patriarchy, there were courageous missionary endeavours, monastic movements, long traditions of state service, education and medical care, a mutual beneficial co-existence with neighbours of other faiths, survival despite repression and persecution, creative biblical interpretation, theology and spirituality.[29] The record of pre-1500 shows a clear signpost of wholistic mission. Christian communities in many countries at that time not only co-existed peacefully with those of other faiths, but also happily exchanged understandings of religious faith and life. For example, Buddhist terms and imageries were used freely to present New Testament teaching. There is also clear evidence of Christian influence in Mahayana teachings. From the earliest period in Persia (pre-400 C.E.), until the later history of Mongol ascendancy (pre-1400 C.E), Christians played key roles in various professions, and their commitment to all that promoted people's welfare is widely recorded. In all these periods, there was a "non-institutional" Christian presence which was authentically rooted in secular worlds and a new pattern of Christian community life, study, and prayer.[30] It is imperative that we revisit these early traditions in our attempt to re-root mission in our context.

Looking Ahead to the Future

a) *Affirming Life*: Christian witness and mission is about bringing healing, wholeness, and new life into the lives of individuals, communities and nations. Any mission that builds barriers, divides the world into the 'saved' and 'unsaved', that makes people narrower, that alienates neighbours, that promotes enmity and rivalry, that is not built on self-giving, is not mission. It is a counter witness to God. It betrays God, and in the Christian context,

---

[28] John C. England, "Historical Notes on Mission and Ecumenism in Asia" in *They Left by Another Road,* 39-42.

[29] Ibid., 40-49.

[30] Ibid.

is alien to the spirit and message of Christ.[31] Breaking down barriers, seeking justice and dignity for all, building community, enabling reconciliation and peace among all peoples are at the heart of mission.

b) *Transforming life*: The churches in India need a transformative mission. Mission in Christ's way is God's mission amidst people in pain is the one which is transformative. It is giving protection and justice for the weak in the house, in the community, in the nation and also in all creation. This is not a mission by conquest but mission according to the way of the cross. Mission amidst people in pain means fellowship and peace among communities and nations. This cannot be attained without justice. It involves struggle for the transformation of a social system that ensures social, economic, political and cultural justice. This peace and fellowship cannot be realized when people still have to struggle to meet their basic needs. Jesus was able to bring justice through organizing people's movement. "Only when people are able to organize themselves for social justice can the oppressed regain their dignity and help secure justice and dignity for all."[32] The churches have to take the position of, and for the poor and become the voice of the poor and exploited.

(c) *Building solidarity*: The World Mission Conference held in Melbourne affirmed that

> There is no evangelism without solidarity; there is no Christian solidarity that does not involve sharing the knowledge of the Kingdom which is God's promise to the poor of the earth. There is here double credibility test: Kingdom to the poor of the earth is a caricature of the Gospel; but Christian participating in the struggles for justice which does not point towards the provision of the Kingdom also makes a caricature of a Christian understanding of justice.[33]

Solidarity is not token partnership with its economic and political agenda; it is not a life of passive indifference but an active and critical engagement in people's concrete needs. Genuine solidarity encompasses interreligious solidarity. To be in solidarity means to be one with another, to identify with the other, to feel strongly for the pain and hurts of the others, to share the burden of the other as if it were one's own. Solidarity implies the self-emptying mindset and attitude of Christ in an effort to lift up those who are downtrodden, oppressed and dehumanized.[34]

d) *Affirming the Integrity of Creation:* The land, the mountain, the desert, the river and forest have been the home and life sustaining source of

---

[31] S. Wesley Arirajah, "Asian Christian Theological Task in the Midst of Other Religious Traditions", in *Visioning New Life Together Among Asian Religions,* eds., Daniel S. Thiagarajah and Wati Longchar (Hong Kong: CCA, 2002), 21.

[32] Ibid., 104.

[33] *Mission and Evangelism: An Ecumenical Affirmation* (Geneva: World Council of Churches, 1085), 58.

[34] Hope S. Antone, "New Paradigm Concepts of Mission" in *CTC Bulletin*, Vol. XXIV, No. 3, December 2008, 58.

tribal people for centuries. But today they are being misused and raped to meet the growing demands of consumerism. Forest and fishing resources are depleted for quick profits. Mining companies rape resources with little regard to the environmental and social costs. The sustaining power of the earth for nurturing life is being destroyed. The whole planet is under threat and climactic change is the biggest side effect of our world today; a world which we see in a serious and complex crisis. Today one cannot deny the fact that land and resources have become the greatest single cause of strife and warfare between nations and people of different communities within a nation. Resources are hoarded by a few and denied to others. Instead of being used as an opportunity for mutual sharing, as of an unmerited gift of God, resources have become a matter of conquest and seizure, a tool of oppression, greed and power. We need to affirm…

- Community over individual interests,
- A logic of relationality or interconnection between every living being, even the inanimate living as rocks, sites, etc,
- Simplicity of function over luxury,
- Respectful and reciprocal logic and use of natural resources,
- Sharing over accumulation of wealth,
- Alternative definitions of privilege, power and prestige.

Subaltern Movements: Insights from Interfaith Dialogue

T. Swamiraju

This is, indeed, a great privilege given me to work along with the study group of "Inter-Faith Relations for Subaltern Cultic Traditions and New Movements", and write on "Subaltern Movements: Insights for Inter-Faith Relations" in view of the centenary celebrations of both Edinburgh 1910 and particularly the formation of the United Theological College (UTC) as the first ecumenical theological institute in India. In the history of Christian Church, 1910 is not only a watershed but also the beginning of the modern ecumenical movement which, in fact, brought about drastic changes in Christian theological thinking and ecclesiological activities. The United Theological College has historical significance due to its formation in 1910 at Bangalore in India, sometime just before the first World Missionary Conference was held in Edinburgh, Scotland in the same year opening the gates for ecumenical thinking. UTC is really a symbol of a wider ecumenism, which has been working for the unity and integrity promoting inter-faith relations in the pluralistic context in India by bringing about awareness and producing scholars all through the past century from its very inception. It is more appropriate to work on inter-faith relations keeping both these historically remarkable events: Edinburgh – 1910 and UTC formation while observing the centenary celebrations to praise God for His theological guidance and divine leadership all through the years of this theological and ecumenical journey.

This article is divided into three sections: the first section deals with conceptual clarifications of key terms; the second one focuses on some important subaltern movements and cults; and the final section investigates insights for inter-faith relations particularly from subaltern cultic practices. At the outset let me express the theatrical difficulty of this topic. The main focus of this topic is on insights for inter-faith relations from the perspective of subaltern movements and cultic traditions, but, as per my little knowledge, many subaltern movements originated and further evolved as the movements of "liberation" rather than "dialogical" or "inter-faith" concerns. However, there are some insights that can be investigated for inter-faith relations and dialogue from the perspective of the subaltern movements and cultic traditions of our country. It is true, perhaps, subaltern people, especially Dalits have a good opportunity of having inter-faith relations and dialogical occasions with upper castes only during the time of subaltern-cultic traditional practices rather than classical Hindu religious cults, which indeed provides insights for inter-faith relations.

Conceptual clarifications: "Subaltern" and "**inter-faith relations**" are two important key terms of this article, which perhaps, need some clarification for better understanding. "Inter-faith dialogue" or "inter-faith relations" is a familiar term to many ecumenical Christians, but many do not access the meaning and use of "subaltern" with much clarity. "Subaltern" is a term that commonly refers to the perspective of persons from regions and groups outside of the hegemonic power structure. In the 1970's the term began to be used as a reference to colonized people in the South Asian subcontinent. "Subaltern" is now regularly used as a term in history, anthropology, sociology and literature.[1] The Oxford Dictionary gives the meaning of the term "subaltern" as "an officer below the rank of captain, esp. a second lieutenant (to its noun and adjective forms), and also uses 1) of inferior rank, 2) particular, not universal (to its adjective form)".[2] A subaltern is a military term for a junior officer literally meaning "subordinate". Subaltern is used to describe commissioned officers below the rank of captain and generally comprises the various grades of lieutenant.[3] Antonio Gramsci, an Italian Marxist, popularized this term while writing to counter Fascism during the 1920's and 1930's, and he substituted the term for 'proletarian class,'[4] possibly as a codeword in order to get his writings past prison censors, while others believe his usage to be more nuanced and less clear cut.[5]

A group of Indian scholars made this term popular and made it the focal point of research, investigation, critical scholarship and publication through their Subaltern Studies. The Subaltern Studies group published nine volumes on South Asian history and society, particularly from the "subaltern perspective" during 1982-1996. From then onwards this term has attracted the attention of many researchers and scholars especially of social scientists and theologians. Ranjit Guha explains further the meaning of this term:

> The word 'subaltern'...stands for the meaning as given in the Concise Oxford Dictionary, that is, 'of inferior rank'. It will be used... as a name for the

---

[1] Gyan Prakash, "Subaltern Studies as Postocolonial Criticism," *The American Historical Review,* Vol. 99, No.5, December, 1994, 1475-1490, particularly 1476.

[2] Judy Pearsall and Bill Trumble (eds.), *The Oxford English Reference Dictionary,* Oxford University Press, Oxford, 1995, 1436.

[3] Retrieved from "http://en.wikipedia.org/wiki/Subaltern

[4] Cf. Sathianathan Clarke, *Dalits and Christianity: Subaltern Religion and Liberation Theology in India,* Oxford University Press, Delhi, 1998, 6

[5] Cf. Stephen Morton, "The Subaltern: Genealogy of a concept," in Gayatri Spivak, *Ethics, Subalternity and the Critique of Postocolonial Reason,* M.A: Polity, Malden, 2007, 96-97. Retrieved from "http://en.wikipedia.org/wiki/Subaltern (postcolonialism)"

general attitude of subordination in South Asian Society whether this is expressed in terms of class, caste, age, gender and office or in any other way.[6]

We need to understand this not only from the social aspect but also from the religious point of view, particularly it's relation to 'religion'. The term 'subaltern' is very generally used by scholars for the 'Dalits' point of view, especially when focusing their attention on oppressive structures of "caste" in the Indian context. I agree with Ranjit Guha about the multi-dimensional reality of this term as "class, caste, age, gender and office" discrimination or categorization, but I will focus my attention on one aspect of "caste" discrimination, which has divided people in India as "superior and inferior" or "touchable and untouchable" or "upper and lower castes". This article mainly focuses on "caste dimension of subaltern people". Sathianathan Clark remarks that "The subordination and subjection that marks the life of Dalits in India bring them into the contours of a particularly contextual assembly of subalternity"[7] Oliver Mendelshon and Marika Vieziany express a similar opinion: "Untouchables (Dalits) have retained their identity as a subordinated people within Indian society, and by this we mean to identify a condition that is far more severe than merely being at the bottom of an inevitable hierarchy".[8]

The term "subaltern" is used in postcolonial theory. The exact meaning of the term in current philosophical and critical usage is disputed. Some thinkers use it in a general sense to refer to marginalized groups and the lower classes – a person rendered without agency by his or her social status.[9] Others, such as Gayatri Chakravorty Spivak argues that subaltern is not:

> just a classy word for oppressed, for other, for somebody who's not getting a piece of the pie....In postcolonial terms, everything that has limited or no access to the cultural imperialism is subaltern – a space of difference. Now who would say that's just the oppressed? The working class is oppressed. It's not subaltern.... Many people want to claim subalternity. They are the least interesting and the most dangerous. I mean, just by being a discriminated-against minority on the university campus, they don't need the word 'subaltern'.... They should see what the mechanics of the discrimination are. They're within the hegemonic discourse wanting a piece of the pie and not

[6] Ranjit Guha (ed.), *Subaltern Studies I: Writings on South Asian History and Society*, Oxford University Press, New Delhi, 1982, vii, quoted in Sathianathan Clark, *loc.cit.*

[7] *Ibid.* 7.

[8] Oliver Mendelsohn and Marika Vicziany, "The Untouchables" in *The Rights of Subordinated People*, Oliver Mendelsohn and Upendra Baxi (eds.), Oxford University Press, New Delhi, 1994, 115.

[9] Refer Young, Robert J.C., *Postcolonialism: A Very Short Introduction,* Oxford University Press, New York, 2003.

being allowed, so let them speak, use the hegemonic discourse. They should not call themselves subaltern.[10]

In several essays, Homi Bhabha, a key thinker within postcolonial thought, emphasizes the importance of social power relations in his working definition of 'subaltern' groups as "oppressed, minority groups whose presence was crucial to the self-definition of the majority group: subaltern social groups were also in a position to subvert the authority of those who has hegemonic power."[11] Here, the term subaltern is used to denote marginalized and oppressed people(s) specifically struggling against hegemonic globalization.

The terms "subaltern" and "dali" are used as synonyms in general by many scholars and theologians in their recent writings.[12] Yes, there are similarities between these two terms, but "dalit" is the term much popularized in the Indian context by Indian Christian theologians, religious scholars and social activists of several dalit movements of the recent past. Both terms indicate subjectivity – objectivity and superior – inferior differences between people and their faiths, religions, traditions and so on. Simultaneously this term is used for people and religion of lower class/caste and called subaltern people and their religion – subaltern/dalit religion; hence, we are identifying now the distinctiveness of dalit/subaltern religion/faith, which is distinctively different from that of the so called upper castes religion. There are several movements now in protest against low class/caste people and also against gender discrimination. Hence, dalit protest movements came into existence fighting against the oppressive social hierarchical structures and inhuman attitudes of the dominant sections.

The second important concept is "**inter-faith relations**", which is the outcome of the ecumenical movement that began from the World Missionary Conference held at Edinburgh in 1910. This ecumenical movement, indeed, brought many changes in Christian ecclesiological

---

[10] Leon de Kock, "Interview with Gayatri Chakravorty Spivak: New Nation Writers Conference in South Africa," *A Review of International English Literature,* 23 (3) 1992, 29-47.

[11] Refer "Unsatisfied: Notes on Vernacular Cosmopolitanism," in *Text and Nation: Cross-Disciplinary Essays on Cultural and National Identities*, eds., Laura Garcia-Moreno and Peter C. Pfeiffer, SC: Camden House, Columbia, 1996, 191-207 and "Unpacking my library....again," in *The Post-Colonial Question: Common Skies, Divided Horizons,* eds., Iain Chambers, Lidia Curti, Routledge, New York, 1996, 210.

[12] For more information on the use of the term 'dalit' and it's meaning, for example, refer Sathianathan Clark, o*p.cit.,* T. Swami Raju, *The Study of Religion: Methods and Perspectives*, BTESSC/SATHRI, Bangalore, 2004, especially fourth chapter on "Distinctiveness of Dalit Folk Religion" 135-163; T. Swami Raju, *Vira Cult in Folk Religion of Guntur District: A Dalit Perspective*, ISPCK, New Delhi, 2005, 12f, 79f, particularly chapter 5, 249-315.

relations not only within inter-denominational circles, but also with the people of other faiths, thus, paving a better way for "inter-faith/religious dialogue" bringing about awareness of the oneness of common humanity irrespective of religion, faith, class, caste, gender, color, racial, national, official discrimination. We thank God for opening our eyes through this ecumenical movement to realize His wider love and concern for all people. Since 1910 inter-faith relations and inter-faith dialogue have become a common theme for all ecumenical conferences and a positive change is evidenced in place of exclusivist attitudes towards other faiths, not only among Protestant Christians, but also Roman Catholics and Evangelicals.[13]

The importance of 'dialogue' is in its potential to improve better inter-faith or inter-religious relations in a pluralistic context i.e., multi-faith or multi-religious contexts such as in Asia or in India. Ecumenical movement has been given much importance in promoting harmonious relations between people of different religious/faith backgrounds. Inter-faith dialogue is a kind of verbal communication and mutual sharing of religious experiences between people of different faiths in an attitude of mutual trust and love for the purpose of mutual learning and enrichment and cooperation in the task of social change.[14] Several debates in ecumenical councils since 1910 have focused their attention on the importance and urgency of 'dialogue with people of different faiths' in order to promote "better harmonious inter-faith relations" and have drafted guidelines and programs on this aspect.[15] But no one so far attempted to investigate

---

[13] For detailed information see, for instance, T. Swami Raju, *Christian Responses to Plurality of Religion*, BTESSC/SATHRI, Bangalore, 2006, 70-103; and in Telugu language T. Swami Raju, *Bahulamatha Bhartadesemulo Kristhava Sakshyam,* Telugu Theological Literary Board, Hyderabad, 2006, 101-150.

[14] Cf. A. Haque, *Mission and Dialogue in the New Millennium*, ISPCK, Delhi, 1999, 1, quoted from "Participants' Report", *Current Dialogue*, 26, June, 1994, 53. This is a report of the Consultation on "The Theology of Religion" held in Baar, Switzerland, on September 3-8, 1993.

[15] More information on dialogue is available now in printed form, for example, refer Jan S.J. Kerkhofs, *Modern Mission Dialogue and Practice,* Ecclesia Press, Shannon, 1969; Hellencruetz, *Dialogue and Community: Ecumenical issues in inter-religious relationships,* WCC, Geneva, 1977; *Guidelines on Dialogue with people of living Faiths and Ideologies*, WCC, Geneva, 1979; S.J. Samartha, *Courage for Dialogue: Ecumenical issues in inter-religious relationships*, Orbis Books, New York, 1982; Arnulf Camps, *Partners in Dialogue: Christianity and Other Religions*, Orbis Books, New York, 1983; Jathanna C.D. (ed.), *Christian Concern for Dialogue in India*, CSI Karnataka Central Diocese, Bangalore, 1987; David Tracy, *Dialogue with the Other: The Inter-Religious Dialogue*, W.M. Eerdmans Publishing Co., Grand Rapids, 1990; J.R. Chandran (ed.), *Third World Theologies in Dialogue*, EATWOT, Bangalore, 1991; Henry Thompson, *World Religions in Dialogue: Cooperating to transform Society,* ISPCK, Delhi, 1993 and there are several articles published in theological journals and periodicals, for instance, T.K. Thomas, "Dialogue as Presence" in *Religion and Society*, Vol. 4, No. 2, 1967, 38-47; Felix Wilfred, "Liberating Dialogue: An Indian Perspective" in

insights for dialogue and inter-faith relations from the subaltern perspective; hence, there is a need for special research in this area to help unearth several aspects helpful to promoting better inter-faith relations. This article is a very brief attempt in this regard.

Subaltern Movements and Cultic Traditions

There are several movements and cultic traditions developed in the history of religious traditions in India related to subaltern perspective either directly or indirectly. Atheistic movements like Charvaka, Lokayata, Jainism and Buddhism developed against the oppressive structures of Brahmanic Hindu ritualism. The bhakti movements are another source of interpretation from the subaltern perspective, which contain resources for inter-faith relations from the inter-religious point of view. Thirdly dalit movements, of course aimed at the liberation of dalit folk from the oppressive structures in Indian society, directly connected to the subaltern movements. There are several folk/popular cultic-traditions in our country providing better position for dalits and giving wider place for inter-faith relations. There is the possibility of relating Neo-Vedantic and Neo-Buddhist movements to the subaltern perspective. Finally the contributions of Protestant Christian Missionary Movements for the social transformation of subaltern people in India and to improve inter-faith relations are indeed noteworthy. It is difficult to justify these movements both from the "subaltern" and "inter-faith" perspectives within the brief discussion of this article, but further studies are needed to uncover the hidden sources from these perspectives. Hence, this article focuses mainly on "dalit cultic traditions and movements," which are related to the subaltern perspective, since the term "subaltern" has been used for the oppressed, marginalized and down trodden people or "dalits".[16] This study confines itself to the dalit movements and cultic traditions of Andhra Pradesh, especially the two popular dalit folk cultic traditions of Guntur district locally known as the

---

Journal of Dharma, Vol. XIX, No. 3, July-Sept. 1994, 235-247; Paul G. Schrotenbour, "Inter-Religious Dialogue", *Evangelical Review of Theology,* Vol.2, No.3, July 1988, 208-225.

[16] Volumes of literature is available now on the use of the term "dalit", dialits history and theological attempts, for example, refer T. Swami Raju, *Vira Cult in Folk Religion of Guntur District: A Dalit Perspective*, 12ff; T. Swami Raju, *The Study of Religion: Methods and Perspectives*, 135ff. For detailed discussion on "dalit" refer James Massey, *Roots: A Concise History of Dalits,* CISRS, Bangalore, 1991; James Massey(ed.), *Indigenous People: Dalits – Dalit Issues in Today's Theological Debate*, ISPCK, Delhi, 1994; R.K. Kshirasagar, *Dalit Movement in India and its Leaders(1857-1956)*, M.D. Publications Pvt. Ltd., New Delhi, 1994; Bhagwan Das and James Massey (eds.), *Dalit Solidarity*, ISPCK, Delhi, 1995; Arvind P. Nirmal (ed.), *Towards a Common Dalit Ideology*, GLTC, Madras, n.d.; and so on.

Chennakesava Cult and the Vira Cult, both having their origin and hold in the Palnad area, the western part of Guntur district.

These two cults, mentioned above, are offshoots of the bhakti movements, perhaps, developed and still continued as distinctively "dalits folk bhakti cults" in Andhra Pradesh. The bhakti movements gave importance not only to the devotional aspect, but also to fight against the social injustices and inequalities in Indian society. It is needless, at this point, to say that the bhakti movement led by the the Nayanars and Alvars of the Tamil poet saints of Saivism and Vaishnavism, was not only active rebellions against the atheistic movements – Buddhism and Jainism in South India – but also a massive uprising against caste discrimination and untouchability, Brahmanic ritualism and their dominance.[17] R.C. Zaehner characterizes it as "an impassioned cry against the ossified ceremonial religion of Brahmins and the ideal of passionlessness that they shared with Buddhists and Jains."[18] The major contribution to the bhakti movement of the Nayanars and Alvars, was to break down the caste barriers of their followers. For instance, the Alvars have belonged to different castes – some were Brahmins, some Sudras and one was an outcaste. The small Vaishnava community that treasured their legacy and sang their hymns was also made up of different castes,[19] which included women and children.[20] Thus, the bhakti movements paved the way, perhaps for the first time, to fight against the cause of subalternity and the subjugation of weaker sections, which attracted people of different faith/class/caste backgrounds.

The bhakti movements which passed through the songs of Alvars, gathered their water in the system of Ramanuja's spirit of reformative bhakti cultic tradition and flowed out later in varied streams all over India. Ramanuja's reformative efforts opened the doors of the popular temple of Sri Venkateswara at Tirupathi to the excluded people called Sudras.[21] The dynamic reformative acts of Ramanuja encouraged his followers and motivated the Vaishnava bhaktas to include subaltern people in the religious life of Hinduism. This spirit of reformation of the bhakti movement brought about many changes in the life of subaltern people – Dalits, particularly the Malas and the Madigas in Andhra Pradesh. Brahmanayudu, the ardent Vaishnava bhakta and follower of Ramanuja introduced these reforms in Guntur district and attempted radical social

---

[17] Cf. R.R. Sundera Rao, *Bhakti Theology in the Telugu Hymnal,* CLS, Madras, 1983, 25f.

[18] T.P. Meenakshisundaran, *a History of Tamil Literature*, Anamalai University, Anamalai Nagar, 1965, 71.

[19] John B. Carman, *The Theology of Ramanuja*, Yale University Press, New Haven and London, 1974, 25

[20] For more detailed discussion on Alvars bhakti tradition, for example, refer S. Robertson, *Bhakti Tradition of Vaisnava Alvars and Theology of Religions*, Punthi Pustak, Kolkata, 2006.

[21] R.R. Sundera Rao, *op.cit.,* 28

reforms in Palnad, the western part of present day Guntur district. Brahmanayudu was the Prime Minister of the Velama family of Haihayas, and well known for his radical social reforms.

Through his radical socio-religious reforms, Brahmanayudu is not only opened the doors of the Chennakesava temple at Macherla town to untouchables "dalits", but also made them priests to the Chennakesava Cult, when Brahmin priests and the upper castes boycotted his reformative activities.[22] Chennakesava is, as per the local peoples' belief, one of the local incarnations of Vishnu. He once arranged for a *chapakudu* – a common cosmopolitan meal to people of all castes sitting together and eating together irrespective of caste and sectarian discriminations. His socio-religious reforms enabled subaltern people to get the status of official priests, thus providing a special identity for the discriminated society. From then onwards the Chennakesava Cult has been continued as a distinctively Dalits popular religion. This cult has spread to many places in Andhra Pradesh and the dalits particularly the Malas are today performing priestly duties in several temples.[23]

Another important and more popular offshoot of the Chennakesava Cult is the "Vira Cult" – the hero worship of Palnad, where the heroes of the Palnad War have been venerated as deified deities even today by local people. According to the history of Palnad, these heroes had laid down their lives in the Palnad War on the battle field in twelfth century AD and had later revealed themselves to the local people as their deities at Karempudi. So people erected shrines to the deified heroes and made Karempudi the centre of the Vira Cult. Along with other heroes, the dalit heroes also have been specially venerated and honoured. This cult depends on the active involvement and ritual performance all through the centuries by dalits. Though all caste people including Brahmins, Kshtriyas, Vaisyas, Sudras – like washer men, potters, barbers and other subaltern sections like the Malas and Madigas have a place in this cult, the dalits have been playing an important role. Hence the Vira Cult is distinctively "Dalits folk religion". This cult is also known as multi-faith and multi-cultural because of which it attracts local people of different faiths – Vaishnavites, Saivites, Muslims and Christians too.[24]

---

[22] Cf. B.S.L. Hanumantha Rao, *Religion in Andhra*, Tripura Sundari, Guntur, 1973, 258.

[23] This author (T. Swami Raju) has an opportunity to do special research on Chennakesava Cult during 1991-1993 and submitted a thesis to Senate of Serampore College (University) for the partial fulfillment M.Th. degree in Religions from Gurukul Lutheran Theological College and Research Institute, Chennai. Refer for details T. Swami Raju, *A Study of Chennakesava Cult as Adopted and Practiced by Dalits in Guntur District of Andhra Pradesh*, Unpublished thesis, 1993. This thesis is now in publication process.

[24] Refer for more information T. Swami Raju, *Vira Cult in Folk Religion of Guntur District: A Dalit Perspective*, ISPCK, Delhi, 2005. This publication is outcome of

The village goddess cults[25] are, in fact, subaltern religious cults now continued within the wider umbrella of Hinduism which are gradually losing their originality through the influences of cross-cultural impacts such as sanskritization or brahminization and modernization. Originally these folk religious cults were distinctively different from that of so called classical Hinduism.[26] Almost all these folk cultic traditions continued as oral forms depending upon the active participation and priestly propitiation of dalits. Hence, these are, indeed, dalits folk religious cults. Folk religious cultic traditions, such as drum beating, blood sacrifices, ritual enactment, propitiation, narration, priesthood, devadasi, matangi and so on are exclusively performed by the subaltern people in villages. However many cults are coming under the influence of Brahmin priests due to the sanskritization/brahminization processes, as cited above. Therefore, subaltern people have been marginalized from their own religion and cultic traditional practices. For example, Poleramma, Mutyalamma, Matamma, Maisamma, Marimma and so on were once with subaltern people, but now many of them have come into the hands of upper caste priests and the original cultic traditions such as blood sacrifices, drum beating etc., are replaced with brahminic traditions like vegetarian offerings and classical music.[27]

The neo-Vedantic Movement of the Ramakrishna Mission is another example of inter-faith relations and working for the poor irrespective of Hindu caste discrimination. "Service to humanity is service to god" was the motto of Ramakrishna Pramahamsa and Swami Vivekananda. The teachings of Christ greatly influenced Swami Vivekananda, who indeed attempted to reinterpret Vedantic teachings from a humanistic perspective. Hence, Neo-Vedanta developed giving importance to practical Vedanta (like practical theology).[28] Swami Vivekananda established the

---

this author's doctoral research under the supervision of Dr.David C. Scott during 1996-2000 and first submitted as a doctoral dissertation to Senate of Serampore University from South Asia Theological Research Institute (SATHRI), Bangalore. And for extensive study on Vira Cult refer G.H. Roghair, *The Epic of Palnad*, Clarendon Press, Oxford, 1982.

[25] Cf. Henry Whitehead, *The Village Gods of South India*, Asian Educational Services, New Delhi, reprinted 1988; W.T. Elmore, *Dravidian Gods in Modern Hinduism*, Asian Educational Services, New Delhi, 1984.

[26] For more details on folk element in village goddess cults, refer, B.K. Sarkar, *The Folk Element in Hindu Culture: A Contribution to Socio-Religious Studies in Hindu Folk-Institutions*, Cosmo Publications, New Delhi, 1981.

[27] For distinctive differences between dalits folk religion and brahminic classical religion, refer T. Swami Raju, *The Study of Religion*, 142-154.

[28] Refer for more information on "Neo-Vedanta" of Swami Vivekananda a recent work of this author in Telugu, T. Swami Raju, *Vivekananduni Naveena Vedantam* (Neo-Vedanta of Vivekananda), TTLB, Hyderabad, 2009, and for direct information on the teachings of Swami Vivekananda, refer for example, *Teachings of Swami Vivekananda*, Advita Ashrama, Calcutta, revised & enlarged, 7th

"Ramakrishna Mission" with a bold vision to revive/reform Hindu ritualism and made this a "movement" of service oriented to meet the basic needs of people – education, health, shelter, food and other rehabilitation and philanthropic activities, taking as a pattern the many Christian missionary activities of his time. The Ramakrishna Mission continue these activities in the spirit of social service. Both Ramakrishna Paramahamsa and Vivekananda stood for the social integration of various castes, including the subaltern people and communal/religious harmony between people belonging to different faiths/religions. The services of the Ramakrishna Mission are available to all people irrespective of caste, gender, or religion.

Another recent movement worthy of mention is the "Neo-Buddhist Movement"[29] of B.R. Ambedkar,[30] which is rightly considered as subaltern socio-religious movement developed during second half of the 20th century in Maharashtra among the Mahar community. This movement was indeed, a protest movement against the oppressive structures of Hinduism, especially, "caste and untouchability". Ambedkar vehemently opposed the Hindu dharmasasthras for their caste hierarchical structures and the inhuman attitude of upper castes towards dalits. Hence, he rightly pointed out that there was no liberation for subaltern people as long as the caste system existed in Indian society. Therefore, B.R. Ambedkar became a Buddhist on October 14, 1956 seeking a new identity and human dignity for Dalits. On the same day nearly 308,000 Dalits took initiation into Buddhism. From then onwards Buddhism attained a revival spirit in India increasing its number and Ambedkar made this movement a Neo-Buddhist movement in his quest for improving the dignity of dalits. Why didn't Ambedkar join Christianity? It is a question not yet answered; however, some analysts assume that due to caste discriminations in the Christian community, Ambedkar didn't join the Church. It is true, indeed, some churches are following the caste system even today especially in South India. There is no unity among Christians of dalit background; Christians converted from the upper castes have their own caste based churches like converts church, the Kammas church, the Reddies church and so on.

---

impression, 1981; Swami Vivekananda, *Chicago Addresses*, Advaita Ashrama, Kolkata, 13th Impression, 2002; *Real Worship*, Ramakrishna Math, Hyderabad, 5th edition, 2005 and also *Swami Vivekananda's Complete Works*.

[29] On Neo Buddhism, see T.S. Wiskinson & M.M. Thomas, *Ambedkar and the Neo-Buddhist Movement*, CLS, Madras, 1972; Alleyamma Zachariah, *Modern Religious and Secular Movements in India*, Theological Book Trust, Bangalore, 2nd revised edition, 1998, 161-172 and T. Swami Raju, *Bharatavanilo Adhunika Chaitanya Udyamalu* (Modern Renaissant Movements in India), Telugu Theological Literary Board, Hyderabad, 2004, 163-174.

[30] On life and mission of Ambedkar, refer, Dhananjay Keer, *Dr. Ambedkar Life and Mission*, Popular Praksshan, Bombay, reprinted 1991.

These are some movements which have worked for the cause of subaltern people, but the social Gospel of Christ builds the bridges between people of different communities removing socio-religio-cultural and economic barriers. Christian missionary movements have indeed transformed to a large extent the lives of subaltern communities in India through their educational, medical, religious and social concerns. Christian missionaries established educational institutions for the oppressed, marginalized, subaltern people and these have transformed their lives from ignorance to wisdom. That education brings transformation is true in the lives of these subaltern people who converted to Christianity. Many dalits were attracted to Christianity not merely for food, clothes and other material benefits, but also to get rid of the oppressive structures of Hinduism in India. Christian dalits are today facing a double problem in India – firstly the Church that once upheld and supported these dalits now neglects them, and secondly dalit Christians are not eligible for government reservations. Unfortunately, the Church today in India seems to have given up on the task of providing educational and medical services to the poor dalits. Hence, many dalits are more interested in identifying themselves as Hindu dalits or Buddhist dalits for the benefits from government reservations. It is a great challenge to the Church in India to serve the poor and the oppressed who are in need.

Insights for Inter-Faith Relations

Dialogue should be an ongoing process and spontaneous in a multi-faith contexts as in Asia/India. Ours is a pluralistic context – religiously, culturally, racially and linguistically. Religiously, the people in India follow different religious traditions and confess various faiths, yet live together. We have religions of Indian origin such as – Hinduism, Jainism, Buddhism and Sikhism; and semitic/foreign religions such as Judaism, Christianity and Islam. There are several regional/village/rural religious traditions that emphasize faith in local deities and also cults of folk, popular, dalit, peasant, tribal and village religions. There are also people who have faith in secular ideologies: Atheism, Marxism, Leninism, Maoism, Communism, Gandhism, Ambedkarism, Naxalism, and so on.[31]

Such is the pluralistic context of our country where dialogue should be a spontaneous ongoing process for better and harmonious inter-faith relations. The World Missionary Conference held at Edinburgh in 1910 not only marked the beginning of the neo-ecumenical movement to unite Christians of different denominational backgrounds, but was also landmark

---

[31] Cf. S.J. Samartha, "Dialogue in a Religiously Plural Society" in *The Multith Context of India*, ed. Israel Selvanayagam, The Board for Theological Text Books Programme of South Asia, n.d., 2; T. Swami Raju, "Re-Visioning Theologies: A Multi-Faith Perspective," in *The SAṬHRI Journal*, Vol. 2, No.1, BTESSC, Bangalore, May 2008, 139 (137-149)

in terms of thinking and working for unity in a diversity of faiths. The Church has opened its door towards developing an openness towards people of other faiths, thus paving the way for a dialogical concept through the debates in the WCC councils since 1910. It should be admitted that this ecumenical movement not only has brought about many changes in the orthodox manner of thinking of Christians – Protestants, Catholics, and Evangelicals; but has also influenced people of other faiths – Jews, Hindus, Buddhists, Muslims, Sikhs and so on. We have an Institute of Multi-Faith Studies, as a separate department, in ACT College, Hyderabad to train our theological students from the perspective of a pluralistic context and so spread awareness among the different congregations about the importance of dialogical relations with people of other faiths.[32]

It is, perhaps the right time to search for inter-faith relations from subaltern movements and cultic traditions. There are some resources for inter-faith relations and dialogue from subaltern religious practices. As I have already mentioned, it is true that folk religious traditions are in fact dalit religious practices and there is place in these for people from different religious/faith backgrounds. Folk religious cultic traditions are open to all people irrespective of caste, religion, color and gender; therefore, peoples' participation is genuine rather than a compulsion. Dialogue between people in such situations is spontaneous rather than rigid or scheduled. Official religions have restrictions when it comes to approaching/appeasing the deity in the temple, i.e., only the appointed priest can enter the temple and perform the rituals, whereas in the folk religions there is a flexibility in approaching the god/deity in the folk shrines and all are welcome since folk shrines are always open to all.

In folk religious practices or subaltern cults, people of other faiths participate without expressing any superiority or inferiority about their own faiths.[33] At the time of folk religious festivals all people of the village community inclusively contribute to and interactively participate in the festivals of the folk deity though they may follow other classical traditions. The local people's strong belief is that the folk deity is the deity of their own village, and hence, this integrates the whole village community. The

---

[32] The "Institute of Multi-Faith Studies" is conducting seminars, symposiums, workshops on "inter-faith relations and working to develop better relations with neighboring faiths by inviting people from other faiths to our programs and we are attending to their programs in a mutual respect. As the Coordinator of this institute recently I attended to and delivered a lecture on "Peace Inter-Faith Dialogue" on November 29th 2008 organized by a Muslim organization called "Islamic Research & Educational Foundation" at Hyderabad. Br. Imran, IREF and Prof. K. Subramanyam, Central University, Hyderabad delivered messages from Islam and Hinduism respectively. Sri. SSP. Yadav, IPS and DGP of Andhra Pradesh is chief guest. (Internet accessed 12 December, 2008 – http://irefworld.net/peace.html).

[33] Cf. T. Swami Raju, *Vira Cult in Folk Religion of Guntur District: A Dalit Perspective*, 325.

people of different faiths don't abuse somebody else's faith, but respect these other faiths without losing faith in their own personal religion or deity. In the context of religious pluralism, there is more possibility of adopting the method of "dialogue" in the study of subaltern folk religion rather than the so-called classical traditions.[34] Such an approach is more helpful for inter-faith dialogue and for the promotion of inter-faith relations. People in subaltern cultic traditions show equal respect for other faiths, and hence, there is no question of the "inferior or superior" or the "impure and pure" or "untouchability or touchability" another religion.

Subaltern people are given a special place of honor at the time of cultic practices. Dalits perform their duties as priests, sacrificers, ritual performers, drumbeaters, propitiators and enactors of important episodes. For example, the Matangi represents the local mata or goddess and the Poturaju the local god. Matangi and Poturaju, both ritual enactors are exclusively from the Madiga and Mala communities. At the time of cultic celebrations, people, even from upper the castes, wash the feet of Dalits and pour that water on their foreheads. There is no question of what is impure or pure, perhaps because it is considered a kind of a ritual enhancement of the dalits. The upper caste people also hold a spontaneous dialogue with subaltern people, who act as the ritual performers and drumbeaters of their deity. As mentioned earlier, the Vira Cult of Palnad is one of the best examples for dialogue and multi-faith relations from the subaltern perspective. All castes and people from other religions join the Vira Cultic ritual enactments. People forget their feelings of superiority or inferiority, perhaps temporarily, and join together in cultic practices. For inter-faith dialogue such a kind of openness is essential.

There is no place for claims of superiority in folk religious cults. Hence, generally there is little chance for conflicts between people of different faith backgrounds. Similarly in inter-faith dialogue, mutual respect and trust are more important between dialogue partners. There is a general notion among non-Christians that Christians are exclusivists in their approach towards other faiths. Christians are perceived as unwilling to come forward and develop good relations with others and that they use dialogue as a means to convert people to Christianity.

In conclusion, let us reexamine our attitudes in the light of Jesus and His disciples' attitudes towards other faiths. Literally, the Bible doesn't exclude people of other faiths, but includes all people in a living hope for divine blessings and eternal salvation. Jesus Christ never condemned or criticized people of other faiths or their scriptures as He did the Jews (perhaps because they were his own people), and their ritualistic interpretation of Judaism (Mathew 23) . Jesus talked with all kinds of people without any discrimination – with the Samaritan woman, the Canaanite woman, the Roman centurion, Magdalene Mary. He healed people belong to different

[34] *Ibid.*

backgrounds. If Jesus, our Lord, has adopted such an attitude towards people of other faiths, why are we – His followers – ready to adopt such a negative attitude towards people of other faiths?

St. Paul rightly called himself an "apostle" to the gentiles (Galatians 1:15; 2:7-9). He spent his whole life crossing Jewish boundaries and undertook three missionary journeys to preach the Gospel and hold genuine dialogues with non-Christians. His arguments regarding the problem of the early Church on "circumcision" (Acts 15; Rom 2:25-29) and his approach towards the people of Athens (Acts 17:16-31) are some of the best examples for our attempts at inter-faith dialogue and multi-faith relations. Paul never condemned other faiths. He, in fact, adopted a more inclusively pluralistic and genuine dialogical attitude towards people of other faiths in his missionary activities and attempted to improved the inter-faith relations of his time. Paul rightly argued with Jewish fundamentalists of his day: "Is God the God of Jews only? Is he not the God of Gentiles too? Yes, of Gentiles too, since there is only one God, who will justify the circumcised by faith and the uncircumcised through that same faith" (Romans 3:29-30).

Such an inclusively pluralistic spirituality is more essential for improving inter-faith relations. On the one hand, we as Christians, must be thankful for the ecumenical movement that began at Edinburgh in 1910, which opened the Church's doors in recognizing the reality of the plurality of faiths and the need for a dialogical relationship in such a pluralistic context with people of other faiths. On the other hand, we need to strive for more viable and sustainable approaches to improve inter-faith relations. The 21st century is the century to practice dialogical relations with people of other faiths. The Church in 21st century needs to continue this dialogical journey begun in the previous century to reach the bold ecumenical vision of "oneness of humanity" irrespective of differences. This oneness doesn't mean "uniformity", but in a strict sense, "unity in diversity". It may not be plausible to bring all human beings in uniformity, but "unity in diversity" is possible because it recognizes that all human beings have one origin though there is diversity in religions, races, castes, colors and languages.

Section V

Interfaith Relations from Feminist Perspectives

Interfaith Relations in Mizoram with Emphasis on Mission from a Feminist Perspective

T. Vanlaltlani

Introduction

It is not common for writers from Mizoram, a state in northeastern India to talk about interfaith relations in Mizoram since the majority of the citizens of the state are Christians. This does not mean that people of other faiths are not found in Mizoram. On the contrary, Mizoram is a state where there have been followers of different faiths for a considerable period of time. So far there has not been any incident of religious or communal/ violence between people of different faiths living in the state. There are even shrines of several religions to be found in and around Aizawl city, and other areas.

People of Non-Christian Faiths and Their Holy Places

Holy Places of Other Religions in and Around Aizawl City and Other Areas

Mizoram is regarded as a Christian state due to its Christian majority population. The state also has had people of other faiths living in the state without any hindrances for a considerable period of time and their places of worship are found within and outside Aizawl.[1] A beautiful Hindu temple (or *mandir*) is situated in central Aizawl, and a Muslim mosque, too, is found in the Bara Bazaar area of Aizawl which is also centrally located. *Gurudwara* (of the Sikhs), Mosque and *Mandir* are found very near each other in the area called Thuampui, only few kilometers from Aizawl Theological College. An apartment in a building very near to the Mizoram Presbyterian Church Synod Office was rented and occupied by Brahma Kumari devotees who named their centre the Raja Yoga Centre. On the

[1] Almost all the religious holy places found in and around Aizawl city have been visited by the writer while showing her students how people of other faiths worship in these religious places.

roadsides of the National Highways and in other similar locations, *Shiv Mandirs* can also be found in good numbers; often banyan trees in unusual shapes are considered holy and are decorated with garlands and small offerings by the worshippers. All these indicate that interfaith relations in the state are a healthy one without any religious or communal violence among people of different faiths.

The Existence of People of Non-Christian Faiths in Mizoram

According to the 2001 census, there are 772809 Christians and 115764 non-Christians in Mizoram. There are Hindus, Muslims, Sikhs and Buddhists working in Mizoram University, various government department offices, different colleges, offices, schools, training institutes and in private businesses. Many Muslim men are working as private employees in houses and multi-storey building constructions. Many Hindus from Bihar and Jharkhand are working as laborers under the BRTF, PWD, and other World Bank aided road construction programmes. Nepali Hindus have been living in Mizoram for a long time (the date of their settlement is unknown). The more that the citizens of Mizoram engage in construction works, the more non-Mizo/non Christian people are employed in these constructions. The effect of globalization has also resulted in people serving in multi-business companies. All this has resulted in more and more outsiders coming to Mizoram. The 2011 census will undoubtedly point to the increase of non-Mizos and people of other faiths living in Mizoram.

Beside the above reasons, there is bound to be an increase in the population of non-Christians and non-Mizos in Mizoram due to the educational and training institutions in the cities. Today, unlike as in 2001, there are several institutions and training centres run by the government and private sectors in the city of Aizawl. Institutes for training those interested in pharmacology, nursing, midwifery, to name a few, have attracted people from other states irrespective of their religious faiths. The Central Residential College for Animal Husbandry and Veterinary Training in Selesih, Aizawl, accommodates a number of students and trainees from outside Mizoram every year. Similarly several private hospitals, multinational companies, restaurants, building and road construction works continue to attract people of other faiths and ethnic backgrounds to the state.

Doing Mission for the Creation of Interfaith Relations

Mizo Christians are missionary minded and different denominations are engaged in evangelization among people of other faiths. For instance, the Presbyterian Church of Indian, Mizoram Synod (PCI MS), began mission work among non-Christians in Mizoram in a systematic manner from the 1940s by sending evangelists (*Tirhkoh*) to the Bru-Chakma community. It is known that there are many evangelists, evangelist teachers and other church workers among the Bru-Chakma community. The Aizawl-centred *Masihi Sangati* mission, focuses on the Hindu and Muslim population in Aizawl city and adjoining areas and was started in the 1980s under the umbrella of the 'Synod Gospel Team'. The team started gathering new converts to form a 'Non-Mizo Christian Fellowship' and began worship services in different places such as the First Assam Rifles Church and the House for Orphans built by Dawrpui Church Women's Fellowship. They began raising funds by collecting donations and sought to buy land for a house as well. After a period of struggle they managed to raise the the required amount of money (i.e. Rs. 60,000/-) from a Mrs. Parkungi and bought the present site in Bawngkawn for the team's Non-Mizo Christian Centre.

A ground-breaking ceremony of the land on which the Centre for non-Mizo Christians was to be constructed was done by the former Moderator of the PCI (MS), Rev. Thangpuiliana on 24th April 1983.[2] The Centre celebrated its Silver Jubilee on 24.04.2008. Today the team is better known by the name *Masihi Sangati*. There are 144 Fellowships (*Sangati)* and 101 persons employed to serve under the *Masihi Sangati*.[3] In the northern area of the *Masihi Sangati*, there is a *Milit Samiti* (a committee consisting of 8 Ex-officio members and 31 members representing different pastorates in Aizawl city) which functions like a working committee to look after the overall programmes of the *Masihi Sangati*. 1408 members were baptized in 2008 while 1616 members were baptized during January-September, 2009.[4] In the southern part of Mizoram there are 17 Fellowships (*Sangati)* and 20 employed workers. 75 people were baptized between January and July, 2009.[5] Let us remember that there are 115764 non-Christians in the state who are considered citizens of Mizoram, and the total number of workers from the PCI (MS) among them is 121 (besides workers sent by other church denominations).

There is another kind of mission done by the PCI (MS) which focuses on non-Christian friends; this is through the Hindi Bible School at Bawngkawn, Aizawl and is located in the same building as the Non-Mizo Christian Centre. This school was inaugurated on 24th Aug.1990 by the then Moderator of the PCI (MS) Rev. C. Vanlalhruaia.[6] The first class of the first batch having 20 students was started on 20th Sept.1990 under the

---

[2] Lalhruaitluanga, *Non-Mizo Christian Centre silver Jubilee:24.04.2008 Secretary Report*, 1.

[3] *Masihi Sangati Bawngbawlna Report Jan-Sept.2009*, 1. One is the Director three are office staff, four are Pastors, eighty three are Evangelists and ten are Gospel Team members.

[4] *Masihi Sangati Bawngbawlna Report Jan-Sept.2009*, 1.

[5] *Ibid*., one Pastor, ten Evangelists and nine Gospel Team members.

[6] *Presbyterian Hindi Bible School Report*, 1. This report was given to the writer on 13th Nov.2009 by the said School Office staff, Mr.Lalthangvunga.

charge of Probationary Pastor Vanlalbela (Head Instructor) and Upa H. Lalchungnunga (Instructor). The duration of the course was 6 months covering 10 subjects. [7] This school is, at present, run by the Managing Committee under the Chairmanship of Rev. Vanlalbela, Secretary, Synod Mission Board. The total enrolment of students, as of date, is 1018 (153 women and 865 men). The number of students who have successfully completed their studies is 945, and those that have not been successful in completing their studies are 73.[8] The 44th batch of students hailing from Mizoram, Assam, the Barak Area of Assam, Siliguri (in West Bengal), Arunachal Pradesh, Varanasi, Chhattisgarh, Lucknow in Uttar Pradesh), Dumka, other parts of Jharkhand, Mumbai (in Maharashtra) and Nepal, are now in the process of completing their studies, and an advertisement for the 45th batch is scheduled for 12th Jan.2010.[9] The Hindi Bible School has been training persons to do evangelism and mission wherever they are. Converts who have been trained here are expected to be living examples of Jesus Christ. Of course there are some other churches, too, which support the work of evangelism in Mizoram by sponsoring several workers living among the Bru-Chakma community.

Difficulties in the Establishment of Interfaith Relations

One rarely hears of communal or religious disturbances in Mizoram. Although there are attempts to convert non-Christians, this is never done through force, fraud or inducement. This does not mean that there is no problem in interfaith relations; rather it means an absence of religious or communal conflicts and riots among citizens of Mizoram.

Socio-Culturally Conditioned Diversity affecting Disunity

Almost all Mizos in Mizoram embraced Christianity within 50 years of Christianity being introduced in the region; on the other hand other ethnic communities have maintained their respective religious beliefs and their religious identities which have in turn caused them to maintain their ethnic identities and distinctiveness. This religious difference between the non-Mizo communities and the Mizo Christian community has resulted in a sense of complacency in the Mizo Christian community with little thought given to consider the community's relations with those belonging to other religious communities. Consequently there is no interest in developing

---

[7] Their subjects are Christian Theology, Homiletic, Pauline Epistles Major Religions, The Acts of the Apostles, Mission & Evangelism, The Life & Ministry of Jesus Christ, Bible Knowledge, History of Christianity and Christian Ethics.

[8] *Presbyterian Hindi Bible School Report*, 3.

[9] *Ibid.*, 4.

relationships with people of all faiths irrespective of their doctrinal difference.

Spiritual Pride of Male-Dominated Churches

The churches in Mizoram are not active in the promotion of interfaith relations except through mission among them. These churches are headed by men and none of the denominations have women in top positions of leadership and administration. Their theological understanding and concept, in academic circles, may be wide and broad-minded; but their understanding of the common people is still fundamental and conservative. They do not have a positive attitude towards people of other faiths; they would rather condemn them to suffer the doom of hell. The understanding of 'Jesus is the only way to God and it is only through him that salvation is attainable' is the standard of understanding held by almost all lay people. Even theologians have no courage to deliver and impart the wider and broader theological interpretations to the common people out of fear that people would complain against them and that the offerings in the churches would decrease. Thus, the spiritual pride of the churches is confined to terms such as 'the Bible alone', 'Jesus alone' and there is little initiative to contact non-Christians or to have any kind of interfaith relations. Instead there is opposition from church members (even from leaders) whenever some theologians have highlighted ideas such as interfaith relations and the idea of religious pluralism. The Christians in Mizoram are institutionalized church based Christians and people of other faiths are not accepted as human beings. Several Mizo Christians refer to non Christians as non believers thereby deliberately not recognizing their faiths and practices. Hence there had been no attempt to build interfaith relations because the Mizos do not feel the necessity for this, or see any value and importance in such an exercise.

In the ministerial formation of the churches in Mizoram, theological institutions such as Aizawl Theological College (ATC), Academy of Integrated Christian Studies (AICS) and other smaller institutions ones, students would go through theological education primarily as the preparation for ordained ministry especially in Presbyterian and Baptist churches. Our students in ATC used to say jokingly 'We start our ministerial preparation with servanthood and end with preparation for leadership'. Since they themselves have never felt the necessity to have interfaith relations with those of other faiths, and when the Christian leadership gives priority to the ecclesiastical structure of the churches it is difficult to establish interfaith relations at the grassroots level.

If women are in decision making body it can be argued that there could be an agenda for relations with people of other faiths because women in the Mizo Christian community are better at building bridges with non-Mizo sand non-Christians. Our next point will indicate how open Mizo women are to people of other faiths.

Denominationalism in the face of Interfaith Relation

Denominationalism among church members comes in the way of promoting interfaith relations. Christians in Mizoram are busy with the welfare of their respective church denominations. We will now briefly look at the various factors responsible for Church denominationalism in Mizoram. V.L. Hruaia identified these factors as socio-economic, political, missiological and because of revivals.[10] There will, of course be other factors besides these four factors listed by Hruaia that have caused divisions in the Church in Mizoram.

Today in Mizoram, there are several denominations, such as the Mizoram Presbyterian Church, the Baptist Church of Mizoram, the Evangelical Church of Maraland, the Roman Catholic Church, the Salvation Army, the Seventh Day Adventist Church, the Lairam Jesus Christ Baptist Church, the United Pentecostal Church (NEI & Mizoram), the Assembly of God Church, the Church of Jesus Christ to name a few. Considering the existence these denominations in a same speaking the same language (except for the Mara community), one needs to raise the question: How far can we be obedient to Jesus prayer 'that they all may be one' (Jn.17:21)?

What effect does the division of the Church in Mizoram have? K. Lalhmingliana has traced two effects.[11] His views on the positive effects of denominationalism may be summarized as: participation and responsibilities carried out by more people; more persons get a chance for ministerial exposure programmes outside Mizoram; also more effort is put into increasing the membership in one's own denomination. This is similar to the Reformation in the history of the Church, which had caused loss of members in the Roman Church; but it also roused and challenged Protestant Church members with a strong zeal for the propagation of the Gospel.

The negative effects of the division of the Church in Mizoram have been listed by Lalhmingliana under two main points, i.e. the effect on the life of the Church and the effect on the ministry of the Church. Lalhmingliana has listed five concrete points highlighting the effects of denominationalism on the life of the Church:[12] (1) This division disturbs the life of the Christian

---

[10] V.L.Hruia Khiangte, *Khawtlang Inthendachw Leh a Nghawngte: Khawtlang nun leh Eibar Zawnnaah*, A paper presented on 25th July 2009 in Mizo Theological Association Silver Jubilee Seminar at Zarkawt Presbyterian Church Hall, 1-3.

[11] K. Lalhmingliana, *Kohhran Inthendachuain Kohhran Nun leh a Rawngbawna a Nghawng Dan*, A paper presented in the Mizo Theological Association Silver Jubilee Seminar on 25th July 2009 at Zarkawt Presbyterian Church Hall, 5.

[12] *Ibid.*, 5-8.

family (2) It creates diverse opinions in the Church (3) It destroys our oneness in Christ (4) It makes the Church leaders more prone to various failings and (5) The pain of denominational division as experienced in the Shillong Mizo Church.

The effects of division on the ministry of the Church are listed as follows:[13] (1) It causes a lot of financial expenditure in other matters rather than in the propagation of the Gospel; (2) It causes negative competition in the mission field (3) It causes disunity among Church members when movements or efforts are undertaken to improve the political atmosphere in the state and (4) The scope of preaching for Revival Speakers is limited.

Division and diversity of the Church have been the cause of considerable negative effects on Mizo Christians. Inter-denominational relationship has been becoming progressively worse. 'Sheep-stealing' is practiced in various ways. A lot of money has been spent by different denominations for buying land for the construction of church buildings. The writer was informed by members of the Bru community, during her empirical study in Bru living areas, that Mizo Christians used them as the victims of denominational battles. Hence, denominationalism is bad for interfaith relations between Mizo Christians and Bru members. People of other faith communities get confused with who is right and wrong among Christians when having to deal with different denominations.

As of now, the Mizo Theological Association appears to be the only Christian association searching for the means of uniting all Mizo Christians. Unless the churches in Mizoram are united they cannot effectively stand against any challenge. To make the Church a living witness to Christ the members have to overcome all denominational barriers and need to live and work in unity. The call to be living witness to Christ in the midst of denominationalism is urgent.

Denominationalism weakens Christian unity in the eyes of people of other faiths. It weakens the unity of Christians and does not show to people of other faiths the unity longed and prayed by Jesus in Jn.17. There has never been an attempt by any of the churches in Mizoram to organize a consultation/workshop/seminar with the purpose of creating interfaith or even inter-denominational relations. Each denomination is busy with their respective activities and programmes, and gives no attention/interest to maintaining good relations with people of other faiths. There have also been instances where non-Christians whom one church denomination had converted were further converted by members of another denomination into their own. Thus, little consideration is given to inter-denominational relationships within the Christian community.

---

[13] *Ibid.*

The Role and Mission of Women in Interfaith Relations

The women of Mizoram are known to be sincere in taking up their responsibilities as church members and co-workers of God through their life and practices. Besides they do more than the menfolk in interfaith relations through their marriage to non-Christians or non-Mizos.

Women in Inter-Religious Marriages

Women in tribal society can be considered to contributing to the fostering f interfaith relations through inter-religious or inter-cultural marriages with people of other faiths or communities. It is rare to find Mizo women marrying Buddhists or Jains. But there have been instances of Mizo women, educated and uneducated, marrying Hindu, Sikh and Muslim men. In doing this, they can be considered to practice interfaith relations. Some of them have converted their husbands to Christianity, not by force but through their practical imparting of Christian knowledge and exemplary lifestyles. There have been cases of divorces too. However, 'inter-religious/inter-cultural marriages are one of the methods applied by Mizo women to recognize people of other faiths.

It is quite rare to find Mizo Christian men getting married with women of other faiths or even to women of non-Mizo communities. Often non-Mizo men of different faiths would hold on to their faiths. But it has often been seen that after a while they become Christians having witnessed the manner in which their wives lead their lives. It must be admitted here that Mizo women who married non-Mizo men of different faiths, were initially, severely looked down upon by their fellow Mizos, both men and women, as well as by their own family members, close friends and relatives. Although they were not considered as the Christian missionaries in the true sense of the term, some Mizo Christian women have maintained excellent interfaith relations through their marriages with people of other faiths. The techniques they applied are prayer and an exemplary life as well as sharing their Christian faith with their husbands.

Competency of Women in Pastoral Service who are Denied Ordination

Women in Mizo Christian churches are very active in attending church services, giving offerings, conducting Bible study groups, being involved in the singing and dancing fellowship ministry, giving charitable gifts to the needy, visiting the sick and bereaved families, caring for and offering prayers for people who are in sorrow and distress. Despite carrying out such pastoral duties, they are denied ordination and therefore the opportunity to minister the sacraments.

This denial of their ordination has disqualified them from holding administration and leadership posts. As of 2010 churches there are only a few women who have been being ordained ministers, namely, Rev. Esther

Chemi of the Church of North India, Rev. Rohmingliani of the Mizoram Baptist Church (who was ordained in London, not in Mizoram), and Rev. Sapthangi of the Wesleyan Methodist Church.[14] Very few women have been elected as lifetime Church Elders in order to assist the celebrant (i.e. the male Minister) in the Holy Communion. No women (except those in the Salvation Army) hold the positions of leadership in any church because these positions are meant for ordained Ministers and Elders (who are men). Even the churches who have elected women to be elders have not yet elected/appointed women to be Ministers and this restriction hinders women's participation in the overall activities and administration of the Church.

Missionary Commitment

Despite these obstacles in Church, Christian women of Mizoram are not discouraged in doing God's ministry. Rather they live out their ministry both outside and inside Mizoram. They carry out direct evangelism in some places; they do mission through teaching in schools and institutions, medical institutions, and some give vocational training such as in tailoring and knitting. Almost 1000 Mizo women today are working as missionaries of whom some have even lost their lives at the hands of non-Christians.

Out of the 60 missionaries under the Council for World Mission (CWM) working in different countries, 26 are from Presbyterian Church of India (Mizoram Synod), of which 20 of them are women. The Mizoram Synod of the PCI has contributed the highest in terms of personnel and in finance/material. Several women groups of local churches are sponsoring missionaries, helping many poor people in cash or in kind.

The Challenge of the Plurality of Faiths

Although Christians in some states in India have suffered sometimes at the hands of Hindu extremists and those of other faiths, Christians in Mizoram rarely face any kind of physical persecution. However, in the present day scenario, how pluralism affects Mizo Christian society needs to be given serious attention.

Several Nepalis belonging to the Hindu faith have been living in Mizoram since their birth, but have never made an attempt to convert Mizos to Hinduism. The ongoing years and changing circumstances have

[14] The first two of these three women Ministers are personally known to the writer because they work together as members of the Association of Theologically Trained Women of India, Mizoram Branch.

brought in many Hindus, Muslims, Buddhists, Sikhs, Jains and others to Mizoram. None of these later entrants seem to have the zeal or the inclination to approach Mizos in order to convert them to their faiths. But today things have changed and some Hindu friends have been making attempts to approach the Mizo youth with this evangelistic purpose and tendency. Mr. Lalthlamuana, as one of the leaders of the Students' Union while in college, came into contact with Hindus involved in the 'Students' Exchange in Inter-State Living' (SEIL).[15] He later became Sub-Coordinator during the first half of the 1990s. But he was unaware of the connection of SEIL with the Akhil Bharatiya Vidyarthi Parishad (ABVP), the students' wing of Hindu right wing Bharatiya Janata Party.

This SEIL-ABVP can be used as an instrument of the Hindutva movement to facilitate students' exchange programmes in other states. Muana has handed over charge of Sub-Coordinator-ship to one of the active members of the Mizoram BJP a few years ago.[16] He said that it was only in 2006 that he came to know that ABVP (to which SEIL was attached) was instrumental in causing disturbances in the context of the revival, which happened in Oriental High School, Silchar, Assam state, in 2006. Members of ABVP had made a lot of trouble for Christian missionaries in the Silchar Mission Compound, and for the teachers and students of Oriental High School, by submitting a letter to the Inspector of Schools, CDC, Silchar.[17] In the letter they accused the school authorities of not following some rules of SEBA[18]. But what they had accused the school authorities of was found to be false. Despite this incident, several non Christian students have been given admission to the school, and there is a cordial interfaith relationship between parents of those students and the school authorities.

Even among the Mizos who were generally known to be Christians there are some who claim that they are followers of another faith which disregards Jesus and Christianity. One such group is known as the *Nunna Lalhnam*[19] and has over 1000 members. Their Vice President Mr. B. Lalthlengliana said that their members are around 1000-2000 in number. He also frankly said that they belong to the *Nunna Lalhnam* family, followers of the traditional Mizo religion who worship ***Chungkhuanu***.[20] According to his version, the Exodus history, the river Jordan, Galilee and

[15] Personal Interview with Mr.C.Lalthlamuana on 31st Oct., 2009 at their home in Mission veng, Aizawl.

[16] *Ibid.*

[17] T.Vanlaltlani, *Yoga leh Kristianna*, Aizawl: M.C.Lalrinthanga, 2007, 92-95. The subject of their letter is written like this: 'Memoruandum highlighting different problems of the Oriental School'

[18] *Ibid.*, 94. Long form of SEBA is Secondary Education Board of Assam.

[19] Personal Interview with the Vice President of the Nuna Lal Hnam community, Mr.B.Lalthlengliana on 11th Nov.2009, 6:30-7:30 A.M. at his residence in Saron Veng, Aizawl.

[20] *Ibid.*

other Biblical places and events are important and significant for the Jews/Israelites; Jesus Christ is for the Christians; but for the people of the Mizo nation, the river Tlawng is much better and more important than the Jordan or any other rivers or lakes in Palestine; and God, *Chungkhuanu* is the true object of worship. Consequently *Nunna Lalhnam* members claim that they maintain the Mizo traditional/indigenous religion (*hnam sakhua*). The members of this group used to be members of the Mizo Evangelical Association, one of the para-church organizations, which was quite active in 1970s. As of now, although they have no single canonized scripture they accept the written books of their four leaders, *puithiam* Rorelliana, *puithiam* Lalchangliana, *puithiam* Chawngpianga and *puithiam* Laldinthara as their scriptures. The most popular one is titled *NunnaThu – Zofate Hnena Chungkhuanu Thuthlung* written by *Puithiam* Rorelliana.[21] But inside the cover of the book the title is elaborated in the words *Nunna Thu Kan Nun In Tan – Zofate Sakhua Thuthlung Dik Chungkhuanu Puanchhuah Chu*. This book has 320 pages containing four main sections.

For a few years now a rumour persist and one that has become stronger when the periodical magazine *Zozam* in its Aug.26-Sept.1, 2009 issue, published articles implying that *Nunna Lalhnam*, along with some other groups [22] were agents of the Hindutva movement. The *Nunna Lalhnam* group is also considered responsible for the translation and publication of the Mizo version of *Srimad Bhagavad Gita*.[23] But the *Nunna Lalhnam* family has denied this, and their response to this allegation was printed in the October 14-20, 2009 issue of *Zozam*.[24] It is true that *Nunna Lalhnam* is not the publisher of the *Srimad Bhagavad Gita;* but the three top leaders and one office staff of *Nunna Lalhnam* wrote the Foreword to the book.[25] Besides two other Mizos, also wrote Greetings for this book.[26] The translator of this book, Mr. Ramthanga Khawlhring, in his introduction, articulates the kernel of the *Srimad Bhagavad Gita*.

It is not clear whether or not the *Nunna Lalhnam* is instrumental in spreading the teachings of Hinduism. The group's Vice President wrote an article clarifying that the group was not involved in the propagation of

---

21 Rorelliana, *Nuna Thu-ZofateHnena Chungkhuanu Thuthlung*. Aizawl: Mizo Sakhaw Vuantute, 2009,front cover.

22 "Mizoramah Kristianna a nghing em? Mizo tawngin Hindu lehkhabu thianghlim" in *Zozam vol-VI*, Issue No.1, Aug.26-Sept.1, 2009, 9-12.

23 *Ibid*.11. The translator of the Srimad Bhagavad Gita is Mr.Ramthanga Khawlhring, and the publisher is Heritage Foundation, K.B. Road, Paltan Bazar, Guwahati.

24 B.Lalthlenglianga, "Hindu Nge Nunna Lalhnam" in *Zozam Oct14-20*, 2009, 28,29.

25 The writers of the greetings are Mr. Rorelliana, Lalpuihtiam, H. Chawngpianga, Lalpuithiam, V.L. Ngaihmawia, Office Assistant, and B. Lalthlenglianga, Vice President.

26 The two greeting writers are Mr. C. Vanlallawma, President, Janajati Vikas Samiti, Mizoram and V.L. Peka Chhakchhuak, Vairengte Mizoram.

Hindu teachings. But the appearance of names of their top leaders and staff in the foreword to the translation of one of the Hindu scriptures has given the impression that they are instruments for the propagation of Hinduism by spreading the message of the Bhagavad Gita.

The members of the *Nunna Lalhnam* are not respected by Mizo Christians, and are considered heretics and not exactly adherents of another religion. The members of the *Nunna Lalhnam* in turn consider Mizo Christians as worshippers of a foreign religion as according to their belief, the Mizos have always had their traditional religion worshipping *Chung Khuanu* and therefore do need not Jesus. The Mizo Christians, so far, have not attempted to form a relationship with the members of the *Nunna Lalhnam* because they look down upon the group. `However they are still considered as members of Mizo community despite the absence of an interfaith relation with them.

What we need to remember is the freedom of religion provided by the Indian Constitution, allows both Christians and non-Christians to reach out to each other from their faiths' points of view. Unless we consciously create good interfaith relationships with people of all faiths the inter-religious enmity and fighting can happen at any time in the state.

The problem of denominationalism among Christians in Mizoram, if accompanied by denominational chauvinism and fanaticism, is very serious and can hinder Christian unity. Therefore the Christians in Mizoram have to carefully guard against denominational competition and fighting amongst themselves. We must strive towards organic unity in Christ. If the Christians do not attempt to create good inter-denominational unity they cannot become an example and witness to those of other faiths.

We have made mention of Mizo women's role in interfaith relations through inter-religious and inter-cultural marriages by highlighting the manner in which Mizo Christian women converted/convinced their spouses to embrace Christianity. There are also women who live happily with their non-Christian husbands where no conversion to Christianity has taken place. They acknowledge the value of their partners' faith and allow them take part in their respective religious functions and activities. Of course, there is sometimes confusion among their children as to whose faith they should follow.[27] Looking at this phenomenon of inter-religious and inter-cultural marriage between Mizo Christian women and men of other faiths and cultures, one can see the contribution of Mizo women towards interfaith relationships.

If women are equal partner in decision making there would, I believe, be lesser difficulty in showing respect to people of other faiths. Hence the active and meaningful participation of women in the church administration

[27] The writer found some children confused about whose parent's religion to follow. During childhood they followed their mother's religion; but on growing a little older the fathers sometimes arranged for the children to be exposed to their faiths.

is necessary towards having good interfaith relations in Mizoram. As long as women are restricted from the Church's decision making bodies and positions of authority, there will never be good interfaith relations in Mizoram because male church leaders hesitate to get into interfaith relation promoting programmes and discussions.

Interfaith Relations in the Context of Primal Women in North East India with Emphasis on Christian Mission

R.L. Hnuni

Introduction

It is a well-known fact that the World Missionary Conference Edinburgh 1910 marks the beginning of the modern ecumenical movement. The Conference appealed to 1200 delegates sent by missionaries to bring about the evangelization of the world in that generation. The ensuing concern which became a central issue in the Edinburgh Conference was the Christian understanding of and relationship to other religious traditions. Asia being the home of major religious traditions, the Conference had to encounter the religious traditions of Asia. While there was a strong evangelical thrust in the Conference, the discussions created and stimulated scholarly interest in the study of comparative religions and in exploring Christian relations to other religious traditions.

Right from the beginning, Christianity came in contact with the Graeco-Roman world that was composed of Jews and Gentiles resulting in the conflict between Jewish and Greek religious traditions. Consequently "the history of Christianity is the history of relations for the most part conflictual, with other faith traditions". The Edinburgh conference of 1910 right from the start had to tackle the same issue as many Christians were converts from other religious faiths in Asia. In the ensuing discussions on interfaith relationships at different meetings, interfaith dialogue became one of the important components and concerns for proclamation in the ecumenical journey of the churches. It is true that Christian mission is a controversial issue for many, particularly for people from other faiths especially when it comes to conversion. In order to carry out a successful mission program, relationships with people of other faiths should be handled very carefully.

The topic assigned to me may be rendered the role and contribution of tribal/primal women in dealing with people of other faiths as they carried out Christian mission in North East India (NEI). I find it rather difficult to synthesize the subject. However, it may be said that since Christian mission has had interfaith relations as one of its components right from the beginning, in the plurality of religions in India as a whole, Christian mission cannot be done without confronting or building relationships with other religious traditions. Then only can Christians achieve their purpose and goal for which they have a mission. In the following paper I will bring out Christian mission in NEI in brief, and in what way primal people particularly women contributed to the process of doing mission and evangelism and handled their relations with non Christians.

Christian Mission in NEI

Though a detailed presentation of Christian mission in NEI cannot be made at this juncture, a few lines may be written for information purposes. NEI is composed of seven states (now eight states with Sikkim), and to write anything about what is happening in NEI is as complex as writing about India. A variety of ethno-cultural groups inhabit the region and consequently various religious traditions are to be found. Most of the people are tribal though the Manipuris identify themselves as a sanskritized group and majority of them are Hindus. The tribal people in Mizoram, Nagaland and Meghalaya are dominantly Christian and the number of Christians among the non tribals in Assam, Manipur and Tripura are relatively small. Arunachal Pradesh is dominantly animist and evangelization has been taking place from different church traditions and it is the state which is the leading recipient in receiving Christian missionaries. The contribution of the indigenous people in mission and evangelism is enormous. The total Christian population in NEI is roughly 4.3 million according to the last census, and this accounts for 22.7 % of the Indian Christians.

A Brief Glimpse of the Role of Indigenous Christians in Mission in NEI

Mission in Assam and Meghalaya

Christianity in NEI was first brought to Assam by Roman Catholic missionaries in the 17th and 18th centuries in Cachar district of Assam and by Protestant Christians, particularly by the Baptist Mission of Serampore in the Nowgong district in 1811. The first contact with the Khasis was made by the Serampore Mission in 1813 when William Carey received a letter from W.N. Garret, the judge at Sylhet suggesting that the Khasi tribes should be evangelized. Krishna Pal took up the task of evangelizing the Khasis. Though he made converts, the work was short lived. The first notable evangelization work took place in Meghalaya in the 19th century and in Assam the Serampore Mission started a small work by opening a school in 1829. This however was closed in 1836 and another school was opened in Cherapunji, Meghalaya at the same time, but was closed down in

1837. In 1836 the missionaries from the American Baptist Missionary Society arrived in Assam. With only a few Assamese converts, and the missionaries were frustrated. They were, however, successful only among the tribal groups. In the other northeastern states, mission work started only in the 20th century.

Mission in Mizoram and Nagaland

The pioneer missionaries to Mizoram were J.H. Lorrain and F.W. Savidge sent by the Arthington Aborigines Mission in 1894. The work of evangelization was done largely by the early converts. They had a great zeal and burden to evangelize the neighbouring villages and so formed groups to preach the Gospel. Within a span of 60 years the whole of Mizoram was evangelized. In this work of evangelization, Khasi men and women played significant role.

The indigenous people's role is noteworthy in the mission work,. Even though western missionaries started the work, the main work of evangelization was done mainly by early converts. This is true of Meghalaya, Mizoram and Nagaland. Once they were converted, these new converts began with great zeal to evangelize their own people. The Khasis being a matriarchal society, women converts lost their rights of inheritance. In Mizoram, converts were excommunicated by village chiefs and found a village of refuge where Christians fled and worshipped together. Their zeal to evangelize their own people led to the establishment of the Home Mission towards the end of the 19th century in the Khasi hills. The Khasi converts' contributions to their own people was significant because of which Christianity grew faster than any other place except in Mizoram which received the Gospel later. It is also noteworthy that the Khasis involved also in cross-cultural evangelization, particularly in Mizoram.

Christianity reached Nagaland particularly the Ao Nagas in 1871 when E.W. Clark and his wife Mary Mead Clark arrived in the Ao dominated areas accompanied by the Assamese convert, Godhula. The Naga converts played a significant role in evangelizing the region. Like Meghalaya and Mizoram, the work of evangelization was carried out mostly by native evangelists as a result of whom they could report that all the churches were self supporting by 1898, within 27 years of the introduction of Christianity.

Mission in Manipur, Tripura and Arunachal Pradesh

There is a mixture of ethnic groups in Manipur – the non tribals called the Meiteis who follow Hinduism and the other tribal groups – the Tangkhul Naga, and other Naga tribal groups, the Thado-Kuki, the Paihte, etc. Like Mizoram the Arthington Aborigines Mission sent Mr. William Pettigrew in 1894 and started work among the Meiteis but he was not successful. He changed his work among the tribal Tangkhul Nagas. He could not do much work there due to political problems. However, the work of evangelism was carried on by early Kuki and Tangkhul converts among their own people. The same is true of the Zeliangrong and Mao Nagas in northern and northwestern Manipur and Christianity spread faster among the different tribes in Manipur only after World War I. In all this the early converts played a vital role.

Christian missionaries from the New Zealand Baptist Mission working in Bangladesh entered Tripura only in 1938. However, Mizo Christians settling in the state had started evangelistic work in as far back as 1917. By then there were Christians who were mainly Mizos, Garos and Khasis residing in the area and the New Zealand Mission along with these Christians formed the Tripura Baptist Christian Union which exists even today.

Arunachal Pradesh received missionaries as long back as 1836 when the American Baptist Union arrived in Sadiya in Assam with the purpose of reaching the Shan tribes in northern Burma and southern China. Later on the pioneer missionaries to Mizoram, J.H. Lorrain and F.W. Savidge were sent to the region probably in 1897, but the people did not welcome them and they returned to Mizoram as missionaries of the Baptist Missionary Society. Arunachal is remote and inhabited by different tribal groups having linguistic diversities. Hence the people living there did not have much interaction with people from other states and mission agencies. Christian missionaries from the neighbouring states – Nagaland and Mizoram and other volunteers started entering the state for evangelization only from 1960s and 1970s. Today there is a considerable growth in the Christian population among some Adi and Nishi tribes who claim to be almost 100% Christian. In this, the role of missionaries from Mizoram and Nagaland is very significant. There are people who still cling to the worship of sun-moon called Donyi Polo and the Ramkrishna Mission has established many school in the Along area that give free education children. This discourages many from embracing Christianity.

It is noteworthy that mission works in NEI was more successful among the tribal groups whose religion was animism than those who adhere to Hinduism, Islam or Buddhism. The hill tribal groups embraced Christianity faster than those who had long embraced these major religions of India. It is indeed hard to convince or convert people from other religious traditions as their faith had long been firmly rooted in their respective religions. Even then, there were converts from Hinduism and Islam.

Interfaith Relations in the Context of Primal Women and Mission

When we speak of interfaith relations in the context of the hill tribals in NEI as a whole, it must be kept in mind that since the NEI primal people, especially those in the hills, lived in isolation from the rest of India they had very little or no contact with people from the major religions found in other parts of India. Therefore interfaith relations point more to the relations between Christians and non-Christians who were animists. It was mainly among the primal people who were animists that Christian mission was carried out. Those who embraced Hinduism and Islam, etc., were mainly the people living in the plains of Assam though the Meiteis in Manipur were sanskritized and have identified themselves as Hindus.

It is only in the last few decades that Hindu fundamentalism has appeared in Arunachal Pradesh where the Anti-conversion Bill was introduced. Since then, missionaries in Arunachal have encountered problems relating to anti-Christian activities. Hinduism is a foreign religion which came from outside to the primal community as such interfaith dialogue with Hindus or Muslims or Buddhists was not a necessity. That problem of anti-Christian sentiments comes from outside and not so much from within, except when the local people were instigated by Hindu extremists groups. Due to these instigations from external forces, a cultural renewal movement that began in the 1960s was correlated with anti-Christian activities. This development contributed to the persecution of Christians which intensified in the 1970s. Churches reported numerous kidnappings and torture of Christians, the dispossession of their belongings, and the burning of their houses.

Interfaith Relations and Primal Women

Interfaith relations in the context of primal women in NEI may be viewed from a historical and modern perspective.

The Historical Perspective

In the past women's interfaith relations with people of other faiths was quite limited for the reasons mentioned above as well as due to their limited role and status in the family and society. In the absence of written record and without empirical research, it is difficult to comment on the manner in which primal women helped build relationships between Christians and non-Christians (animists) in the overall mission endeavour. However, it is the general understanding that women normally could relate others better to non-Christians than their male counterparts, and that they were better at building friendships with people irrespective of whether they were Christians or non-Christians.

Among primal women there were also brave and courageous women who risked their lives for the cause of their own people. For example, at the time that Christianity was introduced in Mizoram, there was a queen called Ropuiliani whose daring act humbled the British colonialists as she refused to conform to their demands and refused to submit herself and her people to British authority. She was the only one among so many chiefs, who dared to stand up to the cultural invasion that came with the territorial invasion by the British. While all the other chiefs, when asked, submitted to the authority of the British soldiers, she refused to submit and keep her integrity as Mizo queen who would not yield to the foreign invaders.

She risked her life protecting her people and religion to the extent of starving to death in 1895 in the Chittagong prison (in present-day Bangladesh) where she was imprisoned, because she refused to eat anything offered by the foreigners. She fulfilled her mission as a queen and protected her honour and that of her people and her culture. Even today, she is known and remembered as a lady who would not submit and yield to British colonizers and as the one who stood firm for what she believed to be right and true. Her bravery and strong personality is an example of primal women in NEI. Mission requires uncompromising people when necessary and when interfaith relations do not work, God's mission should be given priority

After the advent of Christianity, women were compelled to live with women who were animists by religion. Before Christianity, women did not play much role in religion as the father was all in all in religion. After the advent of Christianity, women became catalysts of its spread in the Church and society. This can be seen in the manner in which many women became evangelists.

Because of the need for evangelism and mission, many women became evangelists and even ordained church elders in the Mizoram Baptist Church. It is interesting to note that there was another Christian queen Lalkhumi, who had a great passion for evangelism and she was able convert all her people to Christianity.

We have the record of Siniboni, a Khasi woman who worked very hard for the evangelization not only of the Khasi people, but also among the Mizo people. She is called a Bible Woman. Like many other women evangelists, she crossed cultural and regional boundaries and came into contact with other tribal groups and was instrumental in bringing the Gospel message to the Mizos as well as other people. In Mizoram alone there were at least 26 women evangelists called Bible Women, from both the Presbyterian and Baptist church circles alone. It is good to note that among foreign missionaries who came to NEI, women missionaries stand out prominently and they played an important role in evangelism.

3) Educated women are importance factor for evangelization. Christian women became models for many non-Christian women. After getting an education they became teachers, nurses and worked in different spheres of life, and this became a very important factor that drew other non Christian women to becoming Christians.

The Modern Perspective

A few areas where interfaith relations may be built up are mentioned:

1) Economic life: Economic life is the area in which women can develop interfaith relations. Tribal women have been the backbone of a society's economic life right from the primal period till today. They engage themselves in various spheres of life through trading and marketing, and this is an area where interfaith relations can be developed by women.

2) Business: Business is another area in which interfaith relations can be developed. Women today are involved in carrying out different kinds of business and through this women come in contact with people of different faiths. Today women show that they are in no way inferior to their male counterparts in this regard. In Mizoram particularly, Mizo women are the main persons who run businesses, trade and travel to different corners in India and abroad for such purposes. It has also become a means of evangelization in various mission fields. A woman named Villy for example, runs a beauty parlour. She shares the Gospel message with many of the women who visit her parlour.

2) Education: It was Mrs. Clark the pioneer missionary to Nagaland along with her husband who first introduced education for boys and girls though initially parents refused to send their daughters to school. There have been outstanding educated Naga women who have worked untiringly towards the evangelization of their people. In Mizoram, Miss Chapman (Pi Zirtiri) played a significant role in educating Mizo women. There were more women missionaries than men, and they played significant roles in education, in evangelism and in health and sanitation. But as it is often done in a patriarchal culture, history is silent about the role women have played in mission history. Those whose names are mentioned and recorded are those who were really outstanding figures. This is true in other parts of NEI in which there were many women who made outstanding contributions and played great role in mission and evangelism. But most of the time their names were forgotten or ignored. In most cases history is silent about many women and only a few women have appeared in historical records.

Because of the patriarchal cultural traditions and values which dehumanized women, many daring and courageous women were not able to take up their role in mission as they should have done. They were not allowed to receive an education as women were discouraged from going to school. They were controlled by either their fathers or their husbands, and were required to stay back at home to look after the household duties. In spite of their lower status and the conditions they faced, some women still emerged as outstanding contributors in mission and evangelism.

Right from the primitive period till today, women struggle more with the attitude of men than with people of other faiths so far as NEI is concerned. In spite of the low regard given to them, women, who had the freedom to exercise their faith and passion for mission became fruitful instruments of God. They were accepted as full time missionaries and many committed their lives to mission work even at the risk of losing partners or remaining unmarried. Women converts could cross cultural boundaries and establish relationships with others and their simplicity yet firmness and passion for evangelizing other people made them successful missionaries in their own right even though they were not officially recognized as missionaries in many cases. As they had easy access to others and were easily approachable, right from the inception of Christianity among the tribal communities of NEI, primal women's role and contributions were significant in the mission work.

Conclusion: Women's Contribution Today

Today mission and evangelism is the concern of most churches in NEI, particularly in Mizoram and Nagaland. From experience, I can mention the Baptist Church of Mizoram as an example. There are more women missionaries in different parts of NEI as well as overseas. In many places where schools are established the observations of the Church leaders is unanimous: 'Wherever women take the lead as Principal of Mission Schools either Home or Outreached mission, they do much better than men Principals.' As a result church leaders look out for more educationally qualified women to be the heads of the schools in mission fields.

Women are very much enterprising and I met one of my former students Miss Adono Angami, a Naga in Thailand who went to Taiwan as a missionary, and established an orphanage there. Last April I met a Mizo woman whose husband is a recognized missionary among the Galo tribes in Arunachal Pradesh. She also worked along with her husband, and in fact did a good job as she could sing and preach in Hindi. She formed women's groups and they went and preached the Gospel in Mapu village where no Christians have visited. She along with the other Galo women talked to the village chief to organize a gathering of the villagers and she preached the Gospel and sang songs of praise and love. These women could cross the different social and cultural barriers more easily than men and they were invited to go there again. She hopes that at least some of the villagers will be converted. It was a the Mizo lady who first went to Mendabari in West Bengal as a missionary nurse. Now there are many Christians there and a school has also been established there. There could be many more such women who have carried out such pioneering work, but it is often the ordained men will baptize the converts and become known as the pioneer missionaries.

We can thus see that women have been instrumental and God's agents in building relationship with other peoples, and non-Christians. We have come to a time where we must believe that if women were Church leaders today, there could be a much better relationship between Christians and people of other faiths and between denominational churches and that true ecumenism would have its place so that God's reign would be extended.

SECTION VI

CHRISTIAN RELATIONSHIP WITH MARXIST/HUMANIST/SECULAR IDEOLOGIES

On the Need to End Capitalism and Build a Society of Sharing

Gabriele Dietrich

Locating Myself

I am dedicating this paper to the memory of Dr. Stanley Samartha, who was a pioneer in developing the dialogue with secular ideologies in the WCC. I am thankful that an attempt has been made to uphold the dialogue with secular ideologies in this pre-Edinburgh conference. I also feel it is significant that, in the face of the present world-wide crisis of capitalism, Marxism has been specifically mentioned and remembered as an ideological force which since the first half of the 19th Century has contested the legitimacy of capitalism.[1] I also want to remember that the Edinburgh Mission Conference of 1910 took place between the revolutionary uprisings of 1905 and the Russian Revolution of 1917. These revolutions led to the overthrow of the Zar and contributed crucially to the defeat of Fascism in Europe. The peoples of the Soviet Union have paid an enormous price during World War II. The formation of Socialist regimes in different countries in Eastern Europe in the end forties and the victory of the Chinese revolution led to the formation of power blocks, which brought about the contestations of the Cold War. This period came to an end after the fall of the Berlin Wall in 1989 and the ensuing disintegration of the

[1] The Communist Manifesto, published in 1848, starts with the sentence: "A specter goes round in Europe". This refers to the specter of the rising working class. Now that capitalism is in crisis again, the world is still haunted by "Specters of Marx" (Jacques Derrida: Specters of Marx, Verso 1992). The latest translation by Peggy Kamuf; Jacques Derrida: Specters of Marx. The State of debt, the work of mourning and the new International (Routledge Paperback, 2006). This happens despite the demise of actually existing socialism in Eastern Europe and the sub-version of Socialist countries in Asia by the WTO and corporate forces. In India, Communist Parties are part of the democratic process. The CPI-M has a long record of being in power in West Bengal, Kerala and Tripura, though it has had severe conflicts with peasants in Singur and Nandigram over SEZ policies. Maoist struggles are expanding in many parts of the country and are faced with cleansing processes like Salwar Judum and encounter deaths. They themselves turn more violent in the process. The question how to create a democratic, participatory process of transformation, which is forceful enough to bring change, is wide open.

Soviet Union and Eastern Europe. This led Francis Fukoyama[2] to proclaim "The End of History", which was followed shortly by Huntington's[3] perspective of the possibility of "The Clash of Civilizations". We see the hubris of a single focus capitalist system and the shift from economics to culture and identity politics. The irony is that the theological world has happily followed the path of identity politics at the cost of a critique of what is happening in the economic field. The rhetoric of social justice has also been usurped by the claims to rights of castes, tribes, ethnicities, languages, religions and others minorities, of every description, sub-nationalities, women, third sex, differently abled, HIV positive, subalterns, anybody with a claim to "difference". The legitimate claim of cultural rights has been used to obscure mechanisms of exploitation. The toiling classes of workers and peasants are hardly visible, except when they commit suicide. While global warming and water crisis are now officially admitted, it is the corporates who are claiming to be the guardians of the crisis and the harbingers of any solution. They try to control the educational system and try to sell us crisis as opportunity. The State abdicates social responsibility and becomes more oppressive.

Let me therefore say something very personal: I have an obsession with Peace and an end to hunger. This is possibly, because I was born in Berlin during a civil bombardment in 1943 and the war still went on like this for a year and a half. I saw the first real food at home when I was five. Before that we survived by being trouped to a Swedish soup kitchen, rain or shine. We had to survive the blockade of Berlin, being "the free world in the red sea". I was a third generation refugee.

The greatest strain in our generation was to come to understand how it could have happened that six million Jews had been gassed, neatly industrially annihilated. How could it be that only very few people had resisted, that the vast majority said they had not even known?

It is in this context that I first understood about Christian Marxist dialogue. I discovered the Church, because I realized that there had been a Confessing Church, which was in the resistance against Hitler. I was taken by my youth group to Dahlem, where Martin Niemoeller and Helmut Gollwitzer had been in the resistance. I was also taken to a centre called after Paul Schneider, an ordinary pastor, incarcerated in a concentration camp, whose lonely conviction it was not to salute the Swastika flag. For this, he was beaten to pulp daily. However, he kept shouting bible verses from his cell. There were communists in the same camp, who saluted the flag, because they wanted to survive. Even they drew strength from what Paul Schneider did, though they were atheists. It was his act of disobedience unto death which gave them strength to live. This was my

[2] Fukoyama, Francis: "The End of History" in: National Interest, (Washington DC, July 1989).

[3] Huntington, Samuel P. : The Clash of Civilizations and the Remaking of World Order (Simon and Schuster, New York, 1996).

first encounter with Christian Marxist dialogue. A communist who had met Paul Schneider in the camp told the story to the youth after nearly two decades. Despite the cold war I did not perceive communists as enemies.

I knew there had been a common cause between Christians and communists in the resistance against fascism. I knew this despite having lived for a while under a Soviet occupation army which was known for the rape of the women of the civil population. It happened to our neighbors, nothing was simple. I saw the uprising of the 17th of June 1953, the uprising of the workers in the GDR against an autocratic Workers State. They marched through the road where I came from school. If gave me an abiding faith in workers uprisings and in democracy. I butchered my piggy bank in support and I did it again during the Hungarian uprising in 1956, while everybody around me said I was nuts.

The Indian Anti-Colonial Struggle

The Indian situation developed in its own peculiar ways during the early forties. Mahatma Gandhi launched the Quit India Movement on August 9th 1942, but Marxists and Christians were not much part of that struggle. The Marxists kept out of it, because they sided with Stalin and the "allies" in the anti-fascist struggle. Quit India for them meant weakening one of the "allies". This lack of presence in the anti-colonial struggle stuck on to the Left for many decades.

Christians had pro-colonial leanings and were therefore only very sparingly represented in the anti-colonial struggle.[4] While anti-colonial uprisings from the end of the 18th century onwards had participation of Hindus and Muslims, the Churches kept aloof.[5] Another factor lay in the caste composition of the uprisings. While so-called backward castes and "criminal tribes" were very much in the picture, Dalits initially found some social progress by joining the army. They were excluded from the military only later.[6]

During the Freedom struggle, Dalits identified with the leadership of Dr. Ambedkar, the father of the Indian constitution. He was side-lined by

---

[4] George Thomas: Christian Indians and Indian Nationalism 1885-1950; An Interpretation in Historical and theological perspectives, Frankturt, 1968. An interesting deviation is K.C. Kumarappa, a Christian Gandhian economist. See Solomon Victus: Religion and Economics of Dr.J.C. Kumarappa, Gandhism Redefined, ISPCK, 2003.

[5] K. Rajayya: The South Indian Rebellion: 1800-1801, The First War of Independence (Ratna Publications, Madurai, 2000).

[6] This exclusion happened after the 1857 uprising which led to full-fledged colonialism instead of Company Raj.

Gandhi in the Pune Pact, in which separate electorates for Dalits were turned down and direct political representation for Dalits was denied.[7]

It is important to keep in mind that Dr. Ambedkar was quite inspired by Marxism and the Russian Revolution but differentiated himself from the violent means and the resulting lack of democracy.[8] Ambedkar advocated State ownership of all land and the building of cooperatives to run the agricultural production.[9]

However, he chose the spiritual path of conversion to Buddhism to fulfill his ideal of democracy, non-violence and abolition of caste.

One of his most important contributions is Ambedkar's struggle for Freedom of Religion. He announced already in 1935 that though he was born a Hindu, he was not going to die as a Hindu. He enshrined the Right to profess and proclaims one's religion in the constitution and the right to voluntarily change it. His concept of Freedom of Religion also implied the Right to Freedom from Religion. His re-interpretation of Buddhism is entirely rationalistic and he believed that the values of the French Revolution: Liberty, Equality and Brotherhood were already pre-figured in the teachings of the Buddha.[10] He also did not believe in the existence of a soul and actively discouraged religious rituals. At the same time he was deeply compassionate and practically gave up his life in the struggle for Dalit liberation when he died an untimely death two months after his conversion in 1957 due to heart attack, while working throughout the night on his manuscripts. His greatest heart break was that he was unable to push through the reforms of the Hindu Code Bill, due to the opposition of Rajendra Prasad. The tragedy today is that many Dalit movements do not care to read Dr.Ambedkar's writings in depth. Nor do many of the non-Dalit intellectuals own him as a leader of the nation, not only of Dalits. If India today has one of the best constitutions in the world, it is thanks to his untiring labour. It is not sufficiently remembered that Dr.Ambedkar seriously attempted to build a working class movement and only launched into abolition of caste after realizing that caste was not "division of labour", as Gandhi tended to assume with his concept of "bread labour", but that

---

[7] Despite the Communal Award of August 1932 given by Ramsay McDonald which conceded separate electorates for untouchables, this was reverted due to M.K. Gandhi's resistance. Ambedkar accepted joint electorates with reservation of seats in the Pune Pact in Sept. 1934 in order to prevent the fast unto death which Gandhi was ready to stage. Dalits have remembered this as Ambedkar saving Gandhi's life and the lives of Dalits, not as a defeat. On Pune Pact see W.N. Huber: Dr. Ambedkar A Critical study (PPH 1973) see also Gail Omvedt: Ambedkar. Towards an Enlightened India (New Delhi: Penguin) 37-55.

[8] "Buddha or Karl Marx" in B.R. Ambedkar collected works, vol.3, Chapter 18.

[9] See M.L. Kasare: Economic Philosophy of Dr.B.R. Ambedkar (B.I. Publications, New Delhi, 1996).

[10] B.R. Ambedkar: The Buddha and his Dhamma (Siddhartha Publications, Bombay, 1991) first Ed.1951.

caste was the foundation for the division of the labourers. He consequently advocated inter-caste marriage to break the marriage cycle. Dr. Ambedkar was impressed with the achievements in education, medical services, industrialization, agriculture in the Soviet Union, but he favored non-violent transformation, based on compassion and solidarity. At the same time he whole-heartedly quarreled with what he experienced as Gandhi's patronizing and autocratic ways.

The "Development Decade" and "Limits to Growth"

The sixties were the years which had been declared as the "Development Decade" by the UN and consequently, they brought the upsurge of the "Green Revolution" in India, which led to food self reliance but also to considerable polarization between rich and poor, especially in the country side.[11] The early sixties also brought the War with China in 1964 and the split of the Left into CPI and CPI-M. Towards the end of the sixties, the polarizations in the countryside led to the emergence of the Naxalite movement.

However, during this decade a Marxist ferment swept the globe. The Cultural Revolution in China, though in-sufficiently understood,[12] found echos in Paris and Berlin. Struggles for transformation took place in many of the Latin American countries. Students' uprisings were rife in Berkeley, Berlin, Paris, but also in Thailand and in the Philippines. Tansania underwent a struggle for Ulemia Socialism. The people of Vietnam went on with their heroic struggle against US imperialism, which culminated finally in 1975 and the struggle against Apartheid in South Africa made waves in the Ecumenical Movement.

At the same time, decisive struggles for democracy were lost. E.g. the awakening of democratic socialism in Chechoslovakia, the "Prague Spring" under Dubchek and Svoboda, was once again defeated by the invasion of Soviet tanks in 1969. These failures became decisive twenty years later in the process of the collapse of socialism in Eastern Europe and the unraveling of the Soviet Union. One of the ecumenical bodies which consistently pursued dialogue with Marxism was the Christian Peace conference, in which Christians and Marxists from Eastern Europe were in an enduring dialogue with their counterparts all over the world. This played an important role in India and Sri Lanka. Different ideological streams fed into these dialogues and the contributions of CISRS in Bangalore, led by Paul Devanandan and M.M. Thomas, need to be remembered.

This period coincided with the rising crisis of "development" during the seventies. Ecology first cropped up as a topic in the connotation of

---

[11] Francine Frankel: India's Green revolution: Economic Gains and Political Costs (Bombay, OUP, 1971).

[12] Joan Robinson: The Cultural Revolution in China (Penguin, 1970).

"pollution". There had been considerable optimism of unlimited growth and the blessings of industrialism, which led to hymns like "God of Concrete, God of Steel". But by the early seventies, pollution was clearly identified as a major threat.[13] This coincided with the Limits to Growth report of the Club of Rome[14] and the subsequent discussions on "sustainable development"[1515] which turned out to be a gigantic eyewash. The twenty years after report: Beyond the Limits showed that growth had already gone out of control and had become counter –productive. This was called "overshoot". The forces in power kept their eyes fast shut all the while and produced continuous denials. The most recent report explores scenarios to contain the damage, but denial goes on. The absurd situation was aggravated by the constant arms race during the Cold War. Ironically, the development paradigm of technocratically mediated unlimited growth was common to both the power blocks and the image of Nikita Khrushchev hammering the desk of the UN with his shoe while announcing how the Soviet Union would overtake the US two years hence, was a memorable image of a historical epoch of hubris and blindness. Criticism grew from within the socialist fold, but it was suppressed with a heavy hand. In the GDR, Wolfgang Harich came up with a severe critique of the ecological implications of socialist development, but his suggested solutions only required more State control.[16] Harich emigrated to Austria, as that country had taken a stand against nuclear energy. He later lost his GDR citizenship and went to West Germany. A much broader based critique, which integrated the organizational problems of Socialist societies with the ecological crisis, was The Alternative, developed by Rudolf Bahro.[17] He was forced to emigrate to the Federal Republic and became a member of the Green Party before he died of cancer.

Democratic Upsurge

[13] See e.g. New Songs of Asian Cities published by the Urban Industrial Mission Committee of the CCA in 1972, 46f and 62-64.

[14] For Comparison with the present situation see Donella Meadows, Jorgen Randers & Dennis Meadows: Limits to Growth. The 30 years Update (Earths an UK, 2005, Reprinted 2006 & 2008). The 20 years Review had the title: Beyond the Limits (1992).

[15] Brundtland, Gro Harlem: Our Common Future. World Commission on Development (OUP, Delhi, 1987).

[16] Wolfgang Harich: Communism without Growth (1975). Harich was a staunch fighter against nuclear energy. He had to publish his book in the West and later had to emigrate. See my article on him in The Marxist Review, vol.XIII, no.9, March 1980. 332-336.

[17] Rudolf Bahro: The Alternative in Eastern Europe published in German 1977. English translation by David Fernbach, (NLB 1978). See my Review in The Marxist Review vol.XV, No.2&3 August /Sept.1981.

In the mean time in India, the class polarizations in the end sixties led to severe human rights violations. In 1968, on Dec.25, 44 so-called "Harijans",[18] mostly women and children, were burned alive while seeking shelter from a landlord in a hut in the village of Kizhvenmani in East-Tanjore. This was in the context of a wage struggle led by Marxists against the landlords. When this happened, the Gandhian freedom fighter S. Jaganathan and his Dalit wife Krishnammal Jaganathan moved into the area to "bring peace" and to try to tackle the question of land and production. This Gandhian initiative has endured till today in Vinobha Ashram in Kutthur. One lakh acres of land have been distributed. Recently, Krishnammal and S. Jaganathan received the Right Livelihood Award for their contribution to improve people's life.

This is an area where landlordism and bonded labour were co-existing and where Gandhism, Marxism and popular religion of Christians (Velanganni), Muslims (Nagoor) and Hinduism (from the Thanjavoor temple to countless village shrines) were existing cheek by jowl. I myself did a study of these circumstances in the early seventies, while working with CISRS,[19] staying in the affected villages for longer periods and experiencing full – fledged untouchability. This was the time when Stanley Samartha took on board the dialogue with secular ideologies in the WCC. This was also the period when Abraham Airookuzhiel joined the CISRS and started his deep studies of Dalit popular cultures.[20]

It also happened that 1975 was International Women's Year of the UN, which was later expanded into the UN decade until 1985 and the Churches belatedly had their decade in support of women from 1988 to 1998.

This was also the time of the Emergency declared by Mrs.Gandhi in response to a court case in the Allahabad High Court against her. The suspension of the fundamental rights of the Indian constitution led to formidable democratic resistance. Interestingly, CPI supported the Emergency, while the CPI-M and the Maoists opposed it. Jaya Prakash Narayan, who led the "total revolution" from Bihar, was incarcerated and later died of his kidney ailment. When asked what was the content of the total revolution, he referred to the seven fold revolution of Ram Manohar Lohia,[21] a socialist leader, who had died an untimely death due to medical neglect and who in his untiring campaigns had addressed questions of women, caste and untouchability, language, land reform, workers rights,

---

[18] The Ambedkarite Term "Dalits" was not yet in general use at that time, the patronizing Gandhian term "children of God" was still more prevalent.

[19] Gabriele Dietrich: Religion and People's Organization in East Thanjavur (CISRS, Bangalore, 1977).

[20] Abraham A.M. Ayrookuzhiel: Essays on Dalits, Religion and Liberation (CISRS, Bangalore, 2006) and Dalit Desiyata: The Kerala experience in Development and Class Struggle (ISPCK, 1990).

[21] Lohia's concept of Saptakranti (Sevenfold Revolution) is explained in the Preface of: Marx, Gandhi and Socialism (Delhi, 1963) xxx-xxxx.

peace and disarmament, including the problems of nuclear energy. Both Lohia and J.P. Narayan had been impressed with progress made in the Soviet Union in terms of workers' rights, but like Ambedkar resorted to the non-violent democratic path of struggle.

The unique quality of these confrontations was that they led to ideological battles and new conceptualizations which made the political life exciting and resulted in new insights and even political victories. After all, Ms. Gandhi was defeated when she declared elections in 1977. There was also the railway strike and the epic textile workers strike led by Dr. Dattar Samant.

The women's movements, while starting their long drawn struggles against violence and for gender just family laws, came up with a flood of new insights regarding patriarchy, caste and class.[22]

There were also students' movements and attempts of young people to create "non-party political formations".[23] This was a valid democratic impulse drawing on socialist inspirations and side-stepping the dogmatism of established Marxist parties. However, it led into the build-up of an NGO culture, which ultimately catered to professionalisation of social work and destruction of revolutionary and transformative energy. At the outset of this period there was a strong desire towards conceptual clarification and a serious endeavour to come to understand the connections between economic, socio-cultural, political and religious fields and representations in society.[24] Methods of Social Analysis were developed drawing on the experiences of social movements. The experiences and writings of people like M.M.Thomas and Fr. Sebastian Kappen, who had lived the Christian-Marxist dialogue within their own minds and lives, became very important.[25]

Francois Houtart and Genevieve Lemercinier were instrumental in organizing the First Asian Seminar on Religion and Development in 1973 for three weeks at the NBCLC in Bangalore with over one hundred participants from all over India and from different Asian countries. This led to enthusiasm in learning methods of Social Analysis. The method was

---

[22] See Akerkar, Supriya: "Theory and Practice of Women's Movement in India. A discourse Analysis" in: EPW vol.XXX, no.17, 19 April 1995 W-S-2-W-S-23.

[23] See e.g. Wignaraja, Ponna: New Social Movements in the South: Empowering the People (London, Zed Books, 1993) especially the articles by Rajni Kothari and Samir Amin.

[24] See e.g. the case study on the fish workers movement in Kerala: Nalini Nayak and Gabriele Dietrich: Transition or Transformation? A study on the Mobilization, Organization and Emergence of Consciousness among the Fish Workers in Kerala (CSA, Madurai, 2002).

[25] M.M. Thomas: Response to Tyranny. Writings between July 1975 and Feb 1977 (New Delhi, 1979). Sebastian Kappen: Liberation Theology and Marxism (Putamba 1986) also: Future of Socialism and Socialism of the Future (Visthar 1992). Francois Houtart and Genevieve Lemercinier: The Great Asiatic Religions and their Social functions (Lou vain 1985).

further developed by Indian Social Institute Bangalore and CISRS and was also presented to the CSI Bishops, who adopted it whole heartedly.[26] It was also widely used in Sri Lanka, the Philippines and other Asian Countries. Courses in Social Analysis were developed at TTS since the mid seventies and from 1984 higher studies in Social Analysis were started. In summer 1985, Dr. M.M. Thomas lit the torch to inaugurate Centre for Social Analysis in Madurai. This later led to a M.Th. programme in Social Analysis at TTS. Courses at the B.D. level, especially "Towards Understanding Indian Society" were made compulsory at the B.D. level by the Senate of Serampore. However, a running battle went on whether the teaching was a matter of "Social Issues", or whether serious ideological and conceptual efforts had to be made to clarify perspectives in order to aim at a transformation, which would bring more equality, democracy, social justice and peace. A course in the final year on "contemporary ideologies" in TTS was dropped and has never been re-instated. Likewise, it has been a struggle to sustain biblical theology with an integrated approach.

The End of a Bi-Polar World and the Fragmentations of Post-Modernism

As already mentioned, the end eighties appeared to signify the collapse of a bi-polar world as far as a socialist alternative to capitalism was concerned. It was also the time when Islam as the "new enemy" became visible. However, two things need to be kept in mind: The actually existing Socialism in Eastern Europe was in many ways only a form of state capitalism, as it was modeled after the Western capitalist example and in stiff competition with it.[27] It did not pose a socialist alternative with people's participation. Secondly, the totalitarian take-over by the international finance institutions and the WTO was planned already since the Bretton Woods Conference in 1944. It was a very long term plan which was implemented over half a century, consolidated in the eighties by the Washington Consensus. It has been shown in recent years that this take-over was in fact extremely violent. Naomi Klein has called it the Shock Doctrine.[28] She also dwells on the first 9/11 event, which was in 1973, – the bombing of the Moneda, the Presidential Palace in Santiago de Chile by the CIA, to overthrow the democratically elected regime of Salvador Allende, who died gun in hand, defending democracy. Electoral victories like that of Allende was the real challenge to capitalism. It took decades of fascism under Pinochet to undo this challenge, with tens of thousands of political

[26] See also: The Church and Social Justice, (CSI Publication, Bangalore 1975).

[27] The term State Capitalism was coined by Raya Dunayerskaya. See e.g. Philosophy of Revolution. From Hegel to Mao (New Jersey Humanities Press 1973).

[28] Naomi Klein: The Shock Doctrine. The Rise of Disaster Capitalism (Allan Lane, Penguin 2007).

murders and disappearances. Naomi Klein also analyses in detail the dismantling of Eastern Europe.

The 9/11 of the bombing of the World Trade Centre in New York by Muslim terrorists is a symptom of revolt against the terror of Empire, which went to work so very systematically in the second half of the last century. It is also, very ironically, an outcome of the identity politics, which was unleashed to deflect attention from the economic side of the totalitarian takeover of capitalism since the late eighties and early nineties.

This was also the period when we saw a shift in the Human Rights regime of the UN. While the US and Europe always claimed the monopoly of political human rights, the socialist countries had always been seen as neglecting political human rights in favor of greater economic equality. From the eighties through the nineties we get the struggles for cultural human rights, which are closely related to the struggles of local communities in what was earlier called the "Third World". We get Women's Rights as Human Rights and Dalit Rights as Human Rights. Among other things this had to do with the upsurge of people's movements and non-party political formations mentioned above. There is no doubt that these were genuine emancipatory struggles, be it the fish workers movement, the women's movements, the Dalit movements, the Adivasi struggles, the unions in the unorganized sector, the ecological movements. The presence of numerous people's movements since the sixties and their proliferation through the seventies and eighties created a broad discussion on the phenomenon of social movements.[29] However, during the nineties, it became clear that the terminologies had been drastically changed. This went along with wide-spread NGO isation. E.g. the analysis of patriarchy, caste, class and the State, which was capable of analyzing existing power structures, was systematically changed to "gender-awareness" and formation of self-help groups, which relieved the State of much of the burden of micro-credit and sold self-exploitation as liberation. De-centralisation and local governance were instrumentalised as "social capital" and "stake-holders" were encouraged to come together in Public-Private-Partnership (PPP). Of course the goal of such enterprise was much of the time to take the "nature-capital" out of people's hands and to make it cheaply available to the corporates.

Despite this general trend, people's movements soldiered on untiringly and achieved some victories like the Right to Information, National Rural Employment Guarantee Act, the Forest Act and the Right to Food

[29] See: "Social Movements and Collective Action in India" in: Vikalp Alternatives vol.VIII, no.1&2, 2000, 93-127 with articles by Gabriele Dietrich, Nalini Nayak, Lalrindiki Ralte, John Jayaharan. See also: Gabriele Dietrich: "Loss of Socialist Vision and Options before the Women's Movement" in: EPW, vol.XXXVIII, no.43, Oct, 25, 2003. For a comprehensive theoretical discussion see Neera Chandoke: The State and Civil Society. Explorations in Political Theory (Sage New Delhi, 1995).

Campaign. However, it was very difficult to implement the rights which had been conceded and the rulers virulently pursued their polarizing exploitative policies while appealing to the Aam Admi. In the meantime, the Left had also embarked on modernization and "development", which led to the most painful confrontations in West Bengal's Singur and Nandigram, producing the death through police firing and goonda violence as collateral damage. The Nano car of the Tata's was fittingly moved to Modi's Gujarat.

At the international level, significant advances were made in Latin America, where several countries achieved leftist victories and started to oppose the US hegemony, most notably Venezuela and Bolivia, encouraged by the tenacious, struggle for survival of Cuba. Nicaragua, after a short-lived revolution and manipulated rightist victories, inched ahead towards socialism and the World Social Forum, repeatedly hosted in Lula's Brazil, projected a rainbow coalition of populist forces, while the Zapatista struggle in the South of Mexico made a wider impact with a populist neo-Marxist perspective. The Bamako Appeal and the 6th Declaration of the Zapatista Movement give diverse pictures of such attempts to work out a common direction.[30] Despite India hosting the Arian Social Forum in Hyderabad and the WSF in Mumbai; this has not had a significant impact in India, probably due to the great cultural diversity in the sub-continent.

Much of the political and ideological confusion in these situations was created by the anxiety to stem the tide of Hindutva and Muslim fundamentalism, which after the second 9/11 was characterized as "Talibanisation" of society. There were even debates on the "Talibanisation of Hinduism" after the events in Kandhamal in Orissa in 2007 and 2008 and the anti-Christian incidents in Karnataka under the BJP regime.

The upsurge of religion-and caste-based identity politics went on briskly during the eighties and nineties. It attained academic legitimacy in the identity politics of postmodernism and post-colonialism, which indirectly benefited from the critique of science and technology and of "enlightenment" which had been developed in the women's movement as well as in Gandhian circles.[31] However, a solution to these debates does not seem to be in sight.

One of the early and very sensitive critiques of post-modernism in the UK and in the US was put forward by Chetan Bhatt,[32] who points out the

---

[30] Kolya Abramsky: The Bamako Appeal and the Zapatista 6th Declaration. From Reorganizing the Existing World to Creating New Ones (CACIM, New Delhi, 2006).

[31] E.g. Vandana Shiva: Staying Alive (Kali for Women. New Delhi, 1988) Women, Ecology and Survival in India. Vandana Shiva and Maria Mies: Eco-Feminism (Zed Books 1993) Ashish Nandy: Science, Hegemony and Violence: A requiem for Modernity (New Delhi, OUP, 1988).

[32] Chetan Bhatt: Liberation and Purity. Race, New Religious Movements and the Ethics of Post-Modernity (London, UCL Press, 1997).

totalitarian and fascist trends in the cooked up histories of religion-based identity claims in the Diaspora. He points out the ethical weakness in post-modernism, which has not resisted these totalitarian and often racist tendencies. Other authors have tried to take recourse to rescuing enlightenment and scientific temper, be it in a Marxist perspective[33] or in a rationalistic modern science approach with under pinnings from Dr. Ambedkar.[34] However, the standpoints do not meet, because the Marxist critique trends to be weak on the potential for cultural revolt, while the classical rationality of a scientific temper position is rather blind to the pitfalls of Science and Technology as Ideology[35] and is too trusting about capitalism. Where both these positions are missing out is the question of genuine religious reform and cultural revolt. Genuine religious reform, in my understanding, requires a clear sense of social justice and economics. In Christian terminology: We cannot serve God and Mammon. We need to build a sense of solidarity with the poor and among the poor.

Despite this very basic insight, Christian institutions have much of the time sided with the rich. We have to have the humility to be ready to declass ourselves and to truly be on the side of the poor. My teacher Helmut Gollwitzer called it: relinquishing our privileges.[36] This may require relinquishing cars instead of advertising them as "God's Gift". We have to remember the rainbow after Noah's flood. We have to care for Earth, water and all the creatures therein.

The other crucial aspect of genuine religious reform is that we cannot be totalitarian. We have to step down from the claim to universality of any religion. We have to have the humility to accept other people's faith, as legitimate and mutually enriching. We also have to accept freedom from religion as an option. The Edinburgh vision of Christianizing the world in one generation has to be surrendered. The suffering servant has to take over from the conquering king, to put it in the terminology of M.M.Thomas. So while we have to accept pluralism, we also have to overcome fragmentation, appreciating each other in our humanity and building unity against exploitation of people's labour and of nature, joining struggles for

---

[33] Achin Vanaik: Communalism Contested: Religion Modernity and Secularization (New Delhi, Vishtaar, 1997)

[34] Meera Nanda: Prophets Facing Backward. Postmodernism, Science and Hindu Nationalism (Permanent Black) (Delhi, 2004). See also: Postmodernism and Religious Fundamentalism A Scientific Rebuttal of Hindu Science (Chennai, Navayana, 2003)

[35] "Science and Technology as Ideology" was a very old title by Jurgen Habermas in the late sixties. It is by no means outdated. Interestingly Habermas, a great defender of Enlightenment, has recently exhorted present day intellectuals to take religion more seriously. I owe this information to a personal communication by Neera Chandoke, but I have not had access to Habermas' recent writings.

[36] Helmut Gollwitzer: The Rich Christians and the Poor Lazarus (German) Munich 1968. This book appeared at the time of the Uppsala Conference of the WCC

social justice and trying to build peace in freedom, love and dignity and to sustain what is left of God's good creation under global warming and nuclear threat.

The War on Terror and the Fate of the Earth

Let me sound a somewhat alarming note towards the end of my deliberations, because we happen to live in very dangerous times. One of the most disturbing facts is that "War on Terror" has become a very popular and uniting concept in national and international politics. It is one of the devices with which capitalism keeps itself afloat. War on terror explains and legitimizes so-called encounter deaths. It explains the civil war in Chhattisgarh declared as Salwa Judem. It justifies the arrest of Dr. Binayak Sen for two years of his life, only because as State Secretary of PUCL, in full view of the authorities, he kept contact with political prisoners and documented the human rights violations in Dantewada District.[37] War on Terror justifies arbitrary violence on anybody who happens to be called a Naxalite. After Singur and Nandigram, Lalgarh is the new site. At the same time it is true that the Maoist Left has become more desperate and violent and the local population is getting caught in between.

One of the most disturbing events has been the war to the finish against the Tamil minority led by the LTTE in the North of Sri Lanka. This war has led to disproportionate civilian casualties and large numbers of people maimed. It has displaced 3 lakhs of civilians. President Rajapakshe and his brothers appear as internationally acclaimed heroes. Under international pressure even the UN, who highlighted the problem for a long time, has now ruled out the possibility of prosecuting the war crimes through the International Criminal Court in The Hague. It is highly doubtful what is happening to the Right to Return of the Tamil population. While M.S. Swaminathan has pulled out under pressure from development projects in those parts, we hear that Israel will step in to help changing the face of the northern region. It is also important to understand that the crisis of the Sri Lankan State is not just one of ethnic fragmentation, but constitutes a much more profound crisis of democracy. There is a totalitarian suppression of freedom of speech and public opinion, kept in place by constant threat of disappearances in white vans for anyone who does not comply. The Singhala journalist Lasantha Wickrematunga was murdered within days of having written his own obituary.

The international community condones all this, because Sri Lanka is a hot spot from the point of view of military control of the Indian Ocean and

---

[37] Doctors in Defence of Dr. Binayak Sen: Indian Doctor in Jail: The Story of Binayak Sen (New Delhi 2008) Human Rights Forum Publication 14: Death Displacement and Deprivation in Dantewada: A Report (Hyderabad 2006) see also: Justice Krishna Iyer's letter to the PM on Binayak Sen's incarceration in Mainstream April 25, 2009 vol.XLVII no.19.

access to resources of gas and oil. China, Pakistan and India are vying with each other for influence and Myanmar is another crucial piece in this puzzle of power politics, for the same geo-political reasons connected with the energy crunch.

It is the height of absurdity that the situation of energy crunch and global warming is also used to justify the 123 agreement with the US on supply of materials for "peaceful" production of nuclear energy. Nuclear energy is nowadays depicted as a "clean" energy form, helping to reduce global warming, – never mind the costs of production and the totally unresolved question of nuclear waste. Fortunately, the true constellation became visible when the Prime Minister inaugurated a nuclear submarine on Quit India Day August 9, 2009. This, indeed, is the technology we need to protect our nuclear arsenals. In the National Alliance of People's Movements (NAPM) we have been pointing out since over a decade that the highly hazardous nuclear Reactor in Kudamkulam (VVER 1000) was only agreed upon because buying the reactor technology was a way to acquire the know-how for nuclear sub-marines. This is what we have now achieved. Fooling the nation in this way is the height of cynicism which makes science and technology as ideology so untrustworthy and enormously dangerous. Nuclear energy is a highly militarized energy option and promoting it is built on the fallacious notion of deterrence and the possibility of a limited nuclear war.

The debates on this madness are old. Chernobyl is in stark memory. The Chernobyl reactor before the accident in 1986 was actually a type which was considered to be safer than the VVER technology now employed in Kudamkulam. Rosalie Bertell has extensively documented the hazards of nuclear radiation.[38] Jonathan Shell has clearly led ad absurdum the possibility of a limited nuclear war and has helped us to imagine a real "end of history" in the event of a nuclear war.[39]

The strange thing is that though all this is highly accessible information and in that sense common knowledge, the outrage of it does not register. It is once again most urgent to apply our minds to the Fate of the Earth in the face of the Water crisis, the energy crunch, Global Warming and nuclear threat. We are facing the possibility of a general holocaust caused by the greed of competitive capitalism and the madness of cultural fragmentation and ideological confusion. We are in denial of the seriousness of the situation, while governments and political parties brazenly chase the myth of unlimited growth. Future generations, if they survive, will be as incredulous about this situation as my generation was regarding the holocaust.

---

[38] Rosalie Bertell: No Immediate Danger: Prognosis for a Radio-Active Earth (London: the Women's Press 1985).

[39] Jonathan Shell: the Fate of the Earth (Avon Books, New York ,1982).

What Is to Be Done?

As is expressed in the very title of this paper, it is imperative to work towards ending the exploitative system of capitalism and to build a society of sharing. This, obviously, is an organizational political process, which has been going on since the first half of the nineteenth century and which has led to a history of revolutions and of alternative political systems, which have not been able to deliver the goods and to survive successfully, partly because they followed the destructive development model of industrial capitalism, partly because of lack of democracy. Both aspects led to mindless consumerist expectations which led to political failure.

The anti-colonial struggles of the 20th century and the upsurge of people's movements from the sixties onwards has led to a rich history of organizational experiences and ideological conceptualizations. I myself have been working since decades with women's movements and unions in the unorganized sector. Many of us have been part of an ideological process, which has drawn on Karl Marx, Rosa Luxemburg, Mahatma Phule, Dr. Babasahib Ambedkar, Periyar, Pandit Iyothee Das, Gandhism, Feminism, and Eco-Socialism.[40] I have written in different places on the need to build alliances among the internal colonies of Dalits, Adivasis, Women, small peasants, workers in the unorganized sector. This process is extremely arduous as casteism, patriarchy, racism, authoritarianism and violence are present in the organizational processes and need to be thrashed out. This is tedious and demanding, especially since it has to happen side by side with people's ongoing survival struggles. The patriarchal kinship systems produce tenacious power structures, which are very difficult to live down, especially since they also serve as vote banks.

These struggles have to happen on the road, in the villages and jungles and people have to re-invent the world while the powers that be try to hang on and steer us into the direction of disaster. Let me mention two events in the near future, which give an opportunity for involvement. From 9th August 2009 (Quit India Day) up to October 12th, 2009 a Lohia centenary Yatra will cover the country, starting from Mumbai, going South up to Trivandrum and then turning North, through T.N. Andhra, East and Central India, up to Delhi. The Yatra will cover 21 states in 65 days over a distance of 20000km. Youth from the Yusuf Meherally Centre in Panvel is an important component in this venture. This is to galvanize people's movements to remember the Saptakranti (seven fold revolution) of Dr.

[40] E.V. Ramasamy Naiker, called Periyar, is available only in Tamil, so is Pandit Iyothee Thas. However, The non-Brahmin movement has been extensively documented in English. See S.V. Rajadurai and V. Geetha: Towards a Non-Brahmin Millennium: From Iyothee Thass to Periyar (Calcutta , Samya 1999). On Iyothee Thas see G. Aloysius: Religion as Emancipatory Identity. A Buddhist Movement among the Tamils under colonialism (New Age International New Delhi 1998).

Lohia. This Yatra will raise the issues of land reform, SEZ, caste and untouchability, women, unorganized workers, language, secularism, people's right to water, seeds, natural resources, non-violent energy production, disarmament, right to work, education and health. Organizations working on these issues will come together in this effort, try out different forms of struggle, host the Yatris, share food, water and quarters and develop strategies to carry forward different struggles.

Another important event is the spreading of the campaign against nuclear energy. This is the outcome of an anti-nuclear conference in Kanyakumari June 3-5, 2009, which calls for a clear stand on stopping all nuclear energy production. It this sense, the campaign goes further than the CNDP, which is a broad coalition against nuclear arms. The Coalition against nuclear Energy is calling for a massive manifestation in Delhi on Oct 2, 2009 (Gandhi Jayanthi) to draw attention to the dangers of the present situation.

It is very disturbing that the churches appear to be very indifferent to such processes of uprising and transformation. In the Western countries, the dialogue with ideologies does not seem to be of interest and the inter-religious dialogue has got stuck to sort out the problems between Judaism and Islam, which are indeed complicated. The political and cultural resourcefulness of the Asian situation has not been sufficiently perceived, despite the spaces which have been given to post-colonials and "sub-alterns".

I have earlier raised the question how to be post-colonial under neo-colonial on slaught. It has also been pointed out by intellectuals involved in social history that "subaltern studies" is in danger of solidifying into fragments and to indirectly feed into the hegemony of majoritarian forces.[41] So we can't rest under the label of being "subaltern".[42] A large part of the Indian churches has been co-opted into middle class ideology and prosperity theology, together with a charismatic bent of mind. Theologically the question is how to recapture the connection between resurrection and uprising. What is required is an uprising for life and for the sustenance of God's good creation. This is the only thing which makes sense in the face of the enormous destruction which we are facing. Solidarity with the poor means sharing of scarce resources, not extracting more.

The other thing which needs to be understood is the faith of the Eastern Churches in the apokathastasis ton Pantoon, the redemption of all. It makes sense in the light of World Wars and holocausts that God wants Life for All and can bring it about without everybody first being converted to any one religion or the world to be destroyed. It is much more important to convert

---

[41] See my article "Why does Post-colonial Feminist Theology Need to Relate to Peoples' Movements" in Asia Journal of Theology vol.19, no.1, April 2005.

[42] See Sumit Sarkar: Writing Social History (New Delhi, OUP, 1997) especially chapter "The Decline of the Subaltern in Subaltern Studies".

ourselves from our destructive life styles and to sustain God's good creation. Solidarity with the poor and with all creatures great and small is the key.

It so happens that the comprehensive theological inspiration comes yet again from Latin America. Elsa Tamez,[43] who earlier challenged the macho attitude of run of the mill liberation theology and also took on board the pre-colonial heritage of the indigenous people, has also come up with a radical re-interpretation of Pauline theology, which puts the promise of Life for All into the economic context of a globalised system of exclusion, which amounts to a death penalty for the mass of the excluded and leads to a destruction of people and resources from which even the privileged cannot escape. May her voice be heard. May we have the courage to rise from the dead.

---

[43] Elsa Tamez: Against Machismo (Mayer-Stone Books, 1987)
Elsa Tamez: Through Her Eyes: Women's Theology from Latin America (New York, Orbis, 1989)
Elsa Tamez: Contra toda condena. La justificacion por la fe desde los excluidos (Spanish) Editorial DEI, San Jose, Costa Rica 1991
I am not able to locate the English translation. It is available in German (Edition Exodus, Luzern, 1998)

Challenges to Christian Mission from the Struggle for Human Rights in the South African Setting

Pieter Verster

Introduction

The history of South Africa is a history of conflict, oppression and very often, war. Human rights in South Africa were for many years not viewed as something achievable. Differences between culture groups and language groups in South Africa often led to serious conflicts. Since the arrival of Europeans in South Africa the differences in culture, background and worldview have led to the engagement of people in conflicts. Although it is true that the arrival of the Europeans led to terrible oppression it must be stated that oppression and conflict were present in South Africa even before their arrival and were present within other cultural groups also while they were in South Africa. Most prevalent, however, was the oppression of the indigenous peoples by Europeans (For a comprehensive overview of the history of the "Afrikaners" of European descent, see Giliomee 2003). The system of "apartheid" radicalised oppression in many ways (Manavhela 2009:147 ff. and Van der Ven et al 2006:267). The Truth and Reconciliation Commission had to deal with terrible atrocities in trying to come to grips with South Africa's past (Truth telling in South Africa 1996:503). It had a mandate to study "gross violations of human rights" committed with a political motive during the period from 1 March 1960 to May 1994. Although it did succeed in telling many stories and also in giving people the opportunity to voice their plights, it was criticised from both sides of the spectrum and many limitations remained (Chapman 1999:249-250). To seek understanding for the struggle for human rights engagement with this history remains important.

Human Rights in South Africa

South Africa is a country where human rights were very often not upheld. From the Europeans' side it was often viewed as something not applicable to the original inhabitants in South Africa. From the side of the original inhabitants of South Africa it was unknown as a philosophical idea, although in the African traditional environment, respect for others was also accepted. Human rights in South Africa therefore needs full attention. From the background of a terrible past the task is to build a community in which human rights prevail. At present serious violence is derailing this ideal. Van der Ven et al. (2006:268) write in this regard: "Of course the violence gripping South Africa at present cannot be attributed simply and solely to macro-factors rooted in the apartheid regime and the revolutionary struggle against that regime, nor to the profound discontent inherent in the current economic, social and cultural systems despite the fact that the present political dispensation is a constitutional, non-racial democracy and the rule of law prevails. There is also the many-headed violence emanating from the profit-motivated criminality of powerful syndicates and their almighty godfathers." Therefore, the struggle for human rights is a continuing struggle in South Africa.

Mission and Human Rights

The role of mission in human rights and in the South African situation is also of great importance. Mission in South Africa often struggled to make people aware of human rights. Very often missionaries were rejected because they pleaded for human rights for the indigenous peoples of South Africa. The conflict between Europeans and indigenous people in South Africa often led to a new dispensation and in this dispensation oppression was often present.

The recent history of South Africa highlighted the struggle for human rights for all South Africans. Although "apartheid" – also "separate development" – was seen by some people in South Africa as a possible solution to the problem of cultural, language and worldview differences, it led to serious oppression. Apartheid is therefore a well-known concept as term for oppression in the whole world. During the apartheid years the government of South Africa fully understood the importance of the role of the Church and was therefore eager to have the Church on its side. The Dutch Reformed Church in South Africa was also prepared to give its conditional support for the apartheid policies of the government because it believed that those policies were in the best interests of all the people of South Africa. However, it led to disaster, and the DRC had to change its views radically.

Manavhela (2009:147) concludes on the issue of "apartheid": "It is clear that Apartheid was not invented overnight when the National Party won the 1948 elections. It is the culmination of a long process and it has a complexity of intertwined causes. The church and theology were involved in this process and thus we cannot define their role in a simple way either. For understanding Apartheid and its religious components we have to take into account all the factors of the historical development and all aspects and perspectives that played a role."

The Struggle Against Apartheid

As apartheid progressed and the situation became tenser, different groups in South Africa had different ideas on how to deal with the situation, and had different solutions to the problem. Different documents were written to explain how people felt and how the Church felt about the situation in South Africa. Most English churches in South Africa, as well as churches from the Black community, there was severe criticism against the apartheid policies. Botha, Kritzinger and Maluleke (1994:23ff.) refer to the way in which protest against apartheid was established by the churches and especially the WCC. In South Africa the first major reaction against apartheid came from the WCC-organized meeting at Cottesloe. The Christian Institute of Dr Beyers Naudé played an important role in warning the Church against supporting apartheid. The programme to combat racism by the WCC led to many reactions. Then followed documents of rejection of apartheid (Botha, Kritzinger and Maluleke (1994:23ff).

The Kairos Document

The Kairos Document discussed different possibilities to address the situation during the apartheid years. Firstly the Kairos Document explained that in the then South Africa there existed a "state theology". The "state theology" was the theology in which the state was seen as the people who had to keep order in the name of God. They were of the opinion that the state theology was fully supported by the churches of the Afrikaner community, especially the Dutch Reformed Church. The Kairos Document was highly critical of the state theology. Secondly there was according to them, the so-called "church theology". The Kairos Document was also very critical of the "church theology". Church theology was a non-violent theology rejecting violence, even against the state of the time. The Kairos Document explained that in a situation of utmost oppression, and of structural violence, a struggle against the system was required and that it was totally accepted in the system to rebel against the offices of government to bring about a new situation. The Kairos Document then called for a prophetic engagement of the situation. The Kairos Document called for "prophetic theology". In prophetic theology it was claimed that the situation had to be changed and the only way in which it could be changed was with direct confrontation of the state, which according to them had no authority.

In the Kairos Document participation in the struggle is called for by transforming church activities, special campaigns, civil disobedience and moral guidance. In the preface of the document (The Kairos Document 1990: a) it is described as a Christian biblical and theological comment on a political crisis in South Africa. It was seen as an attempt by concerned Christians in South Africa to reflect on the situation of death in the country. The purpose was a critique of the then current theological models that determined the type of activities the Church engaged in to try and resolve the problems of the country. It was thus an attempt to develop out of the perplexing situation, an alternative biblical and theological model that would in turn lead to forms of activity that would make a real difference in the future of our country (The Kairos Document 1990: a). In the Kairos Document people were called to side with and to participate in the struggle (The Kairos Document 1990:28). Christians were called to participate in the struggle for liberation and for a just society: "The campaigns of the people, from consumer boycotts to stay away, need to be supported and encouraged by the church. Criticism will sometimes be necessary but encouragement and support will also be necessary. In other words, the present crisis challenges the whole church to move beyond a mere "ambulance ministry" to a ministry of involvement in participation" (The Kairos Document 1990:29).

Criticism against the Kairos Document came from many sources, especially from the Dutch Reformed Church. In the end the Kairos Document called for human rights in the sense of prophetic engagement and prophetic voices against the oppression against people. Botha, Kritzinger and Maluleke (1994:29) mention that it was clear that the struggle called for radical action. It was at that time also clear who the oppressed and oppressors were and what the struggle was. They asked whether the Kairos Document's call is not again relevant because of poverty and oppression in a new way. Huber (1991:58) also accepted the stance of the Document and says: "It is this ecclesiological basis that helped the Kairos Document to formulate an insight that is possibly one of the most important contributions of recent theology in South Africa to the ecumenical theology of our day. I mean the insistence on a proper understanding of reconciliation. The clarity in which the Kairos Document and other South African documents unmask an ideological misuse of the concept of reconciliation and in which it opens a way to a better understanding of the indissolvable unity between reconciliation and justice, is of inestimable value for the ecumenical fellowship of Christians." However, Barret (2008:18) refers to Russel Botman who stated that the prophetic theology of the Kairos Document hit something of a dead end after "apartheid" because, according to Botman, it lacked a clear christological backing in its sociological, political and legal concerns. Sincere questions must also still be raised on the Kairos Document's stance on violence. Violence in the then South Africa claimed many lives. Could the Church not have changed the situation by non-violent means, or was violence the only option? This serious question must still be raised.

The Kairos Document in South Africa inspired other documents in other parts of the world, such as the document "Kairos: Central America: A challenge to the Churches of the World" in Central America (Kairos International: call to conversion: 1091).

The Kairos Document was followed by another document, the "Road to Damascus", in which a call for conversion was clearly sounded. Conversion is needed.

The Road to Damascus

Paul was converted on the road to Damascus. In the "Road to Damascus" Document the call was for conversion so that a total new situation could come about in South Africa; a call for people to change totally was very important. People had to become new, but then also in this call for conversion the conversion had to become real, radical and total and it had to change the whole situation of people in South Africa.

The Road to Damascus (Brown 1990:121) mentions that nothing is new about the religious conflicts as such. "Christians or believers in the God of the Bible have been on opposing sides of a political conflict before. What is new today is the intensity of the conflict and the awareness we have of it. And never before have we been so conscious of the political implications of Christian faith. This religious conflict is not a mere academic debate; it is a matter of life and death. What is at stake is the future of justice, peace, freedom and the glory of God." (Brown 1990:121). The conflict among Christians raised some very serious questions which they addressed in the rest of the document: "Is the God on both sides the same God, is God on both sides if not, on whose side is God and what has been revealed to us about God in Jesus Christ and then it comes to the conclusion that faith of the poor?"

In the Road to Damascus Document the faith of the poor is seen as the way in which faith should be established. It clearly states on 43 (Brown 1990:124) "God is on the side of the poor, the oppressed the persecuted." And then (Brown 1990:126) about idolatry it is stated: "Idolatry is the sin of worshipping or being subservient to someone or something which is not God, treating some creative thing as if it were God." The Document stated that the same was true in countries where the worship of money, power, privilege and pleasure had certainly replaced the worship of God. (Brown 1990:128) Heresy is also explained (Brown 1990:128): "The Theological justification of apartheid has been declared a heresy. It is recognized by most Christians today to be a distortion of God's revelation." The theological criticism against apartheid theology was severe. The document did not hesitate to reject it in the strongest terms possible.

The Belhar Confession

In the circles of the Dutch Reformed Church, the sister church of the Dutch Reformed Church, the "Mission Church", or the "Sendingkerk" accepted a confession of faith at Belhar. In the Belhar Confession certain explanations were put forward very clearly. The Belhar Confession clearly states that in no way can cultural differences, differences in language or background be the measure of other people and their commitment to Jesus Christ. Therefore the Church had the calling to become one in all its different offices but also that the Church had to become one to confess to the whole world that it belonged to Jesus Christ. Apartheid in all its different forms was an attack on Christianity because it entrenched being not reconciled as the point of departure of the Church (Botha and Naudé 1998:43 ff). Naudé (2007:21) states that the Belhar Confession had a clear message to the churches supporting the status quo, in which it clearly called for repentance from a political order and theological acceptance of that order because heresy and superstition were represented as the truth. Fromm (2006:14) is of the opinion that the themes in the Belhar Confession of unity, reconciliation and justice are grounded in and lifted from Scripture. Fries (2006:2) refers to the fact that Belhar makes social justice rather than doctrinal purity the cornerstone of the Confession. However, this aspect received criticism from those who were wary of the political overtones. Boesak (2008:152) rejects this criticism and states that Belhar "...is a unique representation of God's identification with the poor, the voiceless and dispossessed." The Belhar Confession had a profound influence on the churches in South Africa and is still discussed vehemently in the call for unity in the Dutch Reformed Church's family.

Church and Society of the DRC

The Dutch Reformed Church replied in a document called "Church and Society". In the document apartheid was also rejected because of it being an ideology of unreconciliation and oppression of other people. "Church and Society" was later accepted at a General Synod of the Dutch Reformed Church in 1986 (Kerk en Samelewing 1986). It also sought unity in the Church and unity among its different sister churches. Once again human rights played a very important role, and in the document "Church and Society", human rights were also explained as the right that people had before God to live and to be in his presence.

After the acceptance of the document Prof Willie Jonker extended an apology to the other churches and communities in South Africa (Allen 1994:214). In November 1990 at a hotel outside the small town of Rustenburg, Transvaal, the site of the first conference in 30 years to bring together a leadership of the white Dutch Reformed Church and anti-apartheid South African churches (Allen 1994: 215), Bishop Tutu (Allen 1994:215) accepted the apology by stating: "If there is to be reconciliation, we who are the ambassadors of Christ, we to whom the gospel of reconciliation has been entrusted, surely we must be Christ's instruments of peace, we must be ourselves be reconciled. The victims of injustice and oppression must be ever ready to forgive."

Reconciliation and church unity however still remain to be achieved by the Dutch Reformed Church community. The confession of Belhar is still debated in the Dutch Reformed Church and the Uniting Reformed Church regards this as lack of true commitment.

The Call for Reconciliation

The Catholic community also called for reconciliation. It is spelled out neatly by Hay (1998:161): "The very pattern of the sacrament of reconciliation suggests the steps that can be followed; examination of conscience (confronting our past), contrition (repenting and sorrow for sins), confession (telling the story), satisfaction (remedy and reparation in the light of the demands of justice) and absolution (proclaiming forgiveness and new relationships)." The catholic community played an important role in reconciliation.

The Change in South African Society

The question may well be asked, what brought about the change in South African society? The answer is complex and difficult. Many issues coincided to lead to a new dispensation. The whole picture in the world changed dramatically when the Berlin Wall fell. It made new political changes also in South Africa possible. However, many other aspects had an influence: the realisation that "apartheid" could no longer be sustained, the Christian conscience of many church leaders, the economic situation and pressure from the outside world. The fact that the change came about with minimum violence must however always be viewed as a miracle.

Human Rights and Mission

In the search for human rights the relation with people to one another in South Africa is still very important. And the question is whether mission in South Africa has learned from the struggle for human rights. The way in which mission in South Africa can establish human rights is very important.

The Theological Conference of the Reformed Ecumenical Synod in 1980 stated that human rights are also on the table for discussion of the Church (Church and Nation 1981:36). The document called for the Church to be committed in the this vast reality of overall threats both to freedom and democracy, and also to individual human existence to a clear and urgent calling to fulfil its prophetic mission: "It has no choice but to find a point of convergence with the present day world enjoining forces on the issue of human rights. In order to bring the world of today a message of relevance, the Church must therefore, out of necessity participate in the ongoing debate on human rights."

Van der Ven et al. (2001:167) refer to the fact that the Jewish and Christian scriptures can be said to have functioned and is still functioning as a rich source of morality, principles, imperatives and rules of conduct in society in which the concept of human rights should be respected. They refer to the way in which the prophets called for justice and Jesus' own announcement of the kingdom of God.

Human rights in all its different aspects should be enhanced, but how can it be enhanced in a situation were different people meet and where they live in one geographical area? Bishop Tutu (1990) called for respect for one another in this situation in South Africa and asked that this new respect for one another should lead to the establishment of human rights in all its different aspects. The question however is: How has mission in South Africa in the missionary movement dealt with the problems of human rights and how can it deal with those problems in future? At present in South Africa there is a terrible problem with crime, in which human rights of many people are also totally disregarded. People are killed and murdered on a large scale. Again human rights are under severe pressure.

A theory of human rights should be Biblical. Marshall (1983:18) called for a theory to be in continuity, and flows from the message of Creation, the Fall and Redemption through Jesus Christ revealed in scripture and, in particular, as this message is fresh out in the biblical teaching of God's righteousness and the consequent human authority and claims to have this situation tightened. He continues that such a theory must be a reflection on justice and politics and a modern world which flows from our knowledge that everything in Creation is a creature, servant, responsible to God and that God orders and upholds Creation, including the ways we are to live with, care for, respect and love one another.

De Gruchy (1995:276) in an important essay emphasizes critical solidarity: "The prophetic vision itself, however, demands critical solidarity, and that means a creative and constructive tension expressing the dialectic between Christian faith and culture; between the reign of the triune God and the sovereignty of the people. This dialectical relationship is a two way process, for the global struggle for a just democratic order has forced complacent churches to re-examine their unprophetic roots and rediscover the vision which is at the heart of Jesus' proclamation of the reign of God. If faithful to that vision, Christianity will continue to contribute to the ferment for democratic transformation and the pursuit of a world order which is not only new but also just, and therefore one in which God's *shalom* will become a reality."

Mission as the Ministry of Reconciliation

Mission should be the proclamation of the ministry of reconciliation. In a ministry of reconciliation God reaches out to people. People are reconciled with God. People are in a new relation to God. People are living with one another in this new relation, and they can also – in this new relation – be able to live in harmony with one another. Through the reconciliation with the living God it is also possible to live in reconciliation with one another.

Cocheran, De Gruchy and Peterson (1991:67) establish a platform for reconciliation and human rights: "Forgiveness in reconciliation does point to the transformation of society, a transformation that is best symbolized by the biblical concept of shalom. Shalom (human and societal wellbeing and flourishing) is where the kingdom of God is ultimately about. In this sense it always stands beyond human realisation and witness to that which God alone can finally bring to reality. Yet in the present the Christian church is called to bear witness to the reality of the shalom of Christ, that is, the reality of his justice and reconciliation in the world." See also Dumas (1978:22).

This reconciliation with one another is possible in the reconciliation with the living God. This all comes about through Jesus Christ and the way in which Jesus being the Crucified One for the others made it possible for so many to live in this new relation with God. The question of human rights is therefore an essential question: Does mission have anything to do with human rights? The only way in which one can establish this is to see human rights as something that has to be established in the sense of Christ being the one for the others on the cross. As the Crucified One, Christ made it possible for people to be accepted as people for God. In his love and in the way that he showed his love on the cross, people can understand that Christ is the one for others. People now have a certain value before God, because they are people paid for by the blood of Christ. They have this value of being in the presence of God, but in mission it will always be understood that this has to be answered by faith in Christ by people healing themselves through Christ, coming to Christ, accepting the total redemption in Jesus Christ (2 Cor. 5:11-21).

Chikani (1985:100) calls for direct action in theology: "No Christian can afford to be left out of the action of God with his people. If a theologian is not part of that action of God, then we must be suspicious of the side on which he or she belongs in the struggle with God to establish a just society."

The South African Perspective and the World

Does this have any bearing on human rights in general? In the South African situation it was clear that very often people did not understand that it is possible to be Christian and also to establish good human relations and to be in favour of human rights. Being before God it always meant that we also have to live with one another in this realisation of one another's value before God. Therefore for mission it is important to establish a core value of human rights. Van der Walt (2003:332) explains that obligations and human rights are inseparable: "Our **obligations** are grounded in the **will** of

God. Our **rights** are grounded in the **love** of God. **Obligations** consist of some good **required** of us. **Rights** consist of some good to which we are **entitled.** The dark side of obligations (when they are not fulfilled) is **guilt**. The dark side of rights when they are not acknowledged) is that someone is **wronged.** The Bible says over and over that the wealthy and powerful are **guilty** because they do tot fulfil their **duties** and that the poor, widows orphans etcetera are **wronged** because their **rights** are not acknowledged." (bold Van der Walt). Vorster (2005:477-479) refers to three aspects that are needed in the quest for human rights, namely human dignity, equality and freedom. According to him human dignity is under threat in South Africa through the ongoing acts of violence. The ethos of equality also needs to be established in a society where inequality reigned for many years. He states that a more optimistic opinion concerning the value of freedom in the present day South Africa, where especially freedom of speech is regarded highly, can be voiced.

It is always the task of the Church to reach out to people so that they can be established as people living with one another, so that they can proclaim the word of God. The Church should be the people of God giving the space for people to understand who they are and how they can live in the presence of God. In this new relation it is possible to establish human relations. In South Africa certain lessons were learned. Lategan, Kinghorn, Du Plessis, and De Villiers (1987:13) give a South African perspective: "Human rights – to be truly human – are based on God's claim on people to treat their fellows in the same way as he does. Whenever God serves humanity with life, love and grace, he creates space for people – space within which they can find fulfilment (Gen. 1 and 2, Acts 17; 24-28). We are expected to be co-creators with God in precisely this sense." (See also Symington 1986.).

It is very easy to forget the calling of Christ to be humble, to be obedient and to praise God. In this situation in South Africa the problems of the country became more important than the solutions. The problems became so dynamic that it changed the way in which people looked at one another and they forgot that it is possible to live in peace with one another. It is however also of great importance that it was through the efforts of many Christian people that in South Africa there came about a new situation. Tutu (1990:31) calls compassionately for this: "The same gospel of Jesus Christ, which compels us to reject apartheid as totally unchristian, it is the very gospel that constrains us to work for justice, for peace and reconciliation. God has given us a mandate to be ministers of his reconciliation." Also Villa-Vicencio (1994:114) calls for justice with human rights: "For those who are not pacifist, no less than for those who are, the challenge is to continue to search for non violent ways of bringing about social justice across barriers of race, economics and what may well prove in South Africa to be even more impenetrable – sex."

In the world it should also be established that conflict can be solved when people are prepared to look at one another from the perspective of peace and not from the perspective of conflict. Human rights in this situation are very important so that the oppressed can be lifted up by looking at one another in a new way. Christianity's stand should be not to enhance violence in any way, but to bring about peace and human rights by reaching out to one another in peace.

Bibliography

Allen, J. (Ed) 1994. *The Rainbow people of God: South Africa's victory over apartheid.* (Foreword by President Nelson Mandela). London: Doubleday.

Barret, P. 2008. The quest for *Ubuntu* in a Coming-of-Age South Africa – questions arising from Dietrich Bonhoeffer's Latter Ideas. *Religion and Theology* 15:8-27.

Boesak, A. 2008. To stand where God stands: Reflections on the Confession of Belhar after 25 years. *Studia Historiae Ecclesiasticae* 34 (1): 143-172.

Botha, J. & Naudé, P. 1998. *Op Pad met Belhar* (On the road with Belhar). Pretoria: Van Schaik.

Botha, N., Kritzinger, Klippies, & Maluleke, T. 1994. Crucial issues for Christian mission – a missiological analysis of contemporary South Africa. *International Review of Mission* 83(328): 21-36.

Brown, R.M. (Ed.). 1990. *Kairos: Three prophetic challenges to the church.* Grand Rapids, Mi.: Eerdmans.

Chapman, A.R. 1999. Coming to terms with the past: Truth, justice, and/or reconciliation. *The annual of the society of Christian Ethics* 19: 235-258.

Chikane, F. 1985. Doing theology in a situation of conflict. (In Villa-Vicencio C and De Gruchy, J.W. (Eds) Resistance *and hope: South African essays in honour of Beyers Naudé.* Cape Town: David Phillips: 98-102.

Church and Nation. 1981. Theological conference papers. The Theological conference of the Reformed Ecumenical Synod 1980 Nimes. France, July 10 and 11, 1980.

Cocheran, J.R., De Gruchy J.W., Peterson, R. 1991. *In word and deed: Towards a practical theology for social transformation.* Pietermaritzburg: Cluster.

De Gruchy, J.W. 1995. *Christianity and democracy.* Cape Town: David Phillips.

Dumas, A. 1978. *Political theology and the life of the church.* (Translation Johan Bowden). London: SCM.

Fries, P.R. 2006. Reflections on confession. *Reformed Review (online)* 61(1): 2-7.

Fromm, D.W. 2006. The Belhar Confession in the South African Context. *Reformed Review (online)* 61(1):11-18.

Giliomee, H. 2003. *The Afrikaners: Biography of a people.* Cape Town: Tafelberg.

Huber, W. 1991.The Barmen Declaration and the Kairos Document: On relationship between confession and politics. *Journal of theology for Southern Africa* 75:48-60

Kairos International: call to conversion. Special report. *The Christian Century.* November 22: 1091-1093.

Kerk en Samelewing (Church and Society). 1986. Accepted at the General Synod of the DRC October 1986.

Lategan, B., Kinghorn, J., du Plessis, L., & de Villiers, E. 1987. *The option for inclusive democracy: A theological ethical study of appropriate social values for South Africa.* Stellenbosch: University of Stellenbosch, Centre for Hermeneutics.

Manavhela, G F.2009. *An analysis of the theological justification of Apartheid in South Africa: A reformed theological perspective.* Ph D-dissertation. Amsterdam: Free University of Amsterdam.

Marshall, P 1983. *Human rights theories in Christian perspectives.* Toronto: Institute for Christian studies.

Mathewes, C. 2007. *A Theology of public life.* Cambridge: Cambridge University Press,

Naudé, P. 2007. Would Barth sign the Confession of Belhar? *Journal of Theology for Southern Africa* 129 (November):4-22.

Symington, HR 1986. *Prophecy of hope for Southern Africa.* Kloof: Southern Life Association Limited.

The Kairos Document, 1990. (Revised second edition): Challenge to the church. A theology comment on the political crisis in South Africa. Braamfontein: Skotaville.

Hay, M. 1998. *Ukubuyisana: Reconciliation in South Africa.* Pietermaritzburg: Cluster Publications.

Truth telling in South Africa. 1996. Christian Century, May 8: 503.

Tutu, D. 1990. *Crying in the Wilderness: The struggle for justice in South Africa.* Mbabane: Bok Books.

Van der Ven, J.A., Dreyer, J.S. & Pieterse, H.J.C. 2001. Human rights in the name of God? *Religion and Theology* 8(1): 165-206.

Van der Walt, B.J. 2003. *Understanding and rebuilding Africa: from desperation today to expectation for tomorrow.* Potchefstroom: ICCA.

Villa-Vicencio, C. 1994. The Church and violence. In Web, P (Ed) *A long struggle: The involvement of the World Council of Churches in South Africa.* Genève: World Council of Churches: 102-115.

Vorster, J.M. 2005. Nation-building in South Africa. *The Ecumenical Review* 57(4): 473-491.

Section VII

Perspectives and Issues in Mission and Interfaith Dialogue

A Christian Ecumenical Exploration of Identity Dynamics

Shanta Premawardhana

A document produced for the World Council of Churches' 9th General Assembly in February 2006 affirmed that "the 'politics of ideology,' which played a crucial role in the 20th century, has been replaced in our day by the 'politics of identity.'"[1] Acknowledging that premise, the assembly featured a major address by the Archbishop of Canterbury, and two workshops that addressed this question. Such high-profile attention placed the question of identity squarely on the agenda of the WCC and particularly on its work on Interreligious Dialogue and Cooperation.

This is indeed a critical distinction. Today's inter-religious dialogue is not simply a sober conversation about ideology, in which we explore the power and meaning embedded in our sacred texts and theological/philosophical traditions on their own merit. Rather, it is a complex negotiation about identity, in which we have learned that religious persons and communities bring to the dialogue table a set of complex dynamics of culture, language, ethnicity, social location and political affiliation among others. How carefully we navigate that complexity – including how rigidly participants maintain those identity boundaries or how much they are able to bend – often determines the fruitfulness of the dialogue and cooperation.

The question of identity is, of course, not new to religion, and certainly not to Christianity. The present manifestation of the question, though, is different from the way it was posed at its beginnings. Our unholy allegiances to, and affiliations with political empires ancient and modern have made our conceptions of identity both rigid and static. This paper seeks to raise a few critical questions with a view to examining its role in the multiple crises we face at the present time.

---

[1] "Christian Self-Understanding Amid Other Religions," a paper presented by the programme on Interreligious Relations and Dialogue (as it was called at the time), Commission on World Mission and Evangelism and Faith and Order. It is available at: http://www.oikoumene.org/en/resources/documents/assembly/porto-alegre-2006/3-preparatory-and-background-documents/religious-plurality-and-christian-self-understanding.html

I approach this question from the point of view of a Christian theologian, who, having roots in Sri Lanka, brings a particular critique from that post-colonial and religiously diverse context. I celebrate that these are the waning days of western political, economic, and indeed religious hegemony. It is my hope that we will emerge from the present crises with new political and economic paradigms that will serve the common good of the whole earth. Religion, as it has for over millennia, will continue to influence these emerging paradigms. Whether our influence will actually support the common good or the interests of the empires of the world will, I suggest, depend at least in some measure, upon how we navigate the question of identity, which in the past has been used by both religious and political powers to support their own vested interests.

Religion, Identity and Empire

In his classic study, *The Meaning and End of Religion* eminent religion scholar Wilfred Cantwell Smith investigates "Religion," a term that is notoriously difficult to define. He begins his study by scrutinizing "our practice of giving religious names [such as Christianity, Buddhism, Hinduism and so on] and indeed of calling them religions"[2] and traces the evolution of the Latin word *religio*. From its early meaning as the human yearning for the divine, faith and piety, it first developed to become a "theoretical entity of speculative interest."[3] Later, it came to denote a community which, in turn led to the popularization of its plural form and to the development of the terms *vera religio* and *falsa religio* (true religion and false religion).[4] Smith's articulation of this history leads to the conclusion that the hardening of binary definitions of identity occurred in the modern period, beginning with the renaissance and expanding with the Reformation into the colonial period.[5] Although Smith did not consider this relevant to his topic, it is important that we note for our purpose that this development was taking place at the height of European colonial expansion.

---

2 Wilfred Cantwell Smith, *The Meaning and End of Religion* (1978; Harper and Row), 15.

3 *Ibid.*, 22.

4 Smith points to a fascinating development in the thinking of the Swiss reformer Zwingli, for whom "false religion" described not religions other than Christianity, but the "oversanctification of popes, councils, church authorities and the like," in other words, those who were believers in the same God as he. Zwingli, says Smith, looked forward to meeting in heaven "all the saints and sages and believers and the steadfast and the brave and the good who have ever lived since the world began" a fellowship among whom he names Socrates, and several others not members of his church. *Ibid.*, 35 and end note p. 224.

5 This is the argument of Smith's first chapter "'Religion' in the West" in his *The Meaning and End of Religion*, particularly 32-50.

The church easily and comfortably imbued the empire's need to objectify those who are different in order to subjugate them. Rather than offer an alternative, prophetic critique that befits its original calling, the church with its long history of being a servant of the empire, not only went along, but often was the force behind the creation of binary identities. Unwilling to acknowledge a common humanity with people of India, for example, and unable to see their yearning for the divine, their faith or their piety as expressions of the *religio* that all human beings held in common, the missionaries of the colonial era sought a new language to distinguish themselves and their religiosity from the religious people of India. The invention of the term "Hinduism" is an interesting example of this. The first instances of this term being used to refer to the people living near the river Indus (or Sindhu), comes from the ancient Persians, and not to a religion. This later turned into "Hindu" to which the suffix "ism" was added to describe the religion of India. The British usage of this term since the 19th century was a convenient shorthand to define those Indians who were not Muslims or Christians regardless of the exceeding variety of their beliefs, rituals and religious structures.[6]

Similarly, in other parts of the world, convinced of the absoluteness of their truth claims and the superiority of the culture that Christianity had produced, the missionaries sought to convert the "heathens." In order to have a clear conception of the "other" they found it necessary to create binary identities even in societies where acknowledging their common *religio,* people who followed different paths in their search for the divine, faith and piety lived for centuries in relative harmony with each other.

Yet, binary identity is not a western colonial invention. Ancient societies too, developed ways to stratify society into tribes, castes, races and other identities that pit one identity against another as a way to benefit the political, economic and religious elites. Religion often served as the ideological basis for justifying such stratification. The ancient Vedic creation myth of Purusa, for example, provided millennia-long religious justification for the caste system, while in the more recent past, the Dutch Reformed Church offered vigorous theological defenses for maintaining the system of apartheid in South Africa. Such religious justifications, endowed with divine affirmations and power, effectively deceive the oppressed into accepting the *status quo*.

Sometimes those of a particular identity, having been oppressed by the empire, use that same identity marker as a way of organizing themselves to gain power. For example, if the then powerless Dalits of India did not with great determination claim their identity over several decades, they would not have been able to come this far in their quest to gain a place in Indian

---

6 For a recent and broader discussion of this subject see, Steven Rosen *Essential Hinduism* (2006: Greenwood Publishing Group), 19ff.

civil society. The same is true for African Americans in the United States whose claim to that identity (specifically the characterization "African-American" rather than Black or Negro which were the terms used in previous generations) provided them an effective means to organizing power, which in turn, led most recently to the election of one of their own to the presidency of the United States.

While these gains are to be celebrated, an uneasy difficulty remains. The use of the same oppressive paradigm of binary identity designation to gain power will inevitably yield to other oppressions rather than to the goal of common good for all the earth. Liberation Theology's use of the model of preferential option for the poor is an interesting example. While this is an important theological claim, it uses the same binary identity designation, setting the theologians apart from "the poor." The theologians, by definition, having received an education, the leisure to think and write and the ability to get their work published or on the other hand, having been inducted into church hierarchies, are in an elite social location, and thus cannot be defined as "the poor." This creates an interesting conundrum. The theologians who proclaim the theological principle of God's preference are themselves excluded from that preference! The problem is that the theologians who think of "the poor" as the "other" are falling into the same trap of binary identity designation.

This is not an argument for abandoning all affirmations of identity. It is an argument for exploring the problem of static and binary expressions that lead to the hardening of identities in the context of increasing international and interreligious tensions. It is a proposal for recognizing that prophetically-oriented religious people find themselves in the borderlands where identity is not static, but evolves through a continuous process of interrelation and differentiation, and for analyzing the often inadequately recognized power dynamics that are at play in all these negotiations.

Identity and Christian Ecumenism in an Inter-Religious World

Institutions of the Christian ecumenical movement such as councils of churches in local towns, to national, regional and the World Council of Churches, having sprung from a missionary paradigm where binary identities were affirmed and strengthened, now find themselves in difficult circumstances. Changing demographics is one of their greatest challenges. Christianity, for example, in recent times has seen very significant growth in the global south. In 1900 about 65% of the world's Christian population lived in Europe or North America. Today that figure is about 35%. In 1900 Christians in Africa, Asia and Oceania, Latin America and the Caribbean represented 17.2% of global Christianity. Today that figure is 60.3%.[7] The shifting of Christianity's center of gravity to the global south necessarily involves a re-evaluation of theological questions and priorities.

At the same time Muslim populations in Europe significantly increased. In a Council for Foreign Affairs background article entitled "Europe: Integrating Islam" Esther Pan writes, "The Muslim population has doubled in the last 10 years to 4 percent of the European Union's population. About 1 million new Islamic immigrants arrive in Western Europe every year, and by 2050, one in five Europeans will likely be Muslim."[8] Over the same period, the Muslim population in the United States grew by 25 percent to 4.9 million. Similar numerical growth in other religious communities has resulted today in the United States becoming the most religiously diverse country in the world.[9] These dynamics have set off a series of tensions for ecumenical and inter-religious relations.

In the immediate aftermath of September 11th 2001, the confluence of religious and national identities resulted in serious harassment of Muslims in the United States, including of those who had lived there for generations – a trend that continues to the present time. Churches for the most part gladly played along with the excessively jingoistic expressions of the civil religion of that time. While Christianity was seen to be able to serve the interests of the empire, the unfamiliar and foreign Islam was seen as its enemy.

In Europe, the publication of the cartoon caricatures of the Prophet Mohammad was a deliberate provocation intended to test the limits of free speech. Christianity's affirmation of the secular state was already tested; Islam's was not. And in this instance, Islam refused to assent. The Pope's speech at Regensburg, seven months after the protests in the Muslim world, can be seen as an expression of his frustration that Europeans may be relinquishing their Christian identity for a secular one, and of his desire expressed in his other proclamations that Europe becomes a Christian continent.[10]

The changing dynamics is causing another tension point for the ecumenical community. In European and US cities that are experiencing unprecedented immigration patterns particularly from Asian, African and

---

[7] Fernando F. Segovia, "Interpreting Beyond Borders: Postcolonial Studies and Diasporic Studies in Biblical Criticism," in *Interpreting Beyond Borders,* ed. Fernando F. Segovia (Sheffield: Sheffield Academic Press, 2000), 21.

[8] Esther Pan, "Europe: Integrating Islam" Council for Foreign Relations (July 13, 2005) http://www.cfr.org/publication/8252/europe.html.

[9] Diana Eck, *New Religious America: How a "Christian Country" Has become the World's Most Religiously Diverse Nation* (2002: HarperOne) see especially 222ff.

[10] For my detailed analysis of these events see: Shanta Premawardhana "Interfaith Conflicts: Lessons from 2006" in Monica J. Melanchthon and George Zachariah (eds), *Witnessing in Context: Essays in Honor of Eardley Mendis* (Tiruvalla, India: Christava Sahitya Samithy, 2007), 70ff.

Latin American countries, many local councils of churches are changing to become interreligious councils by including Jewish, Muslim, Hindu, Buddhist and other religious groups in their membership. The loss of the Christian ecumenical character is causing some in the ecumenical movement to suggest that this change must be opposed since the ecumenical agenda is still unfinished. Others see it as an inevitable shift that recognizes and honors the diversity of God's creation and rather than a threat, a gift to the ecumenical movement.

Identity questions that arise in interreligious relationships are often more complex because they often have to deal not only with the dynamics of religious identities but also with more pronounced and complex racial/ethnic identities. Yet reports from these new Interfaith Councils indicate that the dialogues between religious communities are injecting new learnings and energy for the ecumenical conversation. In other words, at least at the local level, interfaith dialogue seems to be energizing the sometimes stagnant ecumenical dialogue.

How should the ecumenical movement navigate through these tensions? Wesley Ariarajah suggests that since the word "*oikumene*" itself means "the whole inhabited earth," it should not be narrowly applied to the Christian ecumenical table but should encompass the wide diversity of God's creation; that we need to think of it as a New or Wider Ecumenism.[11]

He identifies three areas in which Christians have expressed concern. First is that the wider ecumenism would undercut, and eventually replace, the need for Christian ecumenism. This potential loss of identity is clearly the fear that local church councils express even as they find themselves inexorably moving towards becoming interreligious councils. Ariarajah sees the two levels of ecumenical engagement as two concentric circles both having unity as the center and servicing two overlapping constituencies. Wider ecumenism does not replace Christian ecumenism, he suggests, but gives it a new and vibrant context.

The second arises from the fear that the wider ecumenism is an implicit universalism and leads to the tacit admission that "all religions are the same." Some are concerned that such an ecumenism will lead to syncretism. Wider ecumenism is not a search for a "universal religion'; nor is it an attempt to undermine the specificity of religions, says Ariarajah, rather it is an attempt to see unity in diversity, collaboration in the context of differences, and togetherness in a world that is torn apart by divisions and dissentions.

The third is presumed by those concerned with the mission of the church. Christian mission has often divided the world into those who are "saved" and those who are "in need of salvation," with the implication that other religious traditions are false, or at best inadequate paths to salvation. Throughout the missionary conferences of the 20th century there is a

---

[11] *Current Dialogue*, 47, June 2006, 34-36.

tendency of churches to move away from this dichotomous understanding of the world. For example, the early narrow emphasis on the church's mission to gain converts gave way to a broader understanding of *Missio Dei* (God's mission) which affirmed that God is at work in the whole world and that the church is only a servant in God's mission. Today, says Ariarajah, "we see mission primarily as healing the brokenness of the world, announcing God's forgiving love for all irrespective of their labels and standing in solidarity with those who are poor, oppressed, marginalized and made vulnerable by the powerful economic and political forces of our day." Seen thus, religious traditions which have been a source of much fragmentation in the world, working together, can contribute to the healing of the world.

Despite Ariarajah's hopeful analysis, the question remains that after almost a century of raising these questions, (since the World Missionary Conference, Edinburgh, 1910) a significant proportion of Christians still sees the world in dichotomies. If as Ariarajah suggests "healing the brokenness of the world" is our primary theological task, or if as I suggested at the beginning of this paper that we must seek paradigms that lead to the "common good for all the earth," we, as religious people must have the courage to self-critically examine our own traditions in the light of those tasks. When we do, we will recognize that we are indeed working together in one *oikoumene*, that the purity of traditions that we seek to protect are often those that serve the interests of the empires, and that all of us religious people have a common mission – often obscured by our need to maintain rigid identities – of seeking the common good for all the earth.

Conflation of Identities and Conversion

Christianity's historic relationship with the imperial establishment inevitably required that it had a static identity which often conflated with national identities. This was particularly the case in Europe. If you lived under the jurisdiction of the British monarch, for example, you were presumed to belong to the Church of England; in fact, you are likely to have been baptized as an infant into the King's church. The pastoral needs of people who lived in a particular geographical area called a parish were attended to by the local vicar, just as the law enforcement needs were attended to by the local constable. Religious and national identity was so conflated that the occasional conversion to a dissenting religious community, particularly to one with Anabaptist roots, was deemed to be treasonous.

Conversion as a free expression of changing one's belief, detached from one's loyalty to another identity marker, such as one's nationality, is a relatively recent phenomenon mostly attributable to the modern missionary movement. In many colonized countries those who converted to Christianity did not consider themselves disloyal to their ethnic or cultural roots or to their nation. Yet, they were required to make a hard shift in their religious allegiance, repudiate their Buddhist, Hindu or other religious identity and embrace the new Christian identity. Sometimes, a name change at baptism, usually to one that is biblical (for example, Thomas or Mary), but sometimes to one that is English (for example, William or Victoria), affirmed their new identity.

Despite the converts' continuing loyalty to their ethnic, cultural and national identities, this was questioned by their compatriots. Those who revoked their Buddhist or Hindu identity and received a Christian one were also considered to be "white" and "European," or at least to have characteristics of and loyalties to their white, European colonial masters. The colonial masters, in turn, rewarded these Christians through jobs, prestige and the goodwill of the empire. Following independence and the accompanying shifts in power, Christians began indigenization movements, seeking to cast their lot with the local power structure.

Without properly understanding this changed reality, during the past three decades, mostly US based evangelistic groups have engaged in aggressive evangelism using methods that include the use of allurements to entice poor and unsuspecting villagers into becoming Christians. In many countries, most recently in India and Sri Lanka, this has caused a violent backlash, as Hindu and Buddhist extremists have gone on rampage burning churches and killing Christians.

Additionally, as in several states in India, in Sri Lanka, anti-conversion legislation has been making its way through the parliament. While currently stalled, this legislation is expected to prevent unethical conversions by jailing the converter for up five years, or if the converted is a minor, a woman or one that is institutionalized, up to seven years. The requirement for a hard change of identity, for example from Buddhist to Christian is seen as a threat, not only to Buddhism, but to Sri Lanka as a nation.

Rather than be viewed in isolation, this question should be considered in the context of Sri Lanka's 500 year history of colonialism, during which period Buddhism was disrespected, Buddhist monks and people were persecuted, and the country's natural resources plundered. This colonialism, some argue, was accompanied by an ideology (Christianity) whose missionaries prepared the ground for its success. Today's new missionary movement is therefore viewed with great suspicion, because of the fear that it could pave the way for a new colonialism. Unlike the previous political colonialism, critics argue that this colonialism would be economic, therefore a more insidious one. Therefore, say the proponents of this legislation, it must be stopped at all costs.

Mainstream Christians, who point to the new evangelical churches as the ones responsible for creating the current hostile environment between religious communities that previously co-existed in relative harmony, miss the point. This is an over-simplification that ignores the historical animosities that were generated by the colonial hostility to all non-Christian religious identities and non-colonial national identities. Unresolved hurt from that period adds to the Buddhist anxiety about the new Evangelical presence, which, when conflated with ethnic Sinhala and Sri Lankan national identities, gains significant energy.

We are living through a period in which violence attributed to extremist religion around the world is daily in our televisions and newspapers. The media conveniently reduces these conflicts to religious issues, although there are many geopolitical and economic factors that go in to creating any conflict. They also fail to provide adequate distinctions between mainstream religions and their extremist factions.

In the international scene, the conflation of identities has reached epidemic proportions. The conflict between India and Pakistan is often seen as a Hindu – Muslim conflict and the continuing crises in the Middle East has distinctly religious overtones. For instance, the American military and economic involvement in the Middle East is perceived by some to be a Christian intrusion into the heart of the Muslim world. Threats by the Iranian president Mahmoud Ahmadinejad against Israel are seen as a Muslim war against Jews. Jews as a religious people are seen as intricately involved with the modern state of Israel and its violence against Palestinians, and the Israeli war against Hezbollah in 2006 and its 2009 attacks on Gaza are seen as Jewish wars against Muslims.

When conflated, often because of external threats or anxieties, religious, ethnic and national identities tend to strengthen each other and turn into rigid positions, making it more difficult to engage in inter-religious dialogues or negotiations towards resolving conflicts.

Religious Boundary Violations

Religious authorities work hard to maintain strict boundaries. Some Christian traditions do not even allow Christians of other traditions to participate at the Eucharist, or Holy Communion. Most religious communities prohibit conversions not so much into its community, but out of its community. Most also proscribe inter-religious marriages. Today, however, increasing numbers of religious people are providing an interesting counter-action of boundary violation.

Disenchanted with traditional forms of religion, these religious adventurers are moving towards "spirituality." While each religion has its own contemplative practices that include prayer and meditation, which is often called spirituality, they are going beyond those to both incorporate others' religious practices, and to seek spiritual community and religious authority outside their own tradition. A variety of reasons can contribute to this: discontent with one's family and ethnic affiliation, intellectual discomfort of the veracity of a particular religious belief, unwillingness to accept the required practice or ethical commitment or affirmatively, the desire to realize religious truth, sensibly, emotionally, cognitively and intuitively in ways called "mystical." Indeed, the number of people who identify themselves as "spiritual" but not "religious" seems to be on the rise.

There is also the phenomenon of double or multiple belonging. If a person has crossed boundaries in a spiritual journey, to what community does this person belong? Is it acceptable for a person to be both Buddhist and Christian and identify herself as a Buddhist Christian or a Christian Buddhist? Although some will see this as a clear instance of boundary violation, such fluidity in identity markers has not been an uncommon practice in countries where people from two or more religious communities lived side by side. Even though the church thoroughly discourages this, it is often the case that a Buddhist who converts to Christianity carries some of his or her core worldview and beliefs from the Buddhist tradition to the newly professed theological framework. Also, as inter-religious marriages become more prevalent, and more children have their faith formation at the intersection of two distinct traditions, it is not uncommon to find people who genuinely find themselves in a situation of multiple religious belonging.

While established religious communities want to carefully guard their boundaries and maintain rigid identities, the current trend favors those who are exceedingly uncomfortable with static identities but are eager to seek new hybrid identities. Interreligious dialogue up to the present time has sought to respect religious communities' requirement to maintain hard identities. In today's context, however, the difficulty of maintaining this position becomes increasingly evident.

A Way Forward

Long before post-colonial theology received such sophisticated expression, in one of his early works, theologian Paul Tillich used the image of "an uneasy border" to express a place where a theologian is situated, arguing that the place of the boundary is "the most fruitful place of knowledge."[12] Tillich has described himself as "a man who always lived on the boundary – on the boundary between religion and culture, on the boundary between Europe and American, and on the boundary between being and non-being."[13] In this, Tillich relies on philosopher Martin Heidegger, whose work is picked up also by Homi Bhabha, one of today's premier proponents of post-colonial theory, who quotes Heidegger at the caption of the Introduction to his seminal work *The Location of Culture:* "a boundary is

[12] Michael Nausner in his article, "Homeland as Borderland: Territories of Christian Subjectivity" (in *Postcolonial Theologies,* 122) translates these concepts from Paul Tillich's early German work *Religiose Verwikrklichung* (Berlin: Furche,1930)

[13] Jerald C. Brauer, "Paul Tillich's Impact on America" in Paul Tillich's *The Future of Religions* (New York: Harper and Row Publishers, 1966), 19.

not that at which something stops, but, as the Greeks recognized, the boundary is that from which *something begins its presencing*."[14]

Tillich goes on to describe the Christian existence as at an uneasy border situation and the Christian task as a struggle for realization from the perspective of the boundary. About this writes Kathryn Tanner, "The distinctiveness of a Christian way of life is not so much formed *by* the boundary as *at* it: Christian distinctiveness is something that emerges in the very cultural processes occurring in the boundary."[15] Indeed, Christians are called to boundary dwelling – to live in the borderlands. It is not something to be tolerated as a temporary inconvenience, or a condition to be transcended. Rather, it is to be claimed as home. Christians are called, writes Tillich, "to hold out at the boundary and to resist the temptation to flee this condition of pressure by settling down on one side of the boundary or the other."[16]

The borderland is the opposite of empire. Indeed those in the borderlands are there precisely because they have been marginalized by institutional power. There, one does not have to be concerned with national, ethnic, linguistic or even religious identities that are claimed by empires but finds oneself in common solidarity with other human beings, including religious ones, struggling together to survive. In the midst of that struggle in the borderland, people are conscientized, and creative and revolutionary energies are engaged. To authentic Christianity, divorced from imperial power, this is home. And so it is to authentic Buddhism, Hinduism, Islam, Judaism and others. In this home they begin to recognize that other borderland inhabitants share a common humanity with them.

Mutually exclusive binary identities are social constructs that are fundamentally about power. Political entities, nations and social groups, but particularly religious communities, beholden to the empires of the world, tend to use them as static non-negotiable factors in order to strengthen their allegiances to empire and to maintain their positions of power. In today's world of increased communication, mobility and de-centralized power, religious people are building new alliances and forging new identities, and such static and binary expressions are fading into irrelevance. Churches and other religious communities that have in the past sought to maintain and static binary identity structures would do well to take this opportunity to examine their own allegiances to empire and find their place in the borderlands where a new and creative ways of being will begin their *presencing*.

---

[14] Martin Heidegger, *Poetry, Language, Thought* (New York: Harper and Row, 1971), 154.

[15] Kathryn Tanner, *Theories of Culture: A New Agenda for Theology, Guides the Theological Inquiry* (Minneapolis: Fortress Press, 1997), 115.

[16] Tillich, *Religiose Verwirklichung,* 12 (trans. Michael Nausner, "Homeland as Borderland" in *Postcolonial Theologies,* 126)

Reconceptualizing Religion, Dialogue, Theology and Mission in Plralistic Society: The Contribution of S.J. Samartha

Gaikwad Rogers

One hundred years after the World Missionary Conference 1910 with all its euphoria about evangelization of the world in the generation of the time, we are faced with a world which is impingingly pluralistic and riddled with communal problems. It is in such a context that Stanley J. Samartha (October 7,1920 – July 22, 2001) through his extensive writings on inter-religious relationships makes us rethink the following important issues: the nature and importance of pluralistic religious traditions, the need, nature and practice of dialogue, theocentric Christology in relation to pneumatology; and, the significance of Christian mission in the contemporary context.

The Pluralistic Religious Traditions

The popular conceptions of religions among Christians, reveal diverse views: Christian faith as being God-given while other religions are of Satanic origin; religions (Christianity not being considered as a religion) as human efforts to reach God while the Christian gospel is God's revelation to humans; religions at best containing God's revelation but devoid of salvation, Christianity having not only God's revelation but also exclusive possession of God's salvation; and, Christianity or Jesus Christ being the fulfillment of the spiritual aspirations, hopes and values of other religions. A good number of the participants at Edinburgh 1910 would have also subscribed to the above mentioned views. It is against the background of such Christian perspectives that Samartha, along with other scholars of our times, calls for a reconceptualization of religions.

The impressive phenomenon of religious plurality, according to Samartha, is a clear indication that religions are different responses to the Ultimate Mystery. The nature of this mystery provides the ontological basis for the empirical fact of religious plurality. Hence the nature, and in particular the distinctiveness of every religious tradition should be studied within such a philosophico-theological framework. Only then can the importance of religious pluralism be understood and appreciated.

In a religiously plural world, Samartha considers religions as different responses to God or the Truth. He advances three reasons for the plurality of religious traditions. First, since human beings respond to the Ultimate Reality from diverse chronological, geographical, historical, cultural, existential and other conditions, the responses to the Ultimate are bound to be plural.[1] Second, religious traditions are human expressions of experiences of the Divine or Truth. "How can so great a Mystery be experienced in only one way and expressed through only one set of symbols? Religious plurality, therefore, is the homage which the finite mind pays to the inexhaustibility of the infinite." [2]

Third, an ontological basis for the phenomenon of religious plurality is, as Samartha suggests, the pluralistic nature of reality: "(D)iversity is in the heart of Being itself."[3] The numerous religious traditions may therefore be understood as varied expressions of the heterogeneous essential characteristics of the nature of reality. However the diversities within the being of Mystery need not be interpreted as perpetually separate entities; rather they are all inter-related, constituting a complex whole, an *advaitic* reality.[4]

Thus Samartha recognizes religions as traditions which have responded differently to the mystery of the Ultimate. Furthermore the mysterious ontological basis of Truth gives all religions a relative and interim character. Divine truth is received and preserved in earthen vessels. "No one who is part of a particular community of faith, shaped by linguistic, social and historical factors, can escape this cultural relativity."[5] Being so conditioned, no particular religion can claim absolute significance for all people and for all times.[6] In other words, any particular religion can have decisive but only relative significance.

The degree of the relativity of religious traditions is further heightened by the perceptual realization that the Ultimate Reality or Mystery "is not a static substance but a dynamic process."[7] Therefore any enlightening experience of Truth at a given point in history cannot reveal all of the nature of Reality which while being immanently involved in cosmic history yet continuously transcends it. The attainment of an all-comprehensive

---

[1] Samartha, "Dialogue as a Quest for New Relationships," *Journal of the Chair in Christianity*, Vol. I, No.1(Nov. 1989), 34 -35; see also Samartha, *Courage for Dialogue: Ecumenical Issues in Inter-Religious Relationships* (Geneva: WCC, 1981), 152.

[2] Samartha, *One Christ – Many Religions: Toward a Revised Christology* (Bangalore: SATHRI with Wordmakers, 1992), 5; also see 120, 130.

[3] Ibid., 95; also see 91.

[4] Ibid., 95.

[5] *Courage for Dialogue*, 152.

[6] Ibid., 153.

[7] *One Christ – Many Religions*, 119.

perfect human understanding, as well as the ability of complete human description of dynamic Mystery in all its total fullness is an elusive quest.[8]

Thus there is a kind of 'interimness' about religions; they are relative in relation to Truth or Mystery which alone is eternal. All religions have a pilgrim-like character; each has a contextual realization of the Truth, and is engaged in a deeper search and experience of the Truth.[9] However Samartha does not devalue the particularities of different religions. Every religious tradition, when it reflects or partakes in something of the Truth and leads its adherents towards it, deserves respect and appreciation. In the core of any religion there is something special which belongs to that particular religion alone. It is this specific characteristic which gives it a unique distinctiveness in relation to other religions.[10]

Thus when discussing inter-religious relationships, Samartha says that adherents of particular religious traditions should not operate from within a self-imposed obligation to defend their respective communities of faith over against others. Rather, if

> the great religious traditions of humanity are indeed responses to the mystery of God or *Sat* or the Transcendent or Ultimate Reality, then the distinctiveness of each response… should be stated in such a way that a mutually critical and enriching relationship between different responses becomes naturally possible.[11]

The mysterious nature of Reality provides the ontological basis for edifying inter-religious relationships. When Christians, Hindus, and people of other faiths acknowledge their finite nature and consequent ignorance before the mystery of God, they will realize the importance of coming together for a more comprehensive understanding of Truth and its practical implications.[12] Therefore a frank and humble sense of incompleteness coupled with a genuinely felt need of enrichment are essential pre-requisites for constructive relationships.[13]

However mutual enrichment should be done critically. Without a critical principle there is danger that "plurality might degenerate into a sea of relativity in which different boats flounder aimlessly without rudders."[14] In former times each religious tradition tended to develop its own criteria over against the others. Now as people live in pluralistic societies a critical principle has to be developed by religious traditions in relation to one another.[15] Hence Samartha recommends "a more open conceptual

---

[8] Cf. Samartha, "Indian Realities and the Wholeness of Christ," *Missiology*, Vol X, No. 3 (July 1982), 315.

[9] Cf. *Courage for Dialogue*, 103.

[10] Ibid., 151-153.

[11] *One Christ – Many Religions*, 98.

[12] "Indian Realities and Wholeness of Christ," 315.

[13] Cf. *Courage for Dialogue*, 155.

[14] *One Christ – Many Religions*, 8.

[15] Ibid; also see 167.

framework which could hold together the attitudes of different people in tension but not in conflict." The issue is not so much about the religion of truth, he says, as it is about the truth of religion. Instead of engaging in competitive conversion activities in society, Samartha advocates "a context of day to day living where the realization of the truth needs to be tested."[16]

Thus in the light of the above discussion, Samartha highlights certain important values of religious plurality. First, the different religious traditions provide "spiritual resources for particular communities to survive and retain their identities."[17] Second, quoting Rajni Kothari, Samartha observes that

> a plurality of religions, cultures, languages, and ethnic groups may be a guarantee against fascism in multi-religious society because it would resist the imposition of any 'one and only' religion and ideology on all people.[18]

Third, Samartha points out that the phenomenon of plurality of religions makes possible a whole range of options when people are faced with profound perplexities of life. No single religion has exclusive possession of answers to all the problems of human life. Hence multi-religious traditions which face life and its problems from different perspectives can provide helpful alternative solutions.[19]

Fourth, a context of religious plurality facilitates possibilities of mutual criticism and enrichment.[20] Furthermore religions can play a 'prophetic-critical' role in society purging its evils and moulding public morality. They will also "encourage the emergence of new communities of concerned individuals cutting across visible religious boundaries who, with courage and conviction, can work for fuller life in society."[21]

Along with giving rise to ecumenical religious communities, religious pluralism will also help in drawing attention to a transcendent centre that serves not only as the source of all values but also as the norm to judge all human conduct.[22] Thus it indicates a spirit of open commitment in the lives of the followers of different religious traditions. While being faithful to their experience of Mystery through their respective traditions, they are open to its enrichment through their fellowship with people of other faiths. At the same time a deeper understanding of this Mystery fosters a stronger sense of ethical responsibility in society.

---

[16] Samartha, "Religious Imperatives and Social Concerns," *Religion and Society*, Vol. XXX, Nos. 3 & 4 (Sept. & Dec, 1983), 114..

[17] Samartha, "Religious Identity in Multi-Faith Society," *Current Dialogue*, No.13 (Dec. 1987), 6.

[18] Ibid.

[19] Samartha, "Mission in a Religiously Plural World – Looking beyond Tambaram 1938," *International Review of Mission,* Vol. LXXVII, No. 307 (July 1988), 319.

[20] Ibid.

[21] *One Christ – Many Religions*, 63; also see 64.

[22] Ibid., 63; also see 64-65.

Inter-Religious Dialogue

While the term 'Inter-Religious Dialogue' might not have found explicit mention in the deliberations at Edinburgh 1910, some of the delegates did indicate that one could discern elements of value in other religions. So also the enthusiastic Oriental scholars did attempt to make the then western world appreciate the beauty and spiritual riches of the religions of the Orient. Yet no official theological statement was passed at Edinburgh affirming a positive relationship with people of other faiths. The Jerusalem 1928 Conference however made mention of a possible strategy of cooperation among adherents of different religions in order to withstand the then growing impact of communism. The 1938 Tambaram Conference under Hendrick Kraemer's influence asserted discontinuity between the Christian Gospel and other religions. While the term 'Dialogue' was introduced in the 1961 WCC Assembly (and Vatican II affirmed a positive approach to other faiths since the 1960s), it was almost 10 years later, after Samartha had moved to Geneva in 1968 and was given responsibility of the Dialogue sub-unit in the WCC in the early 1970s, that dialogue was given deeper conceptual meaning and greater practical reality in the ecumenical movement.

For Samartha the context of religious plurality demands a life style that would render philosophical, theological, ethical and empirical justice to every religious tradition as well as promote mutual critical appreciation and edification, thereby enhancing the quality of life on the globe. Samartha advocates the dialogical way of life among people of different faiths. While enumerating different reasons for dialogue, Samartha is also aware of several obstacles in the way of dialogue, but he is hopeful that many of them could be overcome in due course of time.

Samartha understands dialogue as

> a mood, a spirit, an attitude of love and respect towards neighbours of other faiths. It regards partners as persons, not as statistics. Understood and practiced as an intentional lifestyle, it goes far beyond a sterile co-existence or uncritical friendliness. It does not avoid controversies; it does not emphasize only points of general agreement; it recognizes difficulties in relationships as well. It is not a gathering of porcupines; neither is it a get-together of jellyfish.[23]

For Samartha, dialogue is not mere conversation. It is a serious engagement with neighbours of other faiths as all people go through the trials and responsibilities, joys and sorrows, quests and discoveries of existence on earth. It is not a superficial fellowship but a critical cooperative venture, a pilgrimage towards Truth in love, respect and human solidarity.

---

[23] *Courage for Dialogue*, 100; also see "Dialogue as a Quest", 36, and Samartha, "Christians and Neighbours of Other Faiths in Asia: A Search for New Relationships," *Ching Feng*, Vol. XXX, No. 3 (Sept. 1987), 143.

Samartha cites several important reasons for dialogue – historical, socio-economic, and political, empirical, human and theological. Countries which had been under colonial rule for long have experienced a general renaissance giving birth to several socio-economic, political, and religio-cultural movements. The pluralistic heritage of the peoples of Asia and Africa has been brought into sharper focus during the post-colonial years of political independence. In such a situation "where religions divide people into different communities and where political alignments tend to follow religious affiliations it is felt that inter-religious dialogues can help to bring people closer together."[24]

As many countries have become independent since the middle of the twentieth century, national development has become an urgent priority in those countries. In this endeavour there are certain human concerns which are common to people of all faiths. Inter-religious dialogues can prove to be helpful in this task of nation-building by pooling together the different perspectives and resources of the many religious traditions in addressing some of the common problems.[25]

Then again, many people in secularized, scientifically and technologically advanced countries have become alarmed with the adverse effects of their so-called materialistic progress on society. Hence the earnest quest for authentic, relevant and mystical spirituality which can give purpose and direction to life as well as transform it. Inter-religious dialogues assume essential significance in such a quest.[26]

Similarly the importance of personal relationships is being increasingly recognized in pluralistic societies. Religions cannot be known through academic studies of creeds and doctrines. While such knowledge has its value, it cannot compare with the significance of inter-faith personal relationships. "Informed understanding, critical appreciation and balanced judgment – these cannot arise except where people meet in friendliness and trust, in openness and commitment."[27] Furthermore in a world of increasing cruelty and violence there is need for ecumenical religious communities as 'islands of hope in an ocean of despair.' It is dialogue which facilitates the birth of such cross-religious communities.[28]

Samartha presents three theological reasons for justifying dialogue.[29] Firstly, God has entered into a dialogical relationship with all humanity in a very special way through incarnation. Therefore to follow a dialogical life-style is to be part of God's continuing work among human beings. Secondly, the gospel of forgiveness, reconciliation and new creation is full

---

[24] Samartha, "The Progress and Promise of Inter-Religious Dialogues," *Journal of Ecumenical Studies,* Vol. IX, No.3 (Summer 1972), 470.
[25] Ibid; also see "Christians and Neighbours of Other Faiths", 143.
[26] "Progress and Promise of Dialogues," 471.
[27] Ibid.
[28] *One Christ – Many Religions*, 34.
[29] *Courage for Dialogue*, 11-14.

of the promise of the formation of a true ecumenical community in which all barriers are broken down and bonds of love are made stronger. The offer of such a gospel unavoidably depends on dialogue. Thirdly, truth in the Bible is not propositional but a relational concept. One experiences truth in dynamic personal relationships between God and human beings, and among human beings. Thus dialogue becomes a methodological channel in the search for truth.

There are however several obstacles to dialogue. In his writings, Samartha identifies some of them: lack of courage for dialogue; the fear that it dilutes Christian faith commitment and betrays Christian mission; the fear that it leads to religious relativism and syncretism; bitter memories of past relationships among people of different faiths; the presence of evil elements in religious traditions and human encounters; the apprehension of people of other faiths that dialogue is a disguised method of Christian mission to convert people; the perspective that the framework of dialogue is western; and the practical problems of communication in the dialogical relationship.[30]

Samartha is of the opinion that most of the obstacles to inter-religious dialogue are based on unjustified fears and lack of proper understanding about the nature and method of dialogue. He emphasizes that interreligious dialogue can take place meaningfully only when all the partners are genuinely committed to their respective faiths and yet maintain a receptive openness to the spiritualities of other people.[31]It should however be kept in mind that there can be no such thing as pure religious dialogues. Politico-economic and socio-cultural factors also can influence inter-religious relationships.[32] So also there can be no single approach to dialogue, because the partners hail from diverse cultural backgrounds and different historical situations and have developed highly complex attitudes towards the basic questions of life. For instance, some may enter into dialogue as they feel the urgency of cooperation on issues of common human concern, while others may seek dialogue to discover spiritual resources to edify human life and to ward off the ill-effects of secularization. There could be several other approaches to dialogue.[33] Samartha hopes that some of the conceptual and methodological problems would be resolved in the course of the dialogical relationship itself. One way by which some of the barriers to dialogue could be removed is by building a sound theology of dialogue. It is in this area that Samartha has made a significant contribution. His paradigm for inter-religious relationships could be entitled as "A Theocentric Christo-Pneumatological Model."

---

[30] Ibid., x-xi,9; "Progress and Promise of Dialogues," 468-469,472; "Christians and Neighbours of Other Faiths", 145; *One Christ – Many Religions*, 15-16.

[31] "Progress and Promise of Dialogues," 473.

[32] *One Christ – Many Religions, 33.*

[33] *Courage for Dialogue*, 8.

A Theology of Dialogue: Theocentric Christology in Relation to Pneumatology

Samartha advocates a Theocentric Christology which does justice to the Christian experience of Jesus Christ as well as to the empirical reality of religious plurality. When this Theocentric Christology is allied with Pneumatology it enhances one's understanding of the Mystery and gives impetus to inter-religious dialogical relationships.

As the term 'Theocentric Christology' implies, a definite priority of place is given to God. This God is the creator of all life. Therefore all people whether they be Christians, Hindus, Muslims or adherents of any other faith have God as the source of their lives. Consequently they enjoy equality of status and a sense of togetherness in the presence of God. Furthermore this Creator God is concerned with the salvation of all creation and initiates ways and means of reconciling the world to God's own self and imparting eternal life to all creation.[34] Thus a theocentric basis provides a broader framework and more theological space for people of different faiths to live together. However this God has been experienced and understood in different ways by various peoples across the globe. So while each religious tradition maintains its own distinctiveness, the Mystery of God is retained.[35]

The distinctiveness of the Christian religious tradition centres around the life and work of Jesus Christ. Samartha takes a fresh look at the significance of Jesus Christ within the framework of 'Theocentric Christology'. The main focus of Jesus' life and message was not himself, but God and God's Kingdom. He understood himself as a Son living in a bond of love with, and commitment to God as Father. The Kingdom of God was at the very core of Jesus' mission in life. He was totally committed to his God-given vocation of proclaiming and ushering the Kingdom of God on earth. It was to be an open ecumenical kingdom of love for, and obedience to God, and love and justice among all creation.

It is such a person, who was totally dependent upon, open and committed to God, and in whom God was truly present, who is experienced as 'Lord' by Christians. The resurrection is a clear indication of his lordship. "When there is the certainty and assurance that through this particular person, death has lost its hold on life, there is the alternative of hope in the midst of death. That is the sure sign of Christ's lordship."[36]

Jesus' lordship is also experienced through his humility, his self-effacing servanthood. He radically reversed the usual understanding of lordship. Instead of exercising authority over others he surrendered himself to serve

---

[34] *One Christ – Many Religions,* 100; also see Samartha, *The Other Side of the River: Some Reflections on the Theme of the Vancouver Assembly* (Madras: C.L.S., 1983), 47.
[35] *One Christ – Many Religions*, 101.
[36] *Courage for Dialogue*, 94.

others and accepted the burdens of others on himself. His self-emptying service has become a source of empowerment particularly to the suffering and dying.[37] The lordship of Jesus Christ is not an end in itself; it is theocentric and subservient to God's plans and purposes. It is God, whom Jesus calls 'Father' who is previous to Jesus Christ. God is also the eschatological end.[38]

Within the framework of 'Theocentric Christology' Jesus is declared to be the Christ of God, Saviour and Lord. Being a confession of faith articulated by the Christian community, it remains normative to Christians at all times and places.[39]However Jesus is not the absolute complete revelation or only disclosure of Mystery. While for Christians the only way to be in God is through Jesus Christ, "in a religiously plural world to be in Christ is not the only way to be in God."[40]Hence Samartha asserts,

> In our pluralistic situation we have to acknowledge the presence of other 'lords'... the religious 'lords' of Asia who have provided and continue to provide spiritual sustenance, theological strength and ethical guidance for millions of our neighbours. It is not just their religious presence that needs to be recognized, but their theological significance as well.[41]

In the lives of Buddha, Rama or Krishna one may discern a combination of the elements of 'revelation' and 'liberation' which provide the needed meaning, purpose and power in life to their devotees.[42] However the devotees do not quarrel among themselves over the question, 'Which of the lords is most superior?' In fact such a question is a non-issue. God is Mystery and people too are free to meaningfully and dynamically respond to the divine in different ways.[43]

Thus a 'Theocentric Christology' provides more theological space for Christians to live together with neighbours of other faiths in a pluralistic society. Christians can remain committed to God through Jesus Christ without adopting a negative attitude toward people of other faiths. On the contrary, it opens up the possibility of sharing in the abundant riches of God by relating the uniqueness of Jesus Christ to that of other lords, beliefs and practices of other traditions, through dialogue.[44]Inter-religious fellowship within the framework of 'Theocentric Christology' will facilitate mutual enrichment.[45]Furthermore, the theocentrism in

---

[37] Ibid., 95.

[38] Ibid.

[39] *One Christ – Many Religions*, 96.

[40] Samartha, "The Future of the Church in India," *NCC Review,* Vol. CX, No.3 (March 1990), 170.

[41] "Christians and Neighbours of other Faiths", 143.

[42] *One Christ – Many Religions*, 149.

[43] Ibid.

[44] Ibid., 101.

[45] Ibid; also see *The Other Side of the River*, 49, and "Christians and Neighbours of Other Faiths," 144 -145

'Theocentric Christology' grounds cooperation among people of different faiths

> not on expediency, but on theology, providing a vision of participating with all human beings in God's continuing mission in the world, seeking to heal the brokenness of humanity, overcoming the fragmentation of life, and bridging the rift between nature, humanity, and God.[46]

Theocentric Christology gains greater acceptance as it gives importance to the work of the Spirit of God. God is not only ontologically prior, but is also continually related to all creation with the goal of establishing the divine kingdom on earth. Even people of other faiths come within the purview of God's Kingdom. While the Holy Spirit helps Christians to be related to God and the divine kingdom through Jesus Christ, the Spirit also works in different ways among people of other faiths. Theocentric Christology is integrally related to Pneumatology in thought of Samartha.

Samartha is critical of the exclusivistic interpretations of the work of the Holy Spirit. The *filioque* clause in the Nicene Creed, which asserts that the Spirit proceeds from God the Father and the Son, restricts the work of the Spirit to the narrow confines of the history of the Jews and the Christians.[47] Samartha finds the Eastern Church's understanding of the Holy Spirit as conducive to proper and helpful inter-religious relationships. The Eastern Church insists that the Spirit proceeds from the Father alone. While such a theocentric connection does not deny the operation of the Holy Spirit through the Judaeo-Christian tradition, it also provides the Spirit greater freedom and far more theological space to work in the lives of people of other faiths as well.[48]

Though the Bible and Church traditions do not explicitly focus on the larger work of the Holy Spirit, Samartha discerns positive clues in this direction. The Bible testifies that the Spirit has spoken through the prophets and that the Spirit has been operative even before Jesus of Nazareth. The Old Testament also makes brief references, such as in Amos 9:7 to God's concern with nations and individuals other than the Jews.[49]The glowing accounts in the New Testament of the work of the Holy Spirit in the lives of the early Christians should not be interpreted as objective negative judgments on people of other faiths.[50]In the history of Christianity as early Christians came into contact with the different religions and high philosophies of the Hellenistic world, they were confronted with the question of the larger work of the Holy Spirit. Drawing attention to the

---

[46] *One Christ – Many Religions*, 102.

[47] Samartha, "The Holy Spirit and the Revelation of God in Emerging India 2000," *Emerging India and the Word of God,* ed. Paul Puthanangady (Bangalore: NBCLC, 1991), 35; cf. Courage for Dialogue, 63.

[48] "Holy Spirit and the Revelation of God," 36.

[49] Ibid.

[50] *Courage for Dialogue*, 66-67.

struggles of the Church Fathers to grapple with this issue, Samartha concludes, "Irenaeus sums up the general trend in patristic tradition: 'There is but one and the same God who, from the beginning to the end by various dispensations, comes to the rescue of mankind'."[51]

Samartha asserts that the Holy Spirit "often defies control and systematization."[52] Hence one must avoid placing restrictions on the freedom of the Holy Spirit or confining it within one particular theoretical structural framework. Thus a sincere quest for the understanding of the larger work of the Holy Spirit must take one beyond the limits of the Scriptures, through the different trends in the history of the Church and outside it, to the contemporary historical context in which the people of different faiths live neighbourly interdependent lives together. Thus the Theocentric Christology of Samartha is inseparably linked with the activity of the Holy Spirit.[53]

The methodological implications of Samartha's model are: commitment to one's own faith while being open to that of others through dialogue. Such an approach would promote mutual enrichment and global wellness. One may however wonder, "What is the place of mission within such a dialogical framework?" Samartha sees a valid place for mission in pluralistic societies.

The Significance of Christian Mission

Mission is an integral part of the Christian religious tradition. Samartha reiterates the importance of mission in the light of his fresh insights into the nature and characteristics of mission. Furthermore he seeks to understand the positive significance of Christians being a witnessing minority in society. Christian mission should facilitate the emergence of ecumenical communities of justice, peace and growth.

God is not some ontologically prior deistic entity but a Creator who is actively involved in the life of all creation in order to make it a divine kingdom. Samartha therefore defines mission as "God's continuing activity through the Spirit to amend the brokenness of creation, to overcome the fragmentation of humanity, and to heal the rift between humanity, nature and God."[54] Such a mission which has reconciliation, harmony and dynamic ecumenical oneness and growth as its goal has the following important characteristics: First, it is comprehensive. Quoting biblical references such as Col.1: 15-20 and Eph. 1:9-10, Samartha points out that

---

[51] Ibid., 67.

[52] "Holy Spirit and the Revelation of God," 36.

[53] For an extensive discussionon discerning the marks and works of the Spirit, refer "Future of the Church in India", 168-169; Samartha, "The Holy Spirit and People of Other Faiths," *To the Winds of God's Spirit: Reflections on the Canberra Theme* (Geneva:WCC, 1990), 58-59; "Holy Spirit and the Revelation of God," 38-39.

[54] *One Christ – Many Religions*, 170.

God's love is all-embracing; nothing is beyond the scope of the activities of the Holy Spirit. Second, God's mission is wholistic. As seen in Luke 4: 16-21 every aspect of human life is included within God's concern. Third, within the comprehensiveness of God's mission, "Christian mission has a beginning in the incarnation of God in Jesus Christ, in his life, death, resurrection and the coming of the Holy Spirit."[55]Fourth, mission has a congregational character. Christians as the body of Christ and as a community guided and empowered by the Holy Spirit are committed to serve God through their worship, service and witness life.[56]Thus it may be observed that Christian commitment in the world is neither to Christianity as a religion nor to the church as an institution, but to God in Jesus Christ through the Holy Spirit.

A joyful declarative sharing of one's faith and a sincere commitment to the missionary obligations essential to it, do not necessarily imply a critical rejection of other faith commitments or religious traditions. Nor is the mission of the Church to make other people "Christian" by religion. Rather mission is concerned with inviting all people to enter the kingdom of God and to be co-citizens of the same.[57] Hence Samartha is critical of the exclusivistic Christian understanding and expressions of mission. He says, "Terms such as 'evangelistic campaign', 'missionary strategy', 'campus crusade'… sound more appropriate to military enterprises than to Christian witness to God's redeeming love in Jesus Christ."[58] So also the statistical approach implied in terms such as 'the unreached two billion' sounds derogatory. People should not be treated as statistical units but as persons who are co-partners in the common enterprises of the society. They too have experienced something of God's loving grace and revelation.

Samartha however sees a legitimate place for conversion within the framework of mission. Had there been no space for conversion, India would have been impoverished of such great religious traditions as Buddhism, Jainism and Sikhism. So also Christianity would not have emerged out of Judaism in the first century. However the primary concern in conversion should be a theocentric orientation which simultaneously brings about a genuine renewal of life. The focus of conversion should not be horizontal movement of people from one community to another. Samartha does recognize the value of conversion as a form of a social protest movement, but when horizontal conversions are manipulated by economic affluence, organizational strength, technological power, political

---

[55] *Courage for Dialogue*, 79.

[56] Ibid., 79-80.

[57] Samartha, "Christian Commitment and Christian Tolerance in a Pluralistic Society," *CCA News*, Vol. XXII, No.2 (Feb. 15, 1987), 10.

[58] *Courage for Dialogue*, 134.

forces and other factors thereby destabilizing the life of a society, then such conversions are suspect.[59]

Since the word 'mission' has fallen into much disrepute in countries such as India, Samartha suggests the use of the term 'witness' instead of 'mission.' Witness is a biblical term. It involves giving expression to the gospel of Jesus Christ in the living context of relationships. Each new situation requires an appropriate form of witness. For instance in the context of social oppression, Christians should bear witness through their involvement in the struggle for justice. In bearing such witness, "distinctiveness not exclusiveness, uniqueness not only-ness, participation in God's continuing work rather than one way proclamation of the word" will have to be the missional style of the church.[60]

In bearing witness, Samartha assures Christians that they need not be discouraged about their small numbers. Statistics is not the measure of the depth of religious life. Samartha reminds Christians that in the Bible, 'minority' is a good word. "Israel was a minority among the nations. The remnant was a minority within a minority. Jesus and his disciples... constituted a minority."[61]Moreover history bears witness that creative minorities have always played a significant role in renewing and transforming social life. Even the images which Jesus uses for his disciples' life and witness in the world are minority images: light, salt, leaven, mustard seed and treasure hid in the field. The missional style of Christians should be like "salt and leaven and light permeating life around, and unmistakably transforming it."[62] The evangelization of the world in our generation should be thought of in holistic spiritual terms and not in religious conversion language.

The depth of Christian witness should go hand in hand with the breadth of Christian tolerance. When Christians witness to their neighbours, they should also be open to the witness of their neighbours to them. Mutual witness becomes an essential dimension of mission in a religiously plural world. Each particular religion has its unique distinctiveness in relation to other religions. So mutual witness facilitates enrichment of all in the discovery of new dimensions of Truth. Then again, no religious tradition can have sole possession of solutions to the massive problems that contemporary human beings face. While Christians can and should respond by bringing forth biblical insights to tackle these problems they should also be open to the contributions which neighbours of other faiths make.[63]

---

[59] *One Christ – Many Religions*, 169-170; see also Samartha, "Dialogue and the Politicization of Religions in India," *International Bulletin of Missionary Research*, Vol. VIII, No.3 (July 1984), 106.

[60] *Courage for Dialogue*, 102-103; "Future of the Church in India,"167.

[61] "Future of the Church in India," 167-168.

[62] Ibid., 168; "Christians and Neighbours of Other Faiths,"146.

[63] *One Christ – Many Religions*, 171; *Courage for Dialogue*, 152-153; "Progress and Promise of Dialogues," 473; "Mission in a Religiously Plural World,"324.

Samartha discusses two important issues which could bring people of different faiths together: the concerns of liberation and interreligious harmony. In dialogical unity people of different faiths could work in solidarity with the poor, the powerless and the oppressed as they struggle for justice, liberation and dignity.[64] As far as the situation of communalism is concerned, while not absolving religious traditions of their sinfulness and failures, Samartha is convinced that what are usually described as inter-religious conflicts are in reality socio-economic and political conflicts in which religions are cunningly manipulated by people with vested interests. This is what Samartha calls the 'politicization of religions.'[65] Inter-religious dialogue promotes harmony by facilitating informed and mature understanding among people of different faiths. It strengthens resistance against attempts to suppress, exaggerate or distort facts in the history of relationships between different religious communities. However in this endeavour of promoting inter-religious harmony and giving birth to an ecumenical community of communities, "Christians, together with their neighbours of other faiths, need to draw attention to a transcendent centre, the ultimate mystery, the truth of the truth (*satyasya satyam*) which is both the source of all values and the criterion to judge all human efforts."[66]

Hence the call for Christians to enter into dynamic inter-religious relationships with neighbours of other faiths. This is by no means a betrayal of Christian mission; rather it provides "the context in which the Christian witness to God's saving work in Jesus Christ becomes transparently clear"[67]It entails no dilution of the substance of Christian faith nor the contradiction of the distinctively Christian concern for love and justice as manifest in the life and work of Jesus Christ. On the contrary, such dialogical relationships enhance and enrich a Christian's commitment to Jesus Christ.

Edinburgh 2010 is Therefore a Time to Reconceptualize

- *religions* including Christianity as human articulations of the experiences and messages of and about the divine;
- *dialogue* as the methodology of spiritual commitment and openness in the mutually empowering pilgrimage and movement to further actualize the truth;
- *Christian faith* as Theocentric Christo-Pneumatology; and,
- *Christian mission* as cosmic-transforming witness through ecumenical communities of Truth-centredness, justice, love,

[64] *One Christ – Many Religions*, 173; "Progress and Promise of Dialogues," 473-474.

[65] "Religious Identity in Multi-Faith Society," 7.

[66] *One Christ – Many Religions*, 175.

[67] Ibid., 171.

peace and growth.

One of the watch-words for Edinburgh 2010, in line with Samartha's thought, could well be "Dialogical Evangelization of the Pluralistic World in our Times!"

CHALLENGES IN GLOBAL CHRISTIANITY: RELIGIONS AND THE GOAL OF CHRISTIAN MISSION

Jonas Adelin Jorgensen

Abstract

This article identifies and discusses three main missiological challenges present in global Christianity. First, the political challenge is discussed, secondly the ecumenical challenge, and thirdly the challenge from other religions. The political challenge structures and limits everyday life of Christians as well as of other religious groups. Secondly, the ecumenical challenge is discussed as the globalisation of Christianity accentuates it. Thirdly, the challenge from other religious traditions is identified on a number of levels and discussed. The article argues that the main challenge for missiology from other religious traditions is to answer the question: 'what is the goal for Christian mission in relation to believers from other religious traditions?' In conclusion the article answer this fundamental missiological question by pointing out how mission can become a truly joyful message for believers from other religious traditions.

I recently read a number of writings of the Danish theologian and educator L.P. Larsen (1862-1940), who served as a missionary in South India from 1889-1935. While originally sent by the Danish Missionary Society (DMS) to the Arcot Lutheran Church, he soon started working as an independent missionary after a controversy with DMS over the baptism of converts. From 1905 he engaged himself in the establishment of a number of reading rooms for Christian literature in Tamil Nadu, and at some point in the 1930s he was active in the establishment of Kandiswamy's 'Fellowship of Followers of Jesus' in Madras. Furthermore, around 1910 he became increasingly involved in the establishment of the United Theological College (UTC) in Bangalore. From 1911 to 1924 he taught comparative religion and exegesis and served as the first dean of UTC for a number of years.

The reason for mentioning Larsen here is his 1907 article from *Nordisk Missionstidsskrift* entitled "Kristendom og Folkekarakter i Indien" ("Christianity and Folk-Character in India"). In this article, Larsen discusses the 'folk-character' of Indian peoples, that is, the general character which an ethnic group has as a result of its biological, historical, social and cultural development. More specifically, Larsen wants to identify the obstacles which this special folk-character gives rise to in relation to the gospel of Jesus Christ. These very same obstacles are the ones which will be overcome by conversion to Christianity. Larsen identifies three areas in which the folk-character has 'weaknesses and omissions' namely subjectivity, metaphysics, and social solidarity.

The article is interesting in several aspects: First, I agree with Larsen in his identification of subjectivity and metaphysics as areas with a marked difference between Christianity and Hinduism, as well as in his observation that religions influence these concepts. Not only missionaries but anthropologists as well have later argued that one of the transformations implied by conversion to Christianity is discovery (or construction) of a new form of subjectivity and socialisation of a new person with new ultimate reference points. Secondly, I find myself in disagreement with Larsen's unproblematic hierarchical evaluation of the Hindu subjectivity and metaphysical speculations as the result of 'weaknesses and omissions' and thus as inferior in comparison with Christianity: How can we be sure that the Hindu is better off with a new form of subjectivity and a new conscience? And can we rest assured that this new form of subjectivity is really a Christian and not merely a modern Western one?

These introductory remarks lead me to my first point on the challenges from global Christianity to missiology: History has certainly made us more cautious when recommending quick whole-sale solutions to deep-rooted contextual problems, especially if the solution to these problems involves dominion over passive indigenous subjects by external Western agents. My question is now: Has the last hundred years of history with its imperialist, nationalist and totalitarian political regimes – and the reaction against this in post-colonialism and post-modernism – made it impossible to use the very concepts underlying Larsen's vision for mission, that is, the hierarchical thinking, the 'folk-character', and the large-scale descriptions of moral qualities in ethnic groups? Questions like these need to be considered carefully independently of whether or not we are sympathetic to Larsen's overall agenda – the proclamation of Jesus as Christ for all peoples. In the following, I attempt to start such a consideration, first by briefly describing the broader theological background of Larsen's concepts and hierarchical thinking, and secondly by relating this to the present challenges which global Christianity poses to our missiological reflection.

The Broader Background of Larsen's Writings: Liberal Theology, Religion and Mission

Even if neither Larsen nor others described him as 'liberal' in terms of theology or ethics, the broader background for Larsen's writings as well as that of the Edinburgh 1910 conference was liberal theology.

The term 'liberal' should not be understood in a pejorative sense but simply describing a historical phase in Christian theology, a phase with certain agendas, certain concepts and a certain inherent logic of its own.

Especially the idealist philosophy underlying the understanding of concept 'religion' and the role of historical religions seems to be important as an implicitly shared presupposition in the Edinburgh 1910 statements. In the early 20th century, the common European reasoning in relation to religion included the following key elements: First, religions belong to the general sphere of human life and cannot be reduced to other factors. Secondly, revelation is the start of religions and a few chosen individuals had a special psychic or prophetic access to this revelation, typically the founders of religions. Thirdly, far from being lofty speculations for the sake of speculation religions serve to direct attention to the practical world through the psycho-social fellowship which it gives rise to. In this perspective all religions are abstract equivalents to their practical value, that is, the value of a religion depends upon the concrete transformations which the religion facilitates in individuals' lives. This means that religions can and should be evaluated; however, this evaluation is not to take place on the basis of their theological content but according to their effect. Thus, the 'truth' of any given religion is its value, and the 'absolute truth' of a religious tradition is a question of hierarchical superiority in terms of transforming effect. Now, according to this hierarchical value perspective, the Christian religion is identified as the highest and most noble expression of the human spirit. Then, if it is true that humanity finds its fullest expression and culmination in Christianity, and Christianity effectively succeeds in liberating and transforming human beings, Christianity might be said to be the 'absolute religion' on a purely immanent basis, it was argued. That is, the superiority of Christianity need not be argued for from supernatural miracles such as the unique incarnational status of Jesus Christ but could also be argued for from an immanent value basis.

In a broad sense this argument gives direction to a missiological reflection on the role of Christian missions in relation to other religious traditions around the Edinburgh 1910 conference, namely that there is a hierarchical relation between Christianity and other religions and that Christianity is the 'fulfilment' of these religions. The hierarchical thinking surfaced frequently during the 1910 conference, both in the selection of delegates (17 Asians and 1 African out of 1.200 delegates), in the notion of a hierarchy of civilizations with African nations in the bottom, India and China in the middle, and Japan in the top, as well as in the racial thinking underlying the view upon other religious traditions as expressed e.g. in the Commission IV report on the missionary message and non-Christian religions. Furthermore, the very reason for the Edinburgh 1910 conference was a sense of a *kairos* moment, a turn of time, where there was a combination of political openness, Christian economic power, and Western technology which allowed contemporary Christians of all denominations to now fulfil the commandment of Jesus Christ to 'make disciples of all nations' (Matt 28). On the basis of this reasoning Christian mission became a way of helping believers from other religious traditions to reach their true human potential – and reaching this potential would at the same time mean the dissolution of the other traditions. Thus one of the fundamental premises behind the modern global Christian mission as expressed by the Edinburgh 1910 conference was that Christianity should replace other religious traditions because of its hierarchically superior value as witnessed in the economic spending power, political ability, and technological superiority of contemporary Western societies and churches.

Contemporary Challenges to Mission in Global Christianity

At this point I would like to put aside the reflections from Larsen and the reasoning behind the Edinburgh 1910 conference for a moment in order to focus on the actual challenges which face us in globalized Christianity. Even if the Christian Church has been missionary by its very nature from the beginning, the modern understanding of mission as geographically international is relatively new, dating from the establishment of the Roman Catholic *Sacra congregation de propaganda fide* in1622 and the first Protestant mission in Tranquebar, Tamil Nadu, in 1706. Within the last 100 years – from the first Edinburgh conference in 1910 to the second Edinburgh conference in 2010 – Christianity has undergone a global spread, partly due to the conscious missionary efforts of the various Catholic and Protestant missions. From my perspective this globalisation of Christianity has lead to three main challenges to Christian mission: the political challenge, the ecumenical challenge, and the challenge from other religious traditions. Even if this paper focusses on the last of these three challenges let me briefly introduce the two first challenges.

The first and in many places most important challenge is the political situation which structures and limits the everyday life of Christians in many parts of the world. By 'political situation' I do not primarily intend totalitarian political regimes and the reordering of relations between state and religion, which the spread of Christianity has led to in a number of countries, but the socio-political reality which manifests itself in terms of wars, systematic oppression, hunger and violence targeting religious groups. These problems are not specifically Christian problems but common problems for all peoples in a suffering, conflict-ridden, and violent world – and therefore they are also Christian problems. These problems become a challenge for Christian missions in the sense that Christians in many parts of the world live a life which is structured by these political realities and because it is within these structures that discipleship of Jesus is to be realised. The challenge stemming from the political situation to missiology is: how can Christian mission become good news to people whose lives are structured and limited by wars, systematic oppression, hunger and violence?

The second challenge which globalisation of Christianity has brought forth with renewed strength is the ecumenical challenge. The 'ecumenical situation', that is, the fact that the spread of Christianity has caused great cultural and social variety within Christianity itself has caused the difference between traditional denominations in certain geographical areas to appear comparatively smaller than differences within a single denomination across geographical borders. In other words, the variation across different forms of Christianity might be smaller than internal variation within a single form of Christianity. From my perspective, this development raises two important questions: First, is it still relevant to navigate in the present situation after the historical denominational borders? Secondly, is it possible to talk about a single 'Christianity' or should we restrict ourselves to talk about 'Christianities' in the plural without claiming any essential identity between various historical and contemporary forms? Focused on missiology the question here becomes: Should we start speaking about various goals for various forms of Christianity or can we still speak of mission in the singular, presuming a single, overarching goal for Christian missions?

The rest of the article will focus on the third challenge which has its background in what could be termed the 'relative success' of global Christian missions: In Larsen's article as well as in the broader liberal stream of theological thinking which formed the background for the Edinburgh 1910 conference, the presupposition was that Christianity through global missions would replace other religious traditions – 'in our generation' as chairman of the Edinburgh 1910 conference, John R. Mott's personal slogan had it. The absolute value of Christianity was argued for in terms of a hierarchy between religions and the absoluteness of Christianity was identified as its actual value over and against all other religious traditions, as described above. In this perspective global Christian mission seems to have had only relative success because even if it has been instrumental in the global spread of Christianity, and has been partly responsible for maintaining Christianity as the numerically largest religion in the world, it did not succeed in replacing other religious traditions. Quite the opposite is actually the case: The postcolonial situation and suppressive totalitarian systems made fertile ground for a cocktail of national, political and religious resistance: Islam in Egypt, Iran, and Afghanistan, as well as Buddhism in Cambodia, Vietnam, and Tibet have resurged to the public sphere in a way which most commentators thought impossible. The challenge which this development amounts to for missiological reflection is tremendous and might be formulated as the following question: How can the Christian mission and Gospel become a truly joyful message for people from other religious traditions? Do the logics underlying Christian mission thinking require that believers from other religious traditions stop being what they are – believers in a non-Christian religious tradition – in order to participate in the good news which Christian mission truly is? Or are there other options for Christians who want to remain truthful and obedient to their Lord and Saviour but feel a conflict in their respect for people from other religious traditions who do not want to become Christians? These seemingly simple questions contain a number of levels and dimensions which I will now try to unfold under three headings, namely the hermeneutical problem, the dogmatic problem, and the missiological problem.

Religions as a Hermeneutical Problem

The hermeneutical problem in relation to religions concerns whether other religions can be understood at all: If we acknowledge that truth is mediated through religious traditions – as we do as Christian missiologists – can we be sure that we recognise and understand truth outside of our own religious tradition or do the historical and cultural differences make such an understanding impossible, rendering all attempts to understand useless and doomed to fail?

The problem was first described by the historian of religions W.C. Smith in his book *The Meaning and End of Religion* in 1962. Smith criticises the essentialist understanding of 'religion' as something static beyond its historical expressions and argues that the phenomenon 'religion' is more adequately described as historically conditioned expressions of the function which religion has. Exactly because religions are historically conditioned expressions it is wrong to speak about 'religion' as a static analytical concept, Smith argues, and we should instead speak of religions as a phenomenon made up of two qualitative dimensions namely cumulative tradition and individual faith.

In relation to the hermeneutical problem Smith's critique means that what can be seen in religions is not 'religion' as such referring to a fixed theology, ethics or praxis but what 'religion' is, is groups of people behaving religiously. What does this mean for our understanding of religions? It means that the study of religion is not primarily a comparison between different theologies but a comparison of religious lives which both phenomenological and historical are the only comparative element across religious traditions. Going one step further I would argue that a religious experience is more complex that Smith tends to think in his book and that not only cumulative tradition and individual faith should be considered but also human cognition, the human body, and the relation to social and material conditions which make and produce religious experiences. Thus even on a purely phenomenological and historical basis religious experience is a very complex phenomenon, and if we are to engage in the understanding of other religious traditions all these areas need to be addressed insofar as they give meaning and direction to the religious experiences and explicit formulation of theologies.

If we argue that it is possible to understand religious phenomena across religious traditions we are immediately challenged with a second, more philosophical problem. This problem has to do with the criteria and concepts with which we understand and evaluate other religions. If religions are understood and evaluated by the criteria which are most available to us it would mean an understanding and evaluation structured by our own religious criteria. This would involve two things: First, are criteria conditioned by a certain religious tradition able to open up experiences from other religious traditions in a meaningful way? Secondly, can we be sure that these criteria conditioned by our own religious tradition are suitable in the evaluation of other religious traditions?

In his 1993 book *Genealogies of Religion* the anthropologist Talal Asad has answered these questions pointing out and criticizing the Christian dynamics inherent in the concept of religion. Thus what appears as self-evident today when 'religion' is discussed, Asad argues, namely that religion is essentially a matter of symbolic meanings linked to ideas of general order and worldview is to confuse a particular historical and cultural form of religious life – namely Christianity – with the generic concept itself. The concept 'religion' has a specific Christian history itself, he concludes, and if we really want to understand other religious traditions an extraordinary effort is needed. In order to really discover what a religion is and expresses one should not begin with the notion of 'religion' as this symbolic linking but unpack the comprehensive tradition studied in its historical elements thus allowing a deeper understanding of what this particular religion 'is' in its effects, that is, what difference it makes.

On the basis of these reflections, I would argue that an understanding of other religious traditions is possible but only if an effort is done to discover what difference this particular religion makes. However, even if we maintain that we can understand other religions and the possible truth these traditions transmit we have only dealt with one part of the challenge which other religions present to missiology, namely the hermeneutical and philosophical problems. Therefore we must now proceed to the dogmatic aspects of the challenge.

Religions as a Dogmatic Problem

As a dogmatic problem the questions of the role of religions in relation to the Christian understanding of salvation stands forth as the main problem. What is needed in order to start answering this problem is first an attempt to spell out what 'salvation' means as the specific Christian vision for salvation, and secondly on the basis of this, to offer a concrete interpretation of particular religions in the light of God's self-revelation.

If we are able to understand other religious traditions and their analyses of humankind's fundamental problems, the solution to these problems might not be identical with the Christian vision for salvation. Does this disqualify other religious traditions as 'salvific'? From my perspective, two important distinctions need to be made:

First, real religious pluralism seems to lead to real differences which neither should nor can be neglected. A number of metaphors and techniques which Christianity contains are shared with other religious traditions: notions of sin, salvation, mercy, truth, prayer, prophecy, asceticism, blessings, and teleology are found in all theistic religions. However, what makes these concepts and techniques Christian is not their 'conceptuality' but their relation to the word and work of the person Jesus Christ. It is through the connection with the particular and historical – Jesus' life, teachings, death, and resurrection – that the religion which is 'Christianity' is formed. In dogmatic perspective this is expressed through the understanding of faith as formed by the experience of the Spirit of Christ in remembering Jesus. In the New Testament salvation might be seen as a consequence of the relation between the particular human being – Jesus of Nazareth – and the eternal God. This relation is emphasised in Jesus' conception, in his baptism, in his prophetic ministry, in his resurrection and in his eternal pre-existence as the Son. In and through his life, Jesus became and was the Messiah, the Christ, and it is because of his becoming and being Christ that salvation becomes a real option for human beings. In Jesus' incarnational unity of God and man, the divine life becomes a possibility for human life where liberation from sin and redemption from death are manifest. What does this mean for 'salvation'? It means that the Christian vision for salvation cannot be separated from the historical and theological framework giving it its specific meaning namely the experience and remembrance of the person Jesus. Therefore, although universal in scope we cannot talk abstractly and a-historically about salvation in the Christian sense of the word.

The specific Christian vision for salvation might be called naïve in its strong emphasis on the life and deeds of a single human being in the periphery of history for the present transformation of individuals. But the problem is not that it is naïve and bases the possibility for individual transformation upon Jesus' life, death, and resurrection; the problem is that the theological dimensions of the Christian vision for salvation becomes obscured when categories such as 'exclusive', 'inclusive' or 'pluralist' are used to grasp the deepest relation between Christianity and other religious traditions. The Christian vision for salvation is not only historically and theologically connected with the person Jesus but it is also for this very reason clearly different from salvation as envisioned in other religious traditions. Thus, there is no historical or structural basis for arguing that salvation in Christianity and in other religious traditions is identical. In this perspective we must answer the question whether there is Christian salvation in other religions negatively.

Secondly, although salvation is clearly linked to Jesus as Christ it is very unfortunate to term this connection 'exclusive'. The reason for this somewhat counterintuitive conclusion is that faith in Jesus as Christ is possible only on the basis of a confession of one God, the one God who creates and redeems the whole of humanity. It is this one God who reveals himself for salvation in Jesus as Christ – that is, in his life as a totality – and it is only through the confession of the one God that it becomes possible to understand the total life of Jesus as God's self-manifestation, as the content of his will, that is, his 'Word'. It is the one God who has been present from eternity and which is the cause of the world which speaks his Word through the particular life of Jesus of Nazareth and who is universally active as the presence of the Spirit in his church. In other words: the universal life-giving creativity of God cannot be separated or contradicted with the particular revelation of this life-giving creativity in the death and resurrection of Jesus. Thus, the theological premise for the particular experience of salvation in Jesus Christ is God's universal creativity; and Christology can not be meaningfully conceptualised independently of Trinitarian theology, and salvation must reflected upon with this Trinitarian Christological framework.

If both 'logics' are maintained – the intimate connection between salvation and the person Jesus and the Trinitarian Christology – a possible basis for concrete interpretations of particular religions in the light of God's self-revelation becomes possible. As Christian theologians our understanding and evaluation of other religions must be based not only on the exclusive relation between salvation and the person Jesus but also on the inclusive understanding of God's universal creative life-giving. It is God's universal creative will as manifested in Jesus Christ which is the most fundamental theological basis for our interpretation of other religious traditions. We must maintain that salvation must be configured in terms of Christology *and* that God works universally in history. Only this double qualification of the world as created by God and of salvation as Christian is it possible to interpret the meaning of non-Christian religions in terms of salvation: if salvation is the liberation, redemption and restoration of humanity which Christianity envisions, then every attempt to liberate, redeem and restore humanity in God's world might be said to point toward the Christian notion of salvation even if it remains unrelated to the historical and theological particularities of salvation in Jesus Christ.

What, then, is the quality of the relation between religions and Christian salvation if it is not directly historical or theological? I would argue that the way in which God acts in history – and in other religious traditions insofar as they are part of history – follows the way that he acts in Jesus as Christ: He is present but hidden. This does not mean that we can speak of God as the hidden but direct cause of the plurality of religions, such as certain so-called pluralists do. But it means that we must speak of God as the ultimate conditioner and maintainer of the history which also contains the historical religions. In history and in religions God is present in his negativity, as what is waited for, prayed for, hoped for as the ultimate. From a Christian theological perspective, therefore, the universal history is not simply there as something given but is conditioned by and kept within the history of salvation willed by God. This history does not merely illustrate God's acts but it *is* God's acts towards humans for their creation, liberation and redemption. Because of this understanding of God as conditioner and hidden-but-present, we have to not only tolerate but also to respect other religious traditions. This respect is not the product of an immanent, secular and relativistic modernity but based on the notion of the confessed triune God who we confess. And this notion of tolerance and respect transcends the exclusivity of Christianity and opens up Christianity to other religious traditions. This respect gives us reason to hope for liberation, redemption, and restoration of humanity in other religious traditions and motivates a historical and particular interpretation of how this has (or has not) taken place in various religious traditions. This search is not primarily a dogmatic task but a missiological and practical responsibility.

Religions as a Missiological Problem

Finally, and on the basis of the discussion of religions as a hermeneutical and dogmatic problem we are now able to close the circle by returning to the main focus of this paper namely missiology and the problems which the continued existence of non-Christian religions pose to Christian mission. Summing up the findings from above, it was argued that if we are able to understand truth and salvation, our understanding must be based on our own religious tradition. For Christianity this means that our tolerance and respect for other religious traditions must be based on the universal creative will of God as manifest in the particularities of Jesus Christ. A premise to a discussion of religions as a missiological problem is thus that religions can be understood and that the way religions should be thought about is within the framework of God's universal creative will as well as in the particularities of divine action in Jesus Christ. On the basis of this we must now ask: How does Christian mission become a salvific message in a world willed by God but religiously pluralistic? The answer which this article offers is a reconstruction of Christian mission with a focus on salvation, especially bringing out the importance of Christian missions as a sign of the salvation brought by Jesus Christ in a world full of suffering and violence.

With the dogmatic discussion above as a background, we argue that Christian missions do not become a sign of the Kingdom by affirming or denying the self-revelation of God in other religious traditions. Rather, a mission becomes a Christian mission by particular and holistic engagement in the humanization of our common reality across religious boundaries. In modern, affluent Western societies Christianity has degenerated to a civil religion (J.B. Metz), that is, a religious activity which neither claims anything nor gives any comfort. In this situation the radical demands contained in the Sermon on the Mount has lost its relevance. In turn this means that Christianity has lost its ability to be a sign of the Kingdom. But can Christianity exist in the world without following Jesus Christ without hesitation, carrying out its mission, and becoming a sign of the Kingdom? What, then, are these signs of the Kingdom? As pointed out by J. Moltmann, according to the Old Testament the messianic time is characterized by peace, righteousness, justice, and liberation (Is 2:1-5; Micah 4:1-5). According to the New Testament, these signs became manifest, incarnated, in the life, message, death and resurrection of Jesus Christ (Acts 2,14-36), and these are the signs which the Christian church carries on through the Spirit (Rom 8:3-4). Let me briefly expand how these signs might apply on contemporary Christian mission in relation to other religious traditions:

First, as bringers of peace the first Christians spread in the Greco-Roman society, and their lives were driven by a logic which was different from the deadly logic of retaliation and oppression. Isaiah compares peace with a vine or a fig tree which grows organically and gives its fruit to the one who is willing to accept it. Peace spreads through 'fascination' (G. Lohfink) rather than through orders, manipulation, or oppression. But at the same time peace is tangible: wars are ended and conflicts resolved without violence (Is 2:2). In our religiously pluralistic world, a mission becomes Christian by being a sign of peace and by bringing peace.

Secondly, as a sign of a new righteousness and justice we see Jesus' fellowship with the poor, the sick, the sinners, men and women outside the established social hierarchy and its comfortable predictability. It was in relation to these that Jesus became the Messiah, the anointed one, who through healing, feeding, and preaching made the Kingdom tangible and brought the possibility for a new, transformed relationship to God as 'Abba', 'Father'. As the Son of God, Jesus lives in obedience to the Father; as a human being Jesus lives totally for others (K. Barth). Therefore, with the confession of Jesus as Christ we are not only concerned with the theological dimension of his person but also with the social meaning of his life (J. Moltmann). By not sacrificing his obedience to the Father to his living for others, Jesus becomes the new righteousness and invites us to participate in his new righteousness through faith. This second sign, righteousness and justice, is kept in continual tension with the first sign, peace, because in a disobedient and unrighteous world righteousness is not achieved by peace but by the sword (Matt 10:35). But exactly at this point is the logic underlying the Kingdom different from the logic of the world, yes, we might say: it is a blessed difference from the world. A mission becomes Christian by being a sign of righteousness and justice and by working for righteousness and justice in peace.

Thirdly, as a manifest reality for the individual believer, the Kingdom begins and ends with liberation. Entrance into the messianic fellowship of those who do the will of the Father is liberation: it liberates the individual from the demanding task of keeping up a life in opposition to peace, righteousness, and mercy. The most fundamental change which divine mercy brings is the theological and existential liberation which the child-parent relationship to God which the life of Jesus allows the individual to enter into. The relation to God as 'Father' becomes possible only through the Spirit (Rom 8:15), and thus possible only by participation in the reality which the messianic Kingdom manifests. Here all psychological, cultural, social, and economic realities of the world are transcended and lose their power to structure and determine the future of individuals. Here is God the Father of his children and other 'fathers' or authorities are not needed (J. Moltmann). It is *this* reality which from now on structures the life of our existence. A mission becomes Christian by being an open invitation to this relation to God as Father and to others as brothers and sisters.

Conclusion: Christian Mission as a Salvific Sign

To conclude this reconstruction of Christian mission in a religiously pluralistic age: To become a sign of the Kingdom means a practical, ethical and theological engagement in the humanization of the world which we share with believers from other religious traditions. The goal of Christian missions is based upon the vision for the messianic salvation which is proclaimed through the life, death and resurrection of Jesus as Christ and which in Biblical terms is described as liberation, righteousness, justice and peace. This vision forms the goal for Christian mission – also in relation to believers from other religious traditions. The humanization of reality started with Jesus' own ministry which was manifest in a suffering and violent world, and is carried on by the Christian church insofar as it is able to be a sign of the Kingdom. The goal for Christian missions in relation to other religions is not to explain away the universal relevance of the Gospel of the Kingdom or to reduce salvation to a merely secular and immanent restoration of humanity. The goal is the humanization of total reality as a reality dependent upon the creative and salvific will of God for its restoration. Whether this means dissolution of other religious traditions cannot be argued *a priori* and therefore the hierarchical ordering of the relationship between religions as in the inherited logic from Edinburgh 1910 stands in need of critique and revision. As a sign of a blessed difference the Christian church is commissioned to work out room for the reality which our Christian hope is grounded on: the Kingdom of God. The goal for Christian mission in relation to other religious traditions is thus to become a sign of the Kingdom with the radical implications which this implies: the critique as well as common work for liberation, redemption, and restoration of humanity across religious traditions. Only in this way can Christian mission remain a sign of the Kingdom and become a truly joyful message for people from other religious traditions.

Perspective and Issues in Mission and Interfaith Relations: Christian Participation in Nation Building in India

D.K. Sahu

Introduction

Nation-building refers to a process of the constructing a national identity using the power of the state. This process aims at the unification of the people within a state so that it remains politically stable and viable. Nation-building can involve the use of major infrastructural development to foster social harmony and economic growth. The founding parents of our country had envisioned India to be a sovereign, socialist, secular democratic republic. It is enshrined in the preamble of the constitution. India draws the attention of the whole world as the largest democracy. A nation normally means a group of people occupying a given area whose common interests are strong enough to make possible the maintenance of a single sovereign civil authority. To be a nation means to have a common bond among the people. Therefore Nation-building is a process of reinforcing the common bonds among the people of a nation state to the end that there may be general stability and prosperity so that the nation may participate usefully in the community of nations. Nation building is an ongoing task of developing a nation in relation to its own people and also in relation to other nations in the world. Therefore Nation-building does not consist merely in economic progress but means increasing the possibility for *all* of living a fully human life on the physical, cultural, spiritual levels. It also implies the growing ability of a nation as a whole to take its rightful place in the international field, economically, politically, culturally. P.D. Devanandan relentlessly had reminded the Church that she may discharge her responsibility to the nation: "Christian participation in the life of the society and therefore in the building of the nation is a moral duty, a national obligation and the demand of enlightened self-interest," [1]

India has emerged as a nation with functioning democratic institutions that have continued to flourish but some may consider it as an improbable outcome. Many think it improbable on the premise that the diverse and

[1] Devanandan, P.D & M.M.Thoma: *Christian Participation in Nation Building*, 1960, 49.

apparently debatable assortment of religions, languages, regions that consist of one billion people could ever be woven into a modern nation. It is thought even less likely by critics that democracy could take deeper root and flourish in this part of the world. India did not have what many took to be the essential conditions for a functioning democracy. It was an agrarian country with a weak middle class and a comparatively small bourgeoisie. Its population was overwhelmingly poor and illiterate. It was and is one of the more deeply hierarchical societies in the world, which, according to some, had little conception of the egalitarianism and individualism thought to be necessary for a functioning democracy

The Christian vision and commitment of nation building is based on the building up of a "just, participatory and sustainable" society. Common civil values that sustain a society, the common symbols that are the identity of a nation, common decision making processes to give the sense of ownership, equality not just before law but the reality of that equality being expressed in the lives of the people, mutual respect for each other irrespective of caste or creed, mutual respect of each other's faith commitments, and common beneficiaries of the progress and last but not the least fostering of moral and ethical values such as liberty, honesty, integrity, love, are non-negotiable values for building and making of a nation.

Indian Nationalism

Nationalism is a state of mind, permeating the large majority of a people and claiming to permeate all its members. It recognizes the nations-state as the ideal form of political organization and the nationality as the source of all creative cultural life and economic well-being. The supreme loyalty of man is therefore due to his nationality, as his own life is supposedly rooted in and made possible by its welfare. [2] There are as many definitions as there are scholars. It can remind people of various things: fascism, Nazism, wars, massacres and also the liberation of nations from colonial rule. One may discern two kinds of political language. One is the language of nation building and involves the rituals of the state, political representation, citizenship, and citizen's rights. This is the Indian colonial heritage and it is what Indian nationalism owes to the colonial experience. The other language derives its grammar from relationships of power, authority, hierarchy which predate the coming of colonialism but which have been modified by having been made to interact with the ideas and institutions imported by British rule. The Indian elite classes equivocate and use both the languages and Indian history has moved in a direction of greater interlacing of the two languages in Indian institutions and practices. But the first language has been the privilege of the Indian elite classes while the

---

[2] Kohn, Hans: *The Idea of Nationalism* , Macmillan,New York, 1945, 16.

lives and aspirations of subaltern classes have been enmeshed on the whole in relationship articulated in the second. [3]

The awakening of the Indian people to nationalism is of great historical importance. The cultural renaissance and reformation together with the emergence of religious and political nationalism all played their part in this encounter. While the encounter itself cannot be explained in simple terms of western influence and Indian response, the interpretation of nationalism depends in part at least on the understanding of the impact of the west on India. The British rule, the evolution of national political institutions and ideas, the influence of economic thought and practice, the introduction of western education, the emergence of a national intelligentsia, the spread of Christianity and its impact on indigenous life and thought, all these were the channels of the western impact. The elite, being oriented to western education, became the leaders of this national awakening which found expression in the organization of the National Congress in 1885 and in the aspiration for political freedom and national community. In this context the churches in India were faced with a new reality with implications for their own identity.

There were outstanding Indian Christians who responded positively to the national awakening. Among them were Susil Kumar Rudra (1861-1925) the principal of St Stephen College, Delhi, Surendra Kumar Dutta (1878-1942) the Principal of Foreman Christian College, Lahore, K.T.Paul (1876-1931) Secretary of the YMCA, one of the founders of the National Missionary Society and President of SIUC, and Vedanayakam Samuel Azariah (1874-1945) one of the founding parents of NMS, chairman of the National Christian Council, the first Indian Anglican Bishop and a pioneer of ecumenism. They were not narrow in their view. In the words of K.T.Paul, "I fully realize the dangers of nationalism. With that warning clearly in our minds, I invite you to contemplate the infinite significance of all that is connoted by the most sacred entity, 'India'. Let it not stir us to any narrowness or exclusiveness: India herself ever kept an open door, with proverbial hospitality and tolerance".[4]

Their concern was to discern the identity of the Church in the context of India's thought aspiration and action. In analyzing the situation they emphasized the structure of the Christian community in relation to the emerging national community. The impact of the national struggle for freedom developed a new sense of selfhood in the churches and they began to see the Church transcending western culture and western Christian denominations. In the words of M.M.Thomas:"Thus God spoke to the churches through Indian nationalism about the uniqueness of the gospel and the oneness of the body of Christ; and the new understanding has helped

---

[3] Sahu, D.K: *The Church of North India* , Peter Lang, 1992, p75

[4] Paul, K.T: "Responsibility of Christian Citizenship in India", Presidential Address to All India Christian Conference, Bangalore, December 27-29,1923.

the churches without giving up their positive attitude to the Western heritage and partnership with Western churches, on the one hand to relate themselves to the nation in its struggle for selfhood and on the other to work for the unity of the churches in southern and northern India".[5]

A Journey

The experience of democracy during the last sixty-one years has been complex and decidedly mixed. On the one hand, it has brought about an extraordinary politicization of Indian society and the creation of a vibrant civil society. This has resulted in a remarkable shift in the balance of political power. On the other hand, its record in securing social justice and providing the basic amenities for its citizens: decent incomes, health, education, leave a lot to be desired. Its democracy continues to be rocked by violent conflicts that are generated by explorations of collective identities in public contexts, and its institutions often seem overwhelmed by complex political, social and economic pressures..

India is a country of diversities and disparities that makes it difficult to evolve a common denominator. The affinities are actually a brahmnical construct that may be stretched to include only the upper castes. This constitutes only seventeen percent of the population of the country. Therefore a common code of behavior and conduct is largely sought after but not reachable. It was easy to borrow from British institutions but the norms and standards which sustain them had to take roots in the consciousness of the people. The greatest hurdle in the emergence of a healthy consciousness is the highly divisive caste system. It not only marginalizes a large segment of the society but hinders the formation of common societal goals.

All citizens in a nation in any part of the world dream to be free. Liberty is an indivisible whole. Perhaps it begins with our mind: the freedom to think even if one disagrees with other and society. It grows into a freedom to express one's beliefs and thoughts, including the freedom of the press, in order to bring positive change in the society as well as in the nation. It continues into economic freedom, wherein one definitely applies one's thoughts to tie together natural resources for everyone's welfare. However, both freedom of mind and economic freedom are integrally related to political freedom: the right of every individual to be protected from the oppressive structures and powers. To be a nation, any community or society requires political unity or territorial integrity. Christians involved in building a nation are deeply concerned about these constituents including foundational aspects which are: common civil values, common sense of progress, common participation in decision making, equality before the law, mutual respect for others and tolerance, and a feeling of freedom.

---

[5] Thomas, M.M: "Indian Nationalism", *Religion & Society*, June, 1959, 26.

The Christian vision and commitment of the building up of a just, participatory and sustainable society where honesty, love, tolerance, reconciliation, forgiveness, and righteousness are the ideals go a long way in building a just and progressive nation. However at the social level in India the caste plays an important factor in Indian society. Being a discriminatory system it does not see the equality of humans. Finality belongs to the social order of caste; community is supreme; individuals exist for society. Many do not have the rights and privileges, particularly the Dalits. The Church has played a dynamic role for the cause of Dalits and is still pursuing the rights of Dalits. Spirituality and education were the monopoly of the privileged few; and they were all male dominated. Some enjoyed almost divine status while the majority was denied access. Female infanticide was widely common. Child marriage, enforced widowhood etc were the order of the day. Medical care and public health programmes were not available to the majority. The infant mortality rate was high, resulting in the creating a multitude of young widows. The high birth rate was the only answer to the high infant mortality rate. The women were and are still deprived of their dignity in the society. Mass illiteracy, poverty, backwardness, degeneration and dehumanization were the order of the day. India's traditional societal structure was composed of three institutions viz., joint family, caste system and the village community.

The caste order was and is in complete command of the situation.[6] Being a discriminatory system it cannot see the equality of humans. The low status and illiteracy of women wasted half of the total human resources. Status quo, in favor of the privileged, was maintained and the religious ideology of *Karma* and *Samsara* sacralized this stagnation while shutting out any scope for innovation and creativity. Mass illiteracy, poverty, backwardness, degeneration and dehumanization were the order of the day. P.D. Devanandan's societal diagnosis and prescription in post-independent times is a help to imagine how worse the situation was a hundred or two hundred years before: Having observed that India's traditional societal structure was composed of three institutions viz., joint family, caste system and the village community he says, "In their rigid traditional forms, they militate against the new urges of individual freedom, material advance and social equality and should be replaced, by viable alternatives more adequate to the present needs" (1960, p.139).

Contribution

The Christian contribution to the nation-building of India in terms of education has been widely acknowledged and appreciated. Education was an integral part of the missionary commitment, and of the Church. In the length and breadth of this country Christians took the initiative and founded

[6] see Pickett, J.W: *Christian Mass Movement in India* , Lucknow , 1933

schools and other educational institutions and through the newly educated generations brought about radical changes in the value system. It broke the intellectual isolation of the Indian mind and brought it into contact with western science, literature and history. A new world of ideas revealed itself. For example, the education of women had far-reaching effects. It assured the women of their worth and their dignity. They received a new sense of equality. The potential in them became available for building the family and the nation and their active participation in public affairs resulted in an enhanced quality of life. This naturally helped the economic aspect of life as well. Christian worldview acknowledges and appreciates the worth and beauty of the material world, the human body and life in this world. Therefore there was always an urge to improve the quality of life here and now. Jesus went around ***preaching*, *teaching* and *healing*** and that became the moving factor of the Church to take all these three ministries seriously. The very preaching of the Gospel that God loves everyone and has offered abundant life freely available for all was revolutionary in itself. One recent welcome historic move was the one by St Stephen's College to give preferential admissions to brilliant students from the Dalit Christian community in this prestigious institution of higher learning. St Stephen's College has become among the first Church-constituted Institution to take this long due affirmative action which will go a long way in undoing long-held prejudices against Christians from the erstwhile depressed classes and scheduled castes in north and south India. The other welcome move is the New Education Policy announced by the Catholic Bishops Conference of India which reaffirms the commitment of the Church to the education of the marginalized. These moves will go a long way in removing the impression that the Church runs only elite schools for the rich and powerful without concern for the poor. These revolutionary measures will also go a long way in the empowerment of 60 per cent of the Indian Christian community who had fallen out of the development net of the Church and were also ignored by the State. These steps are also in keeping with the recent recommendations of the Justice Ranganath Misra National Commission for religious and Linguistic Minorities which had said Dalit Christians [and Dalit Muslims] must be given scheduled caste status and privileges given to Hindu, Sikh and Buddhist Dalits. It is a call to both the State and the Church to ensure quality education through well equipped schools and modern curricula in districts, towns and Dioceses where Dalit Christians are in reasonable numbers. This is in keeping with the spirit of the recommendations made for the Muslim community by the Prime Minster's Special committee on Minorities headed by Justice Rajinder Sachchar.

The Christian contribution to the nation building of India is best appreciated when we look at the initiatives of the missionaries in India in establishing the institution of press and journalism. A classic example is the modern Indian press of Serampore in West Bengal. That was the year of 1818 that saw launching of *Friend of India* in English, *Sumachar Darpan* in Bengali, and the short-lived *Dig Darshan* in Hindi. The three periodicals, under the general editorship of Joshua Marshman, a colleague of William Carey, were inspired exclusively by a presupposition that liberating power comes from the gospel. The birth of the free press was a non-official and non-commercial initiative. It is the Christian faith that was the basis of the efforts of missionaries to go against the caste system, mass illiteracy and the oppression of women. The Christian understanding of spirituality instills a sense of stewardship and economic responsibility for economic emancipation of the poor. Indian .Christian contribution in the post independent era continued in serving the society in building a healthy, educated and prosperous nation. In the medical, educational and social sectors, the caring for the widows, the aged, the destitute, the orphans, the lepers, the blind, the differently abled and the marginalized still continues.

However despite encouraging initiatives in limited circles, there are some emerging concerns that need proper attention. In course of time the institutional aspect of service in general has slowly deviated from service to commercialization. The Christian educational institutions are mostly English medium institutions and are doing a commendable job but what we need to note is that the majority of our educational institutions cater to the needs of the elite upper classes in our cities and towns, and in the process the vast majority of our people in the villages and those who are poor are kept outside the gates of the centers of learning This is a major failure in the involvement of building the nation of one billion people of whom the majority are in villages and slums.

The other major area of contribution by the Christians has been in the health sector. It goes without saying that the missionaries went, served and established health care centers in those parts of our country where we would not have dared to go and do. Some of those initiates have now become institution of national importance like the Christian Medical Colleges of Vellore and Ludhiana. It is the Christians who largely still go to the villages with their medical missions. But the burden here is not to take comfort in that but to highlight the point that a radical shift in our emphasis has taken place in the last few decades. Our priority does not seem to be any longer the health and wellbeing of the poor and the less privileged. There are a number of mission hospitals in our villages that render valuable services to the marginalized and the dedication of the team of doctors and nurses are incredible. However the modern trend seems to deviate from rural sector of service of heath care. The charge may be leveled against our medical services. Who do we serve today? Having visited a number of leading Christian "Mission" Hospitals in Kerala the former director of the Christian Medical College and Hospital, Ludhiana, Dr. K.N. Nambudripad lamented that these have become "five star hotels for the new rich and the middle and upper classes." This criticism is not untrue when we survey the emphasis of our medical ministries today. Instead of reaching every village and hamlet through community primary health centers for the care of the poor, we are busy building up ultra super specialty hospitals to cater to the rich. In many places these have become commercial centers and not service points. It is not these '5-Star Hospitals' that will bring development to our nation, but our attention and concern for the millions in the villages of India. B.H. Jackayya, in a report on the role of the Indian Church in nation building, makes the following sharp criticism, "Despite the fact that our church serves through institutions such as colleges, medical hospitals etc., these are no longer playing a vital role in nation building. Rather they have become prestigious institutions for the high and rich and a source of discord, disintegration, disunity; thereby they defeat the church's mission and ministry"[7] We have lost our constructive bias towards rural India. Nobel Laureate Prof. Amartya Sen categorically observed that until three traditional curses of our national life *viz.,* mass illiteracy, the lack of primary health care and the disappointingly limited and pathetic infrastructure are squarely dealt with, the nation will not march towards progress and wellbeing. The deviation from reaching every village with community primary health centers for the care of the poor to focusing on building super specialty hospitals to cater to the needs of the rich is a major cause for concern that defeats the mission and ministry of the church. The missionary devotion and commitment are the need of the hour.

Challenges

Indian society now is primarily perceived as being constituted of a number of religious communities. Communalism in the modern Indian context is primarily perceived as a consciousness which draws on a supposed religious identity and uses this as the basis for an ideology. It then tends to demand political allegiance to a religious community and supports a programme of political action designed to further the interests of that religious community. In the present socio-political context, the communities assume political importance and relations between communities are embittered by their relevance to the balance of power. Therefore conversion from one group to another means not only a change in spiritual allegiance but also a shift in political power.

Therefore one of the greatest challenges that we, irrespective of all religions face in nation-building is: communalism and corruption. These forces are formidable and they demolish and destroy a nation if not challenged. They cross all boundaries and it is our common task as Indian citizen to develop leadership by people with *moral integrity* and courage. This is a challenge common to all communities. These forces are formidable and they will demolish and destroy our nation if not challenged

---

[7] Jackayya, B.H: Report of International Consultation, September 2-7,1982, LWF, Geneva.

and nullified. They can be countered, not by going nuclear, but by going moral and spiritual. This is the call and challenge before the Christian community in India as never before in seeking the welfare and good of our nation. We have only to ponder deeply on the Christian values enshrined in the Indian Constitution with its recognition of the inviolability of each human person as the foundation of society, its defense of the rights of minorities and especially of the freedom of conscience and the freedom of religious belief and practice. The identity of the Christian community cannot be confined within the supposed identity of being just another communal group. It is not a community in competition with other communities but as a community called to serve in a particular context.

In the process of building a free and just nation we have gone through times of great peril and darkness. There were times when human rights were abrogated and fundamental rights violated as now also in the case of Kondhmal of Orissa. The innocent victims of violence in 2007 as well as 2008 in Orissa still cry for justice. "The sum total of the death and devastation in Kondhmal speaks for itself: more than 75 Christians killed over weeks of continued violence, over 5000 Christian houses looted and destroyed along with 250 churches, and Christian institutions desecrated, looted and reduced to ashes. To cap it all, nearly half of the 117,000 Christians in the jungle district have been rendered refugees with the Supreme Court itself reminding the Orissa Government on January 5, 2009 that 'it is the duty of the state government to protect the minority community. You (state) have done that only after 50,000 people of the minority community fled to the jungles"[8]These are serious threats to the just and free nation we want to build. The Christian community and the community-at-large rose to the occasion in protesting against the inhuman acts against Christians in Orissa and atrocities in other parts of India.

Romila Thapar in her study of the early history of India says that there were in existence multiple communities based on various identities. In pre-Islamic India, the religious identities seem to be related more closely to a sect than a dominant Hindu community. The notion of a Hindu community does not have as long an ancestry as is often presumed. Even in the normative texts of Brahmanism, the Dharmasastras, it is conceded that there were a variety of communities, determined by location, occupation and caste, none of which were necessarily bound together by a common religious identity. The community had one of its roots in location.[9] Religious pluralism is a reality of Indian society. In the pre-independence period, the emergence of nationalism was a powerful ideology that brought people together to fight for the independence of the nation. But once that

[8] Akkara, Anto: *Kandhamal a blot on Indian Secularism*, Media House, Delhi, 2009 , 15.

[9] Thapar ,Romila: *Imagined Religious Communities?*, Modern Asian Studies, Vol.23,May 1989, 220.

was achieved, the focus shifted to self-consciousness of groups and communities in the nation.

One not-ventured sector in nation building by the Christians is the political life of the nation: parliamentary democracy, the legal and judiciary and the civil administration. Articulation of the political process provides vision, the ability to think, discuss, debate and this helps people to be part of the right decision-making process. The active involvement of the Christian leaders was a priority in the struggle for independence. Clear vision, the ability to think, discuss, debate and articulate convincingly and persuasively, the right decision-making process, the power to execute them – these the political process provides. When Christians stay away from this crucial area of life, besides betraying our lack of wholesome commitment to the totality of life, we deny ourselves the privilege to decisively participate in the mission of nation-building. This is willful abdication of responsibility, and that is criminal. Here too, the vacuum our absence creates will be filled by others – many a time by the ones we criticize and condemn – the all too familiar corrupt elements in our society. Corruption that eats away the vitals of our nation and our people cannot be fought by remote control; it calls for conviction, courage and the humility to challenge and fight this demon head-on. In a parliamentary democratic system like ours the decision-making process is so vital that it demands our concerted involvement. "Politically literate Christians" are crucial for nation-building (Devanandan. 1960, p.49).

Industry and commerce is another area that the Christian community has largely ignored. A strong nation can be built by generating sufficient resources and spending and investing them wisely. Christian disinterest in this field is unjustifiable and inimical to nation building. The same may be said about the lack of contributions from Christians in the area of scientific researches and discoveries. We seem to be happy and settled with some white-collar jobs that guarantee financial stability with which we create our security. We dare not venture into the unknown, labour hard and discover and generate new things and new resources. Nearly forty years ago we were encouraged, "If we can release ourselves to new fields like co-operatives, technical education, and developed forms of service to agriculture and small-scale industries in fruitful ways, and show that the spirit of Christian dedication and the framework of Christian fellowship can enhance their value for society and nation, we shall release healthy influences" (Devanandan. 1960. p.126). It is also vital for the Christian community to penetrate and effectively contribute to the development of this nation in the field of art, architecture, literature, media and journalism – media that can be effectively and powerfully used to fight corruption and create a viable and healthy worldview. This too we have, it appears left for others to do what they think might be profitable to them. Though the Christians constitute one of the most literate communities in the nation, our creative involvement in these fields is pathetically negligible and insignificant.

The Way Forward

We stand at the crossroads of the twenty first century. We have many things to thank for – the privilege and blessing of having a secular democratic republic as our nation and the opportunity to contribute towards its development. There is a crying need on our part to acknowledge our limitations – both of omission and commission. We need a fresh vision for our nation in the 21st century – a nation that is made of *individuals, families, communities* and an assortment of races, language groups, religious traditions and cultures; a vision that seeks the wellbeing of our fellow citizens in a healthy environment and the fulfillment of our national aspirations in healthy fellowship with one another; a vision that promotes a genuinely national consciousness, and social and national integration. It must be a vision that realizes truth, righteousness, justice, freedom, equality, mercy and love.

Nation building is integrally related to management. If asked to define management in textbook fashion, it is a set of activities, including planning and decision making, organizing, leading, and controlling, with the aim of achieving organizational goals in an efficient and effective manner. Management is applied to every aspect of human life. We manage our own lives; we manage our families and our finances. However, management is usually perceived in the context of the organization. For a Christian, the techniques are not as critical as the framework in which management is practiced. The challenge is to reflect the Christian faith in managing people and resources.

The notion of management in the Bible centers on the concept of stewardship. At the centre is the steward, the manager of the household of God, the one entrusted to administer effectively. In Gen 1:26 and 2:15, God indicates that human will have power over the fish, the birds, and all animals, domestic and wild and all the earth and is assigned the work to cultivate (develop) it and guard (take care of) it. So, although there is the function of authority (the right to decide) over resources like the earth and the things on the earth, there is also the responsibility of attaining a goal, which is to develop, improve, and cultivate in harmony with all that is on the earth, guarding it against decay and deterioration. A steward identifies with the interests of the Master. In Jesus' parable of the servants who were entrusted with talents (Matt 25:14-30), the expectation is a return of the capital with growth, i.e. Development and the steward is accountable. A steward has received a tremendous honor by being appointed by God. Yet this authority must be carried and displayed with a large measure of humility, as the steward is but a servant. Stewardship carries authority with servant hood. All humans, both as individuals and communally, are commissioned with the task of management, the duty of stewardship but a few have been called with the additional responsibility of serving others through leadership.

Contemporary management thought often refers to people as 'human resources' implying at best that humans are ranked equally with other resources such as money, land, raw materials and machines. But the human resources school of thought continues to give opportunities for intellectually challenging tasks only in the interests of gain for the organization, extracting their pound of flesh. The prevalent consideration is to keep workers satisfied, happy, and challenged so that they can contribute to a greater degree toward the organization's goal achievements. At worst, the implication of viewing people as human resources is that people are exploited, as other resources are exploited by business and industry in the pursuit of materialistic gain.

A Christian Perspective

The Christian approach to management may be understood as that of the steward as a servant leader with God's created people, take care of resources, God-created and owned, and that have been entrusted for development toward God-directed purposes and to the glory of God. As steward in the role of servant leader, he or she can provide a spiritual dimension in the people's want to contribute to the accomplishment of worthwhile objectives. It is to be part of a mission and enterprise that transcends individual tasks. It is not to work in a job that has little meaning, even though it may tap mental capacities. The purposes and principles are to enable others and empower them.

Christian management is working for people within a system, which meets the psychological, social, intellectual, aesthetic, and spiritual needs while addressing economic, technological, societal, and environmental concerns in a harmonious response that benefits all and brings glory to God. Without the Holy Spirit any management responsibility is impossible to shoulder successfully. It is to realign our measurements of success to the biblical perspective. We often limit the measurement of results to quantitative measures of success, be it financial, market share, or even baptisms. But we need to understand that the true measurement of success for the biblical steward is one's attitude. The reward is given to the steward entrusted with the talents, not because he has done so great a work, but because of his fidelity over a few things. God measures not according to the results, but according to the motives. If the steward is faithful then one is successful, and is sure of the final reward, however small may have been his mission.

Such a perspective of management of a servant-steward model, assumes the possibility of transformation. It is the central image of God's work for humanity. Transformation is God's process of bringing forth the possibilities that are ours by virtue of God's will and grace. It must be viewed in its dynamic inter-connection with the total picture of reality that coheres to our faith. This means initially that transformation is the work of the Triune God carried out in the entire world. Our very existence, as well as that of the entire cosmos and planet earth is grounded finally in nothing else but the intention, the freedom and the grace of the Creator God. We and our world owe our existence to God's will that we exist, and the kind of world that we live in must also be the world that God intended. Our world and we ourselves are constituted by God's action of bringing us to the future that God intends for us. All of cosmic history, human history and our personal lives are defined by this vast work of God perfecting the creation that God initiated. We are what God has created, and our future is the future God holds for us.

The revelation in Jesus Christ speaks to us centrally and concretely of the shape of God's transforming work. Jesus lived a life of availability to God's possibilities. The Crucifixion underscores the sense in which God's possibilities seem to be impossibilities when judged by human criteria. In the Resurrection we receive the word that God's possibilities can indeed become real in the very world of the flesh that God created and in which we live out our earthly existence. God the Holy Spirit accompanies creation at every moment and in every situation, and it is this Holy Spirit that makes the resurrection life actual in every moment of our lives. Transformation here and now is the work of the Holy Spirit. The world in God's hands, as creation under the power of the resurrection, is an essential presupposition of the concept of Transformation. This view is the foundation for our trust, our faith in the process of transformation.

It is at the heart of our conviction that something fundamentally new can be brought about by God's gracious will and work. Paul envisions the transformation of the believer from a position of bondage to the Law to the freedom of justification. Mark's Gospel hopes for transformation from self centeredness and fear to the empowerment that God's reign brings whereas Matthew focuses upon transformation from the hypocrisy that is grounded in a false interpretation of Israel's law to the integrity that flows from repentance and truer obedience as set forth by Jesus, whereas Luke speaks of the transformation from oppression to compassion and mercy, and John speaks for the transformation of the blindness that fails to see God's presence in life to the light that is able to discern eternity under the conditions of history in Jesus Christ.

A Call for Participation

Finding commonalities is extremely important for successful transformation in the context of plurality. However, the emphasis is on diversity--how the groups are different, and whether one group or another is superior. Multiracial policies stress the importance of valuing diversity and honoring the differences between people. People united in well-functioning societies need to be tied together with some sense of commonality. Commonalities can occur in values, roles or needs. Although willful conflicts tend to be characterized by wide and deep-rooted interests and value differences between the opposing groups, usually the groups can find some areas of commonality. Often these revolve around needs. All people have similar fundamental needs of security, a secure sense of identity, a sense of belonging.

Fundamental values are a frequent source of commonality: value of human life and family relationships. Bringing together in dialogues is often a very effective way to create a sense of commonality. As people explore their feelings, their fears, their sense of hurt and hopelessness, they usually can find common ground. The Narrative Theory claims that stories do not just describe reality – "A Story is a powerful category for forming identity. It helps to give a community identity, and therefore helps to constitute community. It can express things for which other idioms would be inappropriate. In particular, the identity of a group can be articulated by stories" [10]Stories or narratives in effect create social realities. Participation, and hence empowerment, may be constrained by both the structure of narratives and by the process by which narratives are created. Narrative coherence and closure are also problematic when the ability to produce coherent narratives is uneven. Stories gain coherence by being more complete, and by resonating more closely with the dominant culture. A more coherent story will tend to dominate and marginalize a less coherent one, and so reduce participation on that part. Thus narrative theory re-describes power imbalances as differing degrees of narrative coherence.

The possibility and reality of mutual service may become important instruments in the growth of trust, the display of mutual love and better service to the world. Common witness through service reflects the unity that already exists and nourishes the unity of humankind. At the same time, one must be prepared to find in situations where the type of services called to offer, creates controversy and even division. "The main characteristics as well as the reason for inter caste tension in Kerala churches is the exclusiveness of the dominant section of the Christian community as a distinct caste. This exclusiveness is based on both the socio-cultural and economic factors"[11] If the unity is strong enough to generate service to humanity, it must also be strong enough to stand up to disagreements on the type of service to be given and to engender a degree of trust which will allow having confidence. In a world in which the reconciling vocation is more necessary than ever, we cannot offer pious counsel to warring factions in humanity without showing that we can overcome our own divisions.

Commonality to be a living reality needs to cross the boundary of conflicts. But we live and operate in a world which is constantly changing.

---

[10] Sahu, D.K: *Church of North India*, Peterlang, op.cit., 229

[11] Chatterjee, Saral K: "Some Ingredients of a Theology of the People", *Religion and Society*, December, 1980, 21.

The world today is dominated by a concentration of extreme power and wealth. The people seek to affirm their identities in the light of globalizing forces. To have a perspective in the context of an overwhelming globalization process is to look for new perspectives in contexts today. It will necessitate creating a space for the marginalized or neglected. Such a perspective is very important in the context of globalization. Globalization may be interpreted as a term to describe "a process" which embodies a transformation. It can be assessed in terms of their extensity, intensity, and impact-generating transcontinental, interregional and networks of activity. From an economic perspective, globalization involves an explosion of global trade, investment and financial flows across the boundaries. With the intensification of international trade, investment and finance, more countries and regions entered the competition for market and capital. From a socio-cultural perspective, globalization involves the massive movement of people across borders and the fusion of cultures on a global scale. From a political perspective, the impact of globalization refers to the tendency for political decisions and actions in one part of the world to generate widespread reactions and consequences elsewhere. The global movement of people and news with the global flow of goods and capital has turned many a local event into international concerns

Conclusion

One of the deepest concerns of our time is the search for true spirituality in nation building. Most often spirituality is misunderstood over and against organized religion. Therefore the question of identity is very important. The problem with the contemporary understanding of spirituality is that often it is confined to psychological orientation. M.M.Thomas in 1975 had spoken of the need for 'spirituality of combat' in confronting the principalities and powers of this life. In other words we need a spirituality of engagement in the world. Prosperity unifies and conciliates people. The pertinent question is – when seventy percent of the population has no stake in the system in terms of accessibility and fights a daily struggle for existence, what sort of shared values could be developed? The concept of 'Congregation' is a helpful paradigm for conversation in developing shared values. The self needs to be put at the periphery and the community must take the center stage. God meets each one of us in our journey of faith but there must be space for the other in this journey. Space can have many round tables so that people need not fight for space but can rather seek to discover which table God is inviting them to join where voices, opinions and contradictions can hear one another without fear and censorship. In this process one is conscious of the changing times in communication and embraces communication as a method to tell its story to those who can join the space and those who will not or need not join; a space where variety and diversity are assets rather than liabilities; and a table where faith and scriptures are taught.

The issue is not just of accommodating the reality of place, language, ethnic identity, culture and work. The question is about being true to one's calling to be an instrument of reconciliation in the context of religious pluralism. Religious pluralism is not entirely a new phenomenon as the people of India have witnessed and lived among major religions of the world. The unfortunate part is of the number of conflicts between communities. The response of Christian thinkers in the context of religious pluralism has been varied. The exclusivist[12] maintains that Christ or Christianity offers the only valid path to salvation, the inclusivist[13] affirms the salvific presence of God in other religions but still maintains the definitive and authoritative revelation of God in Christ, and the pluralist maintains the co-efficacy of all religions.[14] The idea of parity does seem particularly ideal in a pluralistic context but to accept the view of particularity is not to rule out the possibility of universal salvation. Referring to the pluralist position as set out in the Myth of Christian Uniqueness, Newbigin comments that the culture in which this type of thinking has developed is one in which the most typical feature is the supermarket. One may stick to one's favorite brand and acclaim its merit in songs of praise; but to insist that everyone else should choose the same brand is unacceptable.[15]

Christian identity and religious plurality are interconnected. The efforts in certain sector through jargons about tolerant coexistence of different opinions are not the answer. Rowan Williams put it succinctly at the Porto Alegre Assembly by saying, "the nature of our conviction as Christians puts us irrevocably in a certain place that is both promising and deeply risky, the place where we are called to show utter commitment to the God who is revealed in Jesus Christ and to all those to whom the invitation is addressed. Our very identity obliges us to active faithfulness of this two-fold kind. We are not called to win competitions or arguments in favor of our 'product' in some religious market place. Identify yourself! Identify our reasons for living, for living less badly and dying less badly. And we do so by giving prayerful thanks for our place and by living faithfully where God in Jesus has brought us to be, so that the world may see what is the depth and cost of God's own fidelity to the world God has made[16]. We should be confident in saying what we believe in straight and clear language and free from jargons.

---

[12] Kraemer, Hendrik: *The Christian Message in a Non-Christian World*, London, 1938.

[13] Farquhar, J: *The Crown of Hinduism*, Oxford, 1919.

[14] Hick, J: *God has many Names*, London, 1980; Knitter,Paul, *No Other Name*? SCM, 1985.

[15] Newbigin, Lesslie: *The Gospel in a Pluralistic Society*, London, 1989, 169.

[16] Kobia, S: *Calle d to the One Hope*, WCC, 2006, 120.

Christian Education and its Contextual Placements for Dialogue

P.S. Jacob

We live in a world of racial, ethnic, cultural and religious diversity. It is generally acknowledged that awareness of such a global reality has to be facilitated at various levels. The well sought after opportunities for Higher Education, brings in people of divergent faiths together in a campus context. In India we find that the majority of Christian College and Deemed university campuses consist of people of people of other faiths. It brings in an authentic contextual situation. These campuses could be effectively used for comprehending and appreciating the increasing impact of interfaith environment and nurturing of interfaith dialogue.

People also come from differing religious traditions. If we understand what other people believe and practice as their way of life influenced by cultures and conditioned by religions, we could understand each other better and so maintain religious harmony and peace for all. India is known as a land of many religions. The major religions that originated in India are ***Hinduism, Buddhism, Jainism and Sikhism***. Often the religions which originated in India are clubbed together because they are 'culturally' interrelated. Nevertheless they are different from each other. In addition, there are other religions that came to India, from other countries. India's pluralistic tradition welcomed those heartily. **Judaism, Zoroastrianism (the religion of the Parsis), Christianity (*almost all denominations and doctrinal forms*), Islam and the** recently arrived **Baha'i Faith (with its beautiful lotus temple in New Delhi) belong to that group**. Those are referred to as 'minority religions' because the followers are smaller in number compared to those of Hinduism. To get an idea of the 'minority' and 'majority' status assigned to religions, let us look at the national population profile in terms of religious classifications. ***According to the last census (2001) enumerated by the Government of India, the following profile has been itemized.***

Hindu 80.5 %
Muslim 13.4%
Christians 2.3%
Sikhs 1.9%
Buddhists 0.8%

Jains 0.4%
Other religions 0.6%
No religion 0.1%

It gives us a population based profile of the multiplicity of religions in India. A quick review of the formation of Indian culture too will enable us to understand the origin and development of religions of India.

Indian Culture

Indian culture was formed and nurtured in pluralism. The intermingling of a mighty stream of humanity that came to inhabit India contributed to the element of diversity in India. People migrated into the land from divergent racial and cultural traditions over thousands of years. Finally through their interactions and conflicts, different groups evolved into India's cultural force. It changed the land into a nation of many people, many cultures and many religions. It leaves no room for any racial group to claim any authentic purity. Historians refer to them as the Aryan, the Dravidian, the Austric, the Scythian, the Greek, the Hun, the Iranian, and the Mongolian. The theory of identifying the Indian population in the Aryan-Dravidian configuration has been regarded as a western invention of racial classification and an over simplification of a complex subject, by post colonial scholars. Even the Semitic cultures and races came into India. All of them contributed to what is 'Indian'. To begin with, they had a common goal of finding prosperity in India. In the course of time over battles, combats and peace treaties, they settled down and shared 'India'. Thus, we find a large number of sub-cultures, languages, social control through the caste system and differing standards of social morality. They produced diverse systems of philosophy and religious sects and cults.

Indian culture includes the customary daily routine of living, language, costumes (clothing) and ways of worship, religious forms, admiration for different gods, ancestors/elders and people of a high level of accomplishment in spirituality (saints/gurus). What we need to understand is that the nature of Indian culture and way of life, vary widely. Thus, Indian culture came from a wide variety of sources of peoples and periods of history over fifty centuries. In short, Indian culture is a ***'composite' culture*** evolving itself into a unique system combining the contribution of all. The cultural contacts with Dravidian, Sumerian, Assyrian, 'Aryan', Persian, Greek, Hun, Arabian, Islamic, European people have played a role. **The process is still active in relation to contemporary 'globalization' as well**. We generally find a "miniature India" on our campuses of higher education and culturally and historically we are inclined if done in the right spirit. The Christian Higher Educational dynamics provides an amiable contextual placement for dialogue. More than a century-old growth of Christian higher education by now has been rendering quality service to the people of India. Highlights of such a sought after service could provide a contextual placement for dialogue.

Christianity's Service to Education in India: An Opportunity for Dialogue

Modern India emerged as a product of the educational efforts of the eighteenth, nineteenth and early twentieth century pioneers in the field. Its contact with English education paved a new road to progress and opened up a new direction in the accepted wisdom of the educated and enlightened leaders of that time. Christianity has played a leading role in the process of enhancing the foundational efforts. Most private educational institutions during the period were established and run by Christian missionaries. The official policy of education of the British rulers was education in English, with the decisive assertion of McCauley's Minutes in 1835 in its favor. People welcomed the new opportunity of English education with enthusiasm. Most missionaries welcomed it and considered it as a God given opportunity to spread the Christian Gospel. Soon private institutions were considered for Government 'grant-in-aid' for their educational efforts.

The contact with English education and Christianity invigorated the paving of a new way and new direction for the enthusiastic educated young men of the 19th century. Though Christian missionary efforts through educational institutions did not succeed in converting all students to their faith, the people of India gained immensely. The rediscovery of a new significance to the rich heritage of the past was the most important gain (Jacob:1973:75).

The young people who received modern education of that time could not escape learning about Christianity reflected in the moral education class and in the study of English literature.

Christianity arrived in India in three most important stages. The Christian traditions of Kerala strongly hold that St. Thomas, the disciple of Jesus brought the Gospel to the coast of Malabar first in 52 CE and later moved to the Tamil region and got martyred there. It is not clear whether the early Church of Malabar, located in Travancore, Cochin and Malabar engage itself educational activities. Common folks point out that one of the words in Malayalam for school is ***pallikoodam,*** which indicated the precincts of the church; so it could indicate that Christians used the church premises for providing some kind of education. Probably the Church confined its educational effort mostly to training the priests to maintain the religious and social activities of the Church. However the descendents of the St. Thomas Christians known as the Syrian Christians belonging to the Orthodox (Jacobite), Marthoma and Catholic traditions in modern times still engage themselves in establishing schools and colleges in a noticeable manner.

The second stage of the arrival of Christianity is demarcated by the arrival of Vasco da Gama in 1498 at Kodangallur (Cranganore) Kozhikode (Calicut) for trading and the promotion of Christianity. The Portuguese Catholic interest encountered the existing Syrian Christian group and established dominance over them for a short period of time. However, the educational endeavor became visible later in the 16th century by the opening of formal Christian educational institutions, the first formal Christian educational institution being Santa Fe School started by Franciscans in Goa in 1540 CE and followed by a cluster of schools in the nearby areas.(Palackapilly:Ponnumuthan:2004 :84) More schools and colleges became well established and sought after by people of other communities in the modern period (after Independence) covering the length and breadth of India.

The third stage of Christianity's arrival was ushered with the arrival of Protestant Christian Missions. Under the patronage of Frederick IV, the King of Denmark, the first Protestant mission was established in 1706 at Tranquebar (Tarangambadi) and its neighboring areas, with the arrival of B. Zeigenbalg (and Pluetschau). Though they arrived to establish 'missions to the Heathen' with an attitude of superiority, they soon discovered the riches of the Tamil language and its ancient literature. In their enthusiasm to learn Tamil, they found the need for making the illiterate literate by establishing small 'schools'. The modern missionary movement came in by the end of the century with the formation of the major societies, the Baptist Missionary Society (1792), The London Missionary Society (1799), the Church Missionary Society (1799), the Methodist Missionary Society (1813) and the American Board of Commissioners for Foreign Missions (1810). With the establishment of the 'Serampore Mission' under the auspices of the Baptist Missionary Society, the pioneering 'missionary trio' consisted of William Carey, the linguist preacher, Joshua Marshman, the educationist, and William Ward, the printer. Carey with his versatile linguistic genius undertook untiring efforts to systematically present various Indian languages. He was supported by the other members of the team who used education and printing as a means for spreading the Gospel news. Soon other protestant missions found it expedient to make the common people literate for helping them to read the Bible and in the propagation of the Biblical message. As early as 1800, the 'Serampore Trio' made arrangements for two boarding schools for Europeans. Before long, they opened boarding schools for Indian children. In 1813, Marshman drew up a scheme for the development of vernacular schools and founded ten village schools attached to the mission station with Indian teachers in charge. They furthermore gained recognition and encouragement from Governor General the Marquis of Hastings. (Walker:1926:291)

During the early period of all three major forms of Christianity, education was visualized as a primary investment in the task of evangelization often limited to minimum literacy for using the religious literature. Later missionaries entered into the task of secondary, higher education and professional training beginning in the 19th century and consolidating it in the 20th century. Nevertheless some of the missions also discovered a social mission in their educational efforts soon after. Professional education in areas such as medicine, social work, management; engineering, etc. were introduced in addition to colleges of arts, science and commerce. From early times, the need for starting job-oriented courses at a lower level was realized by missions in different parts of the country and they started industrial and technical institutes. Though Christian schools and colleges are not evenly distributed geographically, Christians have expanded their educational work massively considering the minority character of the community. This article will focus more on **areas** of service rather than citing numerical strength by quoting statistics. Besides, updated statistics especially from numerous Protestant Christian groups are not available in complete form. Some regional and denominational reporting is available such as "The Role of the Baptist Missionary Society in the field of Education in Orissa" by Rashmirekha Senapati

Awakening the Modern Character of Restoration

The desire for Western education was kindled in Bengal and spread through out India in different centers and its cumulative effect was a new spirit of inquiry. It found expression in social, political and religious spheres. The demand for English education emerged from Indians supported by Christian missionaries and broad-minded Indians before the British Government policy encouraged it from 1835 onwards. It should be noted that modern education entered India as an enterprise of private individuals. The increase of a large number of missionary educational institutions harmonized with 'the period of Western impact on the non-Western world'. Thousands of young 'non-Westerners eagerly sought after Western education' for 'personal and national advancement'. (Hogg: nd: 163)

The Christian missionaries played the pioneering role both in the area of English as well as vernacular education. For the propagation of Christianity, they found it necessary, to draw out people from the darkness of ignorance, superstitions and reliance on the authority of orthodox practices prevalent in India. They believed that Western/modern education could be used as a means for achieving it.

At a later stage private individuals other than the Christian groups also entered in the arena and are still flourishing in their educational efforts in contemporary India. Western education opened the channel of Western ideas in the beginning of the modern era. The impact of the educational channel to the outside world through modern education influenced modern Indian thought, influencing the social, religious and political life of the country. It also introduced women to modern education. As a result of

McCauley's official advocacy of English, the use of English as the medium of educational communication in schools and colleges became a staple practice. Since the Christian missions started several English medium institutions, ambitious young people and their parents welcomed the opportunity. The leadership of modern India of the time was mostly drawn from groups who gained education from Christian institutions.

During the early years of independence many educated leaders publicly acknowledged the contribution of the Christian educational institutions in shaping their thought patterns and accessing the progress gained by Europe and America. Alexander Duff, the well-known missionary educator of the time reported: "Our English schools are flourishing wonderfully. We find it difficult, indeed, in some places impossible, to provide instruction for all who want it. At the single town of Hooghly 1,400 boys are learning English." (McLean: 1912:188, 89) the Indian renaissance was kindled by Rammohan Roy (1772 – 1833) acknowledged as the Father of modern Indian thought. The revival began with a perspective of the newly emerged spirit of rational inquiry into social, political and religious practices prevalent in India. Consequently it led to the rediscovery of India's own rich heritage. Educational activities of Christian missions also enhanced the activation of the renaissance spirit of India. They also stimulated a refreshing discovery of pride in Hindu religious and Vedic heritage demanding its preservation without succumbing to the appeal of the missionaries' religion.

Literacy, Language Development and Literature

The Christian missionaries expected that their enthusiastic literacy drive would help common people who were mostly illiterate, to read and understand the Christian religious texts. The translation of the Bible and Gospel portions followed. It is a noteworthy fact that the children responded positively in comparison the adults. Hence schools and boarding schools were established soon. They also recognized the value of training the local converts to Christianity for assisting them in the task of evangelization. This facilitated the spread literacy. The Christian missionaries learned the various languages of India and codified those for a systematic expression of new ideas. Along with it printing and publishing became vital for the task at hand. For example, before the death of Serampore missionary, William Carey (1761 –1834), it has been reported that 212,000 copies of the Christian Scriptures in forty different languages were issued from the mission Press and the teachings of Christ were brought within the reach of 300,000,000 human beings. (McLean:62). Carey the linguist and his team even translated portions of the Old and New testaments of the Bible into Sanskrit for the benefit of the Brahmin readers. As an illustration of a glimpse of the extensive work, he is reported to have written:

> " I have just finished for the press my Telinga grammar; the last sheet of Punjabi grammar is the press. I am getting forward with my Kurnata grammar; indeed it is nearly ready for the press. I am also preparing materials for grammars of the Kashmeer, Pushto, and Billochi languages, and have begun digesting those for the Orissa. The care of publishing Felix's Burmah grammar is on me, besides learning all these languages, correcting the translations in them, writing Bengali dictionary and all my personal and collegiate duties."

Such an effort was not confined to the Serampore Mission alone and a number of examples can be cited about the role of missionaries of all branches of Christianity, in the development of regional languages and literature in Indian Christian history. Another excellent illustration is the earlier work of Father Stephen's ***Kristapuran,*** a Marathi rendering of the life of Christ (originally, ***Discurso Sobre a vinda De Jesus Christo nosso Salvador do Mundo)*** in the 'Purana' style in 1616, casing 10962 verses. (Morje:1984:11)

The literary efforts of Christian missions in various parts of India consisted mainly of systematizing grammar and usages of languages, compiling regional language dictionaries, translating religious literature (European languages to Indian languages, Hindu *Bhakti* literature into foreign languages), preparing devotional and worship aids in regional languages (e.g. hymns, devotional books, sermons, etc.), preparing literature for the propagation of the Gospel and historical accounts of similar efforts, preparing biographies of Christian saints (both local and others), printing literature for the eradication of social evils and superstitious practices, preparing Biblical commentaries and doctrinal discourses in a simple style to make it understandable to common people, using stories and novels and plays. This cumulative effort resulted in the development of modern literature by others as well. In addition, Christian educators led the way in the compilation of scattered educational texts/material of social interest by skillfully editing these. The use of material translated from English to the local languages or from one language to the other was also initiated on a wide scale. The translation of the Bible into many languages by constituting teams of linguistic experts drawn from people of other faiths paved the way to later efforts in the translation of other texts including the ancient literary heritage of India like the Bhagavad Gita, the Ramayana, etc. The pioneering efforts of Christian workers in literacy, language development and literature is indeed a very significant contribution to the people of India and a detailed study from various regions of India will prove to be informative and inspiring.

Educational Opportunities for the Disadvantaged

Before the modern era formal education was mostly confined to Brahmins by socio-religious conventions and norms of the caste system practiced at that period. The policy of Christian educators has been that of an **inclusive** approach, irrespective of caste, color, creed, gender or socio-economic status. Those who suffered from socio-religious and economic deprivation and still wanted to get an education received special attention and support.

Christian missionary institutions opened their doors for non-Brahmins, for women, to the disadvantaged and to 'people who otherwise would not have it'. (Profile: 1972:2) In the words of Professor S.M. Dahiwale of Pune University, "It was during the British regime that some non-Brahmins could have modern education, especially in Christian missionary schools, and under the impact of rational thinking, a few rebels emerged to question birth-based inequality, offering opinion that it was man-made, particularly by the Brahmin priestly class in their self interest." (Dahiwale: 2005: 5)

Encouraged by the response to evangelization in tribal and some rural areas, missionaries also pioneered educational efforts among Dalits and Tribals. The oppressed groups were looking for liberation from the socio-religious bondage they were in. Educational opportunities offered by Christians served as an additional encouragement. Thus a good number of schools and colleges were established in regions such as Chotnagapur area and North East India. The keeping open of these establishments to all sections of society anticipated the government's reservation policy. In general Christian educational institutions encouraged and welcomed people from the weaker sections to educational opportunity for personal and social liberation.

Women's Education

Christian missionaries did break a new ground in opening up education for women. The first girls' school was opened as early as in 1819 at Kottayam (Ponnumuthan:2004:89-91), Kerala. Soon schools came up in different parts of India, catering to the special needs of girls. Later, other movements like the Brahmo Samaj in Kolkata also took up the cause.

Women's education meant a lot more than literacy and served to bring about the awareness of a total growth of the girl child. Missions like the Zenana Mission and socially oriented religious orders of nuns also paid special attention to women's education. Schools and colleges were opened separately for their development. But after Independence coeducational institutions also have introduced women's educational programs upholding them as a vital Christian concern. Later, other social and political groups developed educational programmes for women. Christianity's task has been to provide opportunities for women to develop themselves so that they can assume leadership roles in many areas. People of other faiths with social concerns have followed the pioneering work of missions to provide equal opportunities for women.

Innovative Efforts

Some of the Christian schools and colleges have experimented with innovative programs in human development. Moral instruction, which later came to be known, as value education had been introduced by them. The involvement of students and teachers in the development of the less privileged and rural based groups is another example. The widespread National Service Scheme (NSS) is an outcome of an experimental program attempted by Ahmednagar College. (Jacob:NFE: 1983:25,26) Several other examples such as Loyola College's (Chennai) LEAP (Loyola Extension and Awareness Programme), St Joseph College's (Tiruchirappalli) SHEPHERD (SCIENCE AND Humanities for People's Development), Arulandar College's (Karumathur) RADAR (Rural Action for Development and Research), are also excellent pioneering efforts. Ecumenical organizations such as the All India Association for Christian Higher Education (AIACHE) and United Board for Christian Higher Education in Asia, Jesuit Educational Association of India and other denominational groups also have actively strengthened innovations in various degrees.

Women's colleges such as Lady Doak College, Madurai, Stella Maris College, Chennai, have been forerunners in initiating programs involving women students in learning from communities around them. Other Christian colleges have also taken up relevant innovative programs making contribution to the social mission of these colleges. In the early days of innovative education in India, Christian institutions added new dimensions such as 'Service to the Nation'; 'Social Justice' (Mathias: NFE: 1978:1,Jagannathan: 2002).

Education as a Private Venture

Christians also served as originators of education as a private venture. The evangelistic concerns of Christian missionaries for the development of individual and society propelled them to taking up education as a private activity irrespective of whether they received government aid or not. Soon a number of other religious groups like the Brahmo Samaj and the Ramakrishna Mission took to education to transform the minds of young people by catching them young. Today we have a number of institutions started by individuals or social service organizations, even others with commercial interests. Private groups are also collaborating with institutions from developed countries as a part of the enterprise.

A good number of Christian colleges were granted Autonomous status (the first Deemed University from the Christian group being Allahabad Agricultural Institute), providing leadership in autonomous approach to education within the framework of Government run universities. Currently we find a number of other private institutions being granted the Deemed University status.

Holistic Approach of Education

Christian effort in education in India has been using a holistic approach to education. Education was not simply literacy and information but the total development of the individual. Different missions practiced it differently. As they gained experience, some concentrated on spirituality from a Christian and biblical perspective insisting on a spiritual transformation as the ultimate goal of education. Later, some placed emphasis on moral education in addition to introducing the Bible. However after the Government policy excluded religious studies during the school/college hours, some colleges concentrated more on **moral instruction** and limited biblical studies to Christian students outside the class hours. Currently we find that there is an emphasis on **value education** without which education is not considered complete. Excellence in sports, personality development and involvement in social concerns has also became a part of holistic education.

Irrespective of whatever approach various groups have taken, the focus of education has included **character formation**. So implementation of **discipline** became known as an outstanding quality of good Christian educational institutions. Some of the formats were inherited from missionary days but were later modified. Alumni of these institutions have always recalled the disciplinary aspects with great pride even though it was unpleasant initially for some of them. Hindus and other non-Christians gave first preference to Christian institutions for their children because of the holistic approach.

Another feature of the holistic approach has been to maintain **academic excellence** by attracting competent and dedicated teachers and academically motivated students. Presently, a number of good institutions have placed emphasis also on serving society in some way or the other through the NSS and other innovative programs. The concept of 'learning through participation' has become a regular feature of several innovative experiments in different areas of development on campus and off campus.

The mission of Christian educational institutions still includes **spiritual development** as an important aspect of a holistic program. However, the theological perspective applicable in the context has changed considerably. Acknowledgement of the reality of religious pluralism has replaced the earlier emphasis on 'Christianity alone' for spirituality; and this has been widened to include all forms of spiritual experience by most institutions.

The holistic approach is thus centered on character formation, discipline, academic excellence, excellence in sports, learning through participation and spiritual development. In this context the ideal of serving God is visualized as serving people (USangeet:1960:212), not according to one's will but surrendering it to God's will in all these areas. Some of the leading Christian institutions serve as role models for the struggling weaker institutions elsewhere.

The most important areas of Christianity's contribution to education in India have been in Awakening the modern character of restoration in the nineteenth and early twentieth century, Literacy, Language Development and Literature, Educational opportunities for the Disadvantaged, Women's education, Innovative educational leads, and Educational institutions as a private venture augmenting the governmental efforts. Christianity has also contributed in pioneering the approach to education as a holistic development of the students. Christianity's most important and vital contribution has been to pioneer and activate Indian social consciousness in relation to making educational opportunity accessible to all without any barriers of caste, color, creed or socio-economic status. J.P. Naik, a distinguished Hindu and a well-known educationist of modern India has expressed it aptly:

> One of the best things that have happened in the history of modern India has been the confrontation of Hinduism with Christianity. It has been one of the happiest and least painful memories in the life of Hinduism. I do not attach much importance to how many people accept Christianity as a religion: but Hinduism has learnt one great thing from Christianity, the idea that the way to God lies through service of man, I think this is a new concept in Hinduism. We have our ways of reaching God: ***Gnana, Karma*** and ***Bhakti;*** but the emphasis on ***Seva***, the service of man as a method and an important method of realizing God came through our contact with Christianity. (Naik: Development: 1967:134)

Such a vibrant vitality triggered by Christian missions in the early stages of a developing India, has spread out to other voluntary efforts in education beyond the Christian confines: private ventures and mission such as the educational, medical and social services of Mata Amritanandamayi, Satya Sai Baba, the Ramakrishna Mission, the Arya Samaj, the Khalsa, are some outstanding examples.

It is hoped that Christianity's contribution will shine all over India for years to come and continue to contribute towards vigorous educational growth in the service of all in the liberative love of Christ. It could provide challenging opportunities for dialogue and mutual enrichment for all seekers of Higher education.

Contextual Possibilities

The major areas of Christianity's service have been in enhancing the modern character of restoration, literacy, language development and literature, educational opportunities for the disadvantaged, special attention to women's education, innovative educational efforts, education as a private venture and a holistic approach of education. These services have been recognized and have attracted people of diverse faiths to prefer Christian institutions for higher education for their quality of service. It has also stimulated the growth of private venture in education in both general and professional domains. Though there are motivational differences, the brighter side is the acceptance of private educational undertaking for their quality education in comparison to many of the Government run institutions. Some of the private institutions have developed quality education in sought after fields. All these academic communities of higher education do bring in a diversity of people to campuses. Christian colleges should undertake to continue the pioneering efforts in nurturing inter-religious understanding and peaceful harmony by encouraging an understanding of each other's beliefs and practices.

As we have already seen in the earlier review of Christianity's service to the people of India in the field of education, the Christian higher educational scene has been contextually placed to play a constructive role. It has been experientially equipped to take up new challenges such as the promotion of enriching dialogue to meet the emerging challenges today. The following are some of such possibilities to begin with.

Restoration and Recovery of Faith in Dialogue

The nineteenth century challenge was to usher people to the rational approach to understand arts, science and technology and also to help to construct a modern world view by introducing social and religious reforms. It led to a series of reform movements. Today we face the problem of **"secularism vs. religious fundamentalism"**. The religious communal identity has entered the campuses too amidst their diversity. Political parties have exploited the situation to their advantage. People are getting confused over what is 'right' and 'wrong'.

Meaningful programs judiciously implemented could restore the confidence and faith in humanity through dialogue. It is an exercise and expression of our faith that we can be different, and yet be united in upholding and strengthening unity and religious harmony. It is a restoration of "humanness" that has been a divine endowment. It is a message of redemption to the contemporary seekers of education. A new dimension of mission has to include such a restoration and recovery of faith in "humanness", that humanity truly is a divine image intended by the creator. It also implies the restoration of faith in ethical heritage and in the distinction between right and wrong. Innovative programs could be designed and tried out on our campuses to establish divinity in humanness.

Development of Language and Literature of Harmony and Peace

In the present day era of competition in search for wealth, power and fame, higher education has drawn people to the campuses for equipping themselves for such a competition. The emerging language is that of competition and success. We need to help our young people to redefine the language of competition and success. The contextual challenge will be to help the campus community to learn the language of harmony and peace along with a competitive ability. The language of peace in spoken words, greetings, art and literature could be formed into a series of activities in the process. While teachers, administrative personnel and students are getting professional help in the language of competition and success, they could perhaps do better in life with the language of harmony in the pursuit of success. The contextual challenge is to help our young people to understand each other's differences and the possibility of creative achievements in success. In other words, the contextual placement of dialogue urges us to strengthen its development and progression as a part of quality education.

Creating Awareness of Campus Integration of the Disadvantaged

Higher education today in general and Christian higher education in particular brings together the advantaged and disadvantaged. Programs could be organized to learn from each other's 'advantaged' condition and 'disadvantaged'. It is a very essential part of education to learn 'disadvantaged' condition of the 'advantaged' and the 'challenges of advantage' that the 'disadvantaged' are facing. An exchange of ideas will reinforce constructive channels of communication which will serve as a product of dialogue. Even in the diversity of religious persuasion on campus, we find that the follower of a 'majority' religion (e.g. Hinduism in India, Christianity in the European and American continents) has certain 'advantaged' conditions. On the other hand a follower of a 'minority religion has specific disadvantages. Through organizing helpful dialogical sessions, the youth could see each other's predicament. On the other hand we also need to realize that there are some 'advantages' for the 'minority' religion's followers (such as constitutional protection and there are 'disadvantages' for majority religions). A proper understanding of these well help each other to mend tensions and encourage integration.

Gender Discrimination and Disadvantages of Women

Dialogue is essential in the Indian context of a powerful patriarchal system in the socio-religious field. The examination of such a social situation is generally left to the specialist and students of sociology and religions. But in the context of Christian higher education we have to bring out it's inter religious analysis on a common level of interaction. The emphasis of dialogue is not on looking at the differences alone but to understand the dilemma that each religion is facing. We need to help the young people to tackle problems with a humanistic understanding and with a desire to maintain harmony and peace.

Initiating 'Action Programs'

Most of the campuses of Christian higher education have introduced some sort of plan in the area of inter religious understanding. The All India Association for Christian Higher Education (AIACHE), an active ecumenical organization of Protestant, Roman Catholic and Orthodox church-related colleges and deemed universities in India, has been encouraging its member institutions to create dialogical interreligious programs. Some have conducted excellent programs and others have made attempts to engage themselves with different degrees of success. I myself have learned much from valuable experience during my active involvement with Christian colleges some time ago.

One of the popular programs has been to arrange on-campus public talks/lectures on religious tenets drawn from the experts with leadership skills from different religions in India. Another common program has been organizing the common observance of different religious festivals on campus. Another interesting experiment has been to hold Interfaith Camps and Integrated living experiences for college students. These camps generally begin and end each day using different religious traditional practices in worship. In one such experience I found that it was hard for some participants to attend a worship using symbols and images because their own religious practice strictly forbade 'idol worship'. When they agreed to sit in the outer circle for a learning experience without any active participation, they found it a 'tolerable' experience in religio-cultural education.

The contextual placement in Christian Higher Education could profitably activate an "Exposure" program. Exposure brings to light many aspects of other religions, thus revealing the reality of other faiths; such an exposure could be in terms of : (a) exposure to ideas (b) exposure to people (c) exposure to religio-cultural events in society and (d) exposure to an interactive situation by undertaking service projects (Indian colleges could make use of organizations like the National Service Scheme (NSS) and also participate in service programs run by people of other religions.). The purpose of such 'exposures' is to reach the goal of harmony and peace transcending communal identities and the over emphasis on religious differences.

In a Nutshell

Having been a pioneer in serving the people of India in opening up education to all irrespective of caste, class or creed, Christian higher education has been placed in a positive contextual frame for dialogue. The participatory dialogue prospects will bring together various caste groups, different classes of people and people of diverse religious faiths and in a contemporary educational context, people of different nations for ushering in a proper appreciative tolerance, harmony and peace for all. To summarize, we could conclude that feasible action programs may possibly be introduced in the following areas:

1. Learning about other religions, beliefs and practices, worship styles, the reading of scriptures, festival celebrations, studying the sub cultural contexts of religions, moral values, developing friendships across religious barriers, introspection into one's own personal religious beliefs and practices, family practices. The purpose is to develop interfaith-relations and friendship
2. Identifying reforms in each religion and reformulation of one's own religious beliefs in this light
3. Understanding each other's problems of religious identity and attempting to come up with practical solutions
4. Tackling oppressive and liberative elements in each religion
5. Discovering common ground in different religions
6. Sympathetically understanding different concepts of spiritual transformation
7. Checking communalism and placing confidence in transforming spirituality
8. Considering service of fellow beings as service of God
9. Promoting communal harmony in colleges and preparing agents of peace in society
10. Restoring faith in the reality of pluralism and experimenting with an interfaith living experience
11. Nurturing a meaningful appreciation of diversity and common ground of religious music and customary rituals.

This list is to be considered as a starter and each campus could expand it and discover new options and innovations according to local needs and characteristics and talents of the participants. The actuality of religious and other related diversities on our college and university campuses should continue to help us to introspect and seriously prepare action plans in the framework of Christian higher education.

Bibliography

Books

Dahiwale,S.M. (ed) *Understanding of Indian Society*, (New Delhi: Rawat. 2005)

Dickinson, Richard D.N., *The Christian College in Developing India* (OUP,1971)

Ingleby, J.C., *Missionaries, Education and India: Issues in Protestant Missionary Education, etc.*, (ISPCK, Delhi 2000)

Jeyaraj,Nirmala,(ed), *Higher Education* (Madurai: Lady Doak College,1998)

Jagannathan, Milton W.S., *Mission and Education* (Chennai: CSI, 2002)

A. McLean, *Epoch makers of Modern Missions,* (New York: Fleming H. Revell Co, 1912)

G.N.Morje, *Kristi Marathi Vangmaya,* (Ahmednagar College and Snehasadan, Pune, 1984)

Shepherd Samuel T, *Bombay*, (Timesof India Press: Bombay 1932)

Walker, F.D., *William Carey, Missionary Pioneer and Statesman*, (London: SCM, 1926)

Ponnumuthan,Selvister, (ed.), Christian *Contribution to NATION BUILDING: A third Millennium Enquiry* (Aluva: St J.P.Seminary,2004)

Profile of a College: A Self-study Project of The Ahmednagar College, Nachiketa: Bombay ,1972)

Ph.D. Thesis (un published)

Jacob, P.S., *Christian Influence Modern Indian Thought with special reference to the Brahmo Samaj A study in Philosophy of Religion,* 1973, University of Poona Ph.D. Thesis (unpublished)

Articles

Some regional reporting is available; For example, see "Role of the Baptist Missionary Society in the field of Education in Orissa" by Rashmirekha Senapati, *NFE*, (op.cit). Vol XXI No.1, 2001, "The Origin of Female Education in Bassein" by A.A. Tuscano and "The Stages and Dynamics of the Community College Movement in India(1995 –2001) by Xavier Alphonse,*NFE*, Vol.XXI No. 1, 2001.

"The Church and Education in the Service of the Nation" by Fr. George Palackapilly,sdb, *NFE* Vol XXVIII, No.3 1998

"Protestant Missions 1864-1914" by W.R.Hogg in *History's Lessons for Tomorrow's Mission* (Geneva: WSCF n.d.)

See "Christian contribution to the Education of the Indigenous peoples of India" in *Nation Building*

"College and Community: A Case study of Ahmednagar College " By Plamthdathil.S.Jacob in *NFE*, Vol.XII No. 1 1983 pp 25, 26

"Christian Educational Effort in India" by T.A. Mathias S.J. in *New Frontiers in Education,* Vol VIII,No.4, 1978

"Transformation of Society through Education" by Francis P. Xavier S.J., in *New Frontiers in Education,* New Delhi, Vol XXIX, No.3, 1999 pp 273-83 See also "Does the Church have a Specific

Mission for Development through Education? " by Rudlof Ficker, *NFE*, Vol XXIX No.1 1999

"Learning through Participation" by P.S.Jacob in *New Frontiers in Education*, Vol.1, No.1, 1971

'Hi khari Prabhuseva-Janaseva' Narayan Vaman Tilak, Hymn 517, on service of the Lord, Upasana Sangeet: Bombay Tract and Book Society 1960 p.212

"The Role of Private Enterprise in Education" by J.P.Naik in *The Christian College and National Development,* (CLS:Madras, 1967).

"Christian Educational Effort in India" by T.A. Mathias S.J., in *New Frontiers in Education*, New Delhi, Vol VIII No.4 1978, pp 1-21

Appendix

Statement of the Consultation

We the participants of the Edinburgh 2010 preparatory consultation on "Christian Mission among Other Faiths" met during July 17-19, 2009 at The United Theological College, Bangalore. It is significant that The United Theological College, a pioneering ecumenical theological institution in India will also be celebrating its centenary in 2010.

"Christian Mission among Other Faiths" may be re-looked as the term "Mission" can be viewed in its colonial, triumphalistic and exclusivist implications. The word "other" also can create a distance between a community, which assumes superiority and power, and the rest of humanity and creation leading to their 'objectification.' Perhaps Christian mission not to be done among other faiths, but Christ should be witnessed to among people of different faiths. This commitment and relationship is not to be carried out in any isolated academic setting but in the context of the day-to-day life and struggles of the people.

Therefore *we commit ourselves* to "Witnessing Christ in the context of contemporary challenges in the mutually edifying fellowship of neighbors of living faiths and ideologies." Such witnessing involves commitment and openness, mutual sharing of our resources and our good news, leading to the conversion of all to God's purposes, reformation and transformation of society, and the empowerment and growth of all creation. The *ultimate goal* of witnessing is the realization of the reign of God on earth.

The priorities of Christian witnessing are:

- to live in solidarity with the poor, the dalits, the tribals and adivasis, women, and all those on the margins, who would become the subjects of mission;
- to engage in efforts and movements to eradicate injustices in society;
- to mend the brokenness of lives and of all creation.

In committing ourselves to such Christian witnessing, we will have to:

- address the issue of casteism within and outside the Church acknowledging that much have been spoken for long about the sin of casteism but efforts in the 21st century have to be made to transcend and eradicate casteism;
- eliminate the evil of patriarchy that has caused much injustice particularly to
- women, besides breeding power struggles, corruption, exploitation of creation, and the unbearable suffering of its victims.
- work to ushering a new order of justice, partnership, and growth in society;

- cultivate deeper and stronger bonds of intra-faith and inter-faith fellowship, following the models of Hospitality and Friendship in relations;
- address the conversion issue seriously and urgently taking the global and local discussions on conversion and integrating relevantly in the Indian context with the goal of such conversion being discipleship-commitment to the reign of God on earth;
- purge the structure and life-style of the Church of its affinity to capitalism, the
- commercialization of the gospel, and indeed its attraction to Mammon;
- co-labour with neighbouring faith communities in addressing contemporary challenges affecting the world such as the ecological crisis, dangers of nuclearization, HIV and AIDS, poverty, disease and death.

List of Contributors

A Jesuit priest, Dr. A. Alangaram is a professor of theology at Arulkadal, a Jesuit Regional Theologate in Chennai. He earned his Master's degree in Commerce at Loyola College in Madras University (1980), his Master's in Theology at Jnana Deepa Vidyapeeth (Pontifical Athenaeum), in Pune (1992) and his doctorate in theology from the Catholic Theology Faculty of Leopold-Franzens-Universität, Innsbruck, Europe (1998). He has written three books and innumerable theological articles both in Tamil and English. At present he is a visiting professor at Madras University – Chennai, Vidyajyoti – Delhi, Dharmaram Vidya Kshetram -Bangalore and Jnana Bharati College of Theology – Varanasi.

Dr. Kalarikkal Poulose Aleaz, is Professor of Religions at Bishop's College as well as Professor and Dean of Doctoral Programme of the North India Institute of Post-Graduate Theological Studies (NIIGPTS), Kolkata, India. He guides doctoral candidates of the South Asia Theological Research Institute (SATHRI), Bangalore, India as well. Author of 21 books and more than 190 articles, he was William Patton Fellow of the Selly Oak Colleges, Birmingham. He was also a Visiting Professor at Hartford Seminary, USA, as well as at the University of South Africa, Pretoria, in 2002 and Teape Lecturer, in the Universities of Cambridge, Birmingham, Bristol and Edinburgh, in 2005.

Steve Cochrane is Regional Director of YWAM, Asia (South) – South India & Indian Ocean and is a PhD scholar at the Oxford Centre for Mission Studies.

Gabriele Dietrich, born in Berlin, Germany, started her life in India with a research project on Religion and People's Organization at the Christian Institute for the Study of Religion and Society (CISRS), Bangalore. She has been teaching Social Analysis at the Tamilnadu Theological Seminary, Madurai since 1975. She has been deeply involved with women's movements especially among slum dwellers and workers in the unorganized sector including fisheries. She has also been working intensely with the National Alliance of People's Movements (NAPM). She has published widely on women's movements, organizational questions, ecology, communalism and culture. She is an Indian citizen.

Rev Dr. Jhakmak Neeraj Ekka is currently serving as the Vice Principal of Navin Doman Theological College, Malar, Ranchi, Jharkhand.

Dr Martha Frederiks is Professor of Missiology: World Christianity and Interreligious Dialogue, Center IIMO/Department of Theology/Faculty of Humanities, Utrecht University.

Dr. Roger Gaikwad is an ordained minister in the Presbyterian Church of India, Mizoram Synod. He had served as Principal of Aizawl Theological College, Mizoram. He is currently serving as the General Secretary of The National Council of Churches in India. He did his doctoral research under Rev. Dr. S. J. Samartha on "Major Issues in a Dialogical-Pluralistic Paradigm for Inter-Religious Relationships." He is presently a member of the Senate of Serampore College.

Dr R.L. Hnuni, a member of the Baptist Church of Mizoram is currently serving as the Principal of The Academy of Integrated Christian Studies at Mizoram.

Plamthodathil S. Jacob, Ph.D., is an Adjunct Professor of Philosophy and Religion and Head of the Department of Contextual Theology at the Union Biblical Seminary (UBS), Pune, India. He has also served as an interim Principal at Union Biblical Seminary. He is the former Principal of Ahmednagar College, Ahmednagar, Maharashtra and a former President of the All India Association for Christian Higher Education, New Delhi. He has published widely and has been recognized as an eminent ecumenist educator.

Jonas Adelin Jørgensen (b. 1973) holds a PhD in systematic theology from University of Copenhagen, Denmark (2006). He is currently serving as general secretary for the Danish Mission Council and as a lecturer in missiology, theology of religions, and intercultural theology at the Theological Faculty, University of Copenhagen.

Dr Wati Longchar is the Dean of Senate of Serampore Centre for Extension and Pastoral Theological Research (SCEPTRE), Kolkata. Currently, he is also the Director-in-charge of SATHRI, Bangalore.

John Parry teaches Missiology and World Religions at Northern College in the Partnership for Theological Education based in Manchester, UK and also at the University of Bangor in North Wales. He was ordained into the Church of Bangladesh and is now a minister of the United Reformed Church in the United Kingdom. A fuller discussion of the issue of the encounter of Sikhs and Christians is to be found in his book: *The Word of God is Not Bound*, published in Bangalore by the Centre for Contemporary Christianity in 2009.

Rev. Dr. Shanta Premawardhana served as a programme executive for Interreligious Dialogue and Cooperation at the World Council of Churches for the past three years and is presently serving as president of SCUPE (Seminary Consortium for Urban Pastoral Education) based in Chicago. A Baptist pastor originally from Sri Lanka, has lived and worked in the United States for many years. Prior to his work at the WCC, he served as Associate General Secretary for Interfaith Relations at the National Council of Churches of Christ in the USA. He received his MA and Ph.D. from Northwestern University in Evanston, Illinois, USA in Religion specializing in Buddhism and Hinduism.

T. Swami Raju is presently working in the Department of Religion, Culture & Society at Andhra Christian Theological College, Hyderabad in Andhra Pradesh and is Acting Dean for the Department of Practical Work and Co-coordinator for the Institute of Inter-Faith Relations.

Rt. Rev. D.K. Sahu had served as the General Secretary of the National Council of Churches in India (N.C.C.I). Prior to his consecration as a Bishop of the Church of North India he served as the Vice Principal of the Serampore College (Theology Department), Serampore, West Bengal.

Dr David Immanuel Singh is Research Tutor in South Asian Studies, Admissions Tutor and M Phil Programme Leader at the Oxford Centre for Mission Studies. His recent publications include: Sainthood and Revelatory Discourse: An Examination of the Bases for Bayan's Authority in Mahdawi Islam, and Physical Jihad: Current Perspectives on Islamic 'Holy War'. He is presently the editor of the Oxford Centre for Mission Studies Journal *Transformation.*

Dr Bolinkar Sohkhlet an ordained minister of the Presbyterian Church of India, Khasi-Jiantia Synod, is presently teaching Religion subjects at the John Roberts Theological Seminary, Shillong, Meghalaya.

Dr T. Vanlaltlani belongs to the Presbyterian Church of India, Mizoram Synod and is presently serving as a Professor in the Department of Religion at the Aizawl Theological College, Mizoram. She is also actively involved with NGOs working towards developing and empowering women.

Pieter Verster was born in Heilbron, Free State Province, South Africa on 22 October 1954. He holds two doctorates from the University of Pretoria (In Missiology and Religious Studies and also in Dogmatics and Ethics). At present he is Head of the Department of Missiology at the Faculty of Theology at the University of the Free State. He is a graded researcher of the National Research Foundation of South Africa.

Canon Dr Andrew Wingate was the former Director of the St Philip's Centre for Study and Engagement in a Multi Faith Society, Leicester, which he founded in 2004. He had worked in South India and Birmingham in the field of theological education. He is now a Chaplain to The Queen, and Canon Theologian in Leicester, and is a consultant in the inter faith field with the Church of Sweden.

REGNUM EDINBURGH 2010 SERIES
Series Listing

David A. Kerr, Kenneth R. Ross (eds.)
Edinburgh 2010
Mission Then and Now
2009 / 978-1-870345-73-6 / xiv + 343pp (paperback)
2009 / 978-1-870345-76-7 / xiv + 343pp (hardback)

No one can hope to fully understand the modern Christian missionary movement without engaging substantially with the World Missionary Conference, held at Edinburgh in 1910. As the centenary of the Conference approaches, the time is ripe to examine its meaning in light of the past century and the questions facing Christian witness today. This book is the first to systematically examine the eight Commissions which reported to Edinburgh 1910 and gave the conference much of its substance and enduring value. It will deepen and extend the reflection being stimulated by the upcoming centenary and will kindle the missionary imagination for 2010 and beyond.

Daryl M. Balia, Kirsteen Kim (eds.)
Edinburgh 2010
Witnessing to Christ Today
2010 / 978-1-870345-77-4 / xiv +301pp

This volume, the second in the Edinburgh 2010 series, includes reports of the nine main study groups working on different themes for the celebration of the centenary of the World Missionary Conference, Edinburgh 1910. Their collaborative work brings together perspectives that are as inclusive as possible of contemporary world Christianity and helps readers to grasp what it means in different contexts to be 'witnessing to Christ today'.

Claudia Währisch-Oblau, Fidon Mwombeki (eds.)
Mission Continues
Global Impulses for the 21st Century
2010 / 978-1-870345-82-8 / 271pp

In May 2009, 35 theologians from Asia, Africa and Europe met in Wuppertal, Germany, for a consultation on mission theology organized by the United Evangelical Mission: Communion of 35 Churches in Three Continents. The aim was to participate in the 100th anniversary of the Edinburgh conference through a study process and reflect on the challenges for mission in the 21st century. This book brings together these papers written by experienced practitioners from around the world.

Brian Woolnough and Wonsuk Ma (Eds)
Holistic Mission
God's plan for God's people 2010 / 978-1-870345-85-9

Holistic mission, or integral mission, implies God is concerned with the whole person, the whole community, body, mind and spirit. This book discusses the meaning of the holistic gospel, how it has developed, and implications for the the church. . It takes a global, eclectic approach, with 19 writers, all of whom have much experience in, and commitment to, holistic mission. It addresses critically and honestly one of the most exciting, and challenging, issues facing the church today. To be part of God's plan for God's people, the church must take holistic mission to the world.

Kirsteen Kim and Andrew Anderson (Eds)
Mission Today and Tomorrow
2011/978-1-870345-91-0

The centenary of the historic and influential World Missionary Conference held in Edinburgh 1910 presented a unique opportunity for the whole church worldwide to come together in celebration, reflection and recommitment to witnessing to Christ today. Edinburgh 2010 also engaged in serious study and reflection on the current state of world mission and the challenges facing all those who seek to witness Christ today. The results of this research was presented and debated within the context of Christian fellowship and worship at the conference in June 2010. This record of that conference is intended to give the background to that Call, to share the spirit of the conference, and to stimulate informed and focused participation in God's mission in Christ for the world's salvation.

Tormod Engelsviken, Erling Lundeby and Dagfinn Solheim (Eds)
The Church Going Glocal
Mission and Globalisation 2011/978-1-870345-93-4

This book provides thought-provoking and inspiring reading for all concerned with mission in the 21st century. I have been challenged by its contributors to re-think our Gospel ministries in our new local contexts marked by globalisation and migration. With its biblical foundation, its missiological reflection and interaction with contemporary society I warmly recommend this volume for study and pray that it will renew our passion for the Gospel and compassion for people.

REGNUM Studies in Global Christianity

(Previously GLOBAL THEOLOGICAL VOICES series)

Series Listing

David Emmanuuel Singh (ed.)

Jesus and the Cross

Reflections of Christians from Islamic Contexts

2008 / 978-1-870345-65-1 / x + 226pp

The Cross reminds us that the sins of the world are not borne through the exercise of power but through Jesus Christ's submission to the will of the Father. The papers in this volume are organised in three parts: scriptural, contextual and theological. The central question being addressed is: how do Christians living in contexts, where Islam is a majority or minority religion, experience, express or think of the Cross? This is, therefore, an exercise in listening. As the contexts from where these engagements arise are varied, the papers in drawing scriptural, contextual and theological reflections offer a cross-section of Christian thinking about Jesus and the Cross.

David Emmanuuel Singh (ed.)

Jesus and the Incarnation

Reflections of Christians from Islamic Contexts

2011/978-1-870345-90-3

In the dialogue of Christians with Muslims nothing is more fundamental than the Cross, the Incarnation and the Resurrection of Jesus. This book contains voices of Christians living in various 'Islamic contexts' and reflecting on the Incarnation of Jesus. The aim of these reflections is constructive and the hope is that the papers weaved around the notion of 'the Word' will not only promote dialogue among Christians on the roles of the Person and the Book, but, also, create a positive environment for their conversations with Muslim neighbours.

Sung-wook Hong

Naming God in Korea

The Case of Protestant Christianity

2008 / 978-1-870345-66-8 / xiv + 170pp

Since Christianity was introduced to Korea more than a century ago, one of the most controversial issue has been the Korean term for the Christian 'God'. This issue is not merely about naming the Christian God in Korean language, but it relates to the question of theological contextualization—the relationship between the gospel and culture—and the question of Korean Christian identity. This book examines the theological contextualization of the concept of 'God' in the contemporary Korean context and applies the translatability of Christianity to that context. It also demonstrates the nature of the gospel in relation to cultures, i.e., the universality of the gospel expressed in all human cultures.

Hubert van Beek (ed.)
Revisioning Christian Unity
The Global Christian Forum
2009 / 978-1-870345-74-3 / xx + 288pp

This book contains the records of the Global Christian Forum gathering held in Limuru near Nairobi, Kenya, on 6 – 9 November 2007 as well as the papers presented at that historic event. Also included are a summary of the Global Christian Forum process from its inception until the 2007 gathering and the reports of the evaluation of the process that was carried out in 2008.

Paul Hang-Sik Cho
Eschatology and Ecology
Experiences of the Korean Church
2010 / 978-1-870345-75-0/ 260pp (approx)

This book raises the question of why Korean people, and Korean Protestant Christians in particular, pay so little attention (in theory or practice) to ecological issues. The author argues that there is an important connection (or elective affinity) between this lack of attention and the other-worldly eschatology that is so dominant within Korean Protestant Christianity. Dispensational premillennialism, originally imported by American missionaries, resonated with traditional religious beliefs in Korea and soon came to dominate much of Korean Protestantism. This book argues that this, of all forms of millennialism, is the most damaging to ecological concerns.

Dietrich Werner, David Esterline, Namsoon Kang, Joshva Raja (eds.)
The Handbook of Theological Education in World Christianity
Theological Perspectives, Ecumenical Trends, Regional Surveys
2010 / 978-1-870345-80-4/ 759pp

This major reference work is the first ever comprehensive study of Theological Education in Christianity of its kind. With contributions from over 90 international scholars and church leaders, it aims to be easily accessible across denominational, cultural, educational, and geographic boundaries. The Handbook will aid international dialogue and networking among theological educators, institutions, and agencies. The major objectives of the text are (1) to provide introductory surveys on selected issues and themes in global theological education; (2) to provide regional surveys on key developments, achievements, and challenges in theological education; (3) to provide an overview of theological education for each of the major denominational / confessional traditions; and (4) to provide a reference section with an up-to-date list of the regional associations of theological institutions and other resources.

David Emmanuel Singh & Bernard C Farr (eds.)

Christianity and Education

Shaping of Christian Context in Thinking

2010 / 978-1-870345-81-1/ 244pp (approx)

Christianity and Education is a collection of papers published in *Transformation: An International Journal of Holistic Mission Studies* over a period of 15 years. It brings to life some of the papers that lay buried in shelves and in disparate volumes of *Transformation,* under a single volume for theological libraries, students and teachers. The articles here represent a spectrum of Christian thinking addressing issues of institutional development for theological education, theological studies in the context of global mission, contextually aware/informed education, and academies which deliver such education, methodologies and personal reflections.

J.Andrew Kirk

Civilisations in Conflict?

Islam, the West and Christian Faith 2011- 978-1-870345-71-2

Samuel Huntington's thesis, which argues that there appear to be aspects of Islam that could be on a collision course with the politics and values of Western societies, has provoked much controversy. The purpose of this study is to offer a particular response to Huntington's thesis by making a comparison between the origins of Islam and Christianity; the two religions that can be said to have shaped, in contrasting ways, the history of the Western world. The early history of each faith continues to have a profound impact on the way in which their respective followers have interpreted the relationship between faith and political life. The book draws significant, critical and creative conclusions from the analysis for contemporary intercultural understanding, and in particular for the debate about the justification of violence for political and religious ends.

REGNUM STUDIES IN MISSION
Series Listing

Kwame Bediako
Theology and Identity
The Impact of Culture upon Christian Thought in the Second Century and in Modern Africa
1992 / 1-870345-10-X / xviii + 508pp

The author examines the question of Christian identity in the context of the Graeco–Roman culture of the early Roman Empire. He then addresses the modern African predicament of quests for identity and integration.

Christopher Sugden
Seeking the Asian Face of Jesus
The Practice and Theology of Christian Social Witness in Indonesia and India 1974–1996
1997 / 1-870345-26-6 / xx + 496pp

This study focuses on contemporary holistic mission with the poor in India and Indonesia combined with the call to transformation of all life in Christ with micro-credit enterprise schemes. 'The literature on contextual theology now has a new standard to rise to' – Lamin Sanneh (Yale University, USA).

Hwa Yung
Mangoes or Bananas?
The Quest for an Authentic Asian Christian Theology
1997 / 1-870345-25-8 / xii + 274pp

Asian Christian thought remains largely captive to Greek dualism and Enlightenment rationalism because of the overwhelming dominance of Western culture. Authentic contextual Christian theologies will emerge within Asian Christianity with a dual recovery of confidence in culture and the gospel.

Keith E. Eitel
Paradigm Wars
The Southern Baptist International Mission Board Faces the Third Millennium
1999 / 1-870345-12-6 / x + 140pp

The International Mission Board of the Southern Baptist Convention is the largest denominational mission agency in North America. This volume chronicles the historic and contemporary forces that led to the IMB's recent extensive reorganization, providing the most comprehensive case study to date of a historic mission agency restructuring to continue its mission purpose into the twenty-first century more effectively.

Samuel Jayakumar

Dalit Consciousness and Christian Conversion

Historical Resources for a Contemporary Debate

1999 / 81-7214-497-0 / xxiv + 434pp

(Published jointly with ISPCK)

The main focus of this historical study is social change and transformation among the Dalit Christian communities in India. Historiography tests the evidence in the light of the conclusions of the modern Dalit liberation theologians.

Vinay Samuel and Christopher Sugden (eds.)

Mission as Transformation

A Theology of the Whole Gospel

1999 / 0870345133/ 522pp

This book brings together in one volume twenty five years of biblical reflection on mission practice with the poor from around the world. The approach of holistic mission, which integrates proclamation, evangelism, church planting and social transformation seamlessly as a whole, has been adopted since 1983 by most evangelical development agencies, most indigenous mission agencies and many Pentecostal churches. This volume helps anyone understand how evangelicals, struggling to unite evangelism and social action, found their way in the last twenty five years to the biblical view of mission in which God calls all human beings to love God and their neighbour; never creating a separation between the two.

Christopher Sugden

Gospel, Culture and Transformation

2000 / 1-870345-32-0 / viii + 152pp

A Reprint, with a New Introduction, of Part Two of Seeking the Asian Face of Jesus

Gospel, Culture and Transformation explores the practice of mission especially in relation to transforming cultures and communities. - 'Transformation is to enable God's vision of society to be actualised in all relationships: social, economic and spiritual, so that God's will may be reflected in human society and his love experienced by all communities, especially the poor.'

Bernhard Ott

Beyond Fragmentation: Integrating Mission and Theological Education

A Critical Assessment of some Recent Developments in Evangelical Theological Education

2001 / 1-870345-14-2 / xxviii + 382pp

Beyond Fragmentation is an enquiry into the development of Mission Studies in evangelical theological education in Germany and German-speaking Switzerland between 1960 and 1995. The author undertakes a detailed examination of the paradigm shifts which have taken place in recent years in both the theology of mission and the understanding of theological education.

Gideon Githiga

The Church as the Bulwark against Authoritarianism

Development of Church and State Relations in Kenya, with Particular Reference to the Years after Political Independence 1963-1992

2002 / 1-870345-38-x / xviii + 218pp

'All who care for love, peace and unity in Kenyan society will want to read this careful history by Bishop Githiga of how Kenyan Christians, drawing on the Bible, have sought to share the love of God, bring his peace and build up the unity of the nation, often in the face of great difficulties and opposition.' Canon Dr Chris Sugden, Oxford Centre for Mission Studies.

Myung Sung-Hoon, Hong Young-Gi (eds.)

Charis and Charisma

David Yonggi Cho and the Growth of Yoido Full Gospel Church

2003 / 1-870345-45-2 / xxii + 218pp

This book discusses the factors responsible for the growth of the world's largest church. It expounds the role of the Holy Spirit, the leadership, prayer, preaching, cell groups and creativity in promoting church growth. It focuses on God's grace (charis) and inspiring leadership (charisma) as the two essential factors and the book's purpose is to present a model for church growth worldwide.

Samuel Jayakumar

Mission Reader

Historical Models for Wholistic Mission in the Indian Context

2003 / 1-870345-42-8 / x + 250pp

(Published jointly with ISPCK)

This book is written from an evangelical point of view revalidating and reaffirming the Christian commitment to wholistic mission. The roots of the 'wholistic mission' combining 'evangelism and social concerns' are to be located in the history and tradition of Christian evangelism in the past; and the civilizing purpose of evangelism is compatible with modernity as an instrument in nation building.

Bob Robinson

Christians Meeting Hindus

An Analysis and Theological Critique of the Hindu-Christian Encounter in India

2004 / 1-870345-39-8 / xviii + 392pp

This book focuses on the Hindu-Christian encounter, especially the intentional meeting called dialogue, mainly during the last four decades of the twentieth century, and specifically in India itself.

Gene Early

Leadership Expectations

How Executive Expectations are Created and Used in a Non-Profit Setting

2005 / 1-870345-30-4 / xxiv + 276pp

The author creates an Expectation Enactment Analysis to study the role of the Chancellor of the University of the Nations-Kona, Hawaii. This study is grounded in the field of managerial work, jobs, and behaviour and draws on symbolic interactionism, role theory, role identity theory and enactment theory. The result is a conceptual framework for developing an understanding of managerial roles.

Tharcisse Gatwa

The Churches and Ethnic Ideology in the Rwandan Crises 1900-1994

2005 / 1-870345-24-X / approx 300pp

Since the early years of the twentieth century Christianity has become a new factor in Rwandan society. This book investigates the role Christian churches played in the formulation and development of the racial ideology that culminated in the 1994 genocide.

Julie Ma

Mission Possible

Biblical Strategies for Reaching the Lost

2005 / 1-870345-37-1 / xvi + 142pp

This is a missiology book for the church which liberates missiology from the specialists for the benefit of every believer. It also serves as a textbook that is simple and friendly, and yet solid in biblical interpretation. This book links the biblical teaching to the actual and contemporary missiological settings with examples, making the Bible come alive to the reader.

Allan Anderson, Edmond Tang (eds.)

Asian and Pentecostal

The Charismatic Face of Christianity in Asia

2005 / 1-870345-43-6 / xiv + 596pp

(Published jointly with APTS Press)

This book provides a thematic discussion and pioneering case studies on the history and development of Pentecostal and Charismatic churches in the countries of South Asia, South East Asia and East Asia.

I. Mark Beaumont

Christology in Dialogue with Muslims

A Critical Analysis of Christian Presentations of Christ for Muslims from the Ninth and Twentieth Centuries

2005 / 1-870345-46-0 / xxvi + 228pp

This book analyses Christian presentations of Christ for Muslims in the most creative periods of Christian-Muslim dialogue, the first half of the ninth century and the second half of the twentieth century. In these two periods, Christians made serious attempts to present their faith in Christ in terms that take into account Muslim perceptions of him, with a view to bridging the gap between Muslim and Christian convictions.

Thomas Czövek,

Three Seasons of Charismatic Leadership

A Literary-Critical and Theological Interpretation of the Narrative of Saul, David and Solomon

2006 / 978-1-870345484 / 272pp

This book investigates the charismatic leadership of Saul, David and Solomon. It suggests that charismatic leaders emerge in crisis situations in order to resolve the crisis by the charisma granted by God. Czovek argues that Saul proved himself as a charismatic leader as long as he acted resolutely and independently from his mentor Samuel. In the author's eyes, Saul's failure to establish himself as a charismatic leader is caused by his inability to step out from Samuel's shadow.

Jemima Atieno Oluoch

The Christian Political Theology of Dr. John Henry Okullu

2006 / 1-870345-51-7 / xx + 137pp

This book reconstructs the Christian political theology of Bishop John Henry Okullu, DD, through establishing what motivated him and the biblical basis for his socio-political activities. It also attempts to reconstruct the socio-political environment that nurtured Dr Okullu's prophetic ministry.

Richard Burgess

Nigeria's Christian Revolution

The Civil War Revival and Its Pentecostal Progeny (1967-2006)

2008 / 978-1-870345-63-7 / xxii + 347pp

This book describes the revival that occurred among the Igbo people of Eastern Nigeria and the new Pentecostal churches it generated, and documents the changes that have occurred as the movement has responded to global flows and local demands. As such, it explores the nature of revivalist and Pentecostal experience, but does so against the backdrop of local socio-political and economic developments, such as decolonisation and civil war, as well as broader processes, such as modernisation and globalisation.

David Emmanuel Singh & Bernard C Farr (eds.)
Christianity and Cultures
Shaping Christian Thinking in Context
2008 / 978-1-870345-69-9 / x + 260pp

This volume marks an important milestone, the 25th anniversary of the Oxford Centre for Mission Studies (OCMS). The papers here have been exclusively sourced from Transformation, a quarterly journal of OCMS, and seek to provide a tripartite view of Christianity's engagement with cultures by focusing on the question: how is Christian thinking being formed or reformed through its interaction with the varied contexts it encounters? The subject matters include different strands of theological-missiological thinking, socio-political engagements and forms of family relationships in interaction with the host cultures.

Tormod Engelsviken, Ernst Harbakk, Rolv Olsen, Thor Strandenæs (eds.)
Mission to the World
Communicating the Gospel in the 21st Century:
Essays in Honour of Knud Jørgensen
2008 / 978-1-870345-64-4 / 472pp

Knud Jørgensen is Director of Areopagos and Associate Professor of Missiology at MF Norwegian School of Theology. This book reflects on the main areas of Jørgensen's commitment to mission. At the same time it focuses on the main frontier of mission, the world, the content of mission, the Gospel, the fact that the Gospel has to be communicated, and the context of contemporary mission in the 21st century.

Al Tizon
Transformation after Lausanne
Radical Evangelical Mission in Global-Local Perspective
2008 / 978-1-870345-68-2 / xx + 281pp

After Lausanne '74, a worldwide network of radical evangelical mission theologians and practitioners use the notion of "Mission as Transformation" to integrate evangelism and social concern together, thus lifting theological voices from the Two Thirds World to places of prominence. This book documents the definitive gatherings, theological tensions, and social forces within and without evangelicalism that led up to Mission as Transformation. And it does so through a global-local grid that points the way toward greater holistic mission in the 21st century.

Bambang Budijanto

Values and Participation

Development in Rural Indonesia

2009 / 978-1-870345-70-5 / x + 237pp

Socio-religious values and socio-economic development are inter-dependant, inter-related and are constantly changing in the context of macro political structures, economic policy, religious organizations and globalization; and micro influences such as local affinities, identity, politics, leadership and beliefs. The three Lopait communities in Central Java, Indonesia provide an excellent model of the rich and complex negotiations and interactions among all the above factors. The book argues that the comprehensive approach in understanding the socio-religious values of each local community is essential to accurately describing their respective identity which will help institutions and agencies, both governmental and non-governmental, to relate to these communities with dignity and respect.

Young-hoon Lee

The Holy Spirit Movement in Korea

Its Historical and Theological Development

2009 / 978-1-870345-67-5 / x + 174pp

This book traces the historical and theological development of the Holy Spirit Movement in Korea through six successive periods (from 1900 to the present time). These periods are characterized by repentance and revival (1900-20), persecution and suffering under Japanese occupation (1920-40), confusion and division (1940-60), explosive revival in which the Pentecostal movement played a major role in the rapid growth of Korean churches (1960-80), the movement reaching out to all denominations (1980-2000), and the new context demanding the Holy Spirit movement to open new horizons in its mission engagement (2000-). The volume also discusses the relationship between this movement and other religions such as shamanism, and looks forward to further engagement with issues of concern in wider society.

Alan R. Johnson

Leadership in a Slum

A Bangkok Case Study

2009 / 978-1-870345-71-2 xx + 238pp

This book looks at leadership in the social context of a slum in Bangkok from an angle different from traditional studies which measure well educated Thais on leadership scales derived in the West. Using both systematic data collection and participant observation, it develops a culturally preferred model as well as a set of models based in Thai concepts that reflect on-the-ground realities. This work challenges the dominance of the patron-client rubric for understanding all forms of Thai leadership and offers a view for understanding leadership rooted in local social systems, contrary to approaches that assume the universal applicability of leadership research findings across all cultural settings. It concludes by looking at the implications of the anthropological approach for those who are involved in leadership training in Thai settings and beyond.

Titre Ande

Leadership and Authority

Bula Matari and Life - Community Ecclesiology in Congo

2010 / 978-1-870345-72-9 xvii + 189pp

This book proposes that Christian theology in Africa can make significant developments if a critical understanding of the socio-political context in contemporary Africa is taken seriously. The Christian leadership in post-colonial Africa has cloned its understanding and use of authority on the Bula Matari model, which was issued from the brutality of colonialism and political absolutism in post-colonial Africa. This model has caused many problems in churches, including dysfunction, conflicts, divisions and a lack of prophetic ministry. Titre proposes a Life-Community ecclesiology for liberating authority, where leadership is a function, not a status, and 'apostolic succession' belongs to all the people of God.

Frank Kwesi Adams

Odwira and the Gospel

A Study of the Asante Odwira Festival and its Significance for Christianity in Ghana

2010 /978-1-870345-59-0

The study of the Odwira festival is the key to the understanding of Asante religious and political life in Ghana. The book explores the nature of the Odwira festival longitudinally - in pre-colonial, colonial and post-independence Ghana - and examines the Odwira ideology and its implications for understanding the Asante self-identity. The book also discusses how some elements of faith portrayed in the Odwira festival could provide a framework for Christianity to engage with Asante culture at a greater depth. Theological themes in Asante belief that have emerged from this study include the theology of sacrament, ecclesiology, eschatology, Christology and a complex concept of time. The author argues that Asante cultural identity lies at the heart of the process by which the Asante Christian faith is carried forward.

Bruce Carlton

Strategy Coordinator

Changing the Course of Southern Baptist Missions

2010 / 978-1-870345-78-1 xvii + 268pp

In 1976, the Southern Baptist Convention adopted its Bold New Thrusts in Foreign Missions with the overarching goal of sharing the gospel with every person in the world by the year 2000. The formation of Cooperative Services International (CSI) in 1985 and the assigning of the first non-residential missionary (NRM) in 1987 demonstrated the Foreign Mission Board's (now International Mission Board) commitment to take the gospel message to countries that restricted traditional missionary presence and to people groups identified as having little or no access to the gospel. Carlton traces the historical development along with an analysis of the key components of the paradigm and its significant impact on Southern Baptists' missiology.

Julie Ma & Wonsuk Ma

Mission in the Spirit:

Towards a Pentecostal/Charismatic Missiology

2010 / 978-1-870345-84-2 xx + 312pp

The book explores the unique contribution of Pentecostal/Charismatic mission from the beginning of the twentieth century. The first part considers the theological basis of Pentecostal/Charismatic mission thinking and practice. Special attention is paid to the Old Testament, which has been regularly overlooked by the modern Pentecostal/Charismatic movements. The second part discusses major mission topics with contributions and challenges unique to Pentecostal/Charismatic mission. The book concludes with a reflection on the future of this powerful missionary movement. As the authors served as Korean missionaries in Asia, often their missionary experiences in Asia are reflected in their discussions.

S. Hun Kim & Wonsuk Ma (eds.)

Korean Diaspora and Christian Mission

2011-978-1-870345-89-7

As a 'divine conspiracy' for Missio Dei, the global phenomenon of people on the move has shown itself to be invaluable. In 2004 two significant documents concerning Diaspora were introduced, one by the Filipino International Network and the other by the Lausanne Committee for World Evangelization. These have created awareness of the importance of people on the move for Christian mission. Since then, Korean Diaspora has conducted similar research among Korean missions, resulting in this book. It is unique as the first volume researching Korean missions in Diasporic contexts, appraising and evaluating these missions with practical illustrations, and drawing on a wide diversity of researchers.

GENERAL REGNUM TITLES

Vinay Samuel, Chris Sugden (eds.)
The Church in Response to Human Need
1987 / 1870345045 / xii+268pp

Philip Sampson, Vinay Samuel, Chris Sugden (eds.)
Faith and Modernity
Essays in modernity and post-modernity
1994 / 1870345177 / 352pp

Klaus Fiedler
The Story of Faith Missions
1994 / 0745926878 / 428pp

Douglas Peterson
Not by Might nor by Power
A Pentecostal Theology of Social Concern in Latin America
1996 / 1870345207 / xvi+260pp

David Gitari
In Season and Out of Season
Sermons to a Nation
1996 / 1870345118 / 155pp

David. W. Virtue
A Vision of Hope
The Story of Samuel Habib
1996 / 1870345169 / xiv+137pp

Everett A Wilson
Strategy of the Spirit
J.Philip Hogan and the Growth of the Assemblies of God Worldwide, 1960 - 1990
1997 /1870345231/214

Murray Dempster, Byron Klaus, Douglas Petersen (eds.)
The Globalization of Pentecostalism
A Religion Made to Travel
1999 / 1870345290 / xvii+406pp

Peter Johnson, Chris Sugden (eds.)
Markets, Fair Trade and the Kingdom of God
Essays to Celebrate Traidcraft's 21st Birthday
2001 / 1870345193 / xii+155pp

Robert Hillman, Coral Chamberlain, Linda Harding
Healing & Wholeness
Reflections on the Healing Ministry
2002 / 978-1- 870345-35- 4 / xvii+283pp

David Bussau, Russell Mask
Christian Microenterprise Development
An Introduction
2003 / 1870345282 / xiii+142pp

David Singh
Sainthood and Revelatory Discourse
An Examination of the Basis for the Authority of Bayan in Mahdawi Islam
2003 / 8172147285 / xxiv+485pp

For the up-to-date listing of the Regnum books see www.ocms.ac.uk/regnum

regnum

Regnum Books International

Regnum is an Imprint of The Oxford Centre for Mission Studies
St. Philip and St. James Church
Woodstock Road
Oxford, OX2 6HR
Web: www.ocms.ac.uk/regnum